My dearest Reader:

Far be it from me to begin, straight off the bat, as they say, by telling you *what to do*.

It seems however that I ought to inform you that this text boasts two appendices, beginning at pages 277 and 333 respectively, the first a library (so to speak) to which the larger text continually refers, and the other a kind of index to another such library, to which it does not, per se. Both contain other things as well.

If you are particularly intrepid, please, proceed at once into the textual thicket, and when you emerge you may, if you will, peruse these hangers-on to the book.

If you are warier, please, engage with them first; they may serve a *certain* preparatory function; though they will provide no map, for in the text itself maps shift with your eyes. If they *seem* to provide a map, do not trust it.

This is to say, my dearest reader, that they are in effect neither prologue nor epilogue, but merely *inside* yet *outside,* and you may take them as and when you will.

To say this is to say that they are a kind of parasite:

which is important.

I inform you of this out of the greatest concern for your peace of *mind*, the state of which is, my *very* dearest reader, my *very* first concern.

Sincerely

      signed,

Now then, since that is done, please: turn the page.

Olchar E. Lindsann

The Ecstatic Nerve: Speculations on Some Dubious Subjects.

October, A.Da. 91, mOnocle-Lash Anti-Press.

mOnocle-Lash Logo by dadaDavid Hartke

Plagiarism is necessary. Progress implies it. It closely grasps an author's sentence, uses his expressions, deletes a false idea, replaces it with the right one.

-Isidore Ducasse, *Poésies* (1870)

The quote institutes a repetition or an originary reflexivity that, even as it divides the inaugural act, at once the inventive event and the relation or archive of invention, also allows it to unfold in order to say nothing but the same, itself, the dehiscent and refolded invention of the same, at the very instant when it takes place.

-Jacques Derrida, *Psyche: Inventions of the Other* (1987).

Art can cease to be a report on sensations and become a direct organization of higher sensations. It is a matter of producing ourselves, and not things that enslave us.

-Guy Debord, *Thesis on Cultural Revolution* (1958)

There are sophisms infinitely more significant and far-reaching than the most indisputable truths:

    -André Breton, *Nadja* (1928).   (Breton 1960, p 144.)

In reality, the activity of reading has on the contrary all the characteristics of a silent production: the drift across the page, the metamorphosis of the text effected by the wandering eyes of the reader, the improvisation and expectation of meanings inferred from a few words, leaps over written spaces in an ephemeral dance. But since he is incapable of stockpiling (unless he writes or records), the reader cannot protect himself against the erosion of time (while reading, he forgets himself and he forgets what he has read) unless he buys the object (book, image) which is no more than a substitute (the spoor or promise) of moments 'lost' in reading. He insinuates into another person's text the ruses of pleasure and appropriation: he poaches on it, is transported into it, pluralizes himself in it like the internal rumblings of one's body. Ruse, metaphor, arrangement, this production is also an "invention" of the memory. Words become the outlet or product of silent histories.

    -Michel de Certeau, *The Practice of Everyday Life* (1980).   (Certeau 1984.)

I need not add that history itself, even more than the novel, provokes me to indulge in this game of possible alterations, which blend extremely well with the real falsifications to be found from time to time in the most respectable documents. All this is very useful in emphasizing the naïve and curious structure of our belief in the 'past'.

    -Paul Valéry, *Memoirs of a Poem* (1937).   (Valéry 1958, p 105-106.)

The reversal that we are here aiming at corrects the history of the past, rendering it better, more revolutionary, and more successful than it ever was. The 'victories' continue the optimistic and absolute *détournement* by means of which Lautréamont, quite audaciously, already disputed the validity of all manifestations of misfortune and its logic: 'I do not accept evil. Man is perfect. The soul does not fall. Progress exists… Up to now, one has described misfortune in order to inspire terror and pity. I will describe happiness in order to inspire the contrary… As long as my friends are not dying, I will not speak of death.'

    -Guy Debord, *The Situationist International and the New Forms of Action in Politics and Art* (1963.) (McDonough 2004, p 166.)

The one duty we owe to history is to rewrite it.

    […]

Who, again, cares if Mr. Pater has put into the portrait of Mona Lisa something that Leonardo never dreamed of?

    […]

the one thing not worth looking at is the obvious.

    […]

Yet his object will not always be to explain the work of art. He may seek rather to deepen its mystery, to raise round it, and round its maker, that mist of wonder which is dear to both gods and worshippers alike.

    -Oscar Wilde, *The Critic as Artist* (1890).   (Wilde 1999, p 194-207.)

Perhaps I shall manage to control my own thought to my own best interest.

    -Phillippe Soupault and André Breton, *The Magnetic Fields* (1919).   (Breton et. al. 1997, p 75.)

Thought involves a little charlatanism… Deliberately inject into one's thought the element of charlatanry required for it to be thought, rather than oneself be its dupe. In this way one can vary the dosage *as one pleases*.

-Julien Torma, *Euphorisms* (1926). (Cravan et. al. 2005, pp 135-136.)

I offer this book of Truths, not in its character of Truth-Teller, but for the Beauty that abounds in its Truth, constituting it true.

-Edgar Poe, *Eureka: A Prose Poem: An Essay on the Material and Spiritual Universe* (1848). (Poe 1997, p 4.)

that enticement to dream which he craved overflowed from the book, where, beneath the printed line, one could detect another line, visible only to the mind, signaled by a qualifier offering glimpses of passion, by an understatement hinting at depths of the soul which no words could satisfy

-J.-K. Huysmans, *A rebours* (1884). (Huysmans 2000, p 148.)

In vain, to seize life's secrets, would you pore, like Faust, over grimoires, it would remain impenetrable, you would seek in vain in books for that which they do not contain.

- Berthe de Courrière, quoted by Alfred Jarry, *Visits of Love* (1898). (Jarry 1993, p 35.)

Do not read, look at the designs created by the white spaces between the words of several lines and draw inspiration from them.

-Paul Éluard and André Breton, *The Immaculate Conception* (1930). (Breton et. al. 1997, p 215.)

"Not he alone used hidden meanings," answered Conrad. "If you scan the various works of certain great poets you may find double meanings. Men have stumbled onto cosmic secrets in the past and given a hint of them to the world in cryptic words."

-Robert E. Howard, *The Children of the Night* (1931). (Carter 1971, p 174.)

Glorious things lie buried here beneath a tangle of unripened rhetoric that remains abstract.

-Hugo Ball, *Tenderenda the Fantast* (wr. 1915-20.) (Ball et. al. 1995, p 123.)

They recognize, in everything they produce in this fashion, without feeling that they are responsible for it, the incomparable quality of a few books, the few words which still move them. They suddenly realize a great poetic unity that proceeds from the prophetic books of all peoples to *Les Illuminations* and *Les Chants de Maldoror*. Between the lines, they read the incomplete confessions of those who once *maintained the system:* in light of their discovery, *Une Saison en Enfer* sheds its riddles, along with the Bible and several other confessions of man that lay hidden under their masks of images.

-Louis Aragon, *Une vague de rêves* (1924). (Nadeau 1973, p 88.)

Now you must follow this dog's example, and be wise in smelling out, sampling, and relishing these fine and most juicy books, which are easy to run down but hard to bring to bay. Then, by diligent reading and frequent meditation, you must break the bone and lick out the substantial marrow—that is to say the meaning which I intend to convey by these Pythagorean symbols—in the hope and assurance of becoming both wiser and more courageous by such reading. For here you will find an individual savour and abstruse teaching which will initiate you into certain very high sacraments and dread mysteries, concerning not only our religion, but also our public and private life.

-François Rabelais, *Gargantua* (c. 1534) (Rabelais 1955, p 38.)

—Here are two senses, cried Eugenius, as we walked along, pointing with the forefinger of his right hand to the word Crevice, in the one hundred and seventy-eighth page of the first volume of this book of books;—here are two senses—quoth he—And here are two roads, replied I, turning short upon him—a dirty and a clean one—which shall we take?

-Laurence Sterne, *The Life and Opinions of Tristram Shandy, Gentleman* (1760). (Sterne 1995, p 150.)

From an early age he preferred to sit reading in his room rather than play with neighborhood children, but such a preference is not remarkable. Most of the books he read were normal, too, though he tended to concentrate on the more unusual sections; after reading the Bible, for instance, he startled his father by asking: "How did the witch of Endor call the spirit?"

-J. Ramsey Campbell, *The Mine on Yuggoth* (1964). (Carter 1971, p 260.)

Perhaps life needs to be deciphered like a cryptogram. Secret staircases, frames from which the paintings quickly slip aside and vanish (giving way to an archangel bearing a sword or to those who must forever advance), buttons which must be indirectly pressed to make an entire room move sideways or vertically, or immediately change all its furnishings; we may imagine the mind's greatest adventure as a journey of this sort to the paradise of pitfalls.

-André Breton, *Nadja* (1928). (Breton 1960, p 112.)

Hoping promptly to see, some time or other, the consecration of my theories accepted by this or that literary form… This hybrid preface has been set out in a way which may not, perhaps, appear natural enough, in the sense that it—so to speak—surprises the reader, who does not very clearly see where he is at first being led; yet this feeling of remarkable stupefaction, from which one generally seeks to shield those who spend their time reading books or booklets, I have made every effort to produce.

-The Comte de Lautréamont, *Les Chants de Maldoror* (1869), Sixth Canto, First Strophe.

I must rejoice beyond the confines of time . . . though the world be repelled by my joy, and in its coarseness know not what I mean.

-Ruysbroeck the Admirable, Second Canticle (Fourteenth century, quoted by Huysmans in 1884). (Huysmans 2000, p 1.)

The obscurity of our utterances is constant. The riddle of meaning should remain in the hands of children. To read a book in order to know denotes a certain simplicity.

-André Breton, *For Dada* (c. 1921?)　　　　　　　　　　　　　　　　(Motherwell 1981, p 200.)

And, moreover, is it necessary to an author's satisfaction that a book such as this be understood, except by those for whom it is written? Must it have been written for *someone?* But for myself I have so little love for the world of the living that—like those idle, sensitive women who are said to post letters to imaginary friends—I would gladly write only for the dead.

-Charles Baudelaire, *Artificial Paradises* (1860).　　　　　　　　　　　(Baudelaire 1996, p 29.)

There are some trains of certain ideas which leave prints of themselves about our eyes and eyebrows; and there is a consciousness of it, somewhere about the heart, which serves to make these etchings the stronger—we see, spell, and put them together without a dictionary.

    -Laurence Sterne, *The Life and Opinions of Tristram Shandy, Gentleman* (1760-67).   (Sterne 1996, p 244.)

decadence… that point of extreme maturity yielded by the slanting suns of aged civilizations: an ingenious complicated style, full of shades and of research, constantly pushing back the boundaries of speech, borrowing from all the technical vocabularies, taking colour from all palettes and notes from all keyboards, struggling to render what is most inexpressible in thought, what is vague and most elusive in the outlines of form, listening to translate the subtle confidences of neurosis, the dying confessions of passion grown depraved, and the strange hallucinations of the obsession which is turning to madness. The style of decadence is the ultimate utterance of the Word, summoned to final expression and driven to its last hiding-place.

    -Théophile Gautier (1868).   (Huysmans 1931, pp 25-26).

Soon the links that bind your ideas become so frail, the thread that ties your conceptions so tenuous, that only your accomplices understand you. And here again you cannot be certain; perhaps they only think they understand you, and the illusion is reciprocal.

    -Charles Baudelaire, *Artificial Paradises* (1860).   (Baudelaire 1996, p 29.)

It was well said of a certain German book that *"er lasst sich nicht lessen"*—it does not permit itself to be read. There are some secrets which do not permit themselves to be told. Men die nightly in their beds, wringing the hands of ghostly confessors, and looking them piteously in the eyes—

   -Edgar A. Poe, *The Man of the Crowd* (1840.)   (Poe 1975, pp 473.)

I've laid the foundations of a magnificent work. Every man has within him a Secret, many die without having found it and won't find it because, since they are dead, neither it nor them will have any further spiritual existence. I have died and been born again with the gem-encrusted key to my final spiritual casket.

   -Stéphane Mallarmé, Letter to Theodore Aubenal, 16 July, 1866.   (Mallarmé 1988, p 42.)

I liked to hide what I loved. It did me good to have a secret, which I carried within me like a conviction and like a seed. But seeds of this kind nourish their carrier, instead of being nourished by him.

   -Paul Valéry, *Memoirs of a Poem* (1937.)   (Valéry 1958, p 126.)

Concealed actions are the most estimable. When I see a few of these in history, they please me greatly. They have not been completely concealed. They have been known. This small way in which they appeared increases their merit. That they could not be concealed is the finest thing of all.

   -Isidore Ducasse, *Poésies* (1870).   (Ducasse 1978, p 59.)

The *Handbook of Superdadaism* is a hand-made book, a single copy only, 30 x 45 cm and 15 cm thick. A written appointment having been made, it can be viewed at the CENTRAL BUREAU OF DADA—Nevertheless, Dada's innermost being will remain a secret.—Freemasons and Jesuits are not Dada.

("Dada Evenings" are mere camouflage and flying machines.)

The International Superdada.

(Dada will be the death of the entente!)

-Johannes Baader, *A Declaration from Club Dada* (1918). (Huelsenbeck 1993, p 137.)

For that which is secret gathers together and roots itself and grows dark, the more so when it is pointed out, undressed, discovered.

-Antonin Artaud, *Coleridge the Traitor* (1947). (Artaud 1965, p 129.)

Possessed, as we were, of the ability to entrust ourselves to 'chance', to our conscious as well as our unconscious minds, we became a sort of public secret society.

-Hans Richter, *Dada: Art and Anti-Art* (1964). (Richter 1997, p 64.)

We are obviously well situated to discover, some years before others, all the possible tricks of the extreme cultural decay of our time. Since they can only be used in the spectacle of our enemies, we keep some notes about them in a drawer.

-Guy Debord, *Editorial Notes: The Avant-Garde of Presence* (1963). (McDonough 2004, p 148.)

The secret: life begins with an anomaly, with an abnormal function. The wheel which turns, etc. The legs…

-Jacques Rigaut, *Lord Patchogue* (1934.) (Cravan et. al. 2005, p 97.)

-Max Klinger, *Invocation* (1879). (Klinger 1977, p 3.)

Adjusting his monocle, he looked carefully around him.

-Villiers de l'Isle-Adam, *The Future Eve* (1886). (Hustvedt 1998, p 546.)

-George Maciunas, *Self-portrait* (1962). (Williams 1998, p 2.)

I'm bored a lot behind my glass monocle

-Jacques Vaché, Letter to Théodor Fraenkel, 29 April, 1917. (Cravan et. al. 2005, p 196.)

-Felix Vallotton, portrait of Symbolist Edouard Dujardin, 1898   (Gourmont 1994, p 195.)

The young woman, dumbfounded, watched curiously as [Max Jacob,] this bald, monocled eccentric, dressed in a proper, if somewhat threadbare, black coat, told her stories about angels and the baby Jesus.

    -Dan Franck, *Bohemian Paris* (2001).   (Franck 2001, p 40.)

-the Dada Richard Huelsenbeck, 1920. (Marcus 1990, p 158.)

She is blind. On her eyes, as hermetically sealed as her sex, gold monocles glitter, monocles and not a binocle, in keeping with the independence of her chameleon eyes.

Alfred Jarry, 'Visiting the Muse', *Visits of Love* (1898). (Jarry 1993, p 80.)

-Felix Vallotton, portrait of the Decadent, Jean Moréas (1896). (Gourmont 1994, p 29.)

Neither Tzara nor Huelsenbeck, both always monocled, could compete with Serner in this respect. To [Walter] Serner the monocle came naturally. In many ways it was he, rather than Ball the idealist or Tzara the realist, who was the incarnation of revolt in what would now be termed its existential form.

-Hans Richter, *Dada: Art and Anti-Art* (1964). (Richter 1997, p 36.)

-Peter Moore, portrait of Fluxist George Maciunas, 1976. (Jenkins 1993, p 52.)

Prancing on their stage, Huelsenbeck and Hausmann with monocles clamped into their left eye sockets, Grosz's face covered with white pancake makeup, they tried to live out an old, orphaned metaphor as if it weren't a metaphor at all.

-Greil Marcus, *Lipstick Traces* (1990). (Marcus 1990, p 115.)

-Man Ray, portrait of Dada & Surrealist Tristan Tzara, 1931.   (Motherwell 1981, p 74.)

I take my Crystal monocle and a theory for troubling paintings for a walk around villages in ruins.

-Jacques Vaché, Letter to André Breton, 16 Oct., 1916.   (Cravan et. al. 2005, p 192.)

-Felix Vallotton, portrait of Symbolist Henri de Régnier, 1898   (Gourmont 1994, p 224.)

Grasp the eye by the monocle

-Dada Proverb, Benjamin Péret & Paul Éluard, *152 Proverbes mis au gout du jour* (1925)   (Brotchie1991, p 129.)

-Dada Raoul Hausmann, 1916.   (Huelsenbeck 1991, p 77.)

at this period [André Breton] protected his eyes behind green glasses, out of a desire to astound. Occasionally he replaced them with a monocle.

-Maurice Nadeau, *The History of Surrealism* (1964).   (Nadeau 1971, p 93.)

    -George Maciunas, 1976   (Williams 1998, p 275.)

[Jacques Vaché's] red hair, his "dead-flame" eyes, and the glacial butterfly of his monocle perfect this constant, willful dissonance and isolation.

    -André Breton, *Anthology of Black Humor* (1945).   (Breton 1997, p 293.)

-the Dadas André Breton, Phillippe Soupault, Jacques Rigaut, and Benjamin Péret, 1921.
(Cravan et al, 2005, p 80.)

I wake up a Londoner and go to bed an Asiatic—Londoner, monocle—furore and fury—O, you who have known me follow me into life

-Arthur Cravan, *Notes* (1913-1918).   (Cravan et. al. 2005, p 63.)

There roam the world today certain individuals for whom art, for instance, has ceased to be an end.
-André Breton, *Les Pas perdus* (1922).   (Nadeau 1973, p 79.)

I am decidedly far from the literary crowd—even from Rimbaud, I'm afraid, dear friend—ART IS STUPIDITY—Almost nothing is stupid—art must be very funny and a little tiresome—that's all
-Jacques Vaché, Letter to André Breton, 9 May, 1818.   (Cravan et. al. 2005, p 207.)

We eschew the distinctions that separate lived experience from 'what can be known' and spit upon the pimps that profit by slicing these imaginary pies.
    -Warren Fry, *The Dada Cabaret, Happenings, and Brute Salon*.   (Fry 2007, p 19.)

Art, with a capital A, is on the contrary, dear Mademoiselle, literally speaking a flower (oh, my dear child!) which blooms only in the midst of contingencies
    -Arthur Cravan, *Exhibition at the Independents* (1914).   (Motherwell 1981, p 12.)

Art:
    will not be tickled, not by man nor god nor tickling device.
    will not be tolerated (unless we can put it into little plastic bags and let other people have a go, as long as they promise to do it properly).
    must therefore be killed or exploited.
    -David Beris Edwards, *A Brown Trouser Manifesto* (2007).   (Fry 2007, p ii.)

It is not enough to confuse the kettle-drum and toy horn, important and profound symbols though they may be, for the essential thing; a proper understanding of Dada presupposes an absolutely serious engagement with almost all realms of life, metaphysics, psychology, art, etc.
    -Daimonides, *Towards a Theory of Dadaism* (1920).   (Huelsenbeck 1993, p 62.)

The science I undertake is a science distinct from poetry. I do not sing of the latter. I strive to discover its source.

    -Isidore Ducasse, *Poésies* (1870).   (Ducasse 1978, p 79.)

Dada, then, is also an occupation; one could even call it the most elaborate and strenuous occupation there is. Dada has chosen a cultural realm for its activity, although it could just as well have chosen to make its appearance as an importer, a stockbroker, or manager of a chain of cinemas.

    -Richard Huelsenbeck, Introduction to *The Dada Almanac* (1920).   (Huelsenbeck 1993, p 10.)

    -Paul Sérusier, *Paul Ranson in Nabi Costume* (1890).   (Lucie-Smith 1972, p 100.)

Then, when he tired of consulting these timetables, he would rest his eyes by contemplating the chronometers and compasses, sextants and diviers, binoculars and maps that were scattered over a table upon which was displayed only one book, bound in sealskin, *The Adventures of Arthur Gordon Pym,* printed specially for him on pure linen-laid paper, selected by hand, bearing a seagull as its watermark.

    -J.-K. Huysmans, *A Rebours* (1884).   (Huysmans 1998, p. 18.)

Close to your hands lies a little volume, bound in some Nile-green skin that has been powdered with gilded nenuphars and smoothed with hard ivory. It is the book that Gautier loved, it is Baudelaire's masterpiece. Open it at that sad madrigal that begins

> Que m'importe que tu sois sage?
> Sois belle! et sois triste!

and you will find yourself worshipping sorrow as you have never worshipped joy. Pass on to the poem on the man who tortures himself, let its subtle music steal into your brain and colour your thoughts, and you will become for a moment what he was who wrote it, nay, not for a moment only, but for barren moonlit nights and sunless sterile days will a despair that is not your own make its dwelling within you, and the misery of another gnaw your heart away. Read the whole book, suffer it to tell even one of its secrets to your soul, and your soul will grow eager to know more, and will feed upon poisonous honey, and seek to repent of strange crimes of which it is guiltless and to make atonement for pleasures it has never known.

    -Oscar Wilde, *The Critic as Artist* (1890).   (Wilde 2002, p. 214.)

One does not read *Tales of Mystery and Imagination* and *Les Fleurs du Mal* with impunity. It is not without risk that one breathes the rarified air of those gardens "from which the vegetable kingdom has been banished," magical hothouses warm with potent fragrances, artificial paradises saturated with dubious and unsettling scents.

    -Henri Laujol, *Villiers de l'Isle-Adam* (1883).   (Pierrot 1981, p 50.)

I was turning to go into the dining-room when my eye fell upon a book bound in serpent-skin, standing in a corner on the top shelf of the last bookcase. I did not remember it and from the floor could not decipher the pale lettering on the back, so I went to the smoking-room and called Tessie. She came in from the studio and climbed up to reach the book.

'What is it?' I asked.

'The King in Yellow.'

I was dumbfounded. Who had placed it there? How came it to my rooms? I had long ago decided that I should never open that book, and nothing on earth could have tempted me to buy it. Fearful lest curiosity might tempt me to open it, I had never even looked at it in book-stores. If I ever had had any curiosity to read it, the awful tragedy of young Castaigne, whom I knew, prevented me from exploring its wicked pages. I had always refused to listen to any description of it, and indeed, nobody ever ventured to discuss the second part aloud, so I had absolutely no knowledge of what those leaves might reveal. I stared at the poisonous mottled binding as I would at a snake.

-Robert Chambers, *The Yellow Sign* (1895).　　　　　　　　　　　　　(Chambers 2000, p 66.)

But consider how far a handful of completely modern works, about which the very least one can say is that a particularly unhealthy atmosphere pervades them, has already wormed their way, admirably and perversely, into the public consciousness: Rimbaud (despite the reservations I have mentioned), Huysmans, Lautréamont, to mention only poetry.

-André Breton, *Second Manifesto of Surrealism* (1930).　　　　　　　　(Breton 1972, p 152.)

I saw now that the books on the tables were not the usual scholarly tomes I had seen on his Ipswich desk, but with some faint apprehension observed that they were the books condemned by the explicit instructions of Tuttle's uncle, as a glance at the vacant spaces on the proscribed shelves clearly corroborated.

Tuttle turned to me almost eagerly and lowered his voice as if in fear of being overheard. "As a matter of fact, Haddon, it's colossal—a gigantic feat of the imagination; only for this: I'm no longer certain that it *is* imaginative, indeed, I'm not. I wondered about that clause in my uncle's will... and rightly surmised that the reason must lie somewhere in the pages of those books he so carefully condemned." He waved a hand at the incunabula before him. "So I examined them, and I can tell you I have discovered things of such incredible strangeness, such bizarre horror, that I hesitate to dig deeper into the mystery.

-August Derleth, *The Return of Hastur* (1936). (Carter 1971, p 140.)

The volume, the scroll of parchment, was to have insinuated itself into the dangerous hole, was to have furtively penetrated into the menacing dwelling-place with an animal-like, quick, silent, smooth, brilliant, sliding motion, in the fashion of a serpent or a fish. Such is the anxious desire of the book. It is tenacious too, and parasitic, loving and breathing through a thousand mouths that leave a thousand imprints on our skin, a marine monster, a *polyp*.

-Jacques Derrida, *Ellipsis* (1967.) (Derrida 2001, pp 375-376.)

And let it be clearly understood that we are not talking about a simple regrouping of words or a capricious redistribution of visual images, but of the re-creation of a state which can only fairly be compared with madness: the modern authors I have quoted have sufficiently expounded on this point.

-André Breton, *Second Manifesto of Surrealism* (1930). (Breton 1972, p 175.)

I want to make a Book that will derange men, that will be like an open door leading them where they would never have consented to go. A door simply ajar on reality.

-Antonin Artaud, *Here Where Others...* (c. 1925?). (Artaud 1965, p 26.)

But what if the Book was only, in all senses of the word, an *epoch* of Being (an epoch coming to an end which would permit us to see Being in the glow of its agony or the relaxation of its grasp, and an end which would multiply, like a final illness, like the garrulous and tenacious hypermnesia of certain moribunds, books about the dead book)?

 -Jacques Derrida, *Edmund Jabès and the Question of the Book* (1967). (Derrida 2001, p. 94.)

 A storm begins
 and the electricity happens horizontally—
  and I find the book written by the anchoress.
 I never understood what it said
 until I went to sleep.

 The Iuk Kide is a book, a place, and a religion.

  -Imogene Engine, *The Iuk Kide* (2007). (Engine 2007, p 2.)

Books or other notes are kept in which for years have been *written-down* all my thoughts, all my phrases, all my necessaries, all the articles in my possession or around me, all persons with whom I come into contact, etc. I cannot say with certainty who does the writing down… I presume that the writing-down is done by creatures given human shape on distant celestial bodies after the manner of the fleeting-improvised-men, but lacking all intelligence; their hands are led automatically, as it were, by passing rays for the purpose of making them write-down, so that later rays can again look at what has been written.

 -Daniel Paul Schreber, *Memoirs of my Nervous Illness* (1903). (Schreber 2000, p 123.)

you take a white book, you clean it, you immerse it page by page for several minutes in a gooey mixture made from: 500 grams of sheep manure, a pinch of cooking salt, a glass of vinegar to which you add 200 grams of elderberry powder, and you sign.

 -Paul Éluard and André Breton, *The Immaculate Conception* (1930). (Breton et. al. 1997, p 215.)

"here is a book, hand-written by myself, which you can seize as the twenty-eighth volume and read, so that you may not only contain yourself in patience but may also very probably understand me better during the course of our voyage, though I am not asking your opinion about its necessity."

[. . .]

René-Isidore Panmuphle, bailiff, began to read Faustroll's manuscript in deep darkness, substantiating the invisible ink of sulphate of quinine by means of the invisible infrared rays of a spectrum whose other colors were locked in an opaque box

-Alfred Jarry, *The Exploits and Opinions of Dr. Faustroll, Pataphysician* (1911). (Jarry 1996, pp 17-20.)

Here, as they were cleaning the ditches, the diggers struck with their picks against a great tomb of bronze, so immeasurably long that they never found the end of it. For it stuck out too far into the sluices of the Vienne. Opening this tomb at a certain place which was sealed on the top with the sign of a goblet, around which was inscribed in Etruscan letters, HIC BIBITUR, they found nine flagons, arranged after the fashion of skittles in gascony; and beneath the middle flagon lay a great, greasy, grand, grey, pretty, little, mouldy book, which smelt more strongly but not more sweetly than roses. In this book was found the said genealogy, written out at length in a chancery hand, not on paper, nor on parchment, nor on wax, but on elm-bark, so worn however by age that scarcely three letters could be read.

-François Rabelais, *Gargantua* (c. 1564?) (Rabelais 1955, p 42.)

Doublemain murmured that it was time for him to reach into the water with his long arms for the Book, and turn the pages of Hydrophilus.

He exhumed from the depths a monstrous beetle, the colour of pitch, its triangular abdomen glazed like a window over its heart. He placed it in the boat, propped up on its legs, and opening up the two flaps of elytron, he leafed through its folded wings. Glancing towards the marsh I saw the red form reappearing and Xenophon sneered: "You'll not be able to inscribe Solomon's name in there."

[. . .]

"The clatter of your wings about your strident body is fearsome. So Book, close your pages wherein I so nearly inscribed this hideosity without soul. Helena! Helena! Behold this body artificially strangled around the middle which dares, when recumbent, to mimic the sign of infinity…"

-Alfred Jarry, *Visits of Love* (1898). (Jarry 1993, p 71.)

I got my hands on a rather curious book in my sleep, in an open air market out towards Saint-Malo. The spine of this book was formed of a wooden gnome with an Assyrian-style white beard which came down to its feet. The statuette was of normal thickness and yet it in no way interfered with turning the pages of the book, which were made of thick black wool. I hastened to acquire it, and when I woke up I regretted not finding it near me. It would be relatively easy to re-create it.

-André Breton, *Introduction au discours sur le peu de réalité* (1924). (Breton 1972, p 277.)

The Ecstatic Nerve

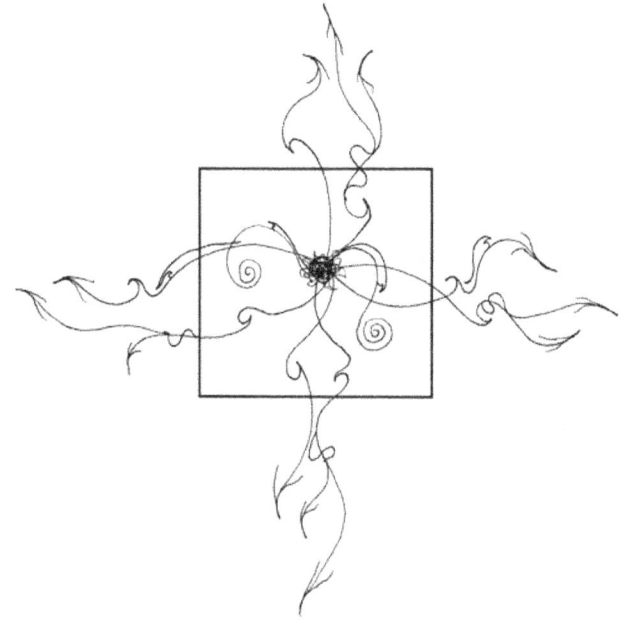

Speculations on Some Dubious Subjects

Olchar E. Lindsann

Now then. It is a time-honoured maxim that when writing fiction, one ought to begin in the midst of an action; far be it from me to break with this tradition.

You see, Charles Baudelaire, along with Gautier and d'Aurevilly, was by the 1850s a leading exponent of Dandyism in France; and the primary goal of their brand of Dandyism was the willful manipulation of one's self as an artistic *figure*. Frantisek Deak, on page 254 of his *Symbolist Theater: Formation of an Avant-Garde*, says of the Dandy at this period that, 'he is someone for whom his appearance and manners are a communicative act, his social gesture, in the contemporary social and aesthetic discourse, as well as a form of spiritual discipline.' Baudelaire himself claimed that, 'dandyism in certain respects comes close to spirituality and to stoicism,' and that, 'I was not far wrong when I compared dandyism to a religion.'[1]

I invite you to consider how this attitude might relate to Percy Shelley's injunction in 1821's *A Defense of Poetry* that:

> We want the creative faculty to imagine that which we know; we want the generous impulse to act out what we imagine; we want the poetry of life: our calculations have outrun conception; we have eaten more than we can digest.
>
> (Perkins p. 1084)

Like many of Mallarmé's later syntactic ambivalences, the first clause can be read in at least two different ways: either an injunction that the known serve as the model of that which we imagine (hardly in keeping with Shelley's conception of Imagination), or that the known be defined as that which is imagined by the creative faculty. Choosing the latter trajectory, and following its implications through the rest of the sentence, the 'poetry of life' appears as the acting out, or lived inscription, of the figures and images of the creative faculty; Mid-19th Century French Dandyism is an articulation of this very principle. But there is a definite difference in tone. For Shelley's erosion of the distinction between poetry and life is closely bound to a generally Positivist—and perhaps even more importantly, optimistic—framework in which the poet, ideally, carries out his or her function from a position of social centrality and authority, serving (as the specific *terms* of Shelley's expansion of the mandate of poetry suggest) as a distillation or idealization of the best of society as a whole (even if a society *of the future*). Baudelaire's Dandyism, on the other hand, is sometimes antisocial and often misanthropic, and his Dandy (and by implication, his poet) carries out her or his function from a

---

[1] Skip this section if you must, my dear reader, but at least read the footnotes before tossing this book into the fire; it will make it burn better. And then, if you will, read it all. Better yet, read it all.

marginal position, opposed to society in general and acting upon it not as society's distilled or idealized self-conception, but as its *other*. In his *Anthology of Black Humor*, André Breton quotes him as writing that, 'the word "dandy" implies a quintessence of character and subtle intelligence, free of the entire ethical mechanism of this world.' (p. 98.) This is a long way from Shelley's assertion that, 'A poet, as he is the author to others of the highest wisdom, pleasure, virtue, and glory, so he ought personally to be the happiest, the best, the wisest, and the most illustrious of men.' (Perkins, 1085.) Even in this latter sentence, we can see that Shelley insists upon an equivalence of the poet *as figure* and the poet *as a producer of texts*. Yet while Baudelaire not only retains but takes this equivalence further in actively shaping both roles, the very nature *of* that relationship is deeply complicated.

Please observe that I determine nothing in all of this—my way is ever to point out to you, my curious reader, various tracks of potential investigation toward multivalent springs. But I feel confident pointing toward a certain realization in Baudelaire, (in his books and in his limbs) which was more fully explicit a few generations later: the Romantic *trajectory*, such as it is, was doomed. Baudelaire and his generation actively resisted in the face of that futility; yet in the wake of this realisation, those artists who, like Baudelaire, refused to give in to the reign of realism, were nonetheless forced to consider how, even in defeat, they might continue to *develop* this impulse, without allowing it to be assimilated into the Bourgeois-Realist order or to fall into nostalgic sentimentality, as happened to a large degree with their British counterparts. It was apparent, I hypothesize, that in order to survive and grow, this Romantic impulse must be radically transformed even, perhaps, in its ideology (for the Yellow Sign—that elusive notion that is not a concept, which without analysis or description shall weave in and out of so much of the text to follow, an always-already vanished term in a trajectory organized around its very *posited* absence—especially among the Decadents, Symbolists, and Dadas—can no more be confined by an ideology than by anything else). It was essential that it ingest its own defeat, and allow its newly—and definitively—*marginal* and oppositional role, to restructure it. In order to continue a project which would be seen increasingly as anachronistic, that project must, paradoxically, be radically rethought and, to the insensitive eye, even broken off.

In fact, the relationship between the French poets of this generation and the Anglophone Romantics of whom they are the (nonexclusive) inheritors is characterized by a strong tension between fissure and continuity. The most obvious discontinuity results from the movement of the principle seat of the Yellow Sign from English poetry to French at this key moment when it starts to become, as it were, recognizable as itself. I am not arguing, of course, that the recent French canon—Hugo, Chateaubriand, and that lot—did not exercise a great influence. Such an argument would be absurd, and I strive to keep my thesis within the firm limits of propriety. But it is the influence of a British tradition that included Matthew Lewis, Charles Maturin, Anne Radcliffe, Samuel Coleridge, Thomas De Quincey, Lord Byron, Percy Shelley, John Keats, Mary Godwin Shelley, and Edgar Poe that, my investigations indicate, catalyzed the Yellow Sign.

It may in fact have been this social fracture that allowed the French writers to re-write the tradition to which they were laying claim; especially since it was a doubled rift. I say this because the most overwhelming influence on the next several generations of French bearers of the Yellow Sign was Edgar Poe, who was himself an outsider from the British tradition, trapped, as he seems very much to have felt, in a country already beginning to succumb to the materialism and aesthetic and intellectual populism that his French counterparts would find themselves opposed to very soon—those counterparts who would transform this tradition into something very different.

I believe that Baudelaire and his circle sensed this. Certainly they were intensely interested in the extrapoetic lives of these figures; and, using the scraps of personal information and various incidents that they could find in memoirs, published letters and journals, and other sources more or less mysterious, they began to form a mythology. This mythology was being assembled from small scraps here and there, isolated among scattered texts and often only ambiguously contextualized. These obscure hints and isolated gestures were merely the peripheral evidences of an essentially *oral* literature that, due to the linguistic and geographic rift in the tradition, had left no trace but these scraps. Around these bare scraps a new mythology could be *written*, a mythology which one could be written *into*, into which one could write oneself. And a mythology that could itself be written *into* society, culture, history, and thus 'reality' itself, opening that 'reality' to textual play and to memetic infection. Edgar Poe, within his own country, was remembered as a vitriolic and erratic critic who had penned a single hit and hovered on the border of degeneracy. At the hands of Baudelaire, who remarks that 'I add a new saint to the martyrology,' (Poe 1980, p 80.) he became Edgar Allen Poe, the hypersensitive and tormented pariah, cradling a bottle in his hands, destroying himself and his own genius in a desperate gesture of contempt for the materialist, philistine society that tormented him with its malicious and concentrated indifference, until one dark night he died, even his own death—hydrophobia? Mugging? Surely it was the alcohol; or was it his own hand?—lost in indifferent obscurity.

While the gap in an oral framework for this mythology heightened Baudelaire's, Gautier's, Nerval's, and others' awareness of the potential significance of that history, enough had been recorded and published that a certain sense of continuity was able to remain at play. Perhaps aware of the tenuousness of any orally-transmitted mythology in an emerging Modern society, the British writers themselves consciously

> A writing that exceeds, by questioning them, the values "origin," "reason," and "history" could not be contained within the metaphysical closure of an archaeology.
>
> -Jacques Derrida, *Cogito and the History of Madness* (1963).
> (Derrida 2005, p 43.)

engaged with the process of leaving *evidence*, as it were, of themselves and each other *as* mythic figures—written engagements with an essentially oral practice, which might serve to establish and maintain mythic themes, cycles, and treatments across the gaps thrown up by temporal or geographic distance; obvious examples are Shelley's *Adonais* and Hazlitt's *My First Acquaintance With the Poets*. (Perkins, pp 1046 & 679.) And mark this:

because these published incidents were often recorded in a number of different forms—published letters, diaries, marginalia, memoirs by associates, largely fabricated albums by third parties, poems and dedications by other poets—and often flatly contradicted each other on nearly every point (a removal from a definitive text of origin), they maintained a mythic, rather than 'historical', structure wherein each instance of a figure, story, or cycle is, as it were, self-contained, and issues of accuracy and consistency become superfluous and inappropriate. A structure that is continually regenerative, always emergent and under erasure; literary history had ceased to be such, and had become a social mythology: social life itself had become a text open to play and to continual re-writing. (For one superbly in-depth example, read Alan Halsey's *The Text of Shelley's Death*.)

> Themes can be split up *ad infinitum*. Just when you think you have disentangled and separated them, you realize that they are knitting together again in response to the operation of unexpected affinities. Consequently the unity of myth is never more than tendential and projective and cannot reflect a state or a particular moment of the myth.
>
> -Jacques Derrida, *Structure, Sign and Play in the Discourse of the Human Sciences* (1967). (Derrida 2001, p 362.)

Discrete myths began to evolve around these (almost necessarily) mythologized figures; and not only separate stories, but common themes providing a structure of symbolic conventions and archetypes. Speaking of Constantine Guys ('M.G.'), graphic chronicler of the dandy community, in *The Painter Of Modern Life*, Baudelaire writes, 'Need I say that when M.G. commits one of his dandies to paper, he always gives him his historical character, we might almost say his legendary character, were it not that we are dealing with our own day and with things generally held to be light-hearted?' (Baudelaire 1972, p 422.) I repeat that in my present condition, unfortunately, I, like the French poets I am writing to you about, can access most of these myths only in the form of their eruptions into print; but they are indicative of an oral mode of transmission between poets within the gradual movement from a state of 'Men of Letters' to a sense of multiple artistic *communities* organized according to theoretical convictions; an oral mode which, as the conditions for it appeared, became the primary vehicle for this literature—thus my description of it as socially inscribed. In relation to these particular artists, of course, I can only intuit and conjecture. My evidence, like theirs, is scattered and largely consequential. In this way, the act of reading becomes one of leaping across gaps, of using the slight handholds that have ruptured into print in order to speculate on a vanished discourse; and having done so, we use these speculations as frameworks for our own traditions.

The story of this, my dear reader, is long and interesting; but it would run my history (such as it is) all upon heaps to give it here. It is for an episode many pages on; and every circumstance relating to it, in its proper place, shall be faithfully laid out before you, I swear it. What was being built was a canon of mythic *literature* with its own system of figurative, iconic, and narrative languages with which each discrete instance could engage.² For instance, we can devise or discern The Addict as a figure, of Addiction as the paradoxical convergence of the willful refusal of society with the ultimate loss of will. And this theme of addiction is often associated with creative engagement: Thus Coleridge, shrinking into a sinister but lisping sleep, sung to by the opium that was introduced to him through a physical illness, but which settled into addiction through an intense anxiety induced by the terrifying and ceaseless trauma of the awareness of exhilarating—and aborted—ideas he could not contain, could not embody, to which he was forever inadequate, continually expiring, helpless, before they could concentrate themselves into marks. And in this oblivion that hides death by resembling it, a terrifying and beautiful vision that evades even that Inner Eye which has taken residence even within him, blocking out the sun—a vision with all the solid and painful vibrancy of phonemes; he attempts to set it down, to inscribe it, to smash his words into mortar; and he awakes in a cold sweat, fumbles for the pen, desperate—but manages no more than 55 lines, warding off reality in order to remain immersed in the text he is struggling to articulate, to embody, grasping desperately with one hand at the disintegrating rags of his rapturous intoxication while scrabbling

---

> **Kubla Khan**
>
> *Or, A Vision in a Dream. A Fragment.*
>
> The following fragment is here published at the request of a poet of great and deserved celebrity, and, as far as the Author's own opinions are concerned, rather as a psychological curiosity, than on the ground of any supposed *poetic* merits.
>
> In the summer of the year 1797, the Author, then in ill health, had retired to a lonely farm-house between Porlock and Linton, on the Exmoor confines of Somerset and Devonshire. In consequence of a slight indisposition, an anodyne had been prescribed, from the effects of which he fell asleep in his chair in the moment that he was reading the following sentence, or words of the same substance, in 'Purchas's Pilgrimage': 'Here the Kubla Khan commanded a palace to be built, and a stately garden thereunto. And thus ten miles of fertile ground were inclosed within a wall.' The Author continued for about three hours in a profound sleep, at least of the external senses, during which time he has the most vivid confidence, that he could not have composed less than from two to three hundred lines; if that indeed can be called composition in which all the images rose up in him as *things*, with a parallel production of the correspondent expressions, without any sensation or conscious effort. On awakening he appeared to himself to have a distinct recollection of the whole, and taking his pen, ink, and paper, instantly and eagerly wrote down the lines that are here preserved. At this moment he was unfortunately called out by a person on business from Porlock, and detained by him above an hour, and on his return to his room, found, to his no small surprise and mortification, that though he still retained some vague and dim recollection of the general purport of the vision, yet, with the exception of some eight or ten scattered lines and images, all the rest had passed away like the images on the surface of a stream into which a stone has been cast, but, alas! without the after restoration of the latter!
>
> -Samuel T. Coleridge's introduction to *Kubla Khan* (1816)
> (McGann 1993, pp 430-431.)

---

². I am emphatically *not* suggesting, like Campbell, Chomsky, or Jung on various registers, the pre-existence of categories, forms, or themic modules into which mythic gestures are fit and by which they are structured in an even remotely rigid or teleologically determined way. On the contrary, I am attempting to formulate a *critical*, rather than prescriptive, strategy that will allow me to trace the work of intertextuality in a way appropriate to this unfixed (orally-*structured*, whether or not orally *transmitted*) form; for specific configurations of letters and words are not, in this socially-inscribed textual practice, the register on which such gestures can be compared. Rather, these (provisionally) posited mythemes can be looked upon as strategies through which a group of related textual occurrences can be (provisionally) looked at in view of a particular set of (provisional) relationships.

equally to concentrate on this hallucination, on the incantatory lines which he feels are inseparable *from*

interruption.

Might I in passing invite you inspect the differences in the way that this figure is treated in the examples of Poe and Coleridge given here? And I might, finally, simply mention that Coleridge's fellow opium-eater, Thomas De Quincey, was perhaps the third major figure of the triumvirate comprising the early manifestations of the Intoxicant, and also engaged artistically with the hallucinations induced. More even than Poe, he helped to establish the *theme* of degeneracy—related to, but not inextricable from (as the example of the bourgeois Coleridge of the *Kubla Khan* period shows) that of intoxication. So obsessed with intellectual pursuit that he ran away at 15 in a failed attempt to enter Oxford early, he was soon living in constant poverty in the slums, protected by a consumptive ex-prostitute known only as Ann as a ward and muse. Breton would later relate that, 'she returned seventeen years later to haunt his opium-eater's dreams... Her luminous apparition again calmed the torments of utter perdition that are, in De Quincey, the terrible underside of "the most astonishing, the most complicated, the most splendid vision." ' (Breton 1997, p 55.)

When Breton says, 'in De Quincey,' does he refer to De Quincey 'himself' or De Quincey the body of texts? De Quincey the subject or De Quincey the author?

I believe that Nerval's and Baudelaire's generation noticed something else—that the British poets had in fact engaged with *their own* myths, crafting *themselves* as figures. For instance, we might compare the above version of the story of Coleridge's composition of 'Kubla Khan' to that of the version first told by himself, which holds an ambiguous position in relation to that poem; for it is attached to the poem itself. Through its claim that the poem is incomplete due to the interruption of its writing by the visitor from Porlock, the introduction in which this myth appears implicitly subordinates the poem itself to the position of a sort of *textual relic* of an event supposed to have occurred in actuality, while at the same time undermining the reliability of that very truth-claim by attaching it to the poem, which is the space where language acknowledges its own opacity; this ambivalence results in the conditions for an a-referential mytheme. Having discerned the iconic and structural language of this nascent canon, Baudelaire and his comrades were quick in inserting themselves into it and in manipulating themselves consciously as figures; in so doing, they were establishing traditions in the treatment of themes (and these themes themselves), and in the nature of individual engagements *with* the mythology of the Yellow Sign. Baudelaire, of course, engaged with both of the mythic themes I have pointed out above. We find him marking his ground in texts which ambiguously suggest the autobiographical, such as in a fairly characteristic poem in which he builds upon the legend of De Quincey's demeaned muse Ann, here in a brutal form as he describes a night with a prostitute:

> In these conditions, thus, art is no longer a question of the creation of a personal myth, but rather, with Surrealism, *of the creation of a collective myth.*
>
> -André Breton, *Political Position of Surrealism* (1935).
> (Breton 1972, p 232.)

> I fell to dreaming, close to that hired flesh,
>
> of the sad beauty that desire denies itself.
>
> (Baudelaire 1993, p 59.)

In the implicitly interrelated world of Baudelaire's *oeuvre,* this mythic engagement is juxtaposed to another on page 49, addressed to another prostitute:

> ...and yet
>
> to wine, to opium even, I prefer
> The elixir of your lips
>
> (Baudelaire 1993, p 49.)

> Six months later, on the day of the Armistice, Guillaume Apollinaire died of influenza, taking, in his delirium, a shout in the streets personally and to heart. The Paris crowds, delighting in the downfall of Kaiser Wilhelm, shouted "*À bas Guillaume! À bas Guillaume!*"
>
> -Donald Revell.   (Apollinaire 2004, p 141.)

Breton (among others) moreover has related how in this world (the 'real' world) Baudelaire searched out constantly more unusual lovers, those marginalized from society either due to economic status and social pressures (such as prostitutes) or to physical abnormalities—giantesses and dwarves, for instance—who often died soon after his acquaintance began due to their bodies being unsuited to develop and operate effectively in this world (the real world). He would sigh despondently, 'One of those dwarves was only twenty-eight inches tall. You can't have everything in this world.' (I would like to add, between these parentheses, that after Baudelaire had thus begun to expand upon the motif suggested by De Quincey's urban muse in a relatively diffused manner, Marcel Schwob would return to a more traditional and centralized treatment in his relationship with a young consumptive prostitute whose given name was Louise but whom he figured as Monelle in the book dedicated to her, published after her death. (Gourmont 1994, p 282.) Breton also reports that, in order to offend the Bourgeoisie, Baudelaire often went out into society sporting a bright green wig. Before *his* death in 1867, Baudelaire succumbed to dementia; shuffling into his room, he greeted himself in the mirror as someone else; and mirrors would continue to figure as complex images in both the fixed published texts *and* in the socially inscribed texts which constitute the doubled flesh of the Yellow Sign. After several months of silence, Baudelaire finally spoke, his voice cracking—

would somebody please pass him the mustard?

These were his last words.

Forgive this apparent digression into the complicated relationship of Baudelaire to the artistic tradition within which he worked; the relationship between Baudelaire's generation of French Dandyism and the traditional British notion of the dandy is equally complicated. During Shelley's own lifetime, the figure of the dandy, as epitomized by its founder Beau Brummell, had yet to acquire any but a very vaguely subversive element; indeed, one of its chief adherents was the Prince Regent himself, and Brummell's influence largely ended when he was excluded by the Regent in 1815. (Hazlitt 1982, p. 433.) Brummell spent five hours each morning preparing his toilet, and his fellow dandies gathered to watch him each morning as he explained each movement in this elaborate ritual.

> After remaining in the Hôpital de la Charité for several days, Jarry's breathing grew labored, his pulse diminished almost to nothing, and he became delirious, mumbling over and over, *"Je cherche... je cherche... j' ch'...* (I seek, I seek)." Then he experienced a lucid moment, raising himself slightly in his bed and looking around him almost hopefully. His attending physician, Dr. Stephen Chauvet, hurried over and asked him if he wanted anything. "His eyes began to sparkle," recalled Chauvet. "There was something which would be very nice... a toothpick." Saltas ran out and bought a box and handed it to Jarry. "He took one between two fingers of his right hand," Saltas wrote afterward. "Pleasure was visible on his face. I had hardly taken several steps to speak to the orderly when the orderly signaled for me to turn around. Jarry was dead."
>
> -Nigey Lennon, *Alfred Jarry: The Man With the Axe* (1984). (Lennon 1984, p. 87.)

Shelley's fellow radical, William Hazlitt, regarded Dandyism with a mixture of intrigue and contempt, calling Brummell 'the greatest of small wits'. (*ibid*, p 430.) Yet he sensed at least an un-activated potential, enough to pen an article on Brummell for *The London Weekly Review* in 1828, and to snare in it no less than ten stories concerning him, together with commentary regarding their relative failures and successes as mythemes; and Hazlitt, the inveterate myth-maker of the Romantic period who was perhaps more responsible than anyone for (for example) the dominant version of the Coleridge myth—where he is not a brilliant polymath but a wasted potential, jack-of-all-trades and master of none[3]—could only have known that through his treatment of Brummell he was setting the co-ordinates for a myth that, through print, could be injected into other languages and social situations—'in so new a species, the theory is unintelligible without furnishing the proofs.' (*ibid.*)

Hazlitt says of Brummell that, 'It is impossible for anyone to go beyond him without falling flat into insignificance and insipidity: he has touched the *ne plus ultra* that divides the dandy from the dunce.' (*ibid.*) Throughout his treatment, Hazlitt reaffirms the essential frivolity of the dandy of his day, yet observes that,

---

[3] See Artaud's *Coleridge the Traitor* for a more incisive and productive re-working of the Coleridge-as-wasted-potential myth.

'The *ideal* is everything, even in frivolity and folly.' (*ibid*, p. 432.) The dandy is in part distinguished by the way in which he approaches this ideal, through increasingly fine distinctions and minute matters of detail that mimic or develop parallel with the increasingly complex critical sensibility marking a rapidly emerging modernity. Through making the transient and insignificant the focus of attention, the dandy locates the ideal not in the object, but in the critical sensibility with which it is approached. Hazlitt presents the following example:

> Thus, in the question addressed to a noble person (which we quoted the other day), 'Do you call that thing a coat?' a distinction is taken as nice as it is startling. It seems all at once a vulgar prejudice to suppose that a coat is a coat, the commonest of all things,—it is here lifted into an ineffable essence, so that a coat is no longer a thing; or that it would take infinite gradations of fashion, taste, and refinement, for a thing to aspire to the undefined privileges, and mysterious attributes of a coat.
>
> (*ibid*, p. 430-431.)

It is not hard to see this obsessive attention to detail, heightened to the point of self-conscious (and sometimes self-induced) 'neurosis', in the work of Flaubert, Poictevin, Roussel, and Huysmans among others; and in the latter case this sensibility may have been activated, as we shall see, as a technique for more radical speculative practices. Nonetheless this brand of Dandyism was quite far from that practiced by or influencing practitioners of the Yellow Sign. Deak notes that, 'Brummell never dressed to attract attention; his dress was always elegant and never eccentric, and only other dandies were able to recognize the significant details and novelties of Brummell's attire. French dandies dressed to be noticed, not because they did not know any better but because they were already a transitional form leading to the aesthetes.' (Deak 1993, p. 254.)

Dandyism began to take on a more subversive quality in France by the 1830s. While the Dandyism of Brummell had taken its coordinates almost entirely from the aristocracy, French dandies, most of them associated with the Jockey Club of Lord Henry Seymour, *adopted* aristocratic postures as part of an attack *on bourgeois* society. The decadent aristocracy became, paradoxically, a space of revolt against the dominant bourgeois order from which most dandies came—few were from

> Since the admiration [Brummell] excited is not justified by facts, which have perished entirely, because they were by nature ephemeral, the weight of the greatest name and the homage of the most enticing genius do but serve to render the enigma more obscure. And in truth, that part of society which leaves the least trace, the fewest remains, an aroma too subtle to last, its manners, manners that cannot be passed on, and it is by them that Brummell was a prince of his time. Like the orator, the great actor, the conversationalist, like all of those minds which speak to the body by the body.
>
> -Barbey d'Aurevilly, *Of Dandyism and George Brummell* (1845.)   (Deak 1993, pp 254-255.)

aristocratic origins and many of them were financially ruined by their lifestyles, dying in abject poverty. (Starkie 1954, pp 72-85.) Elitist rhetoric and aristocratic social signifiers were employed as provocations against the uncritical (and hypocritical) populism and puritanical conformity of bourgeois society. d'Aurevilly wore exclusively 'clothes devised by him and whose cut he had supervised, as a protest against ready-mades, the reach-me-downs of a machine age.' Moreover, he promulgated a notion of Dandyism as the creation of an artificial—and therefore distinct from bourgeois 'common sense'—*personality* for which the clothing and manners were simply a social signifier. (*ibid*, p. 82.) As Baudelaire would insist a generation later,

> If I have mentioned money, the reason is that money is indispensable to those who make an exclusive cult of their passions, but the dandy does not aspire to wealth as an object in itself; an open bank credit would serve him just as well; he leaves that squalid passion to common mortals. Contrary to what a lot of thoughtless people seem to believe, dandyism is not even an excessive delight in clothes and material elegance. For the perfect dandy, these things are no more than the symbol of the aristocratic superiority of his mind.

(Baudelaire 1972, p 420.)

Thus, we do not find, as with Brummell, lords and Princes Regent as the targets of dandies' attacks, but the bourgeois and philistine mass. For instance, Enid Starkie relates a story by the dandy Roger de Beauvoir, who tells us of his fellow dandy that,

> one evening at the theatre Saint Cricq was so disgusted at the applause which greeted a very bad play that, in the interval, he went out and hired all the cabs waiting outside. It was a very wet night and he had assured that none of the smartly dressed men and women of the audience would be able to go home under cover. At the close of the play they applauded more vociferously than ever and he shouted at them from his box: 'Clap away, fools that you are, you'll all get soaked going home!'

(Starkie 1954, p. 75.)

---

1. Prearranged "breakdowns" of a fleet of Fluxus autos and trucks bearing posters, exhibits etc. in the middle of the busiest traffic intersections, such as Times Square, 5th Avenue, 57th and 42nd Streets, tunnel and bridge entries etc.

[…]

2. Clogging up subway cars during rush hours with cumbersome objects (such as large musical instruments…)

[…]

3. Disrupting entries at halls, theaters, museums, galleries, etc. during critical hours by calling (over phone) numbers of taxicabs, trucks, ambulances, firemen etc. etc. (This could be combined with "breakdown" of Fluxus fleet.)

-George Maciunas, *Fluxus Newsletter No. 6* (1963).

(Williams 1997, pp 93-94.)

Despite the more subversive quality of the French dandies of this period, it remains that this subversiveness remained tied to, and tied *down* to, a reactionary and dying social class, and inevitably played into the class structures which not only upheld the aristocracy but gave birth to the Bourgeoisie itself; moreover, it implicitly or explicitly allied itself within the same movement to the ideologies of oligarchy, repression, and

> **WAYWORD YOUTH**
>
> Jean-Michel Mension and Auguste Hommel, 20 years old, are up before Judge Royer of the Twelvth Magistrate's Court.
>
> Their aspect (we refer to their attire) is very curious, including apple-green corduroy pants and ridiculously thick-soled shoes. To complete the picture, wild mops of thick—and possibly inhabited—hair. This is seemingly the uniform of a particular type of fauna found in Saint-Germain-de-Prés, and it is said to be indispensable for shocking the bourgeoisie. Every period, of course, has had young people revolutionary in their morals and ideas: Incroyables during the Directory, Romantics under Louis-Phillippe, Cubists and Fauvists before 1914, Surrealists in 1920, *zazous* in 1943, existentialists courtesy of Monsieur J.-P. Sartre. But at least all those young people, even if they produced lots of noise and very little by way of masterpieces, were not thieves. Mension and Hommel have put the finishing touch to the model: not satisfied with shocking the bourgeoisie, they rob them to boot.
>
> -Crime Report, *Qui? Détective* No. 363 (1953.)
> (Mension 2001, p 21.)

social stasis which in turn legitimized the bourgeois regime through its *professed* opposition to them. The most subversive aspect of the Dandyist programme however, the artificial and conscious re-working of personality, was not inherently tied to this aristocratic posture; and there were other groups and creative communities in France simultaneously exploring other manifestations of this practice.

One was Les Badouilles, a group that adapted the aristocratic and dandyist notion of a closed group of elites, but inverted the terms of elitism in such a way that the 'elite' were characterized by the rowdy, drunken behavior habitually associated by the Bourgeoisie with the lower classes. Initiates were required to recount their various exploits and fights against the Bourgeoisie, and to take an oath of vengeance against that class. They were taught drinking songs declaring republican and democratic ideals in obscene language calculated to offend them. The initiation rite included a full day of eating and drinking of wine, followed by an all-night ball composed of wild dancing, leading directly into another full day and night moving from pub to café to pub in dress calculated to offend the bourgeoisie, the initiate drinking everything put in front of him. (*ibid*, pp 84-85.)

More directly relevant (only) from a genealogical point of view is the Romantic group Le Petit Cénacle, led by a young Petrus Borel, Gérard de Nerval, Théophile Gautier, Aloysius Bertrand, Philothée O'Neddy, and Augustus MacKeat. Like the dandies, Le Petit Cénacle inscribed their social dissent through dress; but in a considerably more outlandish way. Jehan du Seigneur refused to wear anything white, and sported an early prototype of the Punk Mohawk; Nerval often dressed in costume as Goethe's Werther. (*ibid*, pp 25-28 & 72.) The group organized a large-scale intervention at the premier of Hugo's *Hernani* in 1829, recruiting students and, with Hugo's connivance, going through the play with them line-by-line to tutor them on how they ought to react in order to best offend the aristocratic and bourgeois supporters of Classicism in the audience. Fights broke out with crowds on the street before they were even admitted to the theatre, and the production itself, henceforth known as the 'Battle of *Hernani*',

> For the past hundred years summonses of a most serious nature have been issued. We are at a great remove from the sweet, the charming "battle" of *Hernani*.
>
> -André Breton, *Second Manifesto of Surrealism* (1930).
> (Breton 1972, p 137.)

was almost entirely drowned out by the catcalls and shouts of both supporter and detractors, hovering throughout the play on the border of riot. (*ibid*, pp 30-41.)

This alternate form of provocation, quite different from the aristocratic postures of the dandies, was gradually internalized and honed by the group, who began calling themselves the Jeunes France, then (guided largely by Borel, known as the Lycanthrope or Wolf-Man) came to be known as the Bouzingos as the dynamic of their way of living evolved. Gradually withdrawing (or being barred) from the literary salons (*ibid*, p. 91.), the Bouzingos concentrated on the shaping of their own internal social structure, developing a clannishness that manifested itself quite differently from the dandies,[4] choosing as their model the 'degenerate' idiom of Les Badouillards, heavily inflected with macabre Gothic archetypes drawn equally from Byron and from the emerging 'mass literature' that prefigured pulp fiction. The introduction to Borel's *Rhapsodies* declared, 'There are those who will say, This book has something revoltingly lower-class about it, the answer is that indeed the author does not sleep in a king's bed.' (Breton 1997, p 78.) It was not only the class connotations of these models that was calculated to offend both aristocratic tastes and bourgeois pretensions, but also their deliberately over-the-top idiom, a lack of decorum or elegance in their treatment that added adolescent overtones to those of class in order to refuse all notions of respectability.

> In France, higher than the Victor Hugo of 'Fin de Satan' and 'Dieu', the surrealists place Alyosius Bertrand, the 'agitators' Petrus Borel and Charles Lassailly, who give this 'minor' romanticism its tonality of revolt, risk, and authenticity, so different from the rhymed dissertations of Lamartine or Vigny. Above all, Nerval who described his own dream states as 'super-naturalistic' and who so tragically transposed poetry into everyday life, proved to Tzara that poetry escapes the poem, that it can exist without it.
>
> -Maurice Nadeau, *The History of Surrealism* (1964)   (Nadeau 1973, pp 75-76.)

The Bouzingos congregated at the house rented by Borel, where they were forced to sit on the floor for lack of chairs but which had murals painted by Devéria and other members, and was decorated with various parts of human skeletons. Popular report held that their semi-communal quarters were strewn with supposedly-poisoned weapons, scalps, wolf-traps, and human feotuses in jars. As opposed to the explicitly refined idiom of the dandies, the vehemently republican Bouzingos presented themselves as rowdy derelicts. They dressed dummies up in funeral shrouds and flung them from the windows, shouting out into the street that they were corpses. They argued philosophy naked in lawn chairs outside. At their parties, ice cream was served from human skulls, and the basement was reserved for those passed out from too much alcohol. They danced the

---

[4] This clannishness, an aristocratic model in the structuring of its internal dynamic even if re-invested with different ideological implications and positioned differently in relation to class, also signaled what would become almost a defining trait of the avant-garde: the dandies lived essentially solitary lives, their clannishness staging itself only when they *met* within the aristocratic society in which they intervened; both their intervention and the social structure determining it were conceived and experienced as incursions *from outside*. The Bouzingos and other groups, however, maintained this clannishness within their private spaces (both physical and psychological) as well, and their incursions into bourgeois society were determined in such a way as to take on the character of a rupture *from within*.

'Infernal Gallop', its time marked by pistols shot into the ceiling, which left the floor littered with unconscious dancers who collapsed from the strain and excitement. They met in the yard to bash and blow instruments for the sheer love of noise; they roamed the streets in a drunken pack, devising cheers and slogans about one another in turn, or singing songs of their own composition, often attracting enough attention to end up fighting with the police and being hauled off to jail. The name 'Bouzingos' itself—deliberately misspelled to offend the bourgeoisie—is derived from 'bousin' or noise, comes from one of these songs.

But already, some of those within the Bouzingos group, especially Gérard de Nerval, were beginning to explore other routes which incorporated the (relative) subtlety, specificity, interiority, and critical sensibility of Dandyism, while retaining the Bouzingos concern with aggressive public inscription, and pushing and refining the Bouzingo impulse toward outlandishness and absurdity.

These developments also involved a shift away from the mythic model of the Petit Cénacle-Bouzingos, in which the group tended to subsume the individuals involved as the central mythic 'figure', and toward the model provided by the British Romantics as their mythic figurations had begun to be set by themselves and by each other, especially Hazlitt; in the latter model, the individual is the primary mythic unit. The result of the collective model can be seen in the description just given, in which the main mythic figure is the Bouzingo group itself, rather than any individual within it. This model has the advantage of asserting the practices involved as social interventions and not merely individual anomalies, and resists 'heroic' readings that marginalize the social and collective nature of cultural change, but on the other hand it makes effective cross-generational transmission highly problematic; while Enid Starkie, in her study of Borel and the Bouzingos group, makes it clear that Borel's position within that group was largely a result of his mythic status *within* the closed circle of the Petit Cénacle, and perhaps in Parisian creative communities at large, the various individuals involved in the group, and the specific nature of their various contributions *to* this group dynamic, are virtually beyond recovery, and can now be evoked through only lists of their habitual costumes: 'Ourlioff in his Cossack boots; Bouchardy in his bright-blue frock coat, with the gold buttons, like that worn by an Indian Maharaja; the two brothers, one nicknamed 'Le Gothic' and the other 'Le Christ', in their sweeping light-blue cloaks lined with pale pink, and fastened by pearl buttons as large as five-shilling pieces…' and so on. While each of these poets no doubt inflected the group dynamic in an important way recognized by those involved, there is very little for later generations to grasp onto in any attempt to study the tactics and strategies by which similar social interventions and structuration might be approached from the standpoint of the individual subject.

> Cossacks Christ a rotting sun
> Roofs
> Sleepwalkers goats
> A lycanthrope
> Pétrus Borel
> Madness winter
> A genius split like a peach
> Lautréamont
> Chagall
> Poor kid next to my wife
> Morose delectation
>
> -Blaise Cendrars, *Portrait* (1913).
> (Cendrars 1992, pp 61-62.)

It was perhaps in response to this that Nerval began to develop mythic strategies that offered themselves up for more effective transmission; for he deployed distinct mythemes in the form of extreme affectations and habits that offered themselves up for mnemonic retention, that offered the potential for later filling-out and re-working of details to provide a true mythic structure with simultaneous and equally-valid versions, and that served as defined gestures that could engage with intertextual practice and traditional elaboration. At the same time, these habits could serve as catalysts for the inner work and cognitive discipline which Baudelaire would later connect with Dandyism.

> "Yo soy que soy" (I am what I am): this phrase, Borel's motto, was also the last one uttered by Swift three years before is death, as he stared pityingly into a mirror and they hurriedly removed the knife within his reach. And Pétrus Borel, in the portrait used as the frontispiece to his volume of poems, *Rhapsodies,* is also holding a dagger pointed at his breast.
>
> -André Breton, *Anthology of Black Humor* (1945). (Breton 1997, p 75.)

These affectations began as typically Bouzingo, but already betrayed a certain sophistication, weaving in intertextual references from published works; most notably of course his father's skull, which he had made into a cup that he invariably carried to the pub, and from which he always insisted upon drinking his wine. When Nerval first produced the skull, Gautier expressed his surprise, and it was pointed out to him by Célestin Nanteuil that this gesture was also a reference to Hugo's *Han d'Islande*. Nerval then began pitching tents indoors in which to sleep when he spent the night in the homes of friends; this motif was soon expanded when he somehow acquired a huge bed from the Renaissance which he would laboriously haul along with him through the streets of Paris and meticulously set up in the guest room or living room; whereupon he would invariably declare it too precious to sleep on, and go to sleep on the floor beside it. He then stole a lobster and began to parade it about the city, using a pale blue ribbon as a lead; when questioned as to the reason, he remarked archly that lobsters do not bark. Even in his later madness and in his suicide, Nerval's mythic and intertextual sensibility did not leave him; up to the last he protected the length of string that he insisted was the garter of the Queen of Sheba—appearing as an apparition in Flaubert's *Temptation of St. Anthony*—and it was with this garter that he hanged himself from a lamp-post in 1855. Around his head when his body was discovered was the raven he kept as a pet in homage to Poe, whom Nerval had taught only one phrase: 'I'm Thirsty! I'm Thirsty!'

> I don't like to remain cryptic for friends like you, although I'm happy to be so when I want to force others to think of me.
>
> (It seems I forgot to light the lamp? the one from which I hanged myself in times gone by.)
>
> -Stéphane Mallarmé, Letter to T. Aubanel, 28 July, 1866.
> (Mallarmé 1988, p 43.)

By the mid-1830s Nerval was not alone in his intuition that the strategies employed by the Bouzingos to re-write their social and interior lives were limited and must be moved past. A schism occurred between Borel and O'Neddy on the one side and Gautier, Nerval, Camille Rogier, and Arsène Houssaye on the other. Nerval, Gautier, and their group, now calling themselves La Bohême Doyenné, befriended the dandy Roger de

Beauvoir, and their conceptions of social relations and psychological self-discipline became heavily inflected with Dandyism. (*ibid*, p. 123.)

> Two traditions met.
> But our padlocked thoughts
> Lacked the place required,
> Experiment to be tried again.
>
> -Antonin Artaud, *A Cry* (1924).
> (Artaud 1965, p 14.)

One will see now the reason for this long digression, for it was Gautier and Nerval who initiated Baudelaire into Dandyism; and the latter inherited, therefore, a breed of Dandyism that had been passed through the chaos of the Bouzingos and which had therefore developed an especially genuine and complex dissenting impulse.[5] Gautier himself remarked that, 'One might say that [Baudelaire] was a dandy who had strayed into Bohemia.' (Baudelaire 1996, p xiii.) Thus, on the one hand, we find Baudelaire engaging in the kind of witty, cutting small talk superficially characteristic of Brummell, but in fact introducing into the aristocratic discourse a good deal of the vulgarity that, within that discourse, was representative of the threat of 'the rabble' (and which was, perhaps, even more threatening to the moneyed Bourgeoisie aspiring toward aristocratic status, forced to deny their class' relationship with the lower class), as when, upon his introduction to two sisters, he asked the father politely, 'and which of these two young ladies are you grooming for prostitution?' On the other hand, we find him adopting the more flamboyant presentation of the bohemian Bouzingos, sporting a bright green wig and carrying on open affairs with dwarfs, giantesses, and women of other races. Seizing upon Hazlitt's identification of an almost Platonic idealism hidden within the apparent triviality of Brummell's Dandyism, Baudelaire makes explicit the dissenting nature of his own brand of the practice:

> I have a little confession to make. It was while running through, for the twentieth time at least, the pages of the famous *Gaspard de le Nuit* of Aloysius Bertrand (has not a book known to you, me, and a few of our friends the right to be called famous?) that the idea came to me of attempting something in the same vein
>
> -Charles Baudelaire, dedication to Arséne Houssaye of *Paris Spleen* (1869.)
> (Baudelaire 1970, p ix.)

> Fastidious, unbelievables, beaux, lions or dandies: whichever label these men claim for themselves, one and all stem from the same origin, all share the same characteristic of opposition and revolt; all are representatives of what is best in human pride, of that need, which is too rare in the modern generation, to combat and destroy triviality. That is the source, in your dandy, of that haughty, patrician attitude, aggressive even in its coldness.

(Baudelaire 1992, p. 421.)

---

[5] This combination of public rowdiness and cognitive discipline, of individual mythic gestures and thoroughly subsumed group identifications and mythic engagements, would be built on and taken further by the various Dada and Surrealist groups of 90 years later, among others; the trajectory laid out by the Bouzingos would to a large extent be followed by the Lettrists and Parisian Situationists. While its group dynamic was very different, Fluxus, too, would situate their mythic focus more-or-less firmly on the collective, rather than individual level (with the exception of Maciunas, probably the most fully developed post-War figure in the tradition), while the Symbolists and Decadents, via Aestheticism, remained closer to that suggested by Dandyism.

> A game I like to play with readers… is the placement of important information in the footnotes.
>
> -Stewart Home, *Strategies of Writing*. (Home 1995, p 130.)

The Dandyism of Baudelaire was thus necessarily characterized by various tensions. This essential tension was in fact one reason that Baudelaire chose to identify himself with the aristocratic stance of Dandyism, despite his fighting actively on the barricades in the 1848 Revolution; the social codes of the inherently static aristocracy provided a structure within which transgression could be quantitatively managed: 'It is, above all, the burning desire to create a personal form of originality, within the external limits of social conventions,' (*ibid*, p. 420.) and 'Dandyism, which is an institution outside the law, has a rigorous code of laws that all its subjects are strictly bound by, however ardent and independent their individual characters may be.' (*ibid.*, p. 419.) Baudelaire was aware, too, that what made it possible to claim the aristocracy as a space of revolt was precisely its historical status *as* a doomed class faced with dissolution in the face of the encroaching bourgeois order:

> Dandyism appears especially in those periods of transition when democracy has not yet become all-powerful, and when aristocracy is only partially weakened and discredited. In the confusion of such times, a certain number of men, disenchanted and leisured 'outsiders', but all of them richly endowed with native energy, may conceive the idea of establishing a new kind of aristocracy, all the more difficult to break down because established on the most precious, the most indestructible faculties, on the divine gifts that neither work nor money can give.
>
> (*ibid.*)

The aristocracy, then, provided a kind of microcosm of social intervention, with more fixed codes and predictable sensibilities—sensibilities that were all the more raw due to the imminent collapse of the social class. At the same, it provided a model (though again, not the only, or necessarily best) for a nascent Avant-Garde still attempting to establish a social framework through which to solidify and sustain its dissenting impulse.

> Dada strives for total self-knowledge through the unique performance of the personality.
>
> -Richard Huelsenbeck, *Memoirs of a Dada Drummer* (1969).
>
> (Huelsenbeck 1991, p 79.)

One might identify at least two parallel movements implicit in Baudelaire's formulation of Dandyism: on the one hand is the social gesture, or co-ordinated set of gestures, 'of opposition and revolt' *inscribed* within, and only within, a particular socio-economic milieu; on the other hand is that underlying critical attitude or discipline that 'comes close to spirituality and to stoicism', necessarily internalized and integrated into the structure of the subject itself and therefore at play regardless of the presence or absence of the context that would allow for the staged *inscription* of those gestures. In relation to the social or publicly inscribed stratum, one must consider that his access to upper-class circles (which of course by this time were rarely thoroughly aristocratic by birth, but rather by convention and economic status) was based upon his reputation as a critic and to some extent as a poet; his poetry itself, and his engagement with social models deeply opposed to the aristocratic—which permeates his poetry—must then be taken into account as a major element of his practice of this element of Dandyism.[6] At the same time, the critical attitude and subjective, critical, and cognitive practices that constitute the *discipline* of Dandyism are inescapably at play, whether or not in easily recognisable form, in all of his actions, including the production and dissemination of texts. His verse and published writing created a mythic persona which preceded that mythic *subject* he progressively became; while his engagement with Dandyism provided him with the discursive tools to bring about this transformation, as we shall see below.

From both directions then, we find that the aristocratic model alone provides an inadequate picture of his project, and Baudelaire's engagement with aristocratic models cannot be looked at so simply; it is in fact one term of a dialectic. This dialectic could be productively examined on several registers and from several perspectives; in order not to try your patience, my dearest reader (a danger of which I am always keenly alert), I shall choose only one.

Jettisoning or at least bracketing off (as we ought often to do) the notion of the artwork as an aesthetic object, and retaining only the notion of it as a cultural *artifact* in a fairly broad sense (these two notions, besides, *need* not be kept at arms length), we can see how both of these *roles*—'dandy' and 'poet'— while both circumscribed by conventions and culturally-imposed conditions limiting the scope of their effect, in fact served to develop one another and, more importantly, to create in the space where they collapsed into each other a potential mode of *living* that utilized the subversive and decentring potential of self-consciously creative activity while refusing, or beginning to refuse, the social and ideological curtailment and complicity inherent in the modern notion of 'art' considered as a social *edifice* distinct from other areas or registers of life.[7] 'Art' was positioned as escaping *into*, not as *annexing*, 'life'.

---

[6] It should be noted that Baudelaire's comments on Dandyism given in this text, from 1859-60's *The Painter of Modern Life*, describe his practice *after* the scandal that accompanied the 1857 publication of *Les Fleurs du Mal* and the high-profile censorship trials; his position within the circles that provided a playground for Dandyism was, then, heavily informed by, and probably in part due to, his reputation as a poet celebrating 'indecent' and deviant matter. While this raises certain questions as to the practice's efficacy as a truly subversive gesture, it *does* imply that Baudelaire could hardly have failed to consider these two spheres of action as interpenetrating and co-dependant.

[7] For one concise and (appropriately) partisan statement from *within* the tradition here being treated of the role that this edifice plays in maintaining dominant social models, see the introduction to Stewart Home's *Assault on Culture*. By no means am I suggesting that Baudelaire, dandyism, or indeed most of the groups, individuals, or practices at play in this book fully appreciate, much less fully *subvert*, the problem as Home states it. Baudelaire and most others in the 19th Century continued to support without reservation what Home identifies as 'elitist' notions of art/poetry *parallel* with the much more radical practices which shall be posited throughout this book; this is most likely why, in Home's many treatments of a tradition quite close to that which I am assembling here, he very rarely treats 19th century practices, with scattered exceptions such as Lautréamont, Rimbaud, and Jarry. Rather, I am suggesting that an awareness of the (even) deeper implications of this issue, albeit discursively bolstered *by* rather than *escaping* transcendent claims for 'art', developed on the level of the discreet human

subject before being developed in relation to a broader *social* consciousness. This is undoubtedly due in part to the heritage of Romanticism; it is also the result of a set of necessary but flawed strategies (including but not limited to Dandyism) adopted in the attempt to establish a social and discursive position *from which* a project of defiance might be waged (see Richard Cándida-Smith's *Mallarmé's Children*); and indeed a widespread awareness of the full implications of certain cultural models being developed or maintained in the industrialized West might necessarily have awaited the advent and dissemination of dialectical materialism, which finally schematized what many dissenting communities, necessarily groping their way *out of* a society of specialization that they were simultaneously being enclosed *within*, had been unable to comprehensively conceive and comprehensively respond *to*. Thus while I am dealing by and large with practices *emerging from* art and many of the individuals I present were indeed fully 'artists' in the sense that Home (rightly) condemns, it is *not* their status as cultural 'workers' that I am interested in, and their productions are taken not as aesthetic objects, but as relics of lives that were lived and practices of intimate but fundamental revolutionary power. While it goes without saying that the often uncontested containment of these practices within certain limits ('private life') delineated by society excludes many of the figures treated here from Home's 'Utopian current', it seems to me essential to trace not only the history of that current from the moment of its merging with artistic traditions at the turn of the century and the resultant rupture that, to a more radical degree, broke free of traditional notions of 'art' as such; but to trace as well the already-existent traditions which took on that struggle, the practices and discourses within these traditions that prepared them *for* that rupture, and the continuities that underlie this tradition at least as far back as the advent of the dominant system itself—the continuity which provided a stockpile of practical and discursive weapons to the radical tradition that is often *assumed* to find its *'origin'* someplace between Futurism and Dada. The latter groups (and the many still in the fight, amongst whom, since this footnote contains, as few in this book do, a good deal of self-referentiality, I would like to modestly include myself and my comrades) were and are able to act and to *think* as effectively and incisively as they did and do, in part because the *gesture* of revolt, notwithstanding its often misguided terms, had already been established on the levels of theory, strategy, and technique. One might question whether, at present, for a host of reasons it is unnecessary to drearily list, we are not growing closer, within a very few generations, to a major shift certainly not in the *necessity* of continued action, but in the very *coordinates* through which we conceptualize and respond to hegemonic structures. How are we to prepare ourselves for precisely the *condition* of being unprepared? Examining *only* the *most* successful efforts will not be adequate. It is necessary to *begin* a *partisan* examination (partisan on the level of strategy, though as I will explain, partisanship on the tactical level may be more subtle when the strategy demands it) of those efforts which, on the one hand, took a century or so to reach a relatively requisite degree of *comprehensive* critique, but, on the other hand, *did in fact* create the eventual conditions for a cultural activity quite possibly beyond the conception of many of those who, over a number of generations, *had nonetheless striven for it*. We must examine how these early communities and groups *dealt* with their inability to grasp the precise coordinates of the culture they opposed, how they dealt with the need to create new forms of sociality and new forms of *thought* in conditions which had not merely *evolved* from earlier models, but for which they *had* no reliable models; we must attempt to determine both the successes and failures, and develop a discourse concerning the *strategy* of strategy. It is necessary to apply the same rigour, force of detail, and respect (even in, and indeed *through* rigorous critique) to these activities that Home, and a *few* others, apply to the *relatively* more thorough and successful efforts *from within* the struggle—rather than from an ultimately impotent position of academic 'impartiality' (inevitably complicit with the historiography of hegemony). To describe or interpret anything must also be to suggest the possibility and the coordinates of a realm of *praxis*. This is emphatically my intention.

I am very far from claiming that this book achieves *any* of what I have laid out above. It is, rather, a very modest first step in that direction; though, I hope, not so modest as to fail to suggest the seriousness and scope of the work that is to be done if this particular tradition of revolt is to continue to broaden its field and sharpen its attack rather than fall back (as is always the danger) into either vague rebellious theatrics or an empty academicism. For instance, I have mentioned the need for rigorous *criticism*—and it is undoubtedly for this reason that much of this footnote has been oriented in relation to the work of Stewart Home, who (especially in relation to Surrealism and to the Situationist International, or certain elements of it) has incisively acted *against* the more detrimental (because irresponsible) *aspects* of the mythologizing which, nonetheless, I posit as indispensible. This kind of criticism (which might be related, for instance, to Derrida's critiques of Phenomenology, Structural Anthropology, Foucault, etc.) *is absolutely essential* and is the ultimate aim of any such historiographic project as I have suggested. This type of criticism, however, can only be *productively* played out in a context in which a certain amount of detailed understanding of not only the *ideas* of the target group or community, but its social and *psychological* configurations and activities are widely and intelligently understood by the readership, and in which a *certain* enthusiasm and understanding of the relative *importance* of the target has prepared the way; otherwise the result is not a more intelligent, nuanced, and practical approach from which strategies and tactics can be drawn and/or modified, but rather an uninformed rejection of a huge number of *potential* readings. Rather than providing such a *premature* critique, therefore, this text attempts to *begin to lay the groundwork for* such a critique. It can be seen then that on this political register (and it is hopefully apparent that the discussion here deals only with *one* register of the text, that there are other sets of coordinates equally permeating both the

For it was not Dandyism and its aristocratic model alone that offered a productively exaggerated system of codes. Poetry itself also fulfilled, on a different register, this need that Baudelaire identifies for a rigid microcosm within which deviance might be deployed and charted with greater precision—the conditions to develop a subversive *discipline*. These two practices—the one constrained to a craft (the production and arrangement of elements in a discrete *work*) and the other constrained to an extreme historical contingency on the level of an 'everyday life' (specific to very particular social and economic conditions and the codes—both explicit and implicit—that characterized them, and necessitating a high degree of sophisticated spontaneity), might both be looked at as *preparation* for a 'discipline' drawing from both, yet refusing the socially-imposed boundaries limiting, in different ways, the potentials of both.

It is not hard to see how Dandyism proper might, through jettisoning its aristocratic fetters, apply the critical sensibility that it had developed to a much broader field of cultural activity and in a much more comprehensive fashion; and it has already been suggested how it was already beginning to be conceived not

---

structure and 'argument' of the book, and that these registers are by no means really distinct from the present discussion, but rather modulate it from within its own articulation and its own *reading*—you are not at all excluded from this economy, my dearest reader) this book is *strategically* deployed, that is to say that it is conscious of its discursive context, that it *does not* claim to give a 'complete' picture of what it is dealing with; just as I have argued in relation to Baudelaire back where this footnote began, this book is one term in a dialectic, or rather a discussion, a discourse. Therefore, for instance, the book can be seen throughout to emphasize a largely interior or 'personal' practice over the more explicitly 'political' register which is the focus of this footnote (and which, soon, will also need to be rigorously applied to *all* of the movements and currents treated here). This *should not* imply that such an interiorized practice is *sufficient* but that, in most of the *serious* discourse coming from within the struggle of which I am speaking, I identify a lack of focus on revolt in the structures of cognition and the experience of *subjectivity itself* in relation to revolt on the 'social' register; whereas the subject and the *polis* are always already in flux, interpenetrating. (I refer you, for example, to Kristeva's *Revolution in Poetic Language*, especially the conclusion). Any social transformation divorced from transformation of *modes of thought* will become a tyranny in its turn; and it seems likely that the latter must precede the former. There is a sense in which the emphasis in this book on the subject and on personal practices of reading, writing, mythologizing, thinking, and the more radical practices upon which I will speculate might be seen as a counterpoint to the larger number of cogent analyses operating more exclusively from the standpoint of economic and political theory. At the same time, my concerns regarding the form and (Anti-)hermeneutic function of a radicalized historiography should be clear from the structure of the work, though this concern does not exhaust and should not circumscribe the motivations for the book's many idiosyncracies. In all registers, what may seem *tactically* apolitical or uncritical is intended, at the least, as *strategically* practical and motivated.

I do not offer these comments in an attempt at elucidation—on the contrary, the fear of making this book comprehensible to those attempting to *consume* the text therein is the greatest argument against their inclusion. But, firstly, it has appeared necessary to make myself more explicit *in regard to one register,* the polemic (you, my dearest reader, may *initiate your self* into many others), because that register seems to demand at least a modicum of explicit elucidation in order to operate. More importantly, it was finally deemed essential to include, as it were, a palimpsest *within* the book of the larger discourse with which it engages in order to prevent it, through its own coyness or through the laziness of certain readers, from not only failing in its responsibility to the community and the transgenerational project of dissent *from which even its obscurities and its secrets should be inextricable* but from possibly even *aiding* the enemy through failing to *name* the enemy—to place the enemy *in the present* as well as in the past (whatever the difference might be). This book is *not* intended as a de-politicized Post-Modern exercise in clever irony. I am deadly serious, in all of my many voices. There are many forms of death to be read, here and elsewhere. This history and this historiography is a carefully indexed work of fiction, within which I and many others *insist* upon living, and within which many generations always already have.

In any event, this is only a footnote.

only in terms of theatricality and staging, but in terms of subjective process and modes of thinking. However, it must also be considered that the practice of Dandyism within those closed circles might be looked at as a kind of *training* for this potentially broader practice, and was not necessarily exclusive to it. Developing such a practice within the microcosm of a closed code allowed Baudelaire to develop a *technique* of motivated conversational and social exchange through which to articulate a complex network of social, personal, material, and intellectual

> a Place comes forth, a stage, the public enhancement of the spectacle of Self; there, through the mediation of light, flesh, and laughter, the sacrifice of personality made by the inspirer is complete; or else in some foreign resurrection, he is finished: his word from then on, reverberating and useless, is exhaled by the orchestral chimera.
>
> -Stéphane Mallarmé, *Action Restricted* (1886). (Caws 2001, p 22.)

content, utilizing not only spoken language but gesture, deportment, and a host of secondary associations from various areas of social life. This system of technique could then be deployed in other, less predictable social contexts, and could articulate a broader and more complex field of social intervention and inscription with a certain amount of perspicuity and success.

At the same time, the *craft* of poetry can be seen, at least in part, as an analogous preparation. Already largely a matter of technique, of *techné*, the practice of poetry is the manipulation of language; and to manipulate language is to manipulate thought. It might be noted that Baudelaire—whose work is *formally* quite sophisticated and precise—rarely speaks of poetry as an expression of *freedom*, but rather as a duty, an onus, a *discipline*. The practice of verse presents a microcosm of *thought* just as the aristocracy presents a microcosm of *society*.[8] And Baudelaire 'himself' was experienced, *at least* by others, as a kind of living text,[9] where the practices

---

[8] Julia Kristeva: 'Since the end of the nineteenth century, "poetry" has deliberately maintained a balance between sociality and madness, and we view this as the sign of a new era. After the upheavals of the French Revolution, the nineteenth century discovered history: the Hegelian dialectic showed that history constitutes a history of reason or, more profoundly, a history of the subject, and Marxism proved that history is a succession of struggles and ruptures within relations of production. This "discovery" opened up the modern episteme—a historical one—which philosophers today are still exploring. Establishing the bourgeois Republic in the second half of the nineteenth century showed not that history was closed but rather that its logic was henceforth *thinkable*—which is not to say controllable. For a certain "residue" continues to elude the control of the historical *ratio*: the subject. History is not the history of a subject always present to himself; it is a history of modes of production. This is the Marxist correction of this dialectic. But what then becomes of the subject? This is the question that remains unanswered.

The subject never *is*. The *subject* is only the *signifying process* and he appears only as a *signifying practice*, that is, only when he is absent *within the position* out of which social, historical, and signifying activity unfolds. There is no science of the subject. Any thought mastering the subject is mystical: all that exists is a field of practice where, through his expenditure, the subject can be anticipated in an always anterior future: "Nothing will have taken place but the place." This is the "*second overturning*" of the Hegelian dialectic, which came about toward the end of the last century and was as fundamentally radical as the Marxist overturning of the dialectic—if not more so. If history is made up of modes of production, the subject is a *contradiction* that brings about practice because practice is also both signifying and semiotic, a crest where meaning emerges only to disappear. It is incumbent upon "art" to demonstrate that the subject is the absent element of and in his practice, just as it was incumbent upon political economy to prove that history is a matter of class struggle: "… in order to close the gap created by our lack of interest in what lies outside the realm of aesthetics.—Everything can be summed up in Aesthetics and Political Economy."' Both quotes are from Mallarmé. (Kristeva 1984, p 215.)

described in this paragraph and the last came together and acted upon the world. His fellow dandy Gautier describes how the precise control of social and class associations, voice, demeanor, dress, and gesture that characterized Dandyism became in Baudelaire inextricable with a use of language, and a conscious manipulation of his listeners' (i.e. readers') mental processes and practices of listening (i.e. reading) that stemmed from his poetic practice and in fact still seemed to bear the trace of the specifically *printed* text, transcribed into speech and movement:

> He measured his phrases, employing only the most carefully chosen words, pronouncing them in a unique fashion, as if he wished to underline them and clothe them in an air of mysterious importance. He spoke in italics and capital letters. In contrast to the casual manner of most artists, he went to great lengths to uphold the strictest conventions. He would advance some satanically monstrous axiom or introduce a mathematical extravagance with an icy cool detachment. He established connections that the rest of us could only struggle to comprehend but which, nonetheless, struck us by their bizarre sense of logic. His gestures were slow, serious, and held close to the body, for he had a horror of Southern gesticulation.
>
> *Portraits contemporains* (1874).   (Baudelaire 1996, p xii.)

We can see here the evidence of a sustained interior process, a crystallization of theory into cognitive and physical *habit*, without which such behavioural idioms simply could not be consistently sustained; and it is this process of intellectual embodiment, integration, sublimation, and re-creation that, Baudelaire's comments would seem to suggest, were the ultimate goal of Dandyism as he and those around him conceived it, which was on its own therefore a *practice* in every sense of the word.

> Dada was a masque, a peal of laughter. And behind it was a synthesis of the romantic, dandyish and—demonic theories of the 19th century.
>
> -Hugo Ball, *Flight Out of Time*. (Ball et. al. 1995, p 51.)

While chance and contingency must inevitably—and it is no bad thing—remain in play in every condition and articulation of such a mode of living, these things are considered and activated *as such*; while not everything can be *controlled*, there is, ideally, nothing *taken for granted* in the life or constitution of the subject, from mental practices to physiological habits to speech patterns to the cut of a jacket. The notion of 'Human Nature' as a given that is beyond examination *or change*, that offers itself up as a recourse for authoritative rhetoric and propaganda, is thoroughly rejected on every level, from that of thought and social relations (as we have been examining) to the more 'frivolous' concerns that preoccupied Dandyism in its

---

[9] Such a total and detailed manipulation of self as figure, furthermore, requires a certain distancing from 'self', that is, the *subject* must increasingly take on the role of *object* and integrate that foreign-ness into its own structure and functioning; and there is, in this case, no curtain to efface the audience that imposes that objectivity, no stage to mark the limit of this spectre of the subject's ultimate provisionality.

infancy. In the same essay in which he lays out his ideas on Dandyism, Baudelaire proceeds directly to devote a chapter to women's make-up, urging that, 'she must borrow, from all the arts, the means of rising above nature.' (Baudelaire 1972, p 427.) 'Fashion must therefore be thought of as a symptom of the taste for the ideal that floats on the surface in the human brain, above all the coarse, earthly, and disgusting things that life according to nature accumulates, as a sublime distortion of nature, or rather as a permanent and constantly renewed effort to reform nature.' (*ibid*, p 426.)

To attack Nature was to attack the self-satisfied claims of the (merely) liberal bourgeoisie, and to attack the ideology of stasis and limit that silently sustained it; it was also to deny stasis in the status of the subject, and in the fabric of 'reality' as it was defined through the intersection of social, economic, psychological, and other forces. In direct contradiction to their Romantic forebears, whose declarations of the innate positive value of Human Nature had unwittingly contributed to the rapidly-forming hegemony around them, Baudelaire, Gautier, and others aggressively inverted that idiom and claimed *artificiality* as an essential condition for any positive development of cultural or personal identity and experience. Nature, a couple generations ago deployed as the germ of Divinity in Man, was now revealed as a trope for brute instinct:

TRIUMPH OF ART.
" AND NOW, MA'AM, I HOPE THAT'LL PLAZE YE; SHURE THERE'S NIVER A SOUL AS WOULD THINK IT WAS YOUR OWN HAIR ! "

Punch, 2 Feb., 1878

Nature (which is nothing but the inner voice of self-interest) tells us to knock [our dependant parents] on the head. Review, analyze everything that is natural, all the actions and desires of absolutely natural man: you will find nothing that is not horrible. Everything that is beautiful and noble is the product of reason and calculation. Crime, which the human animal took a fancy to in his mother's womb, is by origin natural. Virtue, on the other hand, is *artificial*, supernatural, since in every age and nation gods and prophets have been necessary to teach it to bestialized humanity, and since man by himself would have been powerless to discover it.

Evil is done without effort, *naturally*, it is the working of fate; good is always the product of an art.

(*ibid*, p 425.)

This notion and this rhetoric was to play an essential part in the discourse of the Yellow Sign, and most especially in the development of practices and communities rooted in Dandyism (a largely silent heritage that, in fact, includes most of the Avant-Garde and perhaps the majority of the Yellow Sign). I have already quoted the following sentence from Frantisek Deak: 'French dandies dressed to be noticed, not because they did not know any better but because they were already a transitional form leading to the aesthetes.' (Deak 1993, p. 254.) The Aesthetes, in the word's strict sense, represented the next evolution of that heritage.

Aestheticism as a social (rather than purely 'artistic') phenomenon might be seen as the logical development of Dandyism, drenched in the cult of the artificial as articulated by Baudelaire and, to a lesser extent, Gautier. Developed roughly parallel in England and in France (where it was most enthusiastically engaged with in what became known as the Decadent community, and later in the Symbolist movement)—a development facilitated by intense mutual interest between the communities epitomized by Pater, Swinburne, Rossetti, Morris, and especially Wilde in Britain, and by Moréas, Lorraine, Moreau, Mallarmé, and Louÿs in France (Pierrot 1981, pp 16-24.)—Aestheticism made explicit the subtle but fundamental difference between the construction of *personality* and the transformation of *self-experience*.

Seventeen years after Baudelaire's death, J.-K. Huysmans, in 1884's *Against Nature* (alternatively translated as *Against the Grain*)[10]—referred to famously by Arthur Symons as 'the breviary of the decadence'—describes his alter-ego's transition from Dandyism to Aestheticism:

> Lastly, he had had a high-ceilinged room prepared for the reception of his tradesmen; they would enter and seat themselves side by side in the church stalls, and he would climb up into an imposing pulpit and preach to them of Dandyism, exhorting his bootmakers and tailors to comply in the most scrupulous manner with his briefs on the cuts of his garments, and threatening them with pecuniary excommunication if they did not follow to the letter the instructions contained in his monitories and bulls.
>
> He acquired a reputation for eccentricity, to which he gave the crowning touch by dressing in suits of white velvet and gold-embroidered waistcoats, with, in place of a cravat, a bunch of Parma violets set low in the neck of the shirt. He used also to host dinners for writers which caused quite a stir, one in particular, a copy of an eighteenth-century feast when, to celebrate the most trifling of misadventures, he organized a funerary collation.

---

[10] Throughout this book, *A Rebours* will be referred to in the French or as either of these English translations, as the context and potential connotations of each instance seem to dictate.

[. . .]

But these extravagances in which he had once taken such pride had burnt themselves out; now he was filled with contempt for those outmoded displays, for that eccentric clothing, for that bizarre ornamentation of his apartments. Now he simply wanted to arrange, for his own enjoyment rather than for the amazement of others, a domestic interior that was comfortable yet appointed in an exceptional manner, to fashion for himself a unique and tranquil setting suited to the requirements of his future solitude.

(Huysmans 1998, pp 11-12.)

Huysmans' literary projection, Des Esseintes (who, while not mapping perfectly with Huysmans himself, should be compared to Baudelaire's mythologizing of his own figure within his written work and its relationship to lived practices as discussed above), goes on to create a highly idiosyncratic home for himself, in which every detail is tailored to have particular effects on his various aesthetic, psychological, and physiological *practices*, for which each room is designed; once completed, he leaves this house only once—in an abortive attempt to visit England which shall be discussed elsewhere—before his forced removal by his doctor, which ends the book. He sees no one but this doctor and two servants who have been trained to intrude as little as possible upon his solitude.

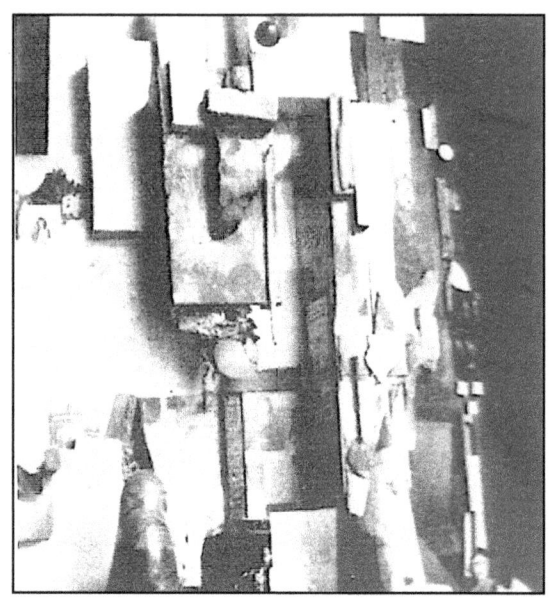

Wall of Kurt Schwitters' Merz-House, c. 1928. (Gamard 2000, fig. 32.)

This radical withdrawal from society—which is continually reexamined throughout the book—signifies an almost equally complete break from the social methodology of Dandyism (though the aristocratic overtones remain), which from Brummell to Baudelaire had always depended upon immediate social conventions for its material. The *sensibility* of Dandyism is even heightened; the detail with which Des Esseintes analyses and lays out his home is little different from a dandy's attention to his clothing or habitual gesture, as is evident in the following palimpsest of his chapter-long rumination on the colour and material in which to dress the walls of his house, which (aside from his servants, treated essentially as nonentities) only he will ever see:

What he sought were colours that increased in intensity by lamplight; little did he care if they appeared insipid or harsh by daylight, for it was at night that he really lived, believing that you were more completely at home, more truly alone, that the mind was only aroused and kindled into life as darkness drew near[11]...

Slowly, one by one, he sorted through the shades of colour. By candlelight, blue is almost an artificial green; a dark shade of blue, like cobalt or indigo, turns black; a pale shade turns grey; a true and gentle blue, like turquoise, looks faded and lifeless....

Tints salmon, maize, and rose were also out of the question, for their effeminizing character would interfere with thoughts inspired by solitude; nor, lastly, could violets be considered, since they lose their colour; only red survives at night, and what a red!...

---

[11] I can only indicate here, but do not have the room to fully engage, the way and extent to which Des Esseintes' house—in fact the other, silent main character in *A Rebours*—acts as a kind of external *machine* to stimulate and sustain a determined synthesis of habits of sensory and physical experience with a certain *form* of thought. By way of example however, one might indicate in one direction its relationship to Roman *exedra* or contemplation chambers, in which the architecture and decoration was conceived as an enveloping mnemonic device that:

> can be used to map out one's topics during invention, somewhat as a mandala-picture does in traditions of Buddhist contemplation. They provide "where" to catch hold of the process of thinking something through. It is the very habitual nature of the pictures in one's familiar place (one's house, indeed one's very bedroom) that makes them inventively fruitful over time for a variety of different matters.

(Carruthers 1998, p 178.)

In the other direction, Des Esseinte's house might be related to Kurt Schwitters' Merz-House, his home in Hannover that he progressively turned into a highly personal and idiosynchratic edifice comprised of assemblage and collage, strange angles, alters and niches dedicated to friends and comrades, secret compartments and passages:

> The literal residence of Schwitters' experience, as well as a primary site of his artistic meditations, the construction did not represent a plan or project in the traditional sense, having no beginning or end... With its labyrinth of associations and inflections, the construction at once responded to the outside world while also remaining wholly removed from it. Representative of the artist's highly individualized cosmology, the *Merzbau* functioned as a safe harbor from the prevailing chaos of Weimar Germany. Yet it also provided material for Schwitters' general resistance to the dominant norms of the social, political, and cultural milieu that surrounded him.

(Gamard 2000, pp 6-7.)

Were we given the space to delve further, we might also examine the entire mythic tradition of the 'home'—including Petrus Borel's home in Algeria, which Enid Starkey informs us is still haunted (or the other residences of the Bouzingos already mentioned); Alfred Jarry's flat on the 2nd and ½ floor, with ceilings less than five feet high and inhabited by his owls and chameleon; or indeed the 'Phalanstary' which he shared with Vallette and Rachilde, or the shack on four stilts in which he lived in utter poverty near the end of his life (which itself could be related to the shack where the destitute and starving Borel wrote *Madame Putiphar*); the 'Ideal Palace' built by Ferdinand Cheval, inspired by the shape of a stone over which he had tripped, and built over several decades from pebbles and rocks picked up along his mail route; the custom-built live-in motorcoach in which Raymond Roussel toured Europe and northern Africa, as well as the fantastic estate which is in fact the main character of the eponymous *Locus Solus*; Jorn's architectural garden; or George Maciunas' loft in Soho, turned into a virtual fortress against both the police and the mafia, complete with re-inforced doors protected by razors, secret rooms and escape passages, and getaway costumes.

Alas, we do not have such space.

> The colour he preferred to all others was orange, thus confirming by his own example the truth of a theory which he asserted was almost mathematically exact: to wit, that there exists a harmony between the sensual nature of a truly artistic individual, and the colour that his eyes perceive as most significant and most vivid.
>
> If, in fact, you disregard the majority of ordinary mortals whose coarse retinas can discern neither the peculiar cadence of colours nor the mysterious charms of their gradations and their subtleties; if you also ignore those bourgeois eyes which are insensible to the triumph of strong, vibrant colours; if you then consider none but those whose discriminating vision has been refined through contact with literature and art, he was convinced that the eye of that individual who dreams of ideal beauty, who craves illusions, who seeks some mystery in his women, is as a rule attracted to blue and its derivatives…
>
> Lastly we have those weak and nervous people whose sensual appetite demands foods enhanced by smoking and pickling, and those with over-stimulated or consumptive constitutions; their eyes, almost without exception, are drawn to that irritating, morbid colour, with all its deceptive splendours, its febrile sourness: orange.
>
> Des Esseintes' choice, therefore, did not admit of the smallest doubt; but very real difficulties still remained. If red and yellow are made more glorious by candle-light, the same is not always true of their compound, orange, which can flare up angrily, often turning a fiery nasturtium red… he decided, at least as far as his own study was concerned, to try to avoid Oriental fabrics and carpets, which now that wealthy businessmen can buy them at a discount in the latest department stores, have become so boring and commonplace.
>
> In the end he decided to have his walls bound like books, in heavy smoothe Morocco leather, using skins from the Cape glazed by huge plaques of steel under a powerful press.
>
> (Huysmans 1998, pp 12-14.)

Despite the obvious influence of Dandyism however, it is an essential difference that nobody else will ever see the result of Des Esseintes' labour; whereas the painstakingly chosen materials and cut of a dandy's clothing or the shocking quality of a green wig or scathing remark is tuned for a social effect on others, the attention paid to the Aesthetic's home is keyed exclusively in relation to the reading and thinking habits of its inhabitant. In Aestheticism, and especially in French Decadence where the solitary role was much more pronounced in the community's discourse and habits than in the British correlative, the essential effect of the practice is internal—the action is cognitive, psychological, and physiological rather than social; the only viewer is the practitioner him or herself, and the practice reveals itself not as a spectacle but as an experience.[12]

---

[12] This internal practice inevitably engages with the social and (ideally) carries on into it its transformative nature, and that matrix of the Imaginary and the Symbolic is (inevitably, as Lacan articulates) always already at stake. It is not a question of maintaining the 'Modern' dichotomy of internal/external, but a matter of the extent to which practices and discourses fully penetrate the process of subjectivity before (or while) being re-introduced in modified form into the symbolic or social economy.

While I have speculated that this condition was most likely the real focus of Baudelaire's Dandyism, as well as Gautier's, Nerval's, and others' before and after him, the Decadents and Aesthetics—especially Huysmans and Wilde—made this focus explicit through their re-working of dandyist praxis. The key goal was the changing not of self-as-image, but of subject-as-self. Deak points out (and many comments by practitioners in this heritage—including Villiers de l'Isle-Adam, Home, Jarry, Mallarmé, Péladan, Sade, Arp, Lautréamont, Ball, Ernst, Chriss, Rimbaud, Borel, Gourmont, Schwitters, Breton, Grimm, Artaud, and Bataille—explicitly confirm the correlation) that this practice can in fact be seen as a continuation of various hermetic, alchemical, and occult traditions:

> Thank you for sending me your study of the esoteric in art, which interests me personally I might almost say, for it would be hard for me to imagine something or to persue it without covering the paper with a geometry which reflects the obvious mechanics of my thought. The study of the occult is a commentary on pure signs, to which literature, bursting almost immediately from mind, is more obedient than to anything else.
>
> -Stépahne Mallarmé, letter to Victor-Emile Michelet, 18 Oct., 1890. (Mallarmé 1988, p 170.)

According to occult doctrine, which in this point is in agreement with the doctrines of various mystical systems, the aim of human life is to abandon or destroy the former self so that a new self can be created. What unites the dandy, the aesthete, and the practitioner of kaloprosopia[13] as well as the Sufi, stoics, gnostics, and all mystics is the heretical idea of self-transformation as self-creation, in which the formal self is replaced by an invented self, or by a multitude of selves. The process, as well as the aim of the transformation, varies from group to group, but the principle remains the same.[14]

(Deak 1993, p 260.)

It might not be completely amiss then to read *Against the Grain* as an *initiatory text;* indeed it has been so read for over

---

[13] Joséphin Péladan's idiosynchratic, highly ritualized development of the set of practices under discussion.

[14] In this sense, the various themes and ideas floating through this book might be looked at as analogous to and, in ways suggested in an earlier footnote, parallel to Stewart Home's suggestion that:

> Since 'art' as a category has been projected back onto the religious icons of the middle ages, it is not surprising that those who oppose it should situate themselves within a utopian current that they, in turn, trace back to medieval heresies. After the event, it is easy enough to perceive a tradition running from the Free Spirit through the writings of Winstanley, Coppe, Sade, Fourier, Lautréamont, William Morris, Alfred Jarry, and on into Futurism and Dada—then via Surrealism into Lettrisme, the various Situationist movements, Fluxus, 'Mail Art', Punk Rock, Neoism and the contemporary anarchist cults. Taking this as our hypothesis—we will not trouble ourselves over whether or not such a perspective is 'historically correct'—we will construct a 'meaningful' story from these fragments.

(Home 1991, p 4.)

as well as his development of this notion in other writings collected in *Neoism, Plagiarism, and Praxis* (1995.)

a century. *A Rebours* did in fact initiate many into the Decadent/Aesthetic community; according to Deak again:

> If among other things it demonstrates the impossibility of a purely aesthetic life, it instructs on what to read, which poets and painters to admire, what to eat, how to dress, and how to cultivate the self one chooses to be. The influence of this literature on everyday life became so pervasive that even those writers that practiced this way of life themselves were appalled by it. Henri de Régnier in "Biographic" parodies the transformation of a young man into an aesthete caused by reading Huysmans.[15]

(p 253.)

Moreover, this transformation was not unlike an initiation into a secret order, albeit a secret order re-inscribed in public, or *to* a *certain* public. For not only were Decadent practices and Decadent books, paintings, music, liquors, fabrics, gems, and everything else invariably those books, paintings, music, liquors, fabrics, gems, and everything else that the bourgeoisie *failed* to appreciate; in fact it was, in large part, their very obscurity and the perceived impossibility of their recuperation into the bourgeois order that singled them out as potential Decadent concerns:

> Dada is an experience of our age, a protest as well as an act of submission. Through its projection into art, dada is a dissolution and synthesis of the idea of the New Man.
>
> -Richard Huelsenbeck, *Memoirs of a Dada Drummer* (1969).
> (Huelsenbeck 1991, p 30.)

> When a writer or artist is praised by the newspapers, it is proof of the intelligibility of his work: wretched lining of a coat for public use; tatters covering brutality, piss contributing to the warmth of an animal brooding vile instincts. Flabby, insipid flesh reproducing with the help of typographical microbes.
>
> -Tristan Tzara, *Dada Manifesto 1918*.
> (Motherwell 1981, p 80.)

> The same was true of his Rembrandts, which from time to time he would examine on the quiet; and, indeed, just as the most charming tune in the world becomes vulgar, intolerable, as soon as the general pubic is humming it, as soon as the street-organs have taken it up, the work to which charlatan art fanciers do not remain indifferent, the work that nitwits do not challenge, which is not satisfied with arousing the enthusiasm of the few, also becomes, by virtue of that very fact, corrupted, banal, almost repellent to the initiated.
>
> (Huysmans 1998, p 83.)

Decadents had no intention of sacrificing the finely-wrought coordinates of their new modes of thinking and living to the banalising mechanizations of the developing bourgeois market, though they could not survive entirely distinct from it. Decadence

---

[15] Note, in relation to certain observations to be made later, that even this protest, in order to be addressed to the Decadent community, must be staged in the form established by Huysmans for the discourse of the community—the semi-biographical novel into which a certain 'reality' is *projected*.

was not a misunderstood tendency that would one day rise triumphant, like Romanticism; Decadence *insisted* upon being and remaining misunderstood and marginal; only from a marginal position could the dominant system be contested—the logical conclusion of the rejection of Nature as a concept typifying and upholding that system, along with every other concept that the reigning ideology used to prop up its regime. Thus Huysmans' friend Gourmont describes, 'that list of works which, to the exclusion of all classicism, forms the abbreviated library and only possible reading of those whose ill-made spirits will not lend themselves to the everyday joys of the commonplace; or of conventional morality.' (Gourmont 1994, p 191.)[16]

It is to precisely this hermetic library, among many other ideas, practices, and notions, that the initiate of *A rebours* is introduced.[17] Des Esseintes' way of life obviates a need for conventional plot; living on inherited wealth (as Huysmans himself could not), his is a life of continuous *derive*, a drift through the chambers of his house, through the aesthetic experiences (both 'artistic' and otherwise) he has prepared for himself, and his memories and thoughts, which are combined in a kind of constant, obsessive inner monologue inflected by and caught up in his increasingly familiar surroundings. Thus, each chapter of the novel serves as a glimpse of one facet of his psychology and of his practice; the initiate gleans the principles, the methodologies that underlie the specific forms that Des Esseintes' individual network of neuroses has dictated (and reciprocally, been dictated by). The obsessive lists and catalogues of information, opinions, and idiosyncratic analyses—the minute

---

[16] The term 'Decadence' itself, which some practitioners adopted and others disliked, can (when adopted) be looked at as a part of this strategy, refusing to play into Positivist, capitalist emphases on 'the new' and on the value of Progress (as most dissenting currents emerging from creative communities would to do to greater or lesser extents, at least on the strategic level, until the advent of Neoism). The emphasis, especially in *Against Nature*, on illness, on un-health as an Anti-heroic quality might be looked at in a similar light (one might see a return to this motif in the person of George Maciunas, whose chronic ill-health and legendary abhorrence of cigarette smoke is reminiscent of Decadent 'neurosis' and physiological hypersensitivities such as that which ultimately makes the Aesthetic lifestyle physically untenable for Des Esseintes). I use the term 'Decadent' here although within *A rebours* itself neither that term nor the term 'aesthetic' is used explicitly in relation to the practice I describe (though dandyism is); the concept of decadence is much discussed there in relation to Huysmans' project, but indirectly, through analyses of decadent Latin literature and the fates of various languages after the fall of Roman hegemony. The term Decadent is generally associated with Huysmans and his milieu, but its use accrued gradually, was never definitively schematized, and is quite fluid in relation to Symbolism, which largely grew from it, and late Romanticism. In any event Decadence represents a broader and less specific worldview than the practice of Aestheticism; while the latter must, I would argue, be looked at as one of the former's salient factors, they do not map perfectly. I employ the term in this section largely to distinguish the French practice of Aestheticism from the British version which, under the influence of Wilde and Morris, assumed a more conventionally utopian and sociable character. (As a system synthesizing practices and discourses from all areas of life generally mandated as separate, Decadence might nonetheless, according to Home's working definition of utopian currents, be looked at as a utopia divorced from the egalitarian).

[17] *A rebours* was not, of course, the only book to serve as both a catalyst and reflection of the French Aesthetic community, as Deak points out (p 253). However, it was by far the most influential, is to my knowledge (unfortunately) the *only* one available in English translation, and seems likely to be the most cogent, condensed, and sophisticated. To a certain extent, therefore, my reading of *Against the Grain* can be seen as an example, proxy, and palimpsest of that community as a whole, limited by a combination of willfulness and necessity.

descriptions of objects, texts, techniques, modes of material production[18]—the sentences, long and sinewy, which convoluting in odd ways and often skimming over the surface of some vague field of reference, some hidden mechanism, seem to infuse what the uninitiated might impatiently shrug off as a gratuitous pedantry with a synthesis of a subtle and anxiously self-reflective mode of thought: all of these elements taken together stage, through the very *manner* of their articulation, the process through which an adventurous mind, willfully and tortuously formed (as one might torture a metal), can engage with the material world *that supports it* in an effort to transform not merely the *contents* of life, but its *form*.[19] [20]

The arrangement of these chapters—there is unfortunately no room to go into any great detail here—suggests both the extent to which traditionally artistic discourse sustained and laid the groundwork for Decadent Aesthetic practice, and the extent to which that practice ultimately escaped the confines of Art as such. On the one hand, whole or partial chapters are devoted to painting, to music, to poetry, to modern and contemporary literature, to ancient and medieval literatures, and to devotional literature. These passages each contain dozens or scores of references, merciless avalanches of names and titles, catching here and there on an aphoristic comment or evaluation, opening intermittently onto long rhapsodies in praise of works which usually

---

[18] On a very superficial level, these passages of intense and detailed description can be seen as a development of Naturalism; but the nature of their deployment and the underlying ideology represent a direct attack on Naturalism, taken as an ideological stance more than a literary school. Indeed, the publication of *A rebours* was taken by Zola and the rest of Huysmans' former literary community as a heresy and a betrayal. (Huysmans 1998, pp ix-x.) Whereas the detail in Naturalist writing is articulated in such a way as to underscore the materiality and specificity inherent in the 'Real' world as such, it is in Huysmans the staging of a certain overstrained sensibility, a consciously self-induced neurosis; it represents not reality, but the specific ways in which the thought of one particular subject fractures and reassembles itself in hurling itself against the perception from which it is indistinguishable.

[19] It is worth keeping in mind, my dearest reader, as you push your way through this book, this potential for *the act of reading* to be an initiatory act, the book as an initiatory text, an alchemical crucible, a challenge which, through denying any 'Natural' intelligibility, forces you to create your *own* intelligibility (always provisional)—that is to say, to *create yourself*: especially the *act* of reading the nearly *un*readable, that is to say the act of *becoming lost in a text* and of *thinking* your way out, back to the relatively firm ground of *some* kind of subjectivity or perspective, through some opening in the text rendered by *your own thought*, an opening certainly unimagined by anyone else, most of all by the 'author'. A 'difficult' text is often a tool for the creation of the reader. There have been many such texts, I might cite for myself some by Coleridge, by Shelley, by Huysmans, by Lautréamont, by Mallarmé, by Bergson, by Jarry, by Roussel, by Tzara, by Artaud, by Derrida, by Kristeva, by Bennett. The attempt to create such a text—an attempt no less disorienting than reading it—is the fulfillment of a kind of debt, a debt with no origin, a debt to no one; a reversal of the process through which one has emerged, and the establishment of another body open to inhabitation and annihilation, another pyre upon which to hurl the world.

[20] or, Kristeva again, via the language of Lacan: 'As the text constructed itself with respect to an empty place ("Nothing will have taken place except the place," writes Mallarmé in *A Throw of the Dice*), it in turn comes to be the empty site of a process in which its readers become involved. The text turns out to be the analyst and every reader an analysand. But since the *structure and function of language takes the place of the focus of transference* in the text, this opens the way for all linguistic, symbolic, and social structures to be put in process/on trial. The text thereby attains its essential dimension: it is a *practice* calling into question (symbolic and social) *finitudes* by proposing *new signifying devices*. In calling the text a practice we must not forget that it is a new practice, radically different from the mechanistic practice of a null and void, atomistic subject who refuses to acknowledge that he is a subject of language. Against such a "practice", the text as signifying practice points toward the possibility—which is a jouissance—of a *subject who speaks his being put in process/on trial through action*.'

were utterly unknown at the time of the writing beyond small communities existing outside or on the fringes of mainstream cultural discourse.[21] The reader-initiate is nearly drowned in this cataract of referentiality, without any hope of keeping up; s/he either closes the book, or learns to swim.[22]

In this way, Huysmans codified and—if only through its codification in a novel both celebrating and (in its counterintuitive way) promoting this community—legitimised a canon *definitively* and not just circumstantially *outside* the 'official' canon (because popularity, in a commercial society, is the standard of officiality). The Decadent community as presented and promoted by Huysmans—and it should be noted in this connection that the canon assembled by Huysmans was not predominantly contemporary, did not reflect a Decadent *style*, but was drawn from throughout the history of Western Culture[23]—*did not*, like Romanticism before it, conceive of itself as the upstart waiting in the wings to take over the reins of the culture; instead, it established itself in a definitively and *permanently* oppositional role. The Aesthetic community would never, even hypothetically, take charge of that culture, for to do so would be tantamount to being recouperated by it.

In this gesture, the dynamics of intra-cultural struggle were radically relocated, in a way which mirrored the social fracturing of Modernity—the loss of a unifying cultural myth identified by Bataille and the Surrealists—while laying bare the Idealist cultural model—in fact the transparent *myth* of unicity itself—that obscured and legitimized it. No longer must each cultural canon (and canons of all kinds serve as the coordinates by which various modes of thought, discourse, and praxis are oriented and organized) conceive of

---

[21] There is virtually no chance that any reader of *Against the Grain* will in fact know what Huysmans is talking about all the time, or quite likely even half the time; but one nonetheless maneuvres a way through the text, internalizes that impossibility, and comes to realise that the mode of discussion is *not* intended only for those familiar with the huge and obscure array of texts; on the contrary, Huysmans is offering to the reader a palimpsest of a certain library, his discussions are written equally for those *unfamiliar* with them, that he is offering them the opportunity to come to a certain understanding of their *salience* to his project, that the reader might track them—some of them—down, to partake in the transformation that Des Esseintes/Huysmans himself has undergone.

[22] Much of *A rebours* could be looked at as criticism and theory radically *contextualized* in relation to a comprehensive system of living. In terms both of the canon he investigates and the practices he describes, it is difficult (and pointless) to tell to what extent or in what forms this community 'preceded' the book (a letter from Mallarmé, as one example, does confirm that this community and lifestyle was certainly at play in some form before the book was written) (Mallarmé 1988, pp 134-136.) and to what extent the creation or condensation of the community was a supremely appropriate example of, if one forgives the expression, 'life following art'. In this sense, of course, *A rebours* is an example of how cultural criticism, theory, biography, history, and fiction can be reduced to a single radical formulation, and how a text conceived and produced accordingly can, potentially, engage in a *praxis* in which the reflection and creation of a community and a tradition, the elucidation of a 'real' world and a fictional intervention into, against, but also *through* it, become one and the same and movement, bringing about a '*reality*', or a-reality, whose essence is fiction, and vice versa; and is this not the Yellow Sign? And might it not be looked at as one formulation of the aspirations (unattainable because worthwhile) of an avant-garde?

[23] That is to say that Decadence is not so much a practice of *writing* or cultural production, as a practice of *reading*, of *active* and motivated consumption, of consumption *against the grain;* in this sense it might be related to (but is not synonymous with) Certeau's ideas put forth in *The Practice of Everyday Life*. It should be mentioned that aside from a few amateur productions, Des Esseintes is *not* an artist or writer, certainly he does not identify himself as such. While his mental processes are derived from an artistic sensibility, it is the sensibility of an appreciator of art, not of an artistic practitioner.

itself as a *future version*, as a *revised version*, as a *better version* of the dominant canon; for all of these conceptions, organizing themselves around the monumentality that is being *fought over*, rather than *fought against*, are ultimately relegated to provisional status. Whatever the arguments they articulate, they ultimately legitimize the dominant canon, and thus the dominant prerogatives of the culture's self-conception, through implicitly buying into the notion *of* an ideal canon, '*the* cultural canon', of which the canons of specific communities, traditions, ideologies, or individuals are merely deviations or idiosyncratic reflections.[24] It might be argued that this revolution in how dissenting communities conceive of themselves and frame their actions, internal relations, and cultural interventions is in fact one point at which an avant-garde as such first appears, as distinguished from a mere power struggle; the level on which revolt is situated and articulated has shifted from enunciation and manifest content to that of a structural insistence upon revolt against all unitary conceptions of power *as such*.

This canonical struggle, moreover, represented only one part of the Aesthetic practice presented in *Against the Grain*. The nature of Huysmans' discussions of artistic practices and artifacts take on an added significance when looked at in order to shed light on other practices he describes. For the same sensibility revealed through his discussions on literature or painting is applied to every other aspect of his daily life; 'art' proper can be seen to serve as preparation and cultivation of a highly refined critical sensibility, which is then to be turned loose on everything it encounters. Thus, we find extended passages and chapters devoted to (and often formulating alternative canons of) gardening, food, interior decoration, drinking alcohol, sex, perfume, travel, gemstones, paper. These things are treated almost identically to 'artistic' topics—long lists and catalogues of obscure examples, attributes, and associations, placing whatever is under consideration in the light of various social, historical, economic, cultural, and personal associations; the *thought* that grasps and defines these things is precisely the same as that which grasps and defines 'artistic' works. The same criteria for their evaluation is applied; thus, to provide only a few easy examples, Des Esseintes' preference first for artificial flowers, then (in order to multiply the departure from Nature) for real flowers mimicking the artificial flowers that mimic the real; or his corresponding delight during his illness in taking his meals in the most artificial way possible—by way of enema; or his assertion that artificial travel is infinitely superior to any Real change of locale.

In examining these practices, we strike upon one reason that Huysmans' gesture needed to be embedded in the form of an autobiographical novel; for such essentially *readerly* practices could only be presented 'accurately' in that form. These practices, due to their intensely private and intangible nature, could only take on a social existence, a status within the symbolic that could thus be passed on and spread, through

---

[24] Plato's persistent phallus raises its ugly head once again.

> If putting people in a book has any meaning to it, then reducing them to the status of thought is the proper way, in accordance with how we read, and truly superior, of communicating with them: and how, after all, it summons forth their true image! For literature continues to be a performance of an act of intellectuality concerning everything to do with life.
>
> -Stéphane Mallarmé, letter to Paul Bourget, 5 Oct., 1890.
> (Mallarmé 1988, p 169.)

conversation or in print; and they could only *survive* beyond the historical moments of their practice (as cultural forms) through print. At the same time, these practices could not be discussed in their ideality, only in their specificity (compare this with the canonical gesture described above), since such a practice takes as its site precisely that point where two irreducible contingencies—the sensory and habitual minutiae of everyday life and the vagaries of a unique consciousness—coincide. Such a practice cannot be postulated and expounded in the abstract beyond the mere assertion of its existence or *possibility*; its *potential* and its *implications* can be engaged theoretically, but its praxis, the nature of its technique, its *form*, can be examined only anecdotally. While *A Rebours* is *in one sense* indisputably didactic as Deak suggests above, no straightforward 'how-to' of Aestheticism, much less an inscribed 'example', would be possible; for Aestheticism does not lie in the opinions, in the particular practices, in the tastes, in the idiom, in any of the *attributes* of Des Esseintes that one might pile up. It is at play in the underlying *logic* rather than the specific outcome of the confrontation between Des Esseintes and the world, and moreover in the relationships *between* that logic—one that is partly created by the practice itself, partly biographical, partly culturally determined—and his own psychology. This suggests, furthermore, why a *novelistic* approach was called for in the writing itself; for that underlying logic, and the traces of other logics that have been partly effaced, partly accentuated, partly sublimated, cannot be *presented* within a text, they must be put into play through the language itself, which provides them with a new body. The reader, subject-ed to the book's often overbearing idiosyncrasies, to its syntactic and stylistic postures, to its state of constant structural anxiety, continuously and simultaneously on the point of both complete pedantry and utter confusion, of identification and dissolution, is forced, in a small way at least, to enter into an inarticulable dynamic which stages on the level of the phenotext what can only be hinted at in the genotext. (Kristeva 1984, pp 86-89.)

One other dynamic is at play in the importance of the *form* Huysmans chose for the articulation of this practice; within the Aesthetic community (whether or not to the extent suggested within the hyperbolized mode of *A Rebours*), the *book* necessarily became the primary locus of social interaction. This seems paradoxical on one level, since the nature of aesthetic practice (like most of the practices presented or speculated upon in the book you are reading now), however literary its inspiration, was in its practice so resistant to any inscription; but it should be noted that, as distinguished from Dandyism, Aesthetic practice is only somewhat more inscribable socially than on the page (and even then indirectly), so that a simulacrum of inner experience inscribed in a book is potentially no less representative than a socially inscribed effect that is, still, merely a *relic* of a practice that in itself remains just as irrecoverable. Moreover, this state of affairs was necessitated by the strategy of social isolation adopted, to greater or lesser extents, within the Decadent community, at least as figured *within* the book. If the Aesthetic was, like Des Esseintes, to live a solitary existence in which his or her thought could be developed to the utmost degree, how were ideas to be exchanged? How to manage a *community of recluses?* The answer was apparent—through the books, the canon, which played so strong a role in identifying that community.

In addition to this (in part) practical consideration, the reinsertion or *projection* of the 'self' one has used artistic principles to create in life, back *into* the text, or the work of art, is also a logical extension of Aesthetic ideas. Why meet, why interact, in *reality*, as Nature demands? Why present oneself *as* such a reality? The auto/biographical novel presents a space analogous to, but more controllable than, the ideal condition of Aesthetic praxis: a space where the fictional and the historical are seen to be inextricable from each other; and the element of greater control, along with the social function of the book, renders it a space perfect for another kind of projection: the projection of what is *possible* into a representation of what *is* and/or *has been*.

The Dandy *Count Robert de Montesquieu* (1897) by Giovanni Boldoni.
(Lucie-Smith 1972, p 53.)

Continuing with the example of *A rebours*, it is well established that the book represents an existent community, and that the character of Des Esseintes contains a strong biographical and autobiographical element;[25] it is equally well established that it served to a very great extent as model *for* that community, and Des Esseintes for individuals within that community. At the same time, certain discrepancies between the book, its sources, and what was modeled after it are indisputable; it is *not* pure biography, or a purely 'factual' representation of the community. But it is precisely due to the

> nothing could interest me as much as the magnificent project you discussed with me [*A rebours*]. It would not have been right for our age to have come to an end without that novel having been written: no other age could have understood it. And it's certainly you alone who ought to assume the responsibility for writing it.
>
> -Stéphane Mallarmé, letter to J.-K. Huysmans, 29 Oct., 1882.
> (Mallarmé 1988, p 134.)

---

[25] While Des Esseintes was inspired in part by the dandy Robert de Montesquieu, he is also very largely a projection of Huysmans himself (Huysmans 1998, pp xvii & xxii.), who is known to have been involved with such practices. (*ibid*, p 211 and Mallarmé 1988, pp 134-136.) While Montesquieu could serve as a model in terms of Des Esseintes' behaviour and more *noticeably* eccentric characteristics (Huysmans did not know him well and worked largely from descriptions by Mallarmé) (*ibid*, p xvii.), the more specifically Aesthetic, as opposed to Dandyist, aspects of Des Esseintes' practice discussed here (and which predominate in the novel) are unlikely to have been gleaned primarily from incidental hearsay, while Des Esseintes' earlier, more flamboyant lifestyle described early in the novel and which has been rejected, bear stronger marks of Montesquieu. Whether Des Esseintes is looked at as primarily *biographical* or *auto*biographical, his ultimately composite nature is another example of the productive ambiguity discussed throughout this paragraph.

book's ambivalent status, refusing to map comfortably to either representation or creation, that the extent to which these deviations occur, or precisely where they may or not be at play, can never be determined; it is impossible to say *how closely* or in *which specific ways* the book represents the Decadent community, Aesthetic practices, or Huysmans' practices himself.[26] The book, and other books in which the discourse of Aestheticism are staged, immerses the entire community within what I have described as a mythic status; and through the form of the novel, it does so without resigning the specificity without which the techniques and strategies of the practice could not be adequately suggested in all their rigour.

For instance: Decadent lifestyles were certainly not *as* solitary and reclusive as that of Des Esseintes; indeed *A Rebours* never mentions explicitly any larger community or practice to which it is related, though of course within its intended readership—that community itself—no such explicit mention would be necessary. Certainly many Aesthetics—Huysmans and Montesquieu included—did maintain personal social networks; but it is impossible to say how many—especially after the publication of *A Rebours*—did in fact adopt such a stance. Likewise, Des Esseintes is

> We wanted to bring forward a new kind of human being, one whose contemporaries we could wish to be, free from the tyranny of rationality, of banality, of generals, of fatherlands, nations, microbes, residence permits and the past.
>
> -Hans Richter, *Dada: Art and Anti-Art* (1964).
>
> (Richter 1997, p 65.)

entirely unfettered by economic limitations, allowing him to engage in the practice to extremes—for instance, buying a tortoise and having its shell encrusted with arabesques of precious and semi-precious stones in order to correct the colour-scheme of a room—utterly impossible by most practitioners, including Huysmans himself, who made his living as a government clerk. While this hyperbolized manifestation of Aesthetic fantasy—or one *particular* fantasy—certainly represents one intense fictionalization of the *forms* Aesthetic practice could take in actuality, it (like Des Esseintes' hyperbolized isolation) allows greater penetration into the underlying *sensibility* at play in existent Aesthetic practice; we can only speculate as to how these sensibilities articulated themselves in relation to the various conditions imposed upon practitioners. And this necessity of *speculation* forces us to reproduce, in our reading and in the use we make of it in formulating continued practice, the book's refusal to adhere to dichotomies of fiction, history, and theory.

This suggests how, not only in the context of Decadence but in relation to such practices—and their traditions, techniques, and strategies—in general, the book as a social form can paradoxically serve as a point of communication and transmission of precisely that which it *cannot* possibly contain: the synthetic *practice* of

---

[26] This approach has continued to be an important historiographic weapon in traditions related to Decadence, though generally (with the qualified exception of Neoism) in a rather piecemeal fashion; for example the account of a Berlin Dada cabaret by Alexis in the *Dada Almanac* (Huelsenbeck 1993, pp 140-145.), Breton's *Nadja*, Home's Account of the Eighth International Neoist Apartment Festival (Home 1994, pp 63-74), and various accounts of (possible) actions by Blaster Al Ackerman (Ackerman 2006, pp 15 & 31-34.)

thought and life. Such a book provides a community or tradition with a model of what is *possible,* but also does so by locating or inserting that potential *within* the present; by fictionalizing current and past practices, such a book makes it possible for potential future developments to have *already occurred.* To depict a community or a practice is to set it into play; to discuss it is to limn its history according to the form of a potential future; to formulate its radicality is to set it and find it always already at play, already waiting, an embedded confirmation of its thinkability and revolutionary potential.

18 May 1884

So here it is, this unique book [*A rebours*]! It had to be written—and you've written it so well!—and it couldn't have been written at any other literary moment than the present.

Truly, as I see it closed on my desk, while under my gaze all the treasure of its knowledge lies stored there, I cannot imagine it other than it is… What is admirable about all this, and what gives your book its strength, (which will be decried as mad imagination etc.) is that there is not an atom of fantasy in it. In this refined tasting of all essences, you have succeeded in showing yourself to be more strictly documentary than anyone else, and in using only facts or reports which are real and which exist just as much as those that are coarse; they're just subtle, and demand the eye of a prince, that's all. But they are truths which, since enjoyment demands stripping one's pleasure more and more, will certainly be attained by all those who are intense and delicate. That is the very point that will be reached, one cannot go beyond it or reach it in any other way.

[…]

Farewell. I laugh as I think of those who believe they now know everything and who have never dreamt of what lies contained in that extraordinary manual, *A rebours.*

-Stéphane Mallarmé, letter to J.-K. Huysmans, 18 May, 1884.   (Mallarmé 1988, pp 135-136.)

Sometimes they effortlessly adopt poses, both provocative and dignified, that would be the joy of the most fastidious sculptor, if only the sculptor of today had the courage and wit to seize hold of nobility everywhere

  -Charles Baudelaire, *The Painter of Modern Life* (1859-1860).   (Baudelaire 1972, p 431.)

  -*Punch*, 14 Dec., 1877.

ERNEST: But what are the two supreme and highest arts?

GILBERT: Life and literature

    -Oscar Wilde, *The Critic as Artist* (1890). (Wilde 1999, p 184.)

That Nature is always right, is an assertion, artistically, as untrue, as it is one whose truth is universally taken for granted. Nature is very rarely right, to such an extent even, that it might almost be said that Nature is usually wrong

    -James Abbot McNeil Whistler, *The Ten O'Clock* (1885). (Caws 2001, p. 7.)

If, however, we are prepared merely to consult the facts that stare us in the face, the experience of all ages, and the *Gazette des Tribunaux,* we can see at once that nature teaches nothing or nearly nothing; in other words it compels man to sleep, drink, eat, and to protect himself as best he can against the inclemencies of the weather.

    -Charles Baudelaire, *The Painter of Modern Life* (1859-60). (Baudelaire 1972, p. 425.)

'There's no doubt about it,' he said to himself, summing up his thoughts, 'man is able to bring about in a few years a range of choice that slothful Nature can produce only after several centuries;'

    -J.-K. Huysmans, *Against Nature* (1884). (Huysmans 1998, p. 78.)

We have all seen in our own day in England how a certain curious and fascinating type of beauty, invented and emphasised by two imaginative painters, has so influenced life that whenever one goes to a private view or an

artistic salon one sees, here the mystic eyes of Rossetti's dream, the long ivory throat, the strange square-cut jaw, the loosened shadowy hair that he so ardently loved

    -Oscar Wilde, *The Decay of Lying* (1891).   (Wilde 1999, p. 158.)

To say to the painter, that Nature is to be taken as she is, is to say to the player, that he may sit on the piano.

    -James Abbot McNeil Whistler, *The Ten O'Clock* (1885).   (Caws 2001, p. 7.)

and as they walked through the meadows, or other grassy places, they examined the trees and the plants, comparing them with the descriptions in the books of such ancients as Dioscorides, Marinus, Pliny, Nicander, Macer, and Galen; and they brought back whole handfuls to the house.

    -François Rabelais, *Gargantua* (c. 1564?)   (Rabelais 1955, p 91.)

[Art's] are the "forms more real than living man", and hers the great archetypes of which things that have existence are but unfinished copies. Nature has, in her eyes, no laws, no uniformity.

    -Oscar Wilde, *The Decay of Lying*, (1891).   (Wilde 1999, p. 157.)

in the past, in Paris, his natural inclination towards artifice had led him to forsake the real flower for its replica, faithfully imitated thanks to the miracles of gums and threads, percalines and taffetas, papers and velvets… he had long been fascinated by this wonderful art-form; but now he dreamt of planning a different kind of flora. After having artificial flowers that imitated real ones, he now wanted real flowers that mimicked artificial ones.

    -J.-K. Huysmans, *Against Nature* (1884).   (Huysmans 1998, p. 73.)

It is not *natural* to think: one must create a veritable stage-setting out of oneself and things, not to mention the inevitable artificial device of reasoning… Without these shams, thought is no more than naïveté (banging on about the obvious) and, basically, stupidity.

-Julien Torma, *Euphorisms* (1926). (Cravan et. al. 2005, p 135.)

It is nature too that drives man to kill his fellow man, to eat him, to imprison and torture him; for as soon as we move away from the order of necessities and needs to that of luxury and pleasures, we see that nature can do nothing but counsel crime.

-Charles Baudelaire, *The Painter of Modern Life* (1859-60). (Baudelaire 1972, p. 425.)

Art is our spirited protest, our gallant attempt to teach nature her proper place.

-Oscar Wilde, *The Decay of Lying* (1891). (Wilde 1999, p. 141.)

Far from a return to nature—the notion of living in a park, as solitary aristocrats once did—we see in such immense constructions the possibility of overcoming nature and regulating at will the atmosphere, lighting, and sounds in these various spaces.

-Constant, *A Different City for a Different Life* (1959). (McDonough 2004, p. 96.)

As he was wont to remark, Nature has had her day; she has finally exhausted, through the nauseating uniformity of her landscapes and her skies, the sedulous patience of men of refined taste. Essentially, what triteness Nature displays, like a specialist who confines himself to his own single sphere; what small-mindedness, like a shopkeeper who stocks only this one article to the exclusion of any other; what monotony she exhibits with her stores of meadows and trees, what banality with her arrangements of mountains and seas!

    -J.-K. Huysmans, *Against Nature* (1884).   (Huysmans 1999, p. 20.)

since he only lived to defy nature and defeat reality, he conceived a dream setting and an artistic composition for his work of the flesh.

    -Joséphin Péladan, *Le Vice suprême* (1884).   (Hustvedt 1998, p. 853.)

Art creates an incomparable and unique effect, and, having done so, passes on to other things. Nature, upon the other hand, forgetting that imitation can be made the sincerest form of insult, keeps on repeating this effect until we all become absolutely wearied of it. Nobody of any real culture, for instance, ever talks nowadays about the beauty of a sunset. Sunsets are quite old-fashioned. They belong to a time when Turner was the last note in art. To admire them is a distinct sign of provincialism of temperament. Upon the other hand they go on.

    -Oscar Wilde, *The Decay of Lying* (1891)   (Wilde 1999, p. 163.)

Espouse within yourself the destruction of Nature. Resist her fatal magnets. Be privation itself! Renounce! Liberate yourself. Be your own victim... What do you think the disciplinary practices of the ascetic are if not the same steps as a spirit freeing and refining itself, retrieving and enlarging its incommensurable entity.

    Villiers de l'Isle-Adam, *Axel* (1890).   (Deak 1993, p. 48.)

The Surrealists' manifesto contains an interesting philosophical introduction. The Surrealists maintain that reality is by definition ugly; beauty exists only in that which is not real. It is man who has introduced beauty into the world. In order to produce beauty, one must remove oneself as far as possible from reality.

-'Professor Janet', discussion in the Société Médico-Psychologique quoted in the *Second Manifesto of Surrealism* (1930). (Breton 1972, p. 121.)

furthermore he was astonished and pleased not to be encumbered with drugs and medicine bottles, and a feeble smile came to his lips when the servant brought him a nourishing peptone enema, warning him that this procedure was to be repeated three times a day.

The operation was successful, and Des Esseintes could not forbear from tacitly congratulating himself on the event, which was in a sense the crowning achievement of the life he had created for himself; his predilection for the artificial had now—without his even desiring it—achieved its supreme fulfillment; one could go no further; to take nourishment in this manner was unquestionably the ultimate deviation from the norm that anyone could realize.

'How delightful it would be,' he said to himself, 'to continue this simple diet once your health has been restored! What a saving of time, what a radical deliverance from the dislike that meat inspires in people who have no appetite! What a complete release from the tediousness that invariably accompanies the necessarily limited choice of dishes! What a spirited protest against the vile sin of gluttony! And finally, what a decided slap in the face for that old Mother Nature whose unvarying demands would be permanently silenced!'

-J.-K. Huysmans, *Against Nature* (1884). (Huysmans 1998, pp 170-171.)

-*Punch.* 1 Nov., 1879.

-Cartoon on Copenhagen Fluxus Festival from *Politikin* Newspaper, 1962. (Williams 1998, p 81.)

SCENE—Her *Boudoir.*   *Enter* He.

He.   What! still that book? Do come into the garden
              And see my roses!

She (languidly).   O, I beg your pardon!
              It's far too hot. Your roses may be pretty,
              But give me coolness, solitude, and Rossetti!

He.   Solitude!

She.   Yes. His dreams are too aesthetic
              To share, unless the sharer's sympathetic.
              There, do not glare upon me like a vulture!
              You're more at home in practical floriculture
              Than culling flowers of fancy.

He.   Now, by jingo:
              I'm sick of all this cant "asthetic" lingo.
              Nature, not mamby-pamby art for me!

She.   Precisely, my dear Faunus. Pan, you see,
              Is quite your natural deity. Go, follow
              His earthly cult, and leave me to Apollo.
              You once,—but there, no matter.

He.   I suppose
              You think there's something earthly in a rose!

She (abstractedly).   Dream-roses are deliciously—

He (drily).   Can you tell
              Where I might buy some?

She (scornfully).   Buy!

He (sardonically).   No! They're a sell!

              (Exit with a bang.)

-Punch, Dec. 1877.

But this definitive choice of the hothouse bloom had itself been modified under the influence of his general ideas, of his now fixed opinions about everything; in the past, in Paris, his natural inclination towards artifice had led him to forsake the real flower for its replica, faithfully imitated thanks to the miracles of gums and threads, percalines and taffetas, papers and velvets.

-J.-K. Huysmans, *Against Nature* (1884). (Huysmans 1998, p. 73)

For what is nature? Nature is no great mother who has borne us. She is our creation. It is in our brain that she quickens to life. Things are because we see them, and what we see, and how we see it, depends on the arts that have influenced us.

-Oscar Wilde, *The Decay of Lying* (1891). (Wilde 2002, p. 163)

Herod: It may be he is drunk with the wine of God.

Herodias: What wine is that, the wine of God? From what vineyards is it gathered? In what winepresses may one find it?

-Oscar Wilde, *Salome* (1894).
              (Wilde1996, p. 46.)

Here the case was very different; as might have been expected from the Duke's love of the *bizarre*. The apartments were so irregularly disposed that the vision embraced but little more than one at a time. There was a sharp turn at every twenty or thirty yards, and at each turn a novel effect. To the right and left, in the middle of each wall, a tall and narrow Gothic window looked out upon a closed corridor which pursued the windings of the suite. These windows were of stained glass whose color varied in accordance with the prevailing hue of the decorations of the chamber into which it opened.

-Edgar Allan Poe, *The Masque of the Red Death* (1842). (Poe 1975, pp 269-270.)

One of our comrades has proposed a theory of states-of-mind districts, according to which each quarter of a city would tend to induce a single emotion, to which the subject will consciously expose herself or himself. It seems that such a project draws timely conclusions from an increasing depreciation of accidental primary emotions, and that its realisation could contribute to accelerating this change. Comrades who call for a new architecture, a free architecture, must understand that this new architecture will not play at first on free, poetic lines and forms—in the sense that today's 'lyrical abstract' painting uses these words—but rather on the atmospheric effects of rooms, corridors, streets, atmospheres linked to the behaviors they contain.

-Guy Debord, *Report on the Construction of Situations* (1957). (McDonough 2002, pp 44-45.)

And then, during that period when Des Esseintes had felt the need to draw attention to himself, he had devised sumptuous peculiar schemes of decoration, dividing his salon into a series of variously carpeted alcoves, which could be related by subtle analogies, by indeterminate correlations of tone, either cheerful or gloomy, delicate or flamboyant, to the character of the Latin or French works he loved. He would then settle himself in that alcove whose furnishings seemed to him to correspond most closely to the essential nature of the work which the whim of the moment induced him to read.

[...]

Now he simply wanted to arrange, for his own enjoyment rather than for the amazement of others, a domestic interior that was comfortable yet appointed in an exceptional manner, to fashion for himself a unique and tranquil setting suited to the requirements of his future solitude.

-J.-K. Huysmans, *A Rebours* (1884).   (Huysmans 1999, pp 11-12.)

Houssaye, who knew Borel intimately as a young man, says, with some acumen, that Borel was always cast for the wrong part, that he deliberately chose one for which he was least suited. He rewrote the part given to him by Nature in accordance with his taste. Houssaye goes on to say that he took infinite pains to cultivate red roses in a garden where white ones would have grown in profusion without effort or care.

-Enid Starkie, *Petrus Borel: The Lycanthrope* (1954).   (Starkie 1954, p 194.)

I can recall the specious distinction that Paul Valéry, in conversation some twenty years ago, tried to establish between what he called "strange" and "bizarre" individuals. Only the first kind found favor in his eyes, Poe naturally belonging to that category. He chided the others, such as Jarry, for being so concerned with their external oddity. But in the man whom Mallarmé physically described as the "devil from head to toe!, his tragic, black stylishness, worried and discreet," we can sometimes recognize, as Apollinaire did, "the marvelous drunk from Baltimore."

-André Breton, *Anthology of Black Humor* (1945).   (Breton 1997, p. 83.)

Subjectivistic ecstatics were not always able to escape being an end in themselves.

-Hugo Ball, *Tenderenda the Fantast* (wr. 1915-1920).   (Ball et. al. 1995, p. 123.)

You must dream your life with great care

Instead of living it as merely an amusement

-Arthur Cravan, *Some Words* (c. 1913?)   (Cravan et. al. 2005, p. 23.)

I wanted, I guess, to be and feel a part of a Fluxus "family"; and to be honest, I could still not approach George as a flesh-and-blood human being. I still saw him as more of a character than a person, a dotty, semi-reclusive paterfamilias who cultivated his peculiarities as part of his art.

-Peter Frank, *Not Wanting To Say Everything About George Maciunas* (1993).   (Williams 1997, p. 152.)

Over and above all this, [Viking Eggeling] had an 'all-embracing philosophy' which had led him to formulate rules of everyday conduct which had, for him, absolute validity. The interplay of 'opposites' and 'affinities' was for him the true principle of creation… But how could one create a new order of things without insisting on dotting all the 'i's? How else could a vision of the world be achieved in which the greatest was exactly mirrored in the smallest and the smallest in the greatest? It was overwhelming. His incisive mind, his intense personality, his whole heart and soul—all were dedicated to the furtherance of his ideas, even in the choice of food. For instance, he refused to have eggs and milk in the same meal on the grounds, expressed in the same terms as he used for his 'linear orchestrations', that "eggs and milk are too 'analogous'."

-Hans Richter, *Dada: Art and Anti-Art* (1964).   (Richter 1997, pp 63-64.)

[Dada] was destined to go beyond the limits of esthetics, to grow venomous, and charged with blasphemy and harshness under the pressure of events. At a time when society refused the right of existence to every being whom it had not incorporated within its warring exigencies, this spirit became, in an indirect form, a protest, the only possible protest of a persecuted individualism.

-Gabrielle Buffet-Picabia, *Arthur Cravan and American Dada* (1938).   (Motherwell 1981, p. 13.)

We must learn to become what we need to be in order to make sense of the circumstances we find ourselves in and to act effectively in them. We must learn to become hard and tempered, attentive, cunning and wholly given over to the visceral act of living.

    -Alan Reed, *Imagining Revolt* (2006).   (Reed 2006, p. 31.)

But dada contained a great deal more: for one thing, a desire for further developments toward a new form and a new life. If art was no longer possible, one might become an adventurer of the body or the mind, change one's creed, turn monk, murderer, Casanova, or religious fanatic. Existence was uppermost in our thoughts, not art.

    -Richard Huelsenbeck, *Memoirs of a Dada Drummer* (1969).   (Huelsenbeck 1991, p 14.)

Maciunas' principal idea, derived mainly from his interpretation of the works made by George Brecht in the early 1960's, La Monte Young's 1960 compositions, and to some extent my own verbal and performance works and those of Dick Higgins, was that there was no need for art. We had merely to learn to take an "art attitude" toward any phenomenon we encountered.

    -Jackson Mac Low.   (Williams 1997, p. 91.)

The word Dada symbolizes the most primitive relation to surrounding reality, a relation with which Dadaism in turn establishes a new reality.

    [. . .]

Dada is a state of mind that can be revealed in any conversation whatever, so that you are compelled to say: this man is a DADAIST—that man is not…. Under certain circumstances to be a Dadaist may mean to be more a businessman, more a political partisan than an artist—to be an artist only by accident

-Richard Huelsenbeck, Tristan Tzara, Franz Jung, George Grosz, Marcel Janco, Gerhard Preiß, Raoul Hausmann, Walter Mehring, O. Lüthy, Fréderic Glauser, Hugo Ball, Pierre Albert-Birot, Maria d'Arezzo, Gino Cantarelli, Prampolini, R. van Rees, Mdme. Van Rees, Hans Arp, G. Thäuber, Andrée Morosini, and François Mombello-Pasquati, *Collective Dada Manifesto* (1918).

(Motherwell 1981, p 246.)

Our companionship (by the way, one in which we all respect each other) dissolved in the acid of a tender or grey desperation…but, nevertheless, upstanding attitude—lies beyond any group, movement, or Dada magazine. A juggling act with one's own bones, including the intestines, on the backstage of the concept of a lost world is, by far, the best method of communication.

-Hans Richter, *Against Without For Dada* (1919). (Caws 2001, p 321.)

If the Yellow Sign is figured as a text within which its initiates are inscribed (though it is not *only* or *completely* this), we might relate its initiates, who have (been) inscribed (themselves) within it, to characters within a fixed, narrative text. We are, all of us, even you, my reader (and perhaps especially you), subject, at various times (at most times) to the conditions set for us by the text; but as you know, narrative relationships constitute only one of many systems at play within any text. Characters in a closed text, by and large, tend to naturalize their own existences. They rarely take the risk of examining their lives outside the context of naturalized existence, to face either their own provisional relationship with the larger text or the provisionality, the erasure of their own discreet existence that is suggested by it. In short, they believe that because they seem to live, they are not characters. Authors of such closed texts, on the other hand, like to make-believe that they stand outside their texts; they have equally naturalized their outlook, convincing themselves that the play of language is confined to the texts that they produce, that because they are not characters *within* that text, and only because of this, *they* escape the spectre of erasure, and so they call themselves existent, present, just as do their characters. Neither could be more wrong. The former attempts to convince himself that he exists by ignoring the potential for manipulating himself as a fully *literary* character, living instead as if the narrow motifs of causality and intention are the only ones he is capable of engaging with as a figure. The latter, on the other hand, attempts to convince herself that she exists in her full plenitude by inserting everything *but herself* into the text which reflects for her the endless manipulability and instability of things. The initiate of the Yellow Sign strives to become both author and character—to live within the text that s/he writes, and to contribute to the writing of the text within which s/he lives in relation to *every* discernible system and motif, with an awareness of the very subject *that* creates as subject *to* the dissemination of what is created—the creation of which involves but exceeds that subject.

-Olchar E. Lindsann, *The Yellow Sign*.

Ah! beware of consoling poets; beware of the Word, of the magic of realisations; beware of Words that rise up and live, of improvised evocations, of creative incantations; beware the logic of Eloquence; not all syllables are ineffectual.

-Remy de Gourmont, 'Prose for a Poet' (1894), dedicated to Saint-Pol-Roux, reprinted in Atlas Press' *The Book of Masks*, p. 21.

A story is told according to which Saint-Pol-Roux, in times gone by, used to have a notice posted on the door of his manor house in Camaret, every evening before he went to sleep, which read: THE POET IS WORKING.

-André Breton, *Manifesto of Surrealism* (1924).   (Breton 1972, p. 14.)

Is simulating a thing any different from thinking it? And what one thinks exists. You will not alter my conviction on this.

-Louis Aragon, *Une vagues de rêves* (1924).   (Nadeau 1973, p. 90.)

If you bury them in enough irrefutable evidence, and create from it an edifice superior to the sordid one in which they are stuck, and invite them in—if only by the slightest gesture of a single finger or inclination of a muscle clinging to your skull—I assure you, they will believe anything.

-Olchar E. Lindsann, *The Yellow Sign*.

In Huysmans' *A rebours*, one of the most unusual rooms in the house of the arch-Decadent Aesthetic, Des Esseintes, is the dining room:

> This dining-room resembled a ship's cabin with its vaulted ceiling, its semicircular beams, its bulkheads and floorboards of pitch-pine, its tiny casement cut into the paneling like a porthole. Like those Japanese boxes which fit inside one another, this room was inserted into another, larger room, the actual dining-room built by the architect.
>
> The latter had two windows; one was now invisible, concealed by the bulkhead which could, however, be slid aside at will by pressing on a spring, in order to renew the air which, entering through this opening, could then circulate around the pitch-pine box and penetrate within it; the other, directly opposite the porthole in the paneling, was visible but no longer served as a real window; in fact, a large aquarium filled all the space between the porthole and the genuine window, housed in the actual wall. Thus, in order to light the cabin, the daylight had to pass, first through the window, where the panes had been replaced by a sheet of glass, then through the water, and finally through the permanent glass pane of the porthole.
>
> [. . .]
>
> Sometimes of an afternoon, when Des Esseintes happened to be up and about, he would set in operation the various pipes and ducts that permitted the aquarium to be emptied and refilled with clean water, and then pour in some drops of coloured essences, thus creating for himself, at his own pleasure, the various shades displayed by real rivers, green or grayish, opaline or silvery, depending on the colour of the sky, the greater or lesser intensity of the sun, the more or less imminent threat of rain... while inhaling the smell of tar which had been pumped into the room before he came in, he would examine some coloured engravings hanging on the walls that depicted—like those in the agencies for steamship lines and for Lloyd's—vessels bound for Valparisio and the River Plate...
>
> [. . .]
>
> ...he would rest his eyes by contemplating the chronometers and compasses, sextants and diviers, binoculars and maps that were scattered over a table upon which was displayed only one book, bound in sealskin, *The Adventures of Arthur Gordon Pym*... In this manner, without ever leaving his home, he was able to enjoy the rapidly succeeding, indeed almost simultaneous, sensations of a long voyage; the pleasure of travel—existing as it does only in recollection and almost never in the present, at the actual moment when it is taking place—this pleasure he could savour fully, at his ease, without fatigue or worry, in this cabin whose

> contrived furnishings corresponded almost exactly with his brief sojourns in it, with the limited time spent on his meals, and which provided a complete contrast with his study, a permanent, orderly, well-established room, fitted out for the solid sustainment of a domestic existence.
>
> (Huysmans 1998, pp 17-18.)

In this passage, Huysmans introduces a notion that runs throughout the book; it merely *suggests* however a more involved *practice* that stems from it, and which takes many of its techniques from the very literal innovations embodied in this dining-room and his use of it.[1] He explains:

> Besides, he considered travel to be pointless, believing that the imagination could easily compensate for the vulgar reality of actual experience. In his view, it was possible to fulfill those desires reputed to be the most difficult to satisfy in normal life, by means of a trifling subterfuge, an approximate simulation of the object of those very desires.
>
> (*ibid*, pp 18-19.)

Huysmans goes on to cite *artificial* wines equal to, or superior to, *natural* wines, and continues:

> By applying this devious kind of sophistry, this adroit duplicity, to the world of the intellect, there is no doubt that you can enjoy, just as easily as in the physical world, imaginary pleasures in every respect similar to the real ones; no doubt, for example, you can embark on long explorations by your own fireside, stimulating, if need be, a reluctant or lethargic mind by reading a suggestive account of distant travels
>
> (*ibid*, p 19.)

It should be pointed out that the practice Huysmans suggests here—and which is at play, to different degrees and at various levels of explicitness, throughout *Against Nature*—goes far beyond what is actually being described in the dining-room; it is both more profound and more subtle. Des Esseintes' extra-gastronomic activity in the dining-room, at least if taken at face value, seems almost entirely dependent upon sensory aids;

---

[1] Note especially the confluence of several contrived sense-impressions—scent (combined with the tactile impression of the flow of air carrying it), sound (or rather its absence, nothing to interfere with potential *remembered* sounds), and of course sight (used both to establish a 'scene'—the cabin interior itself—and to establish the awareness of an *unseen* context—the ship exteriors pictured on the wall); also the implied use of a book as an additional tool in establishing a certain mental context within which his thought can articulate itself.

he is merely *pretending* that his present physical situation is in fact the physical situation it would *seem* to be; the theatrical trappings lull his critical faculty, to whatever extent, into accepting these trappings at face value. In his presentation of the theoretical underpinning of this practice however, Huysmans in facts suggests something much more radical: through internally reproducing *sensory experience* ('an approximate simulation of the object') one can almost literally 'live' in the mind, internalize experiences as integrally with one's sense of 'self' as one can incorporate 'real' experience ('to fulfill those desires reputed to be the most difficult to satisfy in normal life… in every respect similar to the real ones'). Moreover, the amusement-park trappings of the ship's-cabin/ dining-room are not ultimately necessary—one can do this, potentially, without physical aids of any kind, while sitting by one's fireplace.

Why the dining-room then? In part, of course, it represents a part of the hyperbolizing strategy of the book that has been treated elsewhere; blowing out of proportion (though, unfortunately, distorting the practice in the process) the practical and theoretical aspects of the undertaking in order to bring them forcibly to the reader's attention, to provide hand-holds for further examination, and to provide a target for Huysmans' under-remarked self-directed satire which in fact permeates the book. Furthermore however, the two suggestions given in this chapter—a practice of 'pretending' almost completely dependant upon physical stimuli, and a practice of complete introspection—may well mark the two limits of this practice, the beginning and end-points of its development, the nadir and apex of its potential. As we will see, the examples of this practice given throughout the book *tend* to rest somewhere in-between these two extremes.

We can be certain that the dining-room is a particularly far-fetched example of hyperbole; Huysmans' (or most likely even Montesquiou's) resources would not have allowed him to own even the seal-skin copy of Poe let alone the mechanical room in which it was housed. There is however another example of this idea at play later in the novel, which seems much more likely an indication of one mode of actual practice—still largely mediated by physical sense—and which in fact is known to be based upon practices engaged in by Huysmans himself. (*ibid*, p 211.)

In this chapter, Des Esseintes decides, after reading some Dickens (a guilty pleasure), to visit England. He packs, dresses in what he considers to be an English manner, goes into Paris, buys a travel guide, and, with some time to spare, goes to an 'English Pub' near the station. There he is surrounded by Englishmen and Americans; sinking back and taking in the scene, he simultaneously brings to mind the archetypal Englishmen whose absence measures the distance between the 'actual' and the England he desires, 'picturing, under the influence of the crimson tints of the port wine filling the glasses, the Dickensian characters who so enjoyed drinking it'; implicitly withdrawing his attention from the actual condition and inhabitants of the bar, he then replaces them with his preferred characters, concentrating on their physiognomic details, 'in his imagination populating the cellar with quite different beings, seeing here the white hair of Mr Wickfield, there, the cold, cunning expression and implacable eye of Mr Tulkinghorn, the lugubrious solicitor of *Bleak House*.' Finally, he brings this 'approximation of the objects of his desire' away from abstracted imagination and back to bear on the actual scene in front him: 'These characters were actually emerging from his memory and installing themselves, complete with all their exploits, in the Bodega;' that is to say, these *memories* were passing into *perception*—'for his recollections, revived by his recent reading, were uncannily exact.' (*ibid*, p 110.)

After switching locations to another 'English' restaurant, Des Esseintes reflects on the disappointments of past travels, and finally concludes—'In fact, I've experienced and seen what I wanted to experience and see. Ever since leaving home I've been steeped in English life; I would be insane to risk losing, by an ill-advised journey, these unforgettable impressions. After all, what kind of aberration is this, that I should be tempted to renounce long-held convictions, and disdain the compliant fantasies of my mind, that I should, like some complete simpleton, have believed that a journey was necessary, or could hold novelty or interest?' He cancels his plans to travel, and immediately returns to his home, 'feeling as physically exhausted and morally spent as a man who comes home after a long and hazardous journey.' (*ibid*, p 114.)

It becomes increasingly clear that what we are dealing with is something that comes close to self-induced hallucination;[2] and, in fact, there was already a nascent tradition of this within the trajectory with which Huysmans connected himself. Huysmans himself explicitly draws attention to this tradition at several points in

---

[2] 'Hallucination' in its more rigorous sense does not, of course, correspond exactly with the practices being described, in that the practices under examination involve conscious control, and some degree of realisation of the 'fictitiousness', or at least of the difference-from-socially-sanctioned-reality, of the experiences evoked remains at play. (Fink, pp 82-85.) It should therefore be remembered throughout this book that the word 'hallucination' is used quite reservedly, for reasons which will follow. The practices upon which I am speculating are notable (if they can be said to exist) in great part due to the deliberation with which they are intentionally *induced;* any romanticization of (presumably unsuccessful) subjective displacement or other conditions not representing a *choice* but experienced as a 'problem' will most likely be severely detrimental toward both of these modes; though the danger exists of such practices as we *are* discussing *taking on* such a character, for instance in the cases of Nerval and Artaud. Such a practice as that we are speculating upon could, it would seem, only be safely taken on by a subject starting from the position of unitary subjectivity that is to a large degree socially normalized; to add a deliberate instability to a pre-existing one at the core of a person's experience of 'self' or 'reality' could well be disastrous.

Despite these reservations which it seems necessary not to overlook, I nonetheless generally prefer it in this text, once this qualification has been stated, to what seem the other most common terms employed by practitioners across several generations, 'dream' and 'vision'. The former is far too vague, carrying with it connotations of the uncontrolled, and blending into fuzzy Romantic notions of transcendent ideality on the one hand, and into Symbolist notions of the pre- or extra-linguistic on the other (nor are these notions themselves always easily extricable in practice). The other, 'vision', carries a metaphysical or theological connotation of 'revelation' from outside the subjective process that belies its potential for development as a strategic re-structuration of notions of self analogous to (though exceeding) psychoanalytic activity, and furthermore favours the scopic as the primary locus of the practice, a factor whose importance to the potential of this practice will become more clear as the book progresses.

Finally, it should be noted that I use *any* term for this practice at all simply for the sake of relative clarity; such a practice, were it to exist, should have no 'name', which would too easily lend it to conceptualization as a circumscribed 'artistic practice' or 'form', chaining it into a socially- and economically-bounded discourse and realm of cultural activity that it should be precisely an escape from.

A rebours. After a rhapsody on the work of Poe (where he describes his 'delirium-ridden nightmares' and an imagination 'which would conjure up somnambulistic, angelic apparitions like so many delightful miasmas') he goes on to discuss several pieces by his friend Villiers de l'Isle-Adam. (*ibid*, p 156.) One of these is *Vera*, published the year before the publication of *A rebours*, in which the main character willfully ignores the death of his young bride, continuing to act as if she were alive. This begins as a pretence, but gradually becomes a conviction, a conviction so strong that it spreads to his servant, leaves perceptual traces, and is shared between them:[3]

Francisco Goya, *The Dreams of Reason Produce Monsters* (1797-99). (Lucie-Smith 1972, p 25.)

> Here, the hallucination was characterized by an exquisite tenderness; no longer was this one of those gloomy apparitions typical of the American author, but a warm fluctuating vision that was almost heavenly; the opposite (though identical in kind) of the Beatrices and the Ligeias, those pale and dismal ghosts engendered by the inexorable nightmare of the demon opium.
>
> (*ibid, p 157.*)

Huysmans/Des Esseintes gives great weight to the fact that this hallucination is an effort of will, *can be created*, thus opening up a realm of potentially productive inquiry:

> This story likewise involved the operations of the will, but no longer did it describe its failures and defeats under the influence of fear; on the contrary, it studied its moments of exaltation under the impetus of a conviction which had grown into an obsession; it demonstrated the power of the will which could permeate the atmosphere, and impose its belief on its environment.
>
> (*ibid.*)

---

[3] It is worth noting, in relation to the discussion of technique below, that throughout *Vera* are recurrent references to the *objects* in the house confirming her ~~presence~~; this can be related to the significance of sensory objects in Huysmans' own practice.

While this story⁴ provided a detailed thesis on the *potential* of such an undertaking, Huysmans took inspiration in the prior hallucinatory *practice* of Thomas De Quincey, whose *Confessions of an English Opium-Eater* of 1821 famously describes a number of hallucinations induced by opium, and attempts to trace their implications regarding his own psychology. Baudelaire, in his *Artificial Paradises,* presented a translated palimpsest of that book and its successor, *Susperia de Profundis,* along with several essays of his own examining, comparing, and evaluating the use of wine, opium, and hashish in order to reconstruct one's modes of thought and, in many cases, induce hallucination.⁵ Most of the scenes De Quincey describes are in fact dreams, and the status of many others is unclear (see the earlier footnote on the use of that term); in most, De Quincey himself plays a passive role in their conception and unfolding. But just as, when examining Villiers, Huysmans/Des Esseintes calls attention to the role of productive *will*, he cites explicitly the passage from De Quincey most suggestive of a potential, intentionally directed practice, after a long internal disquisition on the (not unrelated) theological questions revolving around virgin birth and the corporeality of Christ:

> For several successive days his brain teemed with paradoxes, with fine distinctions, with a mass of petty quibbles, a tangle of rules as complicated as articles in a legal code, open to every interpretation, to every play upon words, resulting in a body of celestial law of the most subtle and the most elaborate kind; then in turn the abstractions faded away, giving place to the visual, under the influence of the Gustave Moreaus hanging on his walls.
>
> He saw a whole procession of prelates walking past: archimandrites and patriarchs raising their golden arms to bless the kneeling crowds, their white beards moving up and down as they read or prayed; he saw silent columns of penitents descending into gloomy crypts; he saw vast cathedrals rising up, where white-robed monks thundered from the pulpit. Just as De Quincey, after smoking a little opium, would, upon hearing the words 'Consul Romanus,' conjure up entire pages of Livy, watch the consuls solemnly processing and the stately array of the Roman armies beginning their march, he, upon hearing some

---

⁴ This is not the only text in which Villiers explores the notion of willfully re/constructed 'people' occupying ambiguous positions transgressing dichotomies of present/absent, real/hallucinated, subject/image; his novel *The Future Eve* (1886) revolves around the construction of an android whose personality is to be based upon the ideal conception of Lord Ewald, a disillusioned, monocle-wearing Aesthete for whom she is a gift. (Translated in Hustvedt 1998.)

⁵ It will be evident that the practice we are exploring might itself exist or not; first because of the hyperbolized quality of *Against Nature* itself, and secondly because it is woven into the text in such a way that we can read *in detail* only what might be, but cannot be *proven* to be, its relics. We can only ever speculate; and in this sense we are always, inevitably, raising an apparition of this practice, bringing it into a kind of being which cannot be verified according to prevailing social and intellectual imperatives; in speculating, we are willfully calling up a kind of hallucination of this practice which, whether or not it exists, will therefore act, will already have acted.

In this connection, it might be further speculated that Baudelaire engaged with this practice to a greater or lesser extent; and indeed it is a logical extension of the tenants of Dandyism and the cult of the artificial. Throughout *Artificial Paradises* however, he is extremely skeptical of the value of the hallucinations produced, and tends to characterize them as purely passive abnegations of the will. Then again, these objections pertain specifically to the use of narcotics, and not necessarily to the potentially *willful* evocation of hallucination; however, the other suggestions that he may have experimented with such practices are scattered and inconclusive; nonetheless, it is as impossible to deny as to confirm such an engagement.

theological expression, would be left gasping, seeing surging crowds, and priestly presences silhouetted against a background of golden basilicas; these visions held him spellbound, extending through the ages right up to present-day religious ceremonies, cocooning him in infinite swathes of mournful, tender music.[6]

(*ibid*, pp 67-68.)

In this passage, Huysmans not only explicitly links his own or Des Esseintes' practice to De Quincey's, he also highlights the extent to which that practice, or parts of it, were *modeled on* De Quincey's practice, through the form of these two descriptions, in which De Quincey's is embedded in the midst of Huysmans' own; Des Esseintes' hallucination here might almost, if we were to make recourse to the metaphor of artistic pedagogy, be looked at as a Master's Copy or pastiche. He is *learning the craft*. This becomes even more apparent if we glance at the rest of the paragraph in which the passage that Huysmans transcribes appears. *In-between* his explanation of the phrase 'Consul Romanus' as a kind of sigil for evocation, and the description of Roman crowds thus evoked that Huysmans reproduces, De Quincey introduces another hallucinated historical panoply, this one from the English Civil War, which after playing itself out 'would suddenly dissolve; and at a clapping of hands, would be heard the heart-quaking sound of *Consul Romanus*: and immediately,' the Roman hallucination would begin. (De Quincey 1995, pp 61-62.) In this case he makes it plain that these particular hallucinations were not only willed, but *planned in their detail*, rehearsed, and that he was aware of their status as they unfolded:

Often I used to see, after painting a sort of rehearsal whilst waking, a crowd of ladies, and perhaps a festival, and dances. And I heard it said, or I said it myself, "these are English ladies of the unhappy times of Charles I…—The ladies danced, and looked as lovely as the court of George IV. Yet I knew, even in my dream, that they had been in the grave for nearly two centuries.

(*ibid.*)

Only a few pages earlier, too, he had stated:

---

[6] This particular passage from the *Confessions*—accentuated by Baudelaire, reproduced by Huysmans, resurrected by Jarry, referred to by Breton—is possibly the most often cited of all among initiates of the Yellow Sign.

That, as the creative state of the eye increased, a sympathy seemed to arise between the waking and the dreaming states of the brain in one point—that whatsoever I happened to call up and to trace by a voluntary act upon the darkness was very apt to transfer to my dreams;

(*ibid*, p 60.)

In both of these nods to his predecessors—Villiers and De Quincey—in conceiving and practicing this *hallucinatory craft* then,[7] Huysmans emphasizes exactly that nature *as* craft—he proposes not a practice of vague mystical 'vision' nor a proto-Surrealist channeling of the unconscious, but a conscious *discipline* of the mind and of its relationship with the body and the senses.

> We hear it reported of Dryden, and of Fuseli in Modern times, that they thought it proper to eat raw meat for the sake of obtaining splendid dreams.
>
> -Thomas De Quincey, *Confessions*.
>
> (De Quincey 1995, p 63.)

It is only natural that, when beginning to initiate himself into this practice (for despite the *indications* gleaned from earlier practitioners, it can ultimately only be self-initiated, due to its very nature), Des Esseintes would initially latch onto the dominant motif associated with it at the time, via Coleridge, De Quincey, and Baudelaire: drugs. This is quickly discarded however:

In the past he had tried using opium and hashish to generate mental fantasies, but these two substances had brought on vomiting and intense nervous disturbances; he had been obliged to stop using them immediately, and to ask his brain alone to carry him, without the use of these crude stimulants, far from real life into the world of dreams.

(Huysmans 1998, p 140.)

We have already bypassed without comment several clues as to Huysmans' conception of Thought, which is key in reconstructing the coordinates through which he developed this capacity; for despite the sharp

---

[7] It is worth noting that in this same passage, De Quincey in turn goes on to connect *his own* hallucinatory practice to an existent tradition, via Coleridge, Piranesi (to whom Coleridge had in turn connected *his own* hallucinatory practice in conversation with De Quincey), Fuseli, and Dryden. (De Quincey 1995, pp 62-63.) The story of Coleridge's opium-and-reading-induced hallucination leading to the writing of *Kubla Khan*, at the very least, would have been quite familiar to Huysmans and is clearly a latent force behind the motifs and strategies put forth in *A rebours*. This story in itself might be related to Mary Wollstonecraft Shelley's writing of *Frankenstein*, inspired by a dream after reading Erasmus Darwin; both in turn are related to Horace Walpole's description (though like Shelley he does not mention the use of drugs) of the impetus behind his writing of *The Castle of Otranto*, the model of the Gothic form which so heavily influenced both British and French Romanticism, including Coleridge himself—in which Walpole wakes from an uncanny architectural dream that he connects with his reading habits, and feels impelled to, '[begin] to write, without knowing in the least what I intended to say or relate.' Walpole in turn shared Coleridge's later interest in Piranesi, and Praz speculates that Piranesi lies behind Walpole's own dream of Otranto. (Walpole et. al. 1986, p 16-17.)

dichotomy between the physical and mental domains that Des Esseintes' extreme antipathy toward 'the real', his stance *Against Nature,* might suggest, this conception is not so much idealist or even psychological as *physiological.* Thought, for Des Esseintes, is emphatically a function *of* the body—especially of the brain (usually portrayed as a fragile and unhealthy *organ*, not as a metonym for an abstract 'mind') and of the nerves—even if at the same time it can be directed *against* the body. Thus we note that after the hallucinated religious festivities already described, 'he would be left gasping.' After one such hallucination, evoked as he stands before a mirror 'into which his unconscious gaze plunged,' his body falters:

> 'That's all well and good,' he said, interrupted in these reflections by an overwhelming sensation of bodily weakness, 'but I'm going to have to be very wary of these delicious, detestable activities which utterly drain me.' He sighed: 'Well, that means more pleasures to curtail, more precautions to take'; and he sought refuge in his study, thinking that by doing so he could escape the haunting presence of those perfumes.
>
> (*ibid*, pp 100-101.)

Even reading itself can be physically debilitating: 'there were days when he found reading Poe utterly exhausting, days when he was left with trembling hands and ears on the alert'. (*ibid*, p 156.)

It is important not to see such comments as mere hyperbolic indications of *ardour;* it is made clear throughout *Against Nature* that the unique constitution of Thought that Des Esseintes has developed is the cause of the gradual physical dissolution that finally forces him to give up his way of life:

> I waked one morning in the beginning of last June from a dream, of which all I could recover was, that I thought myself in an ancient castle (a very natural dream for a head filled like mine with Gothic story) and that on the uppermost banister of a great staircase I saw a giant hand in armour. In the evening I sat down and began to write [*The Castle of Otranto*], without knowing in the least what I intended to say or relate.
>
> -Horace Walpole, letter of 9 March, 1762. (Walpole et. al. 1986, p 17.)

> And, without giving him time to draw breath, [the doctor] declared that he had set about restoring the digestive functions as rapidly as possible, and that it was now essential to tackle the neurosis which was not in any sense cured, and would require years of diet and medical care. He then added that before trying any kind of medication, before embarking upon any hydropathic therapy (which would in any case be impossible to carry out in Fontenay), he must abandon this solitary existence, return to Paris, get back into ordinary life, and try to enjoy himself, in short, like other people.
>
> 'But I don't enjoy the things other people enjoy!' protested Des Esseintes indignantly.

> Ignoring this observation, the doctor simply assured him that this radical change in lifestyle which he was stipulating was, in his opinion, a matter of life and death, a matter of either a return to health, or of insanity rapidly followed by tuberculosis.
>
> (*ibid*, p 173.)

At the same time, as we shall see, the causes of Des Esseintes' deteriorating health—and for his inability to use opium or hashish—are in fact inextricable from the mental and physiological strategies characterizing his interpretation of Aestheticism and his (possibly) hallucinatory practice.

It would be helpful here to qualify the reference to 'neurosis', a concept which permeates *A rebours* and Decadent discourse in general, and which is vital in unraveling the nature of this hallucinatory practice upon which I am speculating. The term 'neurosis' as used in the late 19th Century, before the influence of Freud, denotes an ill-defined condition, centred in the nervous system, straddling the 'psychological' and 'physical' realms. Characterized by hypersensitivity in the sensory organs, extreme mental anxiety, digestive disorders, the weakening of the 'will' (usually meaning specifically the will to engage with the polis as opposed to, for instance, the will to write, etc.), hot or cold flashes, and pain in the nervous centres, neurosis was widely considered a distinctly *modern* phenomenon, a response to the social, sensory, and environmental conditions typical of Modernity. (Smith 1999, pp 90-91 & Pierrot 1981, pp 47-53.) It was thus a highly *politicized* condition, and a natural space within which a contestation of Modernity might take place—discursively, experientially, and in the collapsing of the distinction between those two modes. And for this reason alone *even if for no other*, Decadent communities were characterized by, and habitually discussed themselves in terms of, this 'malady': which they in fact cultivated. Neurosis is the inevitable result of the mode of perception cultivated in Decadent Aesthetic circles; Maupassant notes that:

> And the amanuensis raised the baking tray as a black sun and said: "Show forbearance, Sire, they are idealists. Thou seest it in the ardour of their inner life. They are born of the twilight and have forgotten to die. Now they're poeticizing for the naked point."
>
> And the putrefaction conductor raised his arms yet three notches higher, blew his nose, spat to the right and left, and said: "Are there any decadents among them, transcendental decadents?"
>
> -Hugo Ball, *Tenderenda the Fantast* (wr. 1914-1920).
> (Ball et. al. 1995, p 134.)

> The artist's mind is so constructed that the repercussions set off within it by external stimuli are much sharper... His specific and morbid sensibility turns him, moreover, into a being flayed alive, for whom all sensations have become painful. I can recall those black days when my heart was so lacerated by things glimpsed only for the merest second that the memories of those visions still live on in me like open wounds.
>
> (Pierrot 1981, p 51.)

Likewise, Huysmans reports of Des Esseintes himself that:

> During the final months of his stay in Paris, when, having lost faith in everything, he was oppressed by hypochondria and ravaged by spleen, he had reached such a pitch of nervous sensibility that the sight of a disagreeable object or person would etch itself into his brain so deeply as to require several days for its imprint to even be slightly dulled; during that period the touch of a human form, brushed against in the street, became one of his most excruciating torments.
>
> (Huysmans 1998, p 20.)

The Dandy Barbey d'Aurevilly, one of the book's keenest critics, observed one aspect of the relationship between Des Esseintes' neurosis and his project of writing on and through himself; for Des Esseintes (like many in the Decadent community) had *written into* his own body and mind a critique of the society of which he was a product and which he intended to *rewrite*:

> Des Esseintes is no longer an organic being in the same way as Obermann, René, Adolphe, those heroes of human, passionate and guilty novels. He is a mechanism breaking down... he has at the same time written the nosography of a society destroyed by the rot of materialism... Make no mistake! For a Decadent of this power to appear, and for a book such as M. Huysmans' to take root inside a human skull, we must truly have become what in fact we are—a race at its last gasp.
>
> (Pierrot 1981, p 48.)

> Without the labor-pain of the body one day, an idea never would have been born,
> and it isn't from the body that it was born, but against it,
> when the idea of a gesture,
> i.e. the shadow of it,
> chose to live its own life.
>
> -Antonin Artaud, *Shit to the Spirit* (1943?)
>
> (Artaud 1960, p 110.)

Indeed, Des Esseintes' physical and psychological suffering is portrayed in *Against Nature* as truly terrible—at once a symptom of the society that produced him, a sign of his estrangement from it, and a punishment for his hubris in refusing it so radically and intimately. Yet despite the agony described by Huysmans and Maupassant and the correlations with cultural decay put forward not only by d'Aurevilly, but Huysmans himself and many others from within and without the Decadent community, the fact remains that this neurosis is claimed and cultivated by them; it is not a disease that *takes one*, it is a disease that is *taken on*. To *read* the Decadents at face value as purely pessimistic, passive, or escapist is to adopt a *passive* attitude toward cultural consumption which *Against the Grain* is a strident manifesto *against*.

To position the society as doomed and to characterize oneself as diseased is not a sign of fatalism; it is a protest against the propagandistic optimism of the Bourgeois order, which founds its authority on the promise of a hypothetical future and the story of an always triumphant recent past. To read these claims as categorically negative is to position oneself firmly within the reigning Positivist order. For this reason alone, the cultivation of un-health (not unrelated to the ascetic and masochistic practices of Medieval mystics) can be seen as a deeply personalized act of revolt, one with particularly high stakes.[8] There were, however, practical reasons as well. At the very least, the nerves themselves, and their *derangement*, are an essential site of aesthetic *and intellectual* significance:

> He had wanted, to satisfy his intellect and give pleasure to his eyes, a few evocative works which would project him into an unfamiliar world, revealing to him evidence of new possibilities, and stimulating his nervous system with learned depictions of frenzy, with complicated phantasmagoria and dispassionate, horrific visions.
>
> (Huysmans 1998, p 44.)

But there may, if my speculations are correct, be another, related reason for the cultivation of this nervous hypersensitivity; for the *nerves*, as they appear in *Against Nature* and in contemporary discussion of neurosis, are themselves the site of a kind of war between matter and mind, and are also the place where any interaction between them, and thus any *subversion*, must take place.

Unlike his predecessors Coleridge and De Quincey, Huysmans' relationship with his own mind was emphatically mediated by a post-Darwinian sensibility, which after all was inextricable from the cult of the Artificial; in fact d'Aurevilly saw *Against Nature* largely as an attempt to come to terms with atheism.[9] Therefore any re-working of it could not escape its physical basis, and any potential hallucinatory process could not merely depend upon 'the inner eye'; it must locate and mediate the relationships between the inner eye, the physical eye, and the functioning of the cognitive machine that was the brain.

---

[8] In light of discussions elsewhere in this book, especially that concerning the (possible) practice of Kurt Schwitters, it might be suggested that the preponderance of this condition within the Decadent community was due to an approach *too* emphatically focused on the sensory, too dependant upon the 'imaging' proper of the object of evocation; for those who we might speculate upon as later practitioners rarely reported such severe conditions. One might, on a further side note, connect Antonin Artaud and George Maciunas to this tradition of chronic nervous debility.

[9] He wrote famously that, 'After such a book, the only thing left for the author is to choose between the muzzle of a pistol and the foot of the cross,' (Huysmans 1998, p 145.) and Huysmans did indeed later convert to Catholicism. *Against Nature*, however ambivalent, was nonetheless written before that *apostasy* (compare to Artaud's arguments about *turning back* in his *Coleridge the Traitor*) and that ambivalence in fact heightens the degree to which the physicality of thought is foregrounded in the novel.

If the body was definitively anterior to 'mind', the latter was therefore essentially conceived of as a *parasite*. And the nerves are sometimes arrayed *against* the body, as if the mind, in its rebellion against its host, had recruited them to its cause; nor is the relationship only one way:

> in the past, he had adored the great Balzac, but at the same time as his constitution had become unbalanced and his nerves had gained the upper hand, his tastes had altered and the objects of his admiration had changed.
>
> (*ibid*, pp 145-146.)

His nerves do not simply *partake* in his body's un-health, they struggle to *bring it about*, they have in a sense seceded from the economy of the body, without at the same time ceding their corporeality. The nerves, as we shall see, are the material through which the *technique* articulated by Des Esseintes is worked out, it is they who grant the escape from the body; but they are also what exacts the price, what will ultimately make Des Esseintes' *particular version* of this practice insupportable at its furthest extreme. They facilitate the practice and take it away; the nerves are what must be *bargained with*.

Henri Bergson (who would later teach Jarry, another probable practitioner, as we shall see elsewhere in this book) explores a related set of issues from a physiological standpoint analogous in many ways to Huysmans' in his *Matter and Memory*, published 12 years after *Against Nature*; and like Huysmans, his system effectively positions memory—and by extension, 'mind' as it is commonly understood[10]—as a parasite inhabiting a nervous system whose anatomical function is directed elsewhere.[11] In this dense text—impossible to adequately condense here, you really ought to read it, dear reader—Bergson begins with the non-idealist view of the body implicit in *Against Nature*, affirming the status of the brain as essentially an organ regulating the nervous system of the human animal. Its function is to organize 'images'[12] according to their relative

---

[10] Bergson carries his explicit argument in this book only as far as memory in the sense of remembered moments, and only gestures vaguely toward abstract thought as such. The implication however is that he considers memory, as he describes it, to be constitutive of the material for imagined images and abstract thought, such as on p 195 where he in passing calls 'true memory' 'co-extensive with consciousness'.

[11] I beg the reader to forgive the following digression, but its relevance will become 'clear'; for the practice that Huysmans portrays and perhaps participates in, while going beyond the *scope* yet remaining largely within the *terms* of Bergson's discussion, could (and will) almost serve as an illustration *of* this theory of cognition.

[12] An 'image' in Bergson cannot be neatly defined, but *might* be conceptualized as that which can be experienced; emphatically *not* as the product of a perceptual operation, but its cause. (See especially pp 1-15, and p 159: 'images can never be anything but things, and thought is a movement.') Perception for Bergson is not additive but discretionary, subtractive; the eye (for instance) does not reproduce an object as a visual 'image', it acts as a filter, allowing in only those aspects of the image it is designed to *snare*.

immanence to affect or be affected by the body; it is an evolutionary extension, specialization, and extreme complication of the same reflex principle that will make single-celled organisms contract upon contact with certain chemicals dangerous to that organism, or to absorb nutrients. It organizes and coordinates perceptual information with muscular action. While this complication allows for learned *response*, there would seem to be no place in this schema for *memory* as such, only for *perception*.[13] There is no biological reason for the brain to interest itself in anything but its immediate situation, much less to 'store' memories (as opposed to learned behaviours); which in any case is shown in many ways to be impossible.[14] (Bergson 2004, pp 17-21.) Memory is therefore a self-supportive phenomenon, and exploits the perceptual economy of the body in order to manifest itself. Bergson implicitly suggests ways in which Decadent practice might have pushed this principle even farther in action. It is evident that the complexity of the cognitive operations in which Des Esseintes is engaged point toward operations both more encompassing and more subtle, and more integral to the functioning of his thought itself, than a mere 'stream of consciousness' reverie. We must, then, examine not only the *role* of memory within his conscious experience, but its mode of articulation within the always already still emerging economy of his subjective structure.

If the brain, as a biological and evolutionary machine, is oriented in its functioning toward organizing and coordinating actions directly useful to the organism, then:

> To recognize a common object is mainly to know how to use it… But to know how to use a thing is to sketch out the movements which adapt themselves to it; it is to take a certain attitude, or at least to have a tendency to do so through what the Germans call motor impulses (*Bewegungsantriebe*). The habit of using the object has, then, resulted in organizing together movements and perceptions; and the consciousness of these

---

> That which is given is the totality of the images of the material world, with the totality of their internal elements. But if we suppose centres of real, that is to say of spontaneous activity, the rays which reach it, and which interest that activity, instead of passing through those centres, will appear to be reflected and thus to indicate the outlines of the object that emits them. There is nothing positive here, nothing added to the image, nothing new. The objects merely abandon something of their real action in order to manifest their virtual action—that is to say, in the main, the eventual influence of the living beings upon them. Perception therefore resembles those phenomena of reflexion which result from an impeded refraction; it is like an effect of mirage.
>
> (pp 29-30.)

[13] See p 71 and others for the basis of Bergson's distinction between the two as separate functions, though the essential logic of it can be gleaned from the present discussion.

[14] For instance, the notion of a discreet 'unit' of memory—simultaneously visual, auditory, tactile, affective, and emotional—nonetheless retaining an awareness of its context, is logically unsustainable. Bergson cites dozens of clinical cases, mostly studies of Aphasia, to show that memories do not exist as discreet units that could be 'stored' but as complex interactions of numerous factors and perceptual and reflex centres. It is beyond the scope of this discussion and my own expertise to evaluate these arguments, and in any case narrow conceptions of factual 'scientificity' are the very least of my concerns; 'For is it not a better test of theory to find out what we can *do* with it?' (Reed 2006, p 19.).

nascent movements, which follow perception after the manner of a reflex, must be here also at the bottom of recognition.

(*ibid*, p 111.)

This principle, of a physiological connection being established between certain perceptions and corresponding physical attitudes—some actual, some prepared for in the brain but arrested—can be applied to the functioning of the human animal in general, surrounded as we are with objects that can affect us or can be affected by us, and which therefore we recognize. It is, furthermore, the principle through which memory as such is able to insert itself into human experience, and the principle we can watch Des Esseintes exploit in the most detailed description of his hallucinatory practice.

Memory proper (as opposed to the habit-memory that is in a way a function of perception, discussed further on) is in Bergson always already integral and homogenous (though capable of partition *into* discrete memories), but is generally not at play, and never in its entirety, within the economy of the human machine. If time is conceived of as a function of the *process* of subjectivity rather than a grid-like context *within which* the subjective process must take place (*ibid*, pp 274-280.), there is no need for memory to be 'stored' in physical form, merely for it to be *perceived*. And for this, it exploits the physiological system that mediates between our perceptions and our actions or motor impulses:

> For, while motor apparatus are built up under the influence of perceptions that are analyzed with increasing precision by the body, our past psychical life is there: it survives—as we shall try to prove—with all the detail of its events localized in time. Always inhibited by the practical and useful consciousness of the present moment, that is to say, by the sensori-motor equilibrium of a nervous system connecting perception with action, this memory merely awaits the occurrence of a rift between the actual impression and its corresponding movement to slip in its images.
>
> [. . .]
>
> By the very constitution of our nervous system, we are beings in whom present impressions find their way to appropriate movements:[15] if it so happens that former images can just as well be prolonged in these movements, they take advantage of the opportunity to slip into the actual perception and get themselves adopted by it.

(*ibid*, p 113-114.)

---

[15] While the notion of these movements will be expanded upon below, it should be remembered throughout that by 'movements', Bergson intends movements both actual or accomplished *and* potential or nascent; such a 'movement' does not require an actual muscular contraction (and if so, it might be quite small—a tightening of the chest, the flick of an eye), merely a physiological preparation *for* one.

Moreover,

> As a rule, when we desire to go back along the course of the past and discover the known, localized, personal memory-image which is related to the present, an effort is necessary, whereby we draw back from the act to which perception inclines us: the latter would urge us toward the future; we have to go backwards into the past. In this sense, movement rather tends to drive away the image.
>
> (*ibid*, pp 113-114.)

As it is for Huysmans then, the nervous system is the *host* for a parasitic memory; and it is memory which, though far from itself *constituting* the subject, provides the vast majority of the coordinates according to which the drives are articulated and the subject is constituted. The memory, and by extension the mind, essentially exists in the spaces *between* the circuits of perception-reaction that constitute our evolutionary mandate.

We can infer an operative grasp of this process in Huysmans'/Des Esseintes' system of technique as revealed within *Against Nature*. This system of technique is in fact quite comprehensive. The hallucinatory practice under discussion, while quite evident throughout the book and not unrecognized by conventional critics, is rarely approached with an awareness of its full potential not only as an imaginary *escape*, but as a sustained intervention in the process of subjectivity itself, a particularly radical extension of the tradition of self-forming represented by Dandyism and Aestheticism; nor is there a full realisation of the sophisticated level to which its technique is developed and indicated within the text—as those reading it willfully as a social document, rather than a work of only vaguely motivated *style*, can find. The present study does not exhaust it.[16] It is my intension here to suggest, even at the risk of overcompensation, the potential depth to which this practice may have plumbed, and the potential rigour with which it might have been approached on the levels of both conception and craft. It must be rescued from vague, platitudinal treatments.

---

[16] One reason that the *fact*, but not the potential *significance* of this practice has not been adequately noted might be that its appearance in the book can often be read, if one is so predisposed, as mere 'reverie' in the Romantic mode, in which the scenes 'relived' are not so much literally and figuratively re-experienced as merely 'pictured'. This impression should be dispelled if we take into account the close relationship in Huysmans' thought—especially as articulated in *Against Nature*—between thought, the senses, and the body. It is also worth recalling, before we decide to take these descriptions only quasi-literally or to filter them through a diluting veil of literary convention, that Huysmans, in his Decadent as much as his Naturalist work, was invariably interested in social *observation* (even if the terms and articulation have changed), and that this was quite manifestly a goal in the writing of *A rebours,* as evinced in his research with (among others) Mallarmé, who remarked as we have noted already that 'what gives your book its strength, (which will be decried as mad imagination etc.) is that there is not an atom of fantasy in it.' (Mallarmé 1988, pp 135-136.)

In teasing out the evidence of this system of technique then, we will notice first that, despite Huysmans' indication that 'this devious kind of sophistry' can be practiced without any kind of external aide, most of the concrete examples given in *Against Nature* do involve at least some kind of physical reference point—some *object* or environment definitively not *of* the subject that goes in this text by the name of Des Esseintes (and therefore not exclusively 'imagined'). And this is to say that they begin with perception, with nervous stimulation. We have looked at several rather elaborate examples here involving immersions in more-or-less contrived environments; but there are much more subtle examples, which are suggestive of how similar practices may have been carried out in the *actual* conditions of Decadent communities and, due to their greater subtlety, more effectively throw light upon the functioning of the Aesthetic subject upon such encounters with objects.

One such example[17] indicates the relationships between such an object, the memories re-*lived*, and the ways in which this practice contributes to Des Esseintes' larger intellectual life and engagement with the world; it occurs during a particularly hot day bringing on a resurgence of neurosis:

> 'What a day!' he said to himself now, mopping his neck and feeling what little strength he still possessed dissolve away in a fresh access of sweating; a feverish excitation still prevented him from remaining in one place; again he roamed through the different rooms, trying every chair in its turn. Finally, giving up the struggle, and slumping into a chair at his desk, he stayed leaning on the writing-table, his mind quite empty, automatically running his fingers over an astrolabe which lay, in place of a paperweight, on top of a pile of books and notes.
>
> [. . .]
>
> This paperweight prompted a host of recollections in him. Prompted by the sight of this ornament, his thoughts left Fontenay for Paris, returning to the dealer who had sold it, then traveled further back to the Cluny Museum, and in his mind he again saw the ivory astrolabe, while his eyes continued to contemplate, though without seeing it, the copper astrolabe that lay on his table.
>
> (Huysmans 1998, pp 140-141.)

One will note, of course, the way that Des Esseintes, in this beginning stage of the evocation to follow, utilizes his mental associations with the object—both its history and its form—as a staging point. But I have not presented this reading to you merely for this obvious point. For Des Esseintes is in no way abandoning himself to passive reverie here; he is carrying out a certain process, probing the relationships between the object, his

---

[17] Another extended example, following the trajectory from object to its various associations to hallucination, can be found on pp 99-101.

store of memories and associations, and his current state of mind, the immediate manifestation of his desire—that is, *the present* as it will be shortly discussed. Already in a hypersensitive, 'nervous' state, he begins by feeling the object, establishing tactile as well as visual contact between it and the nervous system which is the mediator of thought, keying his thought to this sensory focal point; he then allows the recollections it arouses to announce themselves, and he examines them. Note, however, that he *rejects* the first group of associations, those pertaining to the object's history; deeming the recollection of the dealer who sold it, and the trajectory it suggests, a dead end in relation to this present moment, his current state, in relation to his current set of preoccupations; and instead examines another set of recollections, based more on its physical form, which he has been both seeing and feeling. As he evokes the ivory astrolabe, he continues to keep his eyes focused on the copper one which serves him as a model, though *he no longer sees it;* his eyes are engaged, but not in *seeing;* we shall return to this observation shortly.

Through Bergson, we can *begin* to more fully understand the significance of the *object* in Huysmans'/Des Esseintes' practice. The sensory contact that he establishes with the astrolabe—through sight and through touch—stabilizes perception by forestalling action, and thus allows a greater number of images, each representative of a potential trajectory of evocation, to insert themselves into his conscious economy. The object itself, within this stasis of activity, provides the rift into which potentially pertinent associations can penetrate, around which they can proliferate.

Bergson suggests the process through which this insertion takes place, and which Des Esseintes too seems intuitively to take into account; and, tellingly, this analysis is centred on the *object*. He begins with a situation similar to Des Esseintes standing at his desk, feeling and staring at the object, 'attentive perception'. The rift continually opening between the perception and the forestalled actions that could, but do not follow, allow for the insertion of memory. Keeping in mind that memory in Bergson's schema is homogenous, whole, it is not discrete 'memories' that inexplicably find their way *to* this rift; rather, the *filtering* function characterizing the sensory apparatus works upon memory; everything happens as if *the whole* of memory were passing repeatedly through those filters, which catch the aspects of it which the present perception—biologically defined as 'useful'—would seem prepared to accept. (Bergson 2004, pp 126-130.) In this situation, series of nearly identical perceptions, as he continues to stare at the paperweight, allow a greater gradual build-up and reciprocity between the 'actual' perceptual image of the astrolabe and the memory-images inserting themselves, or being netted, in its interstices:

> an act of attention implies such a solidarity between the mind [conceived as inextricable from memory] and its object, it is a circuit so well closed, that we cannot pass to states of higher concentration without creating, whole and entire, so many new circuits which envelop the first and have nothing in common between them but the perceived object. Of these different circles of memory, which later we shall study in detail, the smallest, A, [see diagramme] is the nearest to immediate perception. It contains only the object O, with the

after-image which comes back and overlies it. Behind it, the larger circles B, C, D correspond to growing efforts at intellectual expansion. It is the whole of memory, as we shall see, that passes over into each of these circuits, since memory is always present; but that memory, capable, by reason of its elasticity, of expanding more and more, reflects upon the object a growing number of suggested images,—sometimes the details of the image itself, sometimes concomitant details which may throw light upon it.

(*ibid*, pp 127-128.)

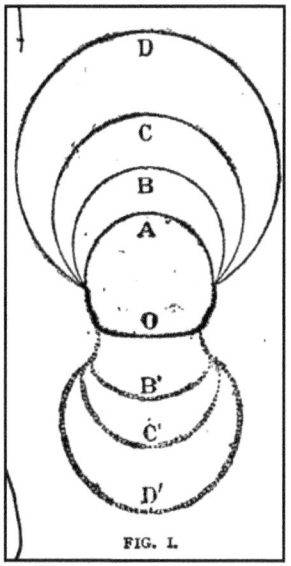

It is, of course, precisely this process in which Des Esseintes is intervening as he stares at the astrolabe, groping his way through the potential trajectories of thought suggested by these various images, rejecting some and throwing his attention *back* upon others in order to call up new associations from the interaction of these images with the perceptual image upon which he is still fixed.

That trajectory chosen, the hallucination now takes root and unhinges from the object:

Then, leaving the museum—though not the city—he sauntered through the streets, strolled down the Rue du Sommerard and the Boulevard Saint-Michel, turned off into adjacent thoroughfares and paused in front of certain establishments, the number and highly distinctive appearance of which had frequently attracted his attention. Inspired, initially, by the astrolabe, this spiritual journey finally led to the dives of the Latin Quarter.

(Huysmans 1998, p 141.)

A key indication of the moment that the hallucination to be embarked upon has been decided, that the transition into an *experience* of it has been accepted, comes when 'he' leaves the museum—the museum does not leave his recollections, for he has now situated his *sense of the present moment within* them—and 'saunters through the streets.' The shops at which he stops are those which he remembers in the most detail. Huysmans is at pains to reiterate both the experience's *origin* in the sensory perception of the astrolabe, and the way in which that perception has been left behind, is possibly even no longer present to the senses, as his eyes stare without seeing. He goes on to describe his memories of the Latin Quarter—remarking upon them now *as* memories at the same time that he describes them as if 'present realities'; this version of the Latin Quarter is characterized by types, caricatures who offer themselves up for mnemonic retention. Des Esseintes evokes the prostitutes lining the streets of the Latin Quarter, and 'every one of them, like automata who were all being wound up at the same time by the same key, proffered the same invitations in the same tone of voice and, smiling in the same way, uttered the same bizarre remarks, the same outlandish reflections.' (*ibid.*)

This concretion of an imagined stroll, this escape from the present of his body,[18] is not however the terminal or, I would argue, most important stage in this hallucinatory *process*. It is, in a sense, a stage of *thought*—thought condensed into experience—to be *passed through*. First, this scene—implicitly built up from 'memories' in the narrow sense—in converted to a scene that can be *inferred* from, but not *reconstructed* from these memories, as he pictures Paris from above. This, however, is merely a visual corollary of a cognitive drawing back, a movement out of the *specificity* that constitutes the hallucinatory *experience* as such, and a return to the severe *abstraction from* perception and perceptual detail and specificity that characterizes *thought* as distinguished from it; this is to say, the *hallucination* is coming to an end, but the hallucinatory *process* is only now coming to its concluding and defining stage as that experience is reintegrated into the linear experience of 'actual' life and into the system of thought and the relationship to time that constitutes (in part) Des Esseintes as subject.

> Now that he was able to conjure up, in memory, a bird's-eye view of that mass of bars and streets, Des Esseintes found that associations of ideas were forming in his mind and that he was reaching a conclusion. He understood the significance of those cafés which reflected the mood of an entire generation, and from them he deduced a synthesis of the period.
>
> And indeed the symptoms were clear and unmistakable; the brothels were disappearing, and as soon as one of them closed, a low-class bar would open. This diminution of licensed prostitution in favour of secret love affairs was obviously a consequence of the incomprehensible illusions of men in matters relating to carnal love.
>
> Monstrous though the idea might appear, the low-class bar satisfied an ideal…
>
> (*ibid*, pp 141-142.)

And Huysmans/Des Esseintes continues into a highly pessimistic analysis of his society's social and moral hypocrisies regarding sex, their relationships to class, and their effects on the self-conceptions and behaviours of individuals. This hallucinated experience has served a purpose, for upon his emergence from it Des Esseintes has come to a new understanding of the society in which he lives and the intersection of the personal and the social within it; it was through this hallucinatory practice that he *read* the 'symptoms' from which his conclusions are drawn, the altered modes of thinking have led to an epiphany. This epiphany regards the

---

[18] Whether the flesh which remains in Fontenay remains, from a certain perspective, precisely his *body* during this period is however, as we shall see, up for debate.

interconnectivity of several registers of human life, associations he has not made in his 'linear' life; Bergson goes on (see diagramme)[19]:

> Thus, having rebuilt the object perceived, as an independent whole, we reassemble, together with it, the more and more distant conditions with which it forms one system. If we call B´, C´, D´, these causes of growing depth, it will be seen that the progress of attention results in creating anew not only the object perceived, but also the ever widening systems with which it may be bound up; so that in the measure in which the circles B, C, D represent a higher expansion of memory, their reflexion attains in B´, C´, D´ deeper strata of reality.[20]

(Bergson 2004, p 128.)

Des Esseintes has, in a sense, intervened in the process through which these systems become manifest to his consciousness, through reproducing an ~~absent~~ sensory 'experience', with its own myriad systems of association constantly modulating in response to the hallucinated ~~sensory~~ environment, all *couched within*, as it were, a sustained effort of thought and the still proliferating associations from his 'actual' perceptual environment, mixing with and mutually inflecting that second, doubly parasitic system of ~~sensory~~ and cognitive action. Thought has not merely been 'quantitatively' doubled (indeed, thought as so conceived is foreign to questions of 'quantity' or 'amount'), it has created a second sphere *in which to act*, and has doubled the *processes at play* in a way which can only constitute a *qualitative* difference in the modes of its own structuration and articulation. His *experience of thought itself* has been altered, its range of action expanded.

A further question now presents itself: during this hallucination, where 'is' Des Esseintes? Upon what register would we locate the locus of his 'experience'? Bergson goes on to remark that:

---

[19] While this claim may initially seem grandiloquent in relation to the fairly modest realization Huysmans ascribes to Des Esseintes, it should be remembered that this realisation is itself the outcome merely of a *particular instance* of this practice; through habitual involvement with the modes thought related to this practice, the unique functioning of thought that they represent will become gradually less localized, will have their effects on the subject's intellectual economy in general, and will affect their modalities of perception and cognition in much greater, though less localizable, ways. A certain distortion between cause and effect is at play because I am treating this instance, due to the specificity of its description, as a metonym for the practice as a discipline.

[20] The possible field of associations that might be 'permitted' by any set of sensory stimuli is potentially quite large and unpredictable, due to this proliferation and to the gradual withdrawal in the process from direct relationship to the perception itself; this is especially true in situations where our physical activity is largely habitual or inactive and the relationship between perception and action is more lax. (for instance *ibid*, pp 93-94 & 109-111.) In light of this observation, the care with which Des Esseintes designs all of the sensory details of his home, his conception of it as a kind of machine for generating thought, and the close relationships he comments on between various colours, fabrics, and spaces and the modes of thought to which they are conducive become more comprehensible.

> The same psychical life, therefore, must be supposed to be repeated an endless number of times on the different stories of memory, and the same act of the mind may be performed at varying heights.
>
> (*ibid*, pp 128-129.)

Surely the practice described by Huysmans involves a kind of productive derangement of these strata of memory, which brings them into contact in unexpected relationships; but this leaves the question—keeping in mind the inherent identification between notions of 'self' and memory—*what is* the subject in the midst of such an operation?

Needless to say, this is an extremely complex question, and it is not my intention to answer it here—indeed, to *approach* an answer, one would have to engage in such a practice her- or him-self, and finding the answer inexpressible, would likely be forced to fall back upon an *ostensibly* deductive approach.[21] I intend merely to suggest several possible *frameworks* for approaching this question, in order to indicate the irreducible subjective crisis—a crisis that can be productive, destructive, or both—that lies at the heart of such a practice.

In order to do so, I shall look at two notions at play within the discourse and organization of the subject—*consciousness*, and *the body*; I shall keep this investigation within the framework of Bergson's system for the sake of (relative) simplicity.[22]

Bergson identifies two forms of memory, one of which we have been dealing with so far, the stock of images from which Des Esseintes' hallucinations are composed. The other he describes as 'memory-image,' or '*habit interpreted as memory*,' and as such an extension of the reflex principle that locates it as, at least in part, *within* the biological order. It is not so much a memory of representations as a mechanism of learned behaviour.[23]

---

[21] Even if memory is (as I would argue, and as Bergson himself suggests (p 186.)) is taken to include the unconscious, neither it nor the notion of 'self' constitute subjectivity itself; see for instance Kristeva's notion of the semiotic chora in *Revolution and Poetic Language*, (pp 21-31.) which is in fact implicit in any psychoanalytic theory of the drives and thus constitutes subjectivity as a *process* and structura*tion* rather than a static or completable structure or entity. At the same time, 'the body' as it functions in Kristeva is *not* analogous to 'the body' in a Bergsonian system; Kristeva's body, as the site and source of biological and energetic rhythms that are organized through the drives, precedes and continues to underlie Bergson's body in any of its manifestations. Bergson's notion of the body is nonetheless, I would argue, not *exclusive to* it, but rather represents a function *and* a controlling image in the economy of self-conception and consciousness itself. While I reiterate that neither consciousness nor the experience of identity *constitute* the subject without excess, both, in *some* form, would seem to be necessary and highly determining factors in any configuration of subjectivity as such.

[22] As always, I am looking out for the patience and the *limits of* you, my reader.

[23] Bergson is unclear on the issue of the biological and evolutionary status of habit-memory. One might speculate that, upon demonstrating its usefulness to the survival of the species, it effectively becomes a part of the animal function,

(*ibid*, pp 88-95.) Perception itself, since it is a *filter* of reality letting through only that which is susceptible to the body's influence or needs in some way, is not continuous but inevitably leaves gaps:

> The diverse perceptions of the same object, given by my different senses, will not, then, when put together, reconstruct the *complete* image of the object; they will remain separated from each other by intervals which measure, so to speak, the gaps in my needs.
>
> (*ibid*, pp 46-47.)

It is this which provides the raw material for 'pure memory', or recollected images, and which provides the opportunity for them to be reintroduced to consciousness—to the present, as we will find:

> Perception is never a mere contact of the mind with the object present; it is impregnated with memory-images which complete it as they interpret it. The memory-image, in its turn, partakes of the 'pure memory,' which it begins to materialize, and of the perception in which it tends to embody itself: regarded from the latter point of view, it might be regarded as a nascent perception.
>
> (*ibid*, p 170.)

As a result, memory and perception are in practice, though not in nature, inextricable in the construction of experience and consciousness itself:[24]

> Your perception, however instantaneously, consists then in an incalculable multitude of remembered elements; and in truth every perception is already a memory. *Practically we perceive only the past*, the pure present being the invisible progress of the past gnawing into the future.
>
> Consciousness, then, illumines, at each moment of time, that immediate part of the past which, impending over the future, seeks to realize and to associate with it. Solely preoccupied in thus determining an

---

perpetuating the biological anomaly that allows it to function; though this is a speculation coming from outside the boundaries of Bergson's discussion itself. Throughout *Matter & Memory*, Bergson refers to evolutionary theory only implicitly, never naming it or mentioning Darwin or his successors by name, though their schema is implicit within his own.

[24] The significance of Des Esseintes *staring at* the copper astrolabe but *seeing* first the remembered ivory one, and then the later images that proliferate around and from it, is hereby partially explained.

> undetermined future, consciousness may shed a little of its light on those of our states, more remote in the past, which can be usefully combined with our present state, that is to say, with our immediate past: the rest remains in the dark.

(*ibid*, p 194.)

Consciousness is a function of the (always absent) present; at the same time, the present *as experienced* (despite its absence *as such*) is always already a function *of memory*. Consciousness marks the moment in which memory and perception *meet* in a non-existent space.

Des Esseintes' groping, then, as he tests the various trajectories which might be followed, is doubly an act of consciousness, and metonym of its own possibility; acting *within* the general mandate of consciousness itself, he is reduplicating its action, 'impending over' a potential future—a future from which, in some cases, he withdraws, a future not accomplished. This is consciousness on the brink, it is thought experienced *exponentially*; but at the same time is merely the inevitable process of *thought*, which is itself a matter, like Bergson's perception, not of *filling* a void but of selection, of drawing a single trajectory from among an infinite number of apprehended, but not *experienced* configurations of the subject made manifest *through* thought.[25] Thought itself, as such, is always on the brink of its own falling-away.

But—what, then, when Des Esseintes makes his decision? When that groping ceases to reject the future it overhangs, and, to use Bergson's word, begins to *gnaw*?

I must enjamb this thought for the moment, let it hang.

In the meantime, let us examine the *body*; for the body, too, represents a certain meeting place of memory, perception, and possible futures. Given the (inevitably inadequate) outline of Bergson given so far, it is not difficult to anticipate his *basic* definition of the body, which he refers to throughout as not *outside* the order of images, but as a 'privileged image' (*ibid*, pp 1-12 and *passim*.):

> Situated between the matter which influences it and that on which it has influence, my body is a centre of action, the place where the impressions received choose intelligently the path they will follow to transform themselves into movements accomplished. Thus it indeed represents the actual state of my becoming, that

---

[25] A footnote, in one sense, denotes just such a groping, a relic of a thought killed in the cradle.

part of my duration which is in the process of growth… it is, in this material world, that part of which we directly feel the flux; in its actual state the actuality of our present lies.

(*ibid*, p 178.)

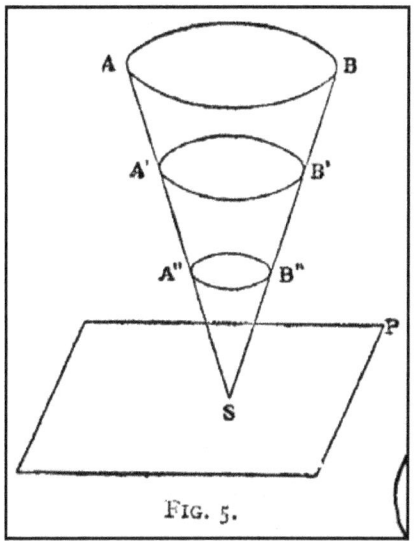

Fig. 5.

The body, then, is defined by its relationship to *action*, it is that which affects, or can affect, what we *perceive*. And yet—do memories not impose themselves to the very degree to which they would *seem* to be related to potential action—to the very degree that their relationship with perception approaches the indistinguishable? Is the body not at stake in the very process of memory?

Already we can see that the body is defined by its own incessant disappearance, for it is a relationship to potential *futures* which is itself constantly converted into a representation *within memory* before it can articulate itself definitively *as* a(n absent) present. Bergson represents the body geometrically as *a point* which is the apex of an inverted cone representing memory itself (see diagramme):

If I represent by a cone SAB the totality of the recollections accumulated in my memory, the base AB, situated in the past, remains motionless, while the summit S, which indicates at all times my present, moves forward unceasingly, and unceasingly also touches the moving plane P of my actual representation of the universe. At S the image of the body is concentrated; and, since it belongs to the plane P, this image does but receive and restore actions emanating from all the images of which the plane is composed.

(*ibid*, p 196.)

Into this moving point which represents the body and, in the same movement, consciousness, those configurations of memory that can insert themselves do so; as the memory continually passes through this point, the remembered images surrounding and partially obscuring the perception 'attract' or make perceptible other images and ideas in turn, and thus a 'cone' of progressively vague but broad memory images makes itself felt; it is in this way that Des Esseintes progressively moves farther and farther from the astrolabe which is his starting point, and the new associations no longer bear *direct* reference to it, but to the associations already hovering around it.

The 'cone' is not in fact the 'shape' of memory, but the momentary organization of potential memory-images, arranged according to the relative possibility of their insertion into present consciousness, at the point S which is the body. (*ibid*, 196-198.)

We might then describe Des Esseintes' movement from the immediate perception of the paperweight into his hallucinated journey, in part, as a progression from that 'point S' into the progressively broader field of mnemonic activity *within* this 'cone', within which he articulates new relationships, organized according to a concept of linear time; this could be seen as a departure from the body at point S, and a re-establishment of *another* body *within* that field of the past—for he does indeed move through, encounter, 'perceive' this amalgamatory world—therefore establishing a secondary present, parasitic in relation to the first, supported by but obscuring the primary present, which, after all, he *no longer sees*, though he is conscious of staring *at* it. It is this surrogate ~~body~~ *within* his hallucination with which he 'directly feels the flux', not the body staring at the astrolabe *without* perceiving it.

This *could* be seen as such a departure, and as such a re-institution; but believe it or not, such an explanation for the subjective crisis so calmly and understatedly inscribed in *Against Nature* is in fact far too simple.

Such an explanation, while potentially productive on many registers, takes Bergson's notion of the cone too literally, treating it as a static 'space' where such a detached but still *internally* coherent subject could 'move' at will. We must recall that memory as experienced is in fact always *passing through* the present, and being modified by it. As has just been pointed out,

> Within the cone so determined the general idea oscillates continually between the summit S and the base AB. In S it would take the clearly defined form of a bodily attitude or of an uttered word; at AB it would wear the aspect, no less defined, of the thousand individual images into which its fragile unity would break up... between the sensory-motor mechanisms figured by the point S and the totality of the memories disposed in AB there is room... for a thousand repetitions of our psychical life, figured by as many sections A′B′, A″B″, etc., of the same cone. We tend to scatter ourselves over AB in the measure that we detach ourselves from our sensory and motor state to live in the life of dreams;
>
> (*ibid*, pp 210-211.)

Des Esseintes' decision to 'leave the museum—though not the city', that is, to *enter into* the state of hallucination and place himself *within* memory, does in one respect then represent a departure from S, a movement 'into' the cone; but in fact he nonetheless continues to inhabit point S, which has not entirely ceased 'moving forward unceasingly' in time. Bergson's qualification just given however, and the diagramme to which it refers, reminds us that at every moment at point S—the body of the 'actual' present—memory, through inserting itself *into* perception, is at the same time *re-inscribed into itself*. Thus we have cone A´B´, A´´B´´, etc. being themselves constantly recalled to point S; but there is a factor missing from this geometrical figuration.

For the memories AB all have one unifying factor: at one point, they passed through point S. That is to say, *they were once perceptions of the subject*. The 'body' is their common denominator, the consciousness their structuring principle. Within A´B´ and A´´B´´, therefore, we must always find: S´, S´´, etc. *The Self*[26] *is re-inscribed within it-self*. And, furthermore, when dealing with memory in its narrow sense—as recollection (including sensory recollections to be re-combined), that reduplicated subject is always present as a center in relation to which to which the recollection is oriented. Thus the 'body' is always already multiple, heterogenous, and subject to the passing physical conditions that limit and de-limit the momentary possibilities of memory and thought. Continuing the geometric framework of Bergson's explanation, we are presented with an infinite number of inscriptions of the body and of sites for consciousness, constantly passing into and through each other. It resembles a constellation, a multiplicity of points between which various connections might be drawn and just as easily erased. Can it therefore still be responsibly conceived as a unitary *point* from which such judgments can be definitively passed? Is it not the body itself that is always already *on trial*?

> Then all my hair, all my mental veins will have been drained in quicklime; then my bestiary will have been noticed, and my mystique will become a hat. Then the joints of stones will be seen smoking, arborescent bouquets of mind's eyes will crystallize in glossaries, stone aeroliths will fall, lines will be seen and the geometry of the void understood: people will learn what the configuration of the mind is, and they will understand how I lost my mind.
>
> -Antonin Artaud, *All Writing is Pigshit* (c. 1925-30?)   (Artaud 1965, p 39.)

For the moment, at the least, I leave this sentence suspended.

We have opened several questions, but it may *seem* initially that, in moving deeper into this speculative and abstract world, like that (as Bergson says) of 'Dream', we have at the same time moved away from the realm of investigative *action*. Starting with the astrolabe of this possible hallucinatory practice at which we gazed (without precisely seeing it), we have moved farther and farther from its source, until the (non-)object under our critical gaze has been almost entirely obscured by the associations it has aroused. Never fear; the

---

[26] I use the term 'Self' here to denote the unifying, rather than modulating and negativising elements of the subjective process; for though the forms and unifying aspects of the subject in a past moment might be re-inserted and even re-inhabited within a present, they would presumably nonetheless be infused with, and thus inflected by, elements of what for lack of a better term I will call the 'biological present', especially thetic forces and their constant regulation by the drives.

hallucination that I am writing and the hallucination that you are reading is[27] slowly but inexorably approaching that critical phase when, in a return to the plane of action, formerly unthinkable avenues are hopefully to be opened up; though the progress will not be as clear-cut or straightforward as the one that Huysmans has provided.

We are not free from this hallucination yet, however; I am merely glancing at my astrolabe to ensure that my various trajectories of thought are *all* remaining at play. First, I must address yet another inaccuracy—for inaccuracies must be managed *very* carefully—in the last argument given.

> This scene from the past came to him suddenly, with extraordinary vividness. Pantin lay before him, bustling with activity and life, in the green, dead-seeming waters of his moonlight-framed mirror into which his unconscious gaze plunged: a hallucination carried him far from Fontenay; the mirror gave him back not only the reflection of the street but also of the thoughts that street once evoked
>
> -J.-K. Huysmans, *Against Nature* (1884). (Huysmans 1998, p 100.)

For the counter-argument could be made that what I have called S´, S´´, etc., above is not in fact another body, but a *representation* of the body, since it has ceased to act. I might counter that as it *does* act within the hallucinatory present within which it operates, and with which Des Esseintes associates him*self* within its duration, it does in fact constitute a *kind* of body, however parasitic, which introduces into the process of the subject a unique factor; I believe, on the whole, I would have a valid point. Nonetheless, you might hold out, arguing that in order to constitute a truly radical modification of subjectivity, such a hallucinatory practice would have to be experienced not only as a system of *representations* acting upon each other, but *as a present,* that is, effectively *perceived*. The body of the past or the imagination would have to be, in some sense, re-*inhabited,* complete with the dynamic of stimulus and action constituting the body, (not merely the body´) as Bergson defines it. And I might agree with you, if for no other reason than that I believe that Huysmans/Des Esseintes, too, was unsatisfied with the *representation* of sensation, feeling that it still remained within the realm of *pretending,* and was determined to go farther. And this was the reason that Romantic notions of 'reverie' were not enough; this *reconstitution* of sensation itself required an especially rigorous discipline.

Once again, Bergson suggests how this might be done, and Huysmans would seem to confirm it. For it is clear that while memory is of a different *order* than perception, it manifests itself through stimulating—essentially through *tricking*—the body's perceptual apparatus. Though not strictly perception itself, memory to be experienced must in some degree *pass for* perception to the body.

---

[27] or 'are'

> My actual sensations occupy definite sections of the surface of my body; pure memory, on the other hand, interests no part of my body. No doubt, it will beget sensations as it materializes; but at that moment it will cease to be a memory and pass into the state of a present thing, something actually lived; and I shall only restore its character of memory by carrying myself back to the process by which I called it up, as it was virtual, from the depths of my past. It is just because I made it active that it has become actual, that is to say, a sensation capable of provoking movements.
>
> (*ibid*, p 179.)

This is precisely the description of a *full* hallucination that must be the ideal goal of such a practice; if the nervous system can be stimulated *by memory* to the point of being experienced *as perception*, one is living *inside thought*. Huysmans' phrase used earlier to describe this practice—'this adroit duplicity'—now becomes clear; in the stance *Against Nature*, Nature herself must be tricked—the biological *body* must be differently inhabited by the parasitic mind, the whole nervous system subverted, or *converted* to mind.

It seems clear that simple 'concentration' would not be enough to achieve this to an extreme degree; such concentration would need to be *trained*. The first issue to address—the objection which I so unceremoniously stuffed into your mouth, dear reader, several paragraphs ago and which has been raised again in the passage just quoted—is the necessity of the memory to demonstrate its capacity for action *in the present* in order to be experienced *as* perception. Several (possible) practitioners of this (hypothetical) practice would seem to have addressed this in a relatively straightforward fashion: Rimbaud describes himself projecting images *onto* the surrounding landscape (Rimbaud 1991, p 37.) and Dali's oneirocritical or 'paranoiac-critical' method involves a similar operation; such a method utilizes the building-up of memory-images around the initial perception, which are therefore pre-determined to be closely related to the motor-functions inspired by the perceptions themselves. In this way, the 'veil' of imagined images is 'thin' enough that both the initial perception and the projected image-perception can coexist, while the aptness for that projected image to its accompanying movement *can* at the same time allow it to approach the sensory-motor *relationship* that characterizes perception and the imminence to consciousness to make it *lived*, especially if the practitioner is applying to that projection a rigorous *technical* sensibility such as that we are in the process of examining.[28] As we shall see elsewhere in this book, Jarry, Mallarmé, Schwitters, and Huysmans himself—in the incident of in the 'English' tavern already discussed and, as we will examine presently, in relation to what he refers to as succubism or pygmalionism—may have developed this trajectory in a more complicated way, by projecting entirely fictional ~~people~~ *into* the actual space within which they themselves moved. While similar to the strategy of projection adopted by Rimbaud and Dali, these ~~people~~ themselves—of whom more will be said elsewhere in

---

[28] It is worth comparing the sensibility of such practices to the Lettrist and Situationist derives, which represent at once a continuation and a reversal of this strategy.

this book—are not mapped to existing objects or (presumably) 'actual' people. However, their positioning in 'actual' space and time similarly relates them directly to the primary Bergsonian body, the biological present; such a practice does not require bodily passivity, and the entire weight of the projective act can be concentrated on these figures, rather than being dispersed in an effort to create a tangible *space* within which interactions can occur. Moreover, while these figures—which are independent of 'actual' objects that might be physically pertinent to the body and are thus perceived—do not correspond to the 'real or virtual movements' that would render them perceptive in as

> I kept gazing at the azure irregular mountains which bounded the view, and in thought was already transported to their summits. Vast and wild were the prospects I surveyed from this imaginary exaltation, and innumerable the chimeras which trotted n my brain. Mounted on these fantastic quadrupeds, I shot visibly from rock to rock, and built castles in the style of Piranesi, upon most of their pinnacles.
>
> -Horace Walpole, *Dreams, Walking Thoughts, and Incidents* (1783).
>
> (Walpole et. al. 1986, p 18.)

direct and relatively effortless a way as would be the case in a more purely oneirocritical approach, the fact of their ~~inhabiting~~ the same space as the practitioner allows for a number of subtle but direct actions that could be specifically aimed at creating such conditions; for example, the 'location' of such a ~~person~~ in actual space could be physiologically 'confirmed' through the movement of eye muscles to focus on the spot; mimicking the habitual contraction of muscles when such a ~~person~~ 'approaches' or 'passes by' in a narrow space; slight muscular inclinations or tics characteristic of an attitude of 'listening' to ~~speech~~; all of these hypothetical techniques might prepare physical attitudes into which images might slip themselves with special effectiveness.[29]

Such strategies, in addition to their more direct appeal to the physiological requirements for *lived* experience which Bergson articulates, also have the advantage of encouraging a greater interpenetration and interplay between 'everyday life', the social register, and these practices and the cognitive states that they develop. Most of the examples Huysmans gives in *A rebours* however are predominantly internal; and action in the 'real' world does not contribute to the *continuity*, only to the initial evocation of the ~~hallucination~~. While the astrolabe might provide the initial impetus and the physiological focus of his evoked trip through Paris, the psychical reality of that trip is *not* supported by him actually walking, to provide the proper physical attitude for the full integration of the remembered image. On the contrary, he is standing still, staring at the astrolabe without seeing it.

---

[29] It should be noted that it would not be sufficient for the practice upon which I am speculating to call up merely a *visual* 'overpainting' of scene; this would amount to mere psychosomatic decoration. Even if certain sensory elements could be kept in their 'purely' perceptive state and not require 'hallucinatory' treatment, such decisions could not be passive; vision, sound, scent, tactility, temperature, internal affection, and psychological and emotional states would all have to be taken into account in the synthesization of the experience.

It is for this reason that the physicality of the brain, the conceiving of it as emphatically an element of the *nervous* system, of matter capable of *action*, is so important to Huysmans' schema. Bergson notes that the brain, as an advanced regulatory apparatus, can not only *prepare* motor reactions but then *hold them back* when a single stimulus suggests (as most in fact will) multiple possible reactions:

> In other words, the brain appears to us to be an instrument of analysis in regard to the [nervous] movement received, and an instrument of selection in regard to the movement executed.
>
> (*ibid*, p 20.)

This capacity of an advanced nervous system to *prepare* an action but then *withhold it from execution* results in what Bergson refers to throughout the book as 'prepared' or 'virtual actions'; an actual 'perception' is capable of producing a physical effect on the brain that *prepares* a certain reflex, but which *is not* ultimately transmitted in order to produce muscular movement. To recall a passage quoted earlier, now further dismembered:

> But to know how to use a thing is to sketch out the movements which adapt themselves to it; it is to take a certain attitude, or at least to have a tendency to do so through what the Germans call motor impulses (*Bewegungsantriebe*).
>
> (*ibid*, p 111.)

In order to approach the physiological status of perception then, the memory being inserted need only *sketch itself out*, find its counterpoint in the form of a motor *impulse*, not necessarily in an *accomplished* movement. One must, then, learn to recognise, isolate, and physically *recreate*—not merely 'remember'—the initial impulse of the nerves that *precedes* movement itself; one must manipulate the brain like one would a muscle; it must be *trained*. In doing so—and admittedly we are, even more than usual, definitively within the realm of pure *speculation*—one must closely study and experiment with our apprehension of what Bergson terms 'affection'—the awareness of the inside of our own body, the 'sense' of physical existence itself. This might be apprehended though an analytical examination of one's own thermoception, equilibrioception, and especially proprioception; within a Bergsonian system this awareness of physical existence, of the spatial localization *of* self, might be none other *than* the apprehension of these millions of conceived but arrested actions.[30] Huysmans provides us with nothing explicit on this matter; but the extreme sensitivity to both internal and external stimuli, the bouts of dizziness, the hyperbolized experience of internal pain, the bouts of hot and cold, that constitute his neurosis—that condition partaking of both the physical and the mental—would be consistent with such a physiological 'training'; it should be remembered in this connection that the hallucination with the astrolabe which we have dissected so interminably was embarked upon during such a spell of neurosis.

In any event, all of the possible strategies just described—oneirocritical, projection, or internal evocation—require for their full effectiveness the application of sensory technique; the practitioner would not merely need to call up the 'pure memory' which remains mostly abstracted from the various sensory *stimuli* which originally produced it. S/he would need to learn to call up, to recall and/or recreate *in detail*, the heterogeneous sensations *as* perceptive sensations which constitute it, and to re-assemble them through their simultaneous re-insertion via the various perception-centres. The syntax of the various senses must be learned and internalized in order to allow the practitioner to manipulate them in detail, while bringing them to bear on the 'present' fully enough to approach the status of perceptions: remembering or 'imagining' with enough *precision* to convince the nervous system that what is being inserted is in fact a perception.

In terms of the *external* senses, the development of such a discipline is easily traced in *Against Nature;* in fact much of the aesthetic practice described throughout the book could be seen as precisely such a discipline. *Sight*, since we are primarily creatures of sight, is the most obvious of the senses to be dealt with, and probably that requiring the least conscious development to reach a pitch necessary for the physiological sleight-of-hand we are suggesting. And in fact Huysmans' background in literary Naturalism had prepared him especially well for this. The detailed *reproduction* of the world in print for which Naturalism strove had necessitated the precise *observation,* analysis, and memorization of that detail—especially visual—which could now be put to other, more obscure uses;[31] so that when we read, for instance, the two pages of vivid and precise description of the rain in all its various attitudes and effects during Des Esseintes' one excursion from his house, ending at the 'English' pub, it might be read as a kind of mnemonic stockpiling, especially when we consider that this observation of the rain was carried out under the aegis of the impending (ultimately ~~hallucinatory~~) trip to England, 'a land of mist and mud'. (Huysmans 1998, pp -107.)

---

[30] Framing the issue in this way, our sense of physical existence would be positioned as the residual apprehension of physiological operations *not* carried out, of what we have *not* done; our physical self-awareness becomes the *trace* of our infinite *non-existences*.

[31] Speaking of the novel *En ménage* from his Naturalist period, Breton remarks upon, 'Huysmans' style, marvelously cast to highlight the nervous communicability of sensations'. (Breton 1997, p 145.)

While vision lends itself relatively easily to such intensification of attention, other senses could not be developed so readily in passing; less often relied upon in habitual life, they required special focus, and many of Des Esseintes' more idiosyncratic aesthetic practices provide this focus. For instance, Des Esseintes has converted his liquor cabinet and bar into a mechanism which he calls his 'mouth organ', to facilitate his highly cultivated sense of *taste*, and the method he has devised for cultivating it:

> A rod linked all the spigots and controlled them with a single action, so that once the apparatus was set up, it only required the touch of a button concealed in the paneling for every tap to be turned on simultaneously and fill the miniscule goblets which stood beneath them. The organ could then be played. The stops labeled 'flute, horn, vox angelica' were pulled out, ready for use. Des Esseintes would drink a drop of this or that, playing interior symphonies to himself, and thus providing his gullet with sensations analogous to those which music affords the ear.
>
> (*ibid*, p 39.)

If music can sharpen our relationship to our sense of hearing and to sound by focusing our perceptual attention on its nature, our cognitive attention on its organization, and our intellectual attention on its logic and potential manipulation, then, Huysmans/Des Esseintes decides, applying those principles to other senses will increase their potential as well. In order to further develop his faculty for differentiation, he has pushed the analogy:

Furthermore, the flavour of each cordial corresponded, Des Esseintes believed, to the sound of an instrument. For example, dry curaçao matched the clarinet whose note is penetrating and velvety; kummel, the oboe with its sonorous, nasal resonance; crème de menthe and anisette, the flute, at once honeyed and pungent, whining and sweet; [etc.]… He was also of the opinion that the correlation could be extended and that string quartets could perform under the palatal vault, with the violin represented by fine old liqueur brandy, smoky, pungent and delicate; [etc.] (*ibid*.)	I had to begin to educate my tactile sense. By sheer will power I localized the confused phenomena of thought and imagination on the different parts of my body. I observed that healthy bodies can use this education to give precise and thorough results…. Among the different experiences, I found the following three preferable: 1. to wear gloves for several days, during which time the brain will force the condensation into your hands of a desire for different tactile sensations; 2. to swim underwater in the sea, trying to distinguish interwoven currents and different temperatures tactistically; 3. every night, in complete darkness, to recognize and enumerate every object in your bedroom. -Filippo T. Marinetti, *Manifesto of Tactilism* (1924). (Caws 2001, p 198.)

In relation to our potential hallucinatory practice, it is important that Des Esseintes teaches himself not just to *recognise* these perceptions, but to *organize* them, to understand their syntax, as it were: to actively manipulate them:

> Once he had grasped these principles he was able, after some erudite experimentation, to play himself silent melodies on his tongue, soundless funeral marches of great pomp and circumstance and to hear, in his mouth, solos of crème de menthe, duets of vespetro and rum. He even succeeded in transferring actual pieces of music to his jaw, following the composer step by step and rendering his thoughts, his effects, his subtleties, through close associations or contrasts, through roughly estimated or carefully calculated blends of liquors.
>
> (*ibid*, p 40.)

When the manipulation of a particular sense had reached a certain pitch, and its organizational principles had been thoroughly internalized—had become in some respect *habitual*—its technique would be further developed by attempting hallucinatory excursions focused on that sense. Huysmans describes such an experiment using the sense of smell. In order to cultivate this sense, he had become a kind of amateur expert in the art of mixing perfumes; while in honing his *taste* he had used methods analogous to musical appreciation and composition, here he had used poetry as a model:

> he used effects analogous to those employed by poets, imitating, in a sense, the admirable ordering of certain works of Baudelaire's, for example *L'Irréparable* and *Le Balcon*, in which the last of the five lines that make up the verse echoes the first and, returning like a refrain, drowns the soul in a measureless ocean of melancholy and languor.
>
> (*ibid*, p 97.)

He then designed a hallucination whose only physical stimulant was this sense:

> His present desire was to wander at will in an unpredictable, ever-changing landscape, and he began with a phrase that was sonorous and full, and afforded him a sudden glimpse of an immense stretch of countryside.
>
> With his vaporizers, he injected into the room an essence composed of ambrosia, Mitcham lavender, sweet pea, and a mixed bouquet, an essence which, when distilled by an artist, does deserve the name it has been given—'extract of meadow flowers'; next, he introduced into this meadow a precisely measured blend of tuberose, orange blossom, and almond blossom, whereupon artificial lilacs instantly appeared, while

> linden trees swayed in the breeze, shedding their pale efflorescence (mimicked by the London extract of tilia) on to the ground.
>
> (*ibid*, p 97.)

While stimulating and training himself in the interpretation and arrangement of scent, Des Esseintes, closing his eyes,[32] *inserts* into the scene the memory-perceptions of sight, whose physiological verisimilitude he has more fully mastered, learning to re-connect the two senses once they have been established:

> With this setting roughed out in a few bold strokes, and stretching, beneath his closed eyelids, far into the distance, he sprayed his room with a light mist of human, half-feline essences, redolent of skirts, heralding the appearance of powdered and rouged womankind…
>
> [...]
>
> Next he let these waves of fragrance escape through a ventilator, retaining only the country scents which he renewed, increasing the dose to ensure that they would return again like the verses of a ritornello.
>
> Little by little, the women had vanished; the countryside had grown deserted; then, on the magic horizon, factories with enormous chimneys rose up, their tops flaming like bowls of punch.
>
> [...]
>
> He then squirted a few drops of 'New-mown Hay' perfume among the now revived fragrances of lime-trees and meadows, and in the middle of the magic landscape—temporarily divested of its lilacs—haystacks appeared, ushering in a new season, releasing their exquisite emanations into the scented summer air.
>
> (*ibid*, pp 97-98.)

In the passage above, note that des Esseintes has developed his relationship to scent to the degree where he can simultaneously distinguish different scents, without them blending together,[33] and that he is using this

---

[32] Since *scent* here serves as the initial 'perception' around which the elements of the hallucination proliferate, rather than a visual object in the earlier examples, the visual information—presumably honed to a point where a memory can be more-or-less fully articulated as perception and connected with the motor-impulses that would tend to follow it—is better inserted into the perceptual economy *without* any directly perceived object, which would only distract his attention from the image being inserted. The same logic explains Des Esseintes' intense need for almost complete silence (Huysmans 1998, p 16).

[33] In fact, this operation is even more complex, for as he is mixing the various perfumes himself from scratch, several scents combine to create even the 'scents' he is able to separately identify; thus his discrimination is able to combine *certain* scents with each other while keeping others separate.

> We are aware of the hypothesis of material essence. This provisional hypothesis considers matter to be a harmony of electronic systems, and through it we have come to deny the distinction between matter and spirit.
>
> When we feel a piece of iron we say: This is iron; we satisfy ourselves with a word and nothing more. Between iron and hand a conflict of preconscious force-thought-sentiment takes place. Perhaps there is more thought in the fingertips and the iron than in the brain that prides itself on observing the phenomenon.
>
> -Filippo T. Marinetti, *Manifesto of Tactilism* (1924). (Caws 2001, p 200.)

ability to create the illusion in his brain of a *spatial grid* apprehensible through scent. He continues elaborating this scene for another page until his nervous system, or its interpretive mechanism, is no longer able to support it; he suffers a renewed attack of neurosis, and is forced to throw open the window to clear out the scents.

The sets of specific formulae that Huysmans provides in such passages (large portions of which have been cut out of these quotations in my merciless insistence upon a lean, spare, and terse prose-style, specially formulated in order to banish any trace of the logos-displacing quality of 'the poetic', banished as it *must* be (for Plato taught us) outside the polis of authoritative discourse, like Foucault's leper; that is to say, my utter and fastidious regard for the patience of you, my dearest reader, for whom I recognize a responsibility to avoid any disorienting eruptions of rhetorical excess, just where they might seem most superfluous, which might upset the project of persuasion which must of course be the ultimate goal of any text clothed in a certain argot and so thoroughly pock-marked with citation. I have no doubt that you have many times remarked upon my singular talent for clarity, compactness, and plain-speaking, upon my complete avoidance of 'unnecessary' and vaguely disquieting verboseness—) are not limited to single sense-systems; once a capacity for such intricate management of sensory data has been established, Huysmans can coordinate all of these systems and offer 'recipes' for the complete combinations of sensory stimulation constituting certain experiences:

> nor is there any doubt that one can—without stirring from Paris—obtain the beneficial sensations of sea-bathing; you would simply have to go to the Vigier baths which are located on a boat in the middle of the Seine.
>
> There, by salting your bathwater and mixing into it, according to the formula given in the Pharmacopoeia, sodium sulphate, hydrochlorate of magnesium, and lime; by taking from a tightly closed, screw-topped box, a ball of twine or a tiny piece of rope specially purchased in one of those huge ship's chandlers whose enormous warehouses and basements reek of sea-tides and sea-ports; by sniffing those fragrances which still cling to the twine or piece of rope; by perusing a really good photograph of the casino and zealously studying, in the *Guide Joanne*, a description of the beauties of the seaside resort where you would like to be; by letting yourself be rocked in your bath-tub by the waves made by the *bateaux-mouches* as they pass close beside the pontoon; finally, by listening to the moaning of the wind gusting under the arches of the bridge, and the rumbling of the omnibuses as they cross the Pont Royal just a few feet above you, the illusion of being near the sea is undeniable, overpowering, absolute.
>
> (*ibid*, p 19.)

Note how, with the exception of taste (though the provisions given here would provide for it—a bit of salt(ed) water in the mouth, for example), each sense is accounted for and brought carefully into play: first touch and *buoyancy*, then scent, then sight and an ~~awareness~~ of context, then balance, then hearing.

Of course, what Huysmans describes here does not in itself constitute what we are *reservedly* referring to as a hallucinatory practice; but it represents a potential final step before the taking on of such a project. On the one hand, there are no memories being *inserted* into the perceptive order; on the contrary, the senses are being 'actually' stimulated in a way as close as possible to that in which they would be stimulated in a 'real' ocean bath, the experience is entirely dependant upon actual perceptive nervous stimulation. The *source* of these sensations, however, is being recast by the mind: while the rumble of buses overhead is immediately perceived and not remembered, a memory is nonetheless being inserted—not into the perceptual apparatus itself, but into the mechanism or mental process *interpreting* that perception and coordinating it with other (perceived *or* remembered) senses, in order to connect it to the rolling of the sea: while the rocking of the boat is 'real', its interpretation requires a specially engineered 'filtering' of the associations clustering around it—reminding Des Esseintes of the actual context—and the insertion of a different set of associations. While the *perceptions themselves* still remain 'real', the cognitive apparatus that *interpret and coordinate* those perceptions are being trained into different modes of operation. Inserting memories or imagined images—via the heightened and trained sensitivity to and management of sensation—*into* this altered process is then the final step.

This is of course to say in part that the centres interpreting the nervous signals of perception have been trained into hypersensitivity. We have noted that in a practice in which a hallucination is not superimposed *upon* an environment but is entirely evoked without 'real' movement, the 'action' which a memory-image must be completed by in order to be taken for a perception must be *virtual,* 'sketched out'. The nervous system, then, must be trained to reach a point of sensitivity in which a virtual action destined to be experienced as a remembered or imagined muscular movement *within* the hallucination can be experienced as such, without ceasing to be a merely virtual or potential movement within the purely physical economy of the body as it exists in socially-defined space. The question of Decadent neurosis already discussed thus takes on an added dimension, for the body and its motor-impulses have no notion of intellectual intension, a phenomenon of a completely different (parasitic) order; this hypersensitivity can enter the perceptual system only as a *habit* that cannot be 'turned off'; it is clearer then why Maupassant, Huysmans/Des Esseintes, and so many others in their community reported such sensory horror at walking into public streets, at the overwhelming and *painful* overload of information attacking them from every side of a burgeoning Modernity, of such agonizing struggles with their *nerves* (Pierrot 1981, pp 47-55.); when he is overcome by his neurosis, in fact, Des Esseintes' malady attacks him along precisely the same order as the hallucinations he induces, which have in turn prepared the way for it: through the progressive activation of each of his senses:

> His malady resumed its progress, accompanied by entirely new symptoms. The nightmares, the olefactory hallucinations, the visual disturbances, the harsh cough as regular as clockwork, the thudding of his arteries and heart and the cold sweats were succeeded by auditory delusions, those disorders which occur only in the final stages of the disease.
>
> (*ibid*, p 164.)

This not unlike the description of the aftermath of one hallucination 70 pgs earlier.

> Emerging, now, from these reveries, feeling drained, exhausted, half dead, he immediately lit the candles and the lamps, flooding himself with light, in the belief that he would not hear, as clearly as he did in the dark, the muffled, persistent, intolerable sound of his arteries beating faster and faster beneath the skin of his neck.
>
> (*ibid*, p 91.)

So. It is now possible to see how a hallucination such as that described earlier in this discussion, wherein, 'you can embark on long explorations by your own fireside' might be evoked. Every step of the process has been accounted for, the perceptual and cognitive systems at play have been explored and understood, their apparatus trained.

Huysmans has given us the clues scattered throughout the text, and in following the mandates of Decadent reading practices, in reading *Against the Grain*, this technique can be reconfigured, or evoked; so long as the apparatus of the 'essay' form (does this word not feel a bit sordid here? But do the terms 'cognitive apparatus' and 'interpretive mechanism' not feel equally so? And yet, must we not face the *facts*, as if in battle?) is satisfied that its function of defining Truth has been fulfilled, so long as the citations point to what is 'out there' to validate this reading, any bit of hallucinatory information might be inserted. (Bergson 2004, pp 113-114.) Huysmans advises us as to the first step of this conjuration (which is in fact taking place on a number of registers): 'The secret is to know how to go about it, to know how to concentrate the mind on one single detail, to know how to dissociate oneself sufficiently to produce the hallucination and thus substitute the vision of reality for reality itself.' (*ibid*, pp 19-20.) At first this detail might be something immediately tangible—look at our detailed discussion of the astrolabe—something the *evaluating* body is immediately able to accept (Bergson 2004, pp 113-114.); as this concentration deepens, one gropes here and there into possible routes to be taken, trajectories sketched out but rejected, like footnotes (Huysmans 1998, pp 140-141.); as thoughts proliferate around that detail in a confusing fashion, a route is sketched out, the field of detail spreads; the different forms through which information can be introduced come under subtle attack, subtly enough that the structure governing their introduction cannot help but accept them, despite their apparent unlikeliness, which is rapidly growing. After all, the rhetoric of these mechanisms has been duly explored.³⁴ (*ibid,* pp 19, 38-40, 87-98.) The proliferating associations condensing around these details offer up the trajectory that is wanted—it is seized—and soon, though our critical gaze would still seem to be directed at that object, we are no longer seeing it, it is obscured by the startling abstractions that have been evoked (*ibid,* pp 140-141.)—our discussion of Bergson should prove this—we move through them at will.

As we have just seen, once the body (whose only purpose, in the end, is to *judge*) has been regularly bombarded with 'this devious kind of sophistry' as Huysmans terms it, we no longer require this discussion on the astrolabe, it is in the end merely a softening-up (*ibid,* p 19.); you will

> Now, whatever is sensation is essentially *present.* There is no other definition of the present except sensation itself, which includes, perhaps, the impulse to action that would modify that sensation. On the other hand, whatever is properly thought, image, sentiment, is always, in some way, *a production of absent things.* Memory is the substance of all thought....
>
> Thought is, in short, the activity which causes what does not exist to come alive in us, lending to it, whether we will or no, our present powers, making us take the part for the whole, the image for reality, and giving us the illusion of seeing, acting, suffering, and possessing independently of our dear old body, which we leave with its cigarette in an armchair until we suddenly retrieve it when the telephone rings or, no less strangely, when our stomach demands provender...
>
> Between Voice and Thought, between Thought and Voice, between Presence and Absence, oscillates the poetic pendulum.
>
> -Paul Valéry, *Poetry and Abstract Thought* (1939).
> (Valéry 1958, pp 73-74.)

recall the discussion where we concluded that certain exercises intended to train the reactive agents receiving and interpreting this questionable information *must* have been involved as well, since the algorithm of proof we have gathered up would seem to demand it. This in turn allows us to begin anew; having mastered now not only the specific *nature* of these various filters which let the world pass through and catch only what is the Truth, but having mastered as well their logic of deployment and the prerogatives of their interpretation (*ibid,* pp 97-98.), we have in effect established a *poetics of Truth,* which is by its very nature as a poetic destined to dismantle it and turn it to its own purposes, a kind of glorious parasite. We can now insert our fictions almost directly, without any longer having to focus our attention critically on a particular piece of 'the world', to a

---

³⁴ It should be evident that the choice of the word 'rhetoric' is not lightly chosen; after all, Huysmans implicitly situates this entire practice in relation to a rhetorical schema when he refers to it a 'kind of sophistry'. In this connection, it may be worth examining the Symbolist poetics extolled by Huysmans in *A Rebours* and developed most forcefully and acutely by Mallarmé, a possible practitioner; the carefully deployed syntactical ambiguity of much of Mallarmé's writing in particular acts analogously to this operation: while meticulously fulfilling the requirements of a grammar which is the very definition and guarantor of 'coherence', he in fact exploits this very system in order to introduce a radical incoherence allowing a text to be read doubly, creating multiple and sustainable potential routes of readerly perception, all validated by the grammatical apparatus, as it were: a truly hallucinatory text, not in what it depicts or the origin of that depiction but within the very structure of the reading experience itself. Expanding this observation, we can see how, for instance, the technique already suggested of directing the muscular movement of an eye to physically mark out a point within the spatial grid within which a remembered or imagined image might be inserted—creating a space of physiological ambiguity to enable this doubling of perceptive possibilities—is none other than an unspecified *index*, a *'this'* or *'that'* or *'it'* that might refer to any of several possibilities (a favourite technique in the *poems* of Mallarmé, for example). Likewise, an oneirocritical approach might develop a system of physiological *puns*. It should go without saying that this observation might be expanded still further, in order to *take in* the economy of Truth on the social and cultural level. Indeed, it already has.

particular *corpus* (recall the discussion with the astrolabe), and reach the same space we had reached in the previous paragraph—in which we are suspended in the startling abstractions which have been evoked, and move through them at will. And *arrange* them at will. (*ibid*, pp 19, 140-141.) And yet so long as the filters of Truth can continue to be exploited, the body can do nothing but accept them; the mechanistic and bureaucratic nature of its functioning and its conception of 'knowledge' has been turned against it; these fictions can be nothing else but ~~truth~~, for they have insinuated themselves into the very apparatus whose function is to define it. (Bergson 2004, p 179.) And when this intricately woven fantasy, which has become inextricable from the weave of what has been determined to be 'real', is about to come to an end, its *logic* remains; we realise that we have lived doubly; and something has been created that was always there already. (Huysmans 1998, pp 141-142 and Bergson 2004, pp 9-16.) The conversion of a living perception to a living ~~perception~~ is, after all, merely a metonym; it is the same operation through which living thought becomes living ~~thought~~, and through which they co-incide; it is a simultaneous living on disparate registers. It is a reading, and it is a writing. And it may be worth re-reading the last two paragraphs, for it is difficult to determine in them which direction the grain runs.

The final test, as Bergson has taught us, is whether these fictions can *act*, can *work;* they can, and they have, my dear reader, it is possible for me to assure you.

I have personal experience of the fact that automatic writing undertaken with any enthusiasm leads directly to visual hallucinations; one need only to refer to Rimbaud's "*Alchimie du Verbe*" to realise he had done the same. But I have difficulty explaining the "terror" which caused him to give up poetry. One of the coolest and therefore most moving psychological texts I know of is the last sentence of M. Pierre Quercy's recently published excellent two-volume work entitled *Hallucination*. With a thoroughly pessimistic statement of fact, he temporarily puts an end to the interminable disputes between mystics and non-mystics, patients and doctors, and the (fanatical) supporters of "perception without an object" verses those of "images dressed up as perception". He writes: "one can assert the presence and perception of an object when it is present and perceived, when it is absent and perceived, and when it is neither present nor perceived." The level of spontaneity of which individuals are capable, when taken in isolation, is the only thing to determine whether one dish or the other will rise or fall on the weighing-scales… "Dissolution" of the senses, all the senses, has yet to be attained; or rather, the education (in practical terms, the diseducation) of all the senses, which amounts to the same thing, has yet to be achieved.

-André Breton, *The Automatic Message* (1933). (Breton et. al. 1997, pp30-31.)

  I mean that I've read, among the youthful poems of Samuel Taylor Coleridge, a little unfinished poem of a few lines where Samuel Taylor Coleridge takes up an old, unfinished, and in a certain respect *aborted* work of Euripides, and undertakes knowingly and firmly to lash with words as if given over to idolatry, to drive the occult into his scheme, to redeem man from God, to transport the occult into the open, to do what one says, I mean what the whole mind (precisely because it is mind and not body, and precisely because it isn't life and has never been part of the living) has always pretended it didn't have to do, which is precisely to practice occultism in public, to convey the occult world into the open in order to show clearly from what nothingness it is created.

  -Antonin Artaud, *Coleridge the Traitor* (1947).   (Artaud 1965, p 129.)

I turn toward those who are not afraid to conceive of love as the site of ideal occultation of all thought. I say to them: there are real apparitions, but there is a mirror in the mind over which the vast majority of mankind could lean without seeing themselves.

  -André Breton, *Second Manifesto of Surrealism* (1930)   (Breton 1972, p 181.)

'Speaking of confessors, if I were a casuist, it seems to me I would try to invent some new sins. Not that I am, of course—but, by dint of searching, I think I have indeed stumbled across one that is original.'

'You?' she said, laughing in turn. 'Can I commit it?'

He scrutinized her features. She had the expression of a greedy child.

'You alone can answer that; I should admit, though, that the sin is not one which is absolutely new, for it comes under the heading of lust. But it has been neglected since pagan times, and it has never been properly defined in any event.'

She listened to him attentively from her armchair.

'Do not keep me on tenterhooks,' she said. 'Tell me, what is it?'

'It is not easy to explain, though I shall try nevertheless. Lust, I believe, as a generic term, can be classified into the following: common sin; sins against nature; bestiality, and let us include here demonality and sacrilege. Well, there is, in addition to these, what I shall call Pygmalionism, which covers at the same time cerebral onanism and incest.

'Imagine, if you will, an artist who has fallen in love with his own creation—an Hérodiade, a Judith, a Helen, a Jeanne d'Arc—whom he has either described in writing or painted; and as a result of this very act of evocation, let us imagine that this same artist finally sexually possesses his creation in a dream. Well, this is a crime of love which is distinctly worse than ordinary incest. In the latter case, the criminal can only commit half an offense, since his daughter is not the product solely of his flesh but is also the child of another. Thus, logically, there is a quasi-natural aspect to incest, one which almost legitimizes the crime. In Pygmalionism, however, the father violates his own spiritual child, the only one which is totally and truly his, the only one which he could have produced without the aid of the flesh and blood of another person. The crime is, thus, entire and complete in itself. The act is a crime against nature, that is to say against God, since the victim is not, as would be the case even with regard to bestiality, a palpable and living creature, but an unreal being created by the use of a talent which is itself being desecrated, a being almost celestial, for is not the aim of art to produce, whether by genius or by artifice, works which will be immortal?

Let us go further, if you wish. Suppose that an artist paints a saint, of whom he becomes enamoured. This raises fresh complications with regard to crimes against nature and crimes of sacrilege. The consequences are extremely far-reaching!'

'Exquisite even!'

-J.-K. Huysmans, *Là-Bas* (1891),   (Huysmans 2001, pp. 155-156.)

Sometimes his dreams presented the image of his favourite Madonna, and he fancied that he was kneeling before her: as he offered up his vows to her, the eyes of the figure seemed to beam on him with inexpressible sweetness; he pressed his lips to hers, and found them warm: the animated form started from the canvas, embraced him affectionately, and his senses were unable to support delight so exquisite. Such were the scenes on which his thoughts were employed while sleeping: his unsatisfied desires placed before him the most lustful and provoking images, and he rioted in joys till then unknown to him.

-Matthew Lewis, *The Monk* (1796), (Lewis 1998, p. 61.)

They offer the Lord the holocaust of their bodily wholeness, those chaste and elegantly adorned virgins who have chosen Christ for their immortal spouse—O marriage of felicity unspotted, without the grave pains of childbirth, without any go-between, any tiresome wet-nurse.—When Christ leaves their beds, angels, guardian angels, enclose them, for fear that incest introduce its pollution, and armed with naked swords, ward off the impure.—For it is in these beds, it is with the Virgins that Christ comes to sleep, happy sleep that refreshes the faithful Virgin clasped in the arms of the divine Spouse…—Clothed in white linen, clothed in Purple, in their left hand lilies, in their right hand rose…—Flowers in which the Lamb delights, flowers His only food…—The Lamb plays and runs, and he leaps in their midst,—and with them he rests in the midday's fervent heat.—He lies down, at midday, on these Virgins' bosoms,—He makes his nest between the Virgins' breasts,—for, a virgin, born on a virgin,—he loves and seeks above all virginal laps,—and it is sweet for him to rest his head on breasts—so pure that nothing blemishes or stains His fleece.—This is the canticle dedicated to the distinguished college of devout Virgins;—may our devotion make of it a further ornament for the temple of the Lord.

-Godeschalk (11th Century monk), quoted by Remy de Gourmont in *Le Latin mystique* (1892), reprinted in Atlas Press' edition of *The Book of Masks*, p. 22.

On his way home, Max [Jacob] would make a detour by the all-night pharmacy near the Saint Lazare station. He would buy a bottle of ether. Locked in his room, he could sniff at his leisure, while conversing with God and with the Virgin Mary. They were on familiar terms. He told them about his day, as if he were chatting with chums.

-Dan Franck, *Bohemian Paris* (2001). (Franck 2001, p 40.)

One day, then, I took her, half-playfully, to the Louvre, telling her, "My dear Alicia, I'm going to give you a little surprise." We passed through the corridors, and I put her without further preparation in the presence of the eternal statue.

This time Miss Alicia raised her veil. She looked at the statue with a certain surprise; then, amazed, she cried aloud childishly:

—Look, it's ME!

The next moment, she added:

—Yes, but I have arms, and besides I'm more distinguished looking.

She shivered; her hand, which had dropped to my arm to seek support from a railing, returned, and she said to me in an undertone:

—These stones… these walls… It's cold in here; let's go away.

-Villiers de l'Isle-Adam, *The Future Eve* (1886)　　　　　　　　　　(Hustvedt 1998, pp 568-569.)

-Max Ernst, from *Une Semaine de Bonté* (1934).　　　　　　　　　(Ernst 1976, p 151.)

The social model of an enclosed 'elitist' micro-society that characterized Decadence and Symbolism did not take its inspiration solely from the Aristocracy; it was also inspired largely by a wide recognition among dissenting creative communities that their project could be seen as a continuation of various secret societies and heresies on the one hand, and of monastic orders on the other, for whom the Church might be seen to have occupied a cultural role analogous in many ways with the ascending bourgeois order.[35] The widespread association made by members of the Decadent community (and initiates of the Yellow Sign in general) between their activities, lifestyles, and thought and the various traditions of hermeticism, occultism, and mysticism have been referred to elsewhere;[36] however, their relationships not only with Dandyist and Aesthetic practices in general, but specifically with the hallucinatory practices that may have been associated with that heritage, remain to be investigated. Once again, Huysmans presents himself as a particularly apt example.

The traditions of monasticism and mysticism are heavily at play throughout *A Rebours* and are constantly evoked; Des Esseintes' home at Fontenay is likened to a cloister, and in fact he has his bedroom done up like one; though, of course, it is a cloister read through a Decadent sensibility, articulated in such a way as to subvert its own form:

> the bedroom must be contrived so as to resemble a monastic cell; but this gave rise to endless difficulties, since he refused to accept, for his own use, the ugly austerity characteristic of places of penitence and prayer.
>
> By dint of considering and reconsidering every aspect of the problem, he concluded that the effect for which he was striving could be summed up in the following way: to furnish a depressing space with joyous objects, or rather, without sacrificing the ugly character of the room, imprint upon it, by this treatment, a kind of overall elegance and distinction… in a word, to fit out a monastic cell which appeared to be genuine without, of course, actually being so.

---

[35] Of course these represent a number of distinct traditions, but the various secret societies and heresies were inevitably affected by the less deviant practices and structural models, due to the monastic backgrounds of most participants if nothing else; in this discussion the focus will be on Mystic practices that while outside the main stream of the Church were not necessarily heretical. This entire issue, in relation to the formation of dissenting communities attempting to articulate a position in relation to an emerging social order, warrants further attention which cannot be given here, anxious as I am, as I am ever anxious to remind you, mindful of your patience and its limits. For the influence of ideas farther from Catholic orthodoxy, see the following footnote.

[36] Pierrot's *The Decadent Imagination* devotes a chapter to reiterating the pervasiveness of occult ideas in Decadent circles, while Deak's *Symbolist Theater: Formation of an Avant-Garde* presents throughout a cogent and thorough analysis of the various ways that these different steams of thought were internalized, developed, conceptualized, discussed, and articulated in practice within these communities. Ben Fisher's *The Pataphysician's Library* also examines in detail the engagements with esoteric systems of a number of individuals, especially Péladan, Bloy, Mendès, and Jarry. Stewart Home emphasis the line of continuity between these traditions in *The Assault on Culture* but does not examine the connections in detail.

> He set about it in this way: to imitate that dark yellow paint favoured by administrators and clerics, he had his walls hung with saffron silk; to imitate the chocolate brown wainscoting customary in that kind of room, he covered those lower areas with thin strips of dark purple kingswood... [etc.]
>
> [...]
>
> And, on the whole, the illusion was easy to maintain, since he led a life almost analogous to that of a monk...
>
> Like a hermit, he was ripe for seclusion, worn out by life and expecting nothing more of it; and also like a monk, he was overcome by a tremendous lassitude, by a need for contemplation, by a longing no longer to have anything in common with the heathen—which was what he called Utilitarians and fools.
>
> In short, though he experienced no vocation for the state of grace, he felt a sympathy for those who are confined to monasteries and persecuted by a vindictive society...
>
> (Huysmans 1998, pp 55-56.)

Nor is the need for solitude Des Esseintes' only connection with monasticism; in fact this connection goes back to his childhood, and might be read as key to the approach that he might take to any hallucinatory practice.

Des Esseintes was in fact raised in such an environment; scarcely even acquainted with his parents, he grew up in a college run by monks of the Jesuit order, whose founder, St. Ignatius Loyola, developed a technique for producing hallucinations that corresponds quite closely with that described by Huysmans in the book; in fact, a number of practitioners of this hypothetical practice were avid readers of Loyola, especially Jarry and Huysmans himself. (Jarry 2001, p 285.)

In this respect Loyola's schema is related to Mystic notions of prayer, which often involve hallucination. Mysticism provides a hierarchy of various forms of prayer: vocal prayer, mental prayer, mystic prayer, ecstatic prayer—a progression through which one passes, without necessarily abandoning earlier stages. (Lash 1947, 9-15.) Even in 'mental prayer', which is accessible to the non-mystic, 'a picturing of the scene of the incident to be meditated upon is advised (if the subject allows of this) called *composition of place*.' (*ibid*, p 30.) Loyola provides a practical scheme of developing this notion into a practice we can recognise as quite close to that we are examining.

In his *Spiritual Exercises*, which form the programme for a four-week meditational retreat, a series of biblical situations are to become the focus of concentrated mental activity, with techniques introduced to ensure that this activity is articulated through both psychological and cognitive registers; these exercises might be seen as an attempt to *live* the scenes 'remembered' from the text, without sacrificing their textual, in this case allegorical status. (Loyola 1999, p 229, 246.) One first reads the text which is the focus of this activity, and focuses one's attention in turn upon its narrative and textual context (Huysmans: 'stimulating, if need be, a reluctant or lethargic mind by reading a suggestive account'—*A rebours*, p 19.); picturing or 'composing the place' which is the narrative, psychological, and cognitive space within which, or in relation to which, the work of thought is to be done (Huysmans: 'by perusing a really good photograph of the casino and zealously studying, in the *Guide Joanne*, a description of the beauties of the seaside resort where you would like to be'—*ibid*); addressing that which lies 'outside' the subject ('god'). One next concentrates on the nature and roles of the images to be figured—their bodies, their histories, and their symbolic resonance. One then moves on to concentrate in a similar way exclusively on the speech that will transpire; and finally to internalize the gestures that will transpire. (Loyola 1999, pp 246-249.) We can see in this elaborate preparation for the hallucination (for lack of a *better* term) a strategy similar to De Quincey 'preparing his canvas against the dark', but in this case there is a much greater emphasis on manipulating the ways in which the perceptual hallucinations will intersect with cognitive processes and with the psychological structure of the subject producing them:

> By the imagination, the soul can render an object present, and as it were see it, hear it, taste it, etc…The application of the senses differs from meditation in this: that in the one the intelligence proceeds by reasoning… while in the other, it is confined solely to sensible objects… It is not that the application of the senses, in order to be useful, does not require some reasoning and reflections, but that they should be short, simple, and rapid.
>
> (Loyola 1999, pp 249-250.)

This rapidity mentioned last is of course acquired through the habituation of interpretation achieved through the preliminary steps.

The induction of hallucination itself is quite evidently a model for the process Huysmans recommends—a bringing into play, one by one, of each of the senses: first sight, then hearing, then taste, then scent, then feeling, both touch and inner sensation. Each of these, in its articulation, involves the development of its intellectual relationships within the same movement as the development of its sensory representation: 'Taste interiorly the sweetness, or bitterness, or any other sentiment, of the person you are considering,' and 'Respire, as it were, the perfume of the virtues, or the infection of the vices, the sulphur of hell, the corruption of dead bodies, etc.' (Loyola 1999, p 250.) In this way, the body is being re-mapped as an instrument for rhetorical organization, the senses *themselves,* and not merely their representation within written texts, are being fully *experienced* as tropes; the body as such is quite literally being placed within the intellectual realm, the full cognitive and interpretive experience of reading is becoming *embodied.*

The process Loyola proscribes can therefore be seen as an almost circular—via Jarry's gidouille we might conceptualise it as spiraling—movement from reading to reading, but to a radically expanded and internalized notion (or reading) *of* reading;[37] which is in turn a reading quite in keeping with the practices of initiates of the Yellow Sign. And many of the practitioners of hallucinatory practice within that tradition, especially from the mid-18th to late 19th Centuries—Walpole, Coleridge, Des Quincey, Huysmans—similarly describe following this model of a movement from reading of the book to reading the perception itself. But while Loyola begins with a specific reading and strives, in the course of its expansion from a *reading-of-a-book* to a *reading-through-the-body*, to remain within the compass of that particular initial reading—thus constraining such a hallucinatory practice to a more restricted conception of reading—the way in which initiates have read this practice is such that while such a specific reading might indeed serve to initiate the hallucination, as that reading expands to a *reading-through-perception* the original reading is abandoned, and replaced by a writing through the reading, a reading what might be. This passage through the hallucinatory experience is explicitly encoded when we read the writings-through-reading of Coleridge or Walpole, and in a modified form—where the connections between the reading, the writing it engenders, and the subsequent reading of that writing become more indirect—the automatic writings of the Surrealists, writing the un-read texts of themselves; Breton and Aragon, after all, both explicitly linked their writing to sensory hallucination—not necessarily to a description of it, or vice-versa—and moreover appropriated Rimbaud as another instance of this connection. In all of these cases, perception is being used not to mandate Truth, but to read *through* the body a text of the mind.

In *The Craft of Thought*, Mary Carruthers examines the ways in which this textualization of the body and of perception was in fact an operating principle of Medieval monastic life and an organizing logic of thought itself as well as communication: perception (both socially-shared and 'hallucinatory') as mnemonic and cognitive device. Loyola's strategies are not an isolated, idiosyncratic gesture but reflect the practices and modes of thinking characterizing a long-standing and highly developed community. The revelatory 'visions' of Saints and monks were conceived, reported, and *experienced* through this matrix of intertextuality that *integrally* involved written texts, visual texts, and *lived* texts in a way which refused any stupidly rigid distinctions between these registers. (Carruthers 2000, 171-172 & *passim*.) The fact that the *experience* of these visions was often either directly or indirectly *written* was irrelevant to their existence or 'truth' which is after all, as on the registers of rhetoric, history, and perception itself a matter of use-value, either positively or negatively construed.[38] The

---

[37] It would be worth speculating how the development of the role of the Flaneur—from Poe to Baudelaire and eventually, through quite modified forms, to elements of Lettrist and Situationist psychogeography—might be looked at as a similar expansion and activation of the notion of productive reading to address the social body.

[38] 'Monastic seeings, deriving from the orthopraxis of prayerful meditation, occupy an ambiguous ontological ground, at least according to our modern notions of the relative truth status of "real" and "fictional" images. In many of them, their ethical and meditational usefulness is foregrounded to the question of their authority as "objective" truth. Even the having of visions, as the compositional circumstances of the *Vision of Wetti* show, was regarded as a practical cognitive act in

preparatory reading of a book or written text, then, does not merely 'remind' one more forcibly of the scene to be depicted or even create a 'suitable frame of mind' in which to create and/or interpret it; it is in fact an initiation *into* the hallucination itself, establishing the cognitive context within which it is to be read/written/remembered/imagined/lived. The book acts not (only, or necessarily) as a conveyor of 'scenes' or 'ideas', but as a palimpsest of the textual experience toward which one is moving, as a certain *form* of textual experience that leads into *other* forms.[39] It is, moreover, never entirely absent from those other forms or textual modes, any more than they are absent from it. In the Abbot Heito's 9th Century account of the *Vision of Wetti* of Reichenau, Wetti's attempt to evoke a vision is aided by his fellow monks chanting psalms, and then, in order to focus his efforts, he requests they read him a specific passage—one from Gregory the Great's *Dialogues,* also dealing with the perception of ~~absent~~ figures; 'Heito [an *eye*-witness] makes very clear the literary basis of Wetti's visions: the psalms, the prayers, the teachings and stories of Gregory. They do not come from some unanticipated divine seizure, but are built in a consciously remembered, highly "literary" manner, from the matter he has just been reading.'[40] (*ibid,* pp 181-182.) And even once the vision is underway, the *inscribed* text continues to play a role in an experience of a much more *broadly* textual nature, as the angel guiding him through this carefully prepared hallucination instructs him *within* the 'vision' to repeat to himself the words of Psalm 118.

These hallucinations are not only experienced and discussed without reference to mutually exclusive categories of 'actual' or 'imagined', 'present' or 'absent' (*ibid,* pp 185-189.); they can also be shared, can take on a *social existence* that fulfils on the social level Bergson's requirement for perception to be experienced as 'actual'—that is, of course, they can *act*. In the *Life of St. Benedict,* written by Gregory, whose writings served to initiate Wetti above into his hallucination, is the story of a monk unable to concentrate on his prayers; during the time set aside for group silent prayer, he physically leaves the congregation to wander both in mind and body. After an unsuccessful attempt to help him, Benedict looks up and 'saw that a kind of little black boy was drawing this monk… outside by the hem of his garment.' Nobody else sees this figure, but after two days of further prayer, his companion Maurus sees the hallucination as well. Nor does this social dimension mean that the hallucinatory nature of the boy is not recognised; for in order to cure the trouble, Benedict strikes with his stick (as one would a child) not the hallucinated boy, but the monk himself—and the boy disappears. (*ibid,* p

---

Carolingian rhetoric, an effective device for the machinery of thinking, and closely related to the cognitive act of making pictures as "ways" for composing meditation.' (Carruthers 2000, p 184.)

[39] It is worth remembering this point in our eventual discussion of Lautréamont.

[40] Compare this strategy to Des Esseintes' own invocation of the text describing De Quincey's hallucination in the process of articulating his own.

188.) The figure was recognised simultaneously as a social agent, as a projected hallucination of Benedict (and later Maurus), as a literalization of the monk's psychological economy—and as a literary reference:

> Again, no one can see the figure but Benedict, at least at first. Both Maurus and then Pompeianus must pray, that is engage in meditative memory work (as Benedict needed to do), in order to "see" the phenomenon that is physically drawing the monk out of the oratory…Indeed, the "little black boy" has been invented from Benedict's memory store. In the *Life of St. Anthony*, Gregory's literary model and an essential monastic text, the devil in the guise of a little black boy, "his appearance matching his mind," tempts Anthony, while he is at prayer, to engage in fornication.
>
> (*ibid*, p 189.)

It is this aspect of hallucination as literary reference articulated via the perceptual system that allows it to take on its social nature; for the intellectual life of monastic communities was developed and maintained within closed communities, whose training and meditation was mediated through a relatively limited stock of canonical texts, stories, and rhetorical devices. Monastic texts, architecture, and visual art were all integrated to create a complex and, because closed, relatively stable system of rhetorical and figurations and tropes *through which* to think, communicate and act. (*ibid, passim.*) While the three monks might not have perceptually 'seen' the *same* boy in terms of the precise detail constituting his reality *for* each of them, their shared cognitive training, and common stock of literary images with their rhetorical functions, allowed this hallucination to occupy a social space in which their different understandings experiences of the figure, without being equivalent to each other, nonetheless provided a means of common action and social interaction. And, it is no doubt unnecessary to point out, this is precisely one definition of a *text*.

Carruthers notes that in the story of the wayward monk that I have evoked above, 'a continuity between the physical postures (being bent over in prayer or standing and walking outside) and what we now think of as separate, the mental "state," is apparent here. The one flows seamlessly into the other, in a dialogue of corporealities of brain and muscles.' (*ibid*, p 189.) The connection with Bergson's notion of muscular movement validating images inserted into the perceptual system is clear, as are, consequently, the potential strategies of oneirocritism and projection proposed earlier.[41] In order to extend the cognitive processes and psychological focus entered into through these practices, this relationship between thought and the body is sometimes developed even farther than Huysmans suggests; Loyola suggests the recital of texts keyed to the

---

[41] The apparent correlations with the physicality of thought in Huysmans' schema also extend to some extent to the associations with illness. The vision of Wetti already described is signaled when he begins to vomit after taking a medicinal potion that does not affect anyone else in the community. (Carruthers 2000, p 180.) Huysmans himself explores this connection at length in his 1901 narrative of *St. Lydwine of Schiedam*. (Gourmont 1994, pp149-156.)

> Without unleashing a storm of delirium one can work systematically to deprive the distinction between subjective and objective of both necessity and value. Myers wrote that, "There exists a form of (very strange) inner hearing... There are complex, powerful groups of concepts which are formed outside (some will say beyond) articulate language, and reasoned thought. There is a path, upwards through ideal space, which some see as the only genuine ascent; an architecture which some see as the only place of rest...
>
> For the simple fact of having seen her wooden cross change into a jewel-studded crucifix, and having held this vision to be at once *imaginative and sensory*, Theresa de Avila can be seen to command this line on which both mediums and poets sit. Unfortunately, for the time being she is merely a saint.
>
> -André Breton, *The Automatic Message* (1933). (Breton et. al. 1997, p 32.)

rhythmic inhalation and exhalation of the lungs (*ibid*, pp 31-32.) while some methods of Eastern Orthodox Mysticism key the repetition of a phrase to the beating of the heart, so that eventually the phrase sinks into nearly-pure physicality to become an automatic chant operating, at least in theory, unconsciously, keyed to the body's natural processes. (*ibid*, p 33.)[42]

This method leads toward the state of 'mystic prayer' where the cognitive state developed through such practices becomes habitual and nearly constant. 'With this prayer comes the accompaniment of almost unconscious recollection of God's presence throughout the day, a recollection which is noticed chiefly when something happens momentarily to disturb it.'[43] (*ibid*, p 35.)

This in turn leads to *Ecstasy*, the final stage of Mysticism, which is in effect the kind of entirely 'interior' hallucinatory state that Huysmans has described as possible while sitting at one's own fireside, with the important exception that the hallucination is conceptualized as being received, rather than created as in the Modern examples we have been primarily considering.

> Ecstasy is due to a degree of abstraction from normal life even more profound than the abstraction we have already considered. In Ecstasy it affects the physical senses. The attention is so withdrawn from the sensory world that the mind no longer has control over the body. To the onlooker it appears insensible.
>
> (*ibid*, p 41.)

This is of course also consistent with Bergson's assertion that *action*, when it is not, or to the *degree* that is not in accordance with memory, will tend to interrupt it. (Bergson 2004, pp 201-202 & *passim*.) Occasionally the

---

[42] This practice could be fruitfully thought of in relation to the Kristevan thetic.

[43] If we remember the extent to which sensory images are bound up in this tradition with prayer and recollection, we can detect parallels, even without the visual hallucinations which are after all metonymic with the cognitive state that characterizes them, with projective and oneirocritical practices.

mystic *will* move, and as Bergson would tend to suggest, will map his or her moves to the grid of the hallucinatory space being inhabited. (Lash 1947, pp 42-43.)[44]

Mysticism also sometimes posits a kind hierarchy of hallucination that clarifies the relationship of this hallucinatory practice to the cognitive and subjective modes which it represents; this hierarchy presents fully sensory hallucination as a stage to be passed through, beyond which the experience is largely stripped of its perceptual nature and is concentrated on the thought itself that underlies it; though these stages are not necessarily mutually exclusive.[45] The first is 'corporeal', in which the terms of hallucination are entirely perceptual, and is the initial goal of Loyola's training of the senses *and* of the (possible) practice of Des Esseintes that has been most closely speculated upon; in 'imaginative' hallucinations, the sensory perceptions remain at play, but there are other factors recognizable as belonging emphatically *to* the hallucination, yet not corresponding to the senses; we might conceptualise this as the *textuality itself* of the hallucination announcing its presence in the subjective order. The final stage is 'intellectual vision', in which the perception—'actual' or exploited—is no longer in play, yet where the ~~presence~~ of the hallucination's *focus*—and the use of this term is of course here even more tenuous than usual—is still announced as a *disturbance* in the subjective order—as an object without a body. I have of course shifted the terms of this development, but it should be noted that we are not dealing with a simple *diffusion* of thought or structuration as a result of the abandonment of the sensory image around which it has heretofore organized itself; though such a movement might be at play, a *spectre of localization* remains, a residual sense of the image as something resisting subjective apprehension, and thus definitively 'outside': 'nothing is seen either corporeally or with the imagination, but the percipient knows that the object or objects of his vision are present, and can even suggest the direction of it or them in relation to the percipient.' (Lash 1947, p 44.) In still other words, the hallucination itself, defined as an imposture upon and/or through the senses, is no longer at play; rather than seeing 'what is not there,' the mystic has passed into *not* seeing 'what is not there'. But this is not a return to normalcy; for the sense persists of 'not seeing what *is* there, but once was not there, when I saw it'. Which is also not seeing what is not there, and was *never* there, but now is *here,* a part of him or her, that within him which must always already be outside of him, which he once saw,

---

[44] It should be understood that the application of these various interpretive frameworks do not represent an attempt either to mystify science nor to scientize mysticism, much less to suggest an equivalence between them. Both are equally to be opposed and ab-used.

[45] In cases where a good deal of what *might possibly* be very solid and detailed information regarding hallucinatory practice can be gathered up, it is possible to employ an analogous framework, though it should be remembered that these categorizations are not exclusive and might, in a continuing practice, be mutually supportive. In this book for instance, Huysmans' practice (especially in *A rebours*) is depicted as largely 'corporeal', Jarry's accounts suggest a state near the 'imaginative', while Anna Blume seems to occupy a cognitive ~~space~~ similar to that of the 'ecstatic' object. There are of course others who might be as closely examined but whom I have not looked at closely here for various reasons, foremost among them being to avoid foreclosing the issue by providing what might somehow be twisted into a closed set of 'authoritative' readings. In addition to others, whom I will *not* even name here for the same reason, I might suggest Blake, Darger, Breton, Ernst, etc…

and does not exist. She has (re)internalized the negativity that is the condition of her own subjectivity, as for her own impossibility; he has (re)internalized by expelling it, out there, as an other, and no longer (necessarily) *needs* to perceive it, always in front of him, in order to understand the impossibility of its existence. (to ~~productively~~ complicate this passage, see Kristeva 1984 pp117-127 & 202-214; and Derrida 1991, p 209.)

Of course I digress.[46] We have, after all, been discussing theology (of all things!) for some time, haven't we? It nearly had us transfixed, as is its way—I mentioned, after all, that the Mystic conception of hallucination, unlike that of Des Esseintes,[47] was external, *possessive*, and often beyond the control of the subject. Well, now you have the proof; but as you can see above, I found a way to escape it; though the path I took is itself dangerously apt to become a kind of possession as well, if one lacks rigour or charm. And now that I am free, you can see that I have become a bit manic, and am ever so glad to see you, again, my dearest reader; and now I am nearly speaking nonsense, delighting in the sheer joy of that freedom, abandoning my habitual argot for a few short moments, and though I may *seem* to have temporarily abandoned the requisite rigour, nonetheless at least, for the moment, I consider myself very charming.[48]

Oh dear—before that long discussion, I believe that I had made several rhetorical gestures seeming to indicate an intention to extend my interminable soliloquy—is that really the right word? I ask you—concerning Huysmans. Never fear: at least this time I shall bring another book into play. And Bergson shall watch quietly, behave himself, and speak only after politely raising his hand.

I had merely wanted to say, before I was caught unawares, that it would be worth our while to take note that the religious practices which I have—at such woefully great length—described are vital to an understanding of what may have been Huysmans' hallucinatory practice; and the religious influence can be assumed to grow as he moves closer to (and passes) his conversion, and his own time spent in monastery. This is especially true when we consider that his next novel, *Là-Bas*, is an exploration of religion; though, in a way typical of Huysmans, it is explored in a way decidedly against the grain: a fictionalized study of Parisian Satanist circles, intercut with the story of the medieval Satanist child-murderer, Gilles de Rais. And while the hallucinatory practices that permeate the text of *A Rebours* play a relatively small role in the latter novel, one can speculate upon a decided development of those practices under these deepening religious influences.

---

[46] It is a part of my function.

[47] We can begin to understand now how it possessed Huysmans as well, turning him, ever so slowly, into a Catholic.

[48] Huysmans, perhaps, forgot to be charming. Some others ensured that they would not.

For example: in discussing *A rebours*, the ambiguity inherent in Bergson's schema between 'memory', 'thought', and 'imagination' has been only occasionally problematic, for most of the hallucinations evoked by Des Esseintes are memories, or are in themselves relatively banal adventures easily reconstructed from fairly congruous *elements* of memories; what gives them their remarkable quality is not the adventure itself (a walk through Paris, a field in the country, an English pub), but the cognitive and psychological systems through which they are staged, and which are coordinated by them. The uses to which Loyola, for instance, puts these strategies, are situated more definitively and explicitly in the otherwise impossible, in the 'imaginary'.

One recurring theme of *Là-Bas* is incubism. We shall immediately take note that the succubus is a creature occupying an ambiguous ontological ground, present yet not existent, or vice versa:

> If the woman is not the victim of a spell, if she voluntarily consorts with the impure spirit, then she is always awake during the carnal act. If, on the other hand, she is the victim of sorcery, the sin may be committed either during sleep or while she is awake, but in the latter case she is in a cataleptic state which prevents her from defending herself.
>
> -J.-K. Huysmans, *La-Bâs* (1891).
> (Huysmans 2001, p 123.)

> In addition to the motif, found in both Ezekiel and John's Apocalypse, of the visionary "eating the book" as a prelude to a vision of heaven, Ezekiel also fell ill with a stroke-like paralysis when he experienced his visions; Daniel fainted... While Wetti is resting on his bed *not asleep but with his eyes closed*, he sees the devil in the guise of a monk, who puts him in great fear—he is then comforted by an angel... Wetti "wakes up" ("expergefactus") from his vision (though—notice—he was earlier described particularly as *not asleep*) and then dictates this vision to two monks whom he summons to his bed.
>
> -Mary Carruthers, *The Craft of Thought*.
> (Carruthers 2000, pp 180-181.)

'Del Rio and Bodin, for instance, believe that incubi are male demons who enter into sexual congress with women and that succubi are female demons who consummate the act with men.

'According to these theories, incubi steal and make use of the semen discharged by men during their dreams...'

'For Sinistrari d'Ameno,' observed Durtal, 'incubi and succubi were not precisely demons, but animal spirits, intermediaries between demons and angels, some sort of satyr or faun of the kind revered in pagan times, or imps of the type exorcised in the Middle Ages.

(Huysmans 2001, p 121.)

Gévingey, the expert on the occult, goes on:

'However that may be, Messieurs, to instruct you completely in this matter, I must divide those assailed with incubacy or succubacy into two classes.

'The first is composed of people who have directly and voluntarily surrendered themselves to demonic spirits. Such people are quite rare; and they all either commit suicide or meet with some other form of violent death.

'The second is composed of people who have been visited by demonic spirits as the result of spells that have been cast on them....'

(*ibid*, pp 122-123.)

In the same conversation just quoted from is another theme pervading the novel, the evocation of the dead. This notion is by no means entirely distinct from that of incubism:

> 'At present, it is far more usual to employ, not demons, but bodies raised from the dead in the timeless role of incubus or succubus. In other words, the term "possession", which refers to a living being who is the victim of succubacy, has become redundant. This evocation of the dead, which combines demonism with the charnel horrors of vampirism, is far worse; strictly speaking, cases of simple possession no longer exist.'
>
> (*ibid*, p 122.)

Now, the 'protagonist' of *Là-Bas* (if such a term can be applied), Durtal, an 'interested skeptic,' is keenly interested in these practices and has steered the conversation in this direction; and in expressing his horror of necromancy, and of the extent with which it was rumoured to be practiced in spiritualist circles, he makes what might seem to be a rather odd comment:

> As for evoking the dead, the mere thought that the butcher on the corner could force the soul of Hugo, Balzac, or Baudelaire to converse with him is enough to drive me demented, were I to give it the slightest credence. No! However abject materialism is as a philosophy, it is not as vile as that!
>
> (*ibid*, p 118.)

Why does this rather odd example of the potential uses of necromancy come to Durtal's mind? And why is he so keenly interested in the various forms of occult *evocation*?

His interest proves prophetic. Durtal, a writer, has been engaged in a frustrating and as yet unconsummated affair with the admiring wife of an acquaintance; as the affair progresses he gradually discovers the extent of Madame Chantelouve's connections with Satanism and occult practices—especially evocation. Finally his attempts to consummate the affair come to a head, and he learns the learns the reason for her hesitation: she has *evoked* him already, and has often evoked the dead for, presumably, sexual purposes:

> 'But what I want is to posses you when and how I please, just as for years I have possessed Byron, Baudelaire, Gérard de Nerval, all those whom I love.'
>
> 'What do you mean?'

'I mean that I have only to desire them, as I have only to desire you, before I go to sleep and…'

'And?'

'The reality of you could not live up to the chimera I have invented for myself, the Durtal I adore, whose caresses make me delirious with pleasure every night.'

He looked at her in stupefaction. She had a troubled, fearful look in her eyes; she seemed no longer to even see him, but appeared to be staring into space. He hesitated for a moment. Suddenly, the scenes of incubacy of which Gévingey had spoken flashed before his eyes.

(*ibid*, pp 134-135.)

While articulated through a different discourse, and greatly modified by the terms and traditions of it, what is suggested is a practice contiguous with that speculated upon in relation to *A rebours;* indeed, as in the former book, this hallucinatory practice is at least in part grounded in a contempt for 'actual' life; the 'Natural' Durtal must inevitably be inferior to the sublimated Durtal which can be (re)created.

While she has developed this practice through occult discourse and practice, what she describes is not pure incubism, nor the necromantic incubism described by Gévingey. Chantelouve, who has, she mentions, engaged in this practice for years, shows none of the anguish ascribed to those who intentionally evoke incubi; moreover, Gévingey adds that, 'if the woman is not the victim of a spell, if she voluntarily consorts with the impure spirit, then she is always awake during the carnal act.' (*ibid*, p 123.) Chantelouve asserts that while prepared in wakefulness (as is the case with De Quincey and Loyola), the hallucination itself occurs in her sleep. And though these quasi-incubi do indeed sometimes take the form of those who are now dead, they are not the called-up corpses of Baudelaire, Nerval, or Byron inhabited by demonic spirits, as Gévingey would suggest; they seem, rather, to be projected images. Moreover, Durtal himself is apparently evoked in the same way; there would appear to be no flesh involved in the practice Chantelouve describes. She is creating, in her own words, *chimeras*.[49]

Moreover, the character of Chantelouve is largely a hybrid of two people engaged in similar practices; one was Henriette Maillat, the former mistress of the Sâr Péladan, founder of the *Rose + Croix* Group; her initiation into the latter's kaloprosopic practice as 'Princess d'Este' is described in his *Le Vice supreme* (published in the same year as *Against Nature*), and she was therefore already engaged in projects of willful self-

---

[49] It is worth noting as well that two of the figures she mentions are connected to what we might call this hallucinatory tradition; Baudelaire introduced De Quincey to the Francophone world and authored *Artificial Paradises*, while Nerval was eventually deprived of his volition by his hallucinations.

transformation approached through an occult framework.[50] (Huysmans 2001, p xx.) The other was Berthe de Courrière.

Berthe de Courrière had actively promoted an image of herself as a devout practitioner of black magic and as a flamboyant nymphomaniac, two proclivities not at all separate in her practice. (*ibid*, pp xiii-xiv.) She attended confession regularly in order to force confessing priests to listen to the most outrageous blasphemies she could conceive; she managed to keep a large carpet bag constantly stocked with consecrated communion hosts, and wandered about Paris feeding them to stray dogs. After escaping from a Black Mass gone too far in Belgium, she was found hiding nearly naked in some shrubbery, and authorities interred her in an asylum for the insane until she was finally released through the intervention of Remy de Gourmont.

Carlos Schwabe, *Poster for the 1st Rose + Croix Salon* (1892). (Gibson 1999, p 53.)

Gourmont, one of the leading theorists, publishers, and writers of Decadence and Symbolism, was Courrière's lover and one of Huysmans' closest friends during the writing of *La-Bàs*. Gourmont would later befriend Alfred Jarry as well; and seven years later, would fall out with him over a letter from Courrière published in Jarry's *Visits of Love*, resulting in Jarry's exclusion from his Symbolist anthology *The Book of Masks*. The contents of this letter not only suggest that the hallucinatory practice described by Chantelouve in *La-Bàs* is based in actual practices engaged in by Courrière, but also indicate a direct line of personal transmission of this (possible) hallucinatory tradition from one generation to the next.

This letter, in which Courrière invites Jarry (in the awkwardly flowery language typical of Aesthetic-Occult writing, such as Péladan's) to join her in creating another world in dreams in which the two would rule together as sovereigns, is remarkably explicit: 'I possess the golden keys that open the ivory portals of the realm of dreams... I will cause every image that exists to pass before your eyes... ideas will hasten to your brain, forms will take on life and furnish us a cortege such as no dictator ever

---

[50] Kaloprosopia was Péladan's highly idiosynchratic, heavily ritualized, liturgical, and (mysogenistically) sexualized process for self-transformation, a heteroclite combination of Decadent Aesthetic, Alchemical, Catholic, Dandyist, Occult, Psychological, and Eastern and Western Mystic traditions. I have not addressed this practice more in this book because it has proved impossible to locate a complete work by Péladan in English translation. Several chapters of *Le Vice suprême*, including the initiation ceremony based on that of Maillat, do however appear in Asti Hustvedt's *The Decadent Reader*. Deak also discusses kaloprosopia at some length in *Symbolist Theatre: Formation of an Avant-Garde*.

had… we shall reign with an uncontested power over a people created by ourselves… Pygmalion will no more animate a futile shade…' (Jarry 1993, pp 33-35.) Taken together with Huysmans' description of Madame Chantelouve, it seems reasonable to assume that Courrière was engaged, at least to a certain degree of technical sophistication, with such hallucinatory practices at the time of the writing of *La-Bâs*, and that it was a matter of discussion between them[51] as she introduced Huysmans to Satanist circles in preparation for his writing of the book. (Huysmans 2001, p xv.) Whatever his reservations may or may not have been about the occult rhetoric through which this practice was, if this letter is any indication, deeply couched (Jarry would later be deeply contemptuous), the more thoroughly *inventive* uses to which Courrière put this practice—including the evocation of specific people, whether 'historical' (Natural) or 'fictional' (Artificial)—as opposed to the primarily *recollective* practice presented in *Against Nature*, could not have failed to have been of interest to him.

> Pataphysics will… explain the universe supplementary to this one; or, less ambitiously, will describe a universe which can be—and perhaps should be—envisaged in the place of the traditional one'
>
> -Alfred Jarry, *Dr. Faustroll, Pataphysician* (1911).
> (Jarry 1996, pp 21-22.)

There is in fact some precedent for such a practice presented in *A rebours*, and Courrière's personifying mode of evocation may have spoken to a trajectory that Huysmans was already following; certainly there are passages of *Against Nature* that can be read as preparation or training for such a practice, though nothing in that book suggests a level of development comparable to that claimed by Chantelouve in *La-Bâs*.

One such passage is remembered by Des Esseintes from the early stages of his practice, before his move to Fontenay. In it, Huysmans describes a former mistress, a ventriloquist from a café. With her he sets out to recreate in his room the dialogue between the Sphinx and the Chimera from Flaubert's *Temptation of St. Anthony*:

> One evening he had a little sphinx of black marble brought in; it lay couched in the classic pose with outstretched paws and rigidly upright head; he also obtained a polychrome clay chimera with a bristling, spiky mane, that flashed its ferocious eyes and with its ridged tail fanned flanks as puffed-up as a pair of blacksmith's bellows. He placed one of these creatures at each end of the room and put out the lamps, leaving the reddening embers in the hearth to cast an uncertain light round the chamber, and magnify the objects which were almost engulfed in shadow. Then he lay down on the sofa, beside the woman whose motionless face was lit by the glow from a half-burnt log, and waited.

---

[51] As there are clues, noted in earlier footnotes, that Huysmans may have discussed these practices—in a very different idiom—with Mallarmé.

> Using strange intonations which he had slowly and patiently made her rehearse beforehand, she, without so much as moving her lips or looking at the mythical creatures, brought the pair of them to life. And in the silence of the night, the wonderful dialogue of the Chimera and the Sphinx began, recited by guttural, deep voices, now raucous, now shrill, almost supernatural.
>
> (Huysmans 1998, p 88.)

Like the practices described by Courrière in her later letter to Jarry, this heavily-aided hallucination attempts to create a fantastic, mythological setting that could not be experienced in any other way; like those presented by Courrière/Chantelouve in *La-Bâs,* they are sexualized, though more subtly so. While the elaborate staging and perceptual aides confirm this as an early stage in the training of the senses and mind and is more indicative of a goal than of a technique, the psychological drama being articulated through it is considerably more complex and underlies a more substantial relationship to the later endeavours of Courrière/Chantelouve.

While the setting has a definite sexual undercurrent and is recalled during a rumination on his eventual impotence, Des Esseintes' mistress here is not the object of Des Esseintes' lust; she is essentially a prop for the artistic experience into which Des Esseintes is gradually sublimating his sexuality, an experience inextricable from the hallucinatory *sensibility* that he is attempting to develop;

> Lulled by Flaubert's splendid prose… shivers ran down him from head to foot when the Chimera uttered the solemn and magical line: 'I seek fresh perfumes, larger blossoms, pleasure yet untried.'
>
> (*ibid*, p 88.)

And it is indeed a 'pleasure yet untried' for which Des Esseintes is striving. Des Esseintes' impotence is a theme running throughout *A rebours*, and it would be difficult (and perhaps pointless) to determine to what extent it feeds *into* his extreme brand of Aestheticism, and to what extent it is a *result* of the sublimating action integral to it, diverting his source of jouissance away from the sexual act and into the critical/readerly/hallucinatory process.[52] In any case Des Esseintes expresses little regret once he has reached a certain stage in his practice and has set himself up at Fontenay.

---

[52] Impotence, as a denial of the 'Natural' *drive* (a carefully chosen word here) toward reproduction, can also be seen as an (anti-)heroic act in reference to Decadence's reversal of Bourgeois values, and the refusal to reproduce was a common theme in Decadent circles, especially under the influence of the ideas of Eduard von Hartmann, a disciple of Schopenhauer who called for a voluntary celibacy that would eventually, it was to be hoped, result in the extinction of the human species. (Pierrot 1981, pp 55-60.)

The passage that he has chosen to recreate and attempt to inhabit reflects this knot of themes. The narrative of the dialogue centres around unsatisfied desire; when the chimera finally accepts the Sphinx's entreaties, the latter turns away from satisfaction at the last moment, for, 'by dint of long dreaming I have no longer aught to say.' (Flaubert 1930, p 176.) 'Chimera' is, of course, the word that Chantelouve would later employ to describe her quasi-incubi; and the dialogue is permeated with language and themes of hallucination, and of hallucinated landscapes and intelligences. As the vision is forming within his confused thoughts, St. Anthony muses that, 'Somewhere there must be primordial figures, whose bodily forms are only symbols. Could I but see them, I would know the link between matter and thought; I would know in what Being consists.' (*ibid*, p 174.) This, of course, describes almost perfectly the goal of the hallucinatory practice of Loyola, as is appropriate in a religious (at least in form) hagiography written by Flaubert, who had rigorously experimented with hashish- and opium-inspired hallucination for years. And the dialogue form itself, in connection with hallucination, also has a long tradition in Mystic practice; an imagined 'colloquy' with the biblical characters involved in a meditation is often included as a part of Mystic 'mental prayer' (Lash 1947, pp 30-31.), and Loyola's hallucinatory 'Meditations' are punctuated by colloquies—

> familiar conversations in which we speak to God like a son to a father, a servant to a master [etc.]… These colloquies are addressed to the Blessed Virgin, to our Saviour, or to God the father, sometimes all three successively. This is the part of the meditation requiring the most liberty and confidence, but also the most respect.[53]

(Loyola 1999, p 57.)

Huysmans, as mentioned earlier, was certainly influenced quite heavily by Loyola, and Flaubert would have had a certain familiarity at least with such practices in Christian Mysticism, so that it is hardly surprising that Des Esseintes—raised as he was by Jesuits—would attempt to import this model into his own secular practice, however awkwardly.

It is this awkwardness—which is, incidentally, manifested, in different terms, even in Courrière's letter more than a decade later—which gives this scene its poignancy and renders it a representation of this practice at its most uncomfortable stage of development, in which everything is half-achieved: Des Esseintes' desire half-integrated into its new structure of sublimation, his senses half-trained to accept images and his faculties half-trained to interpret and co-ordinate them, his practice half-way between private theatre and hallucination,

---

[53] After his conversion to Catholicism, Max Jacob was known to converse with the Virgin Mary every day in precisely these terms, suggesting that he may well have been initiated into hallucinatory practices directly through the Christian Mystical tradition.

his life and personality half-recreated in a way which only aggravates his awareness of the tension between his half-transformed ways of living and the normative expectations, both personal and social, from which he has not yet completely broken:

> It was to him that this voice, as mysterious as an incantation, was speaking; it was to him that it was describing its feverish craving after the unknown, its unattained ideal, its need to escape the horror of existence, to pass beyond the confines of thought, to cast about, without ever arriving at a certainty, in the misty reaches that lie beyond art! All the miserable inadequacy of his own efforts chilled his heart. Gently he embraced the silent woman by his side, taking refuge in her like an inconsolable child, not even seeing the sulky expression of the ventriloquist who had to play a part and ply her trade, at home, in her leisure hours, far from the footlights.
>
> [. . .]
>
> Unfortunately these sessions were of brief duration; despite the exorbitant prices he was paying her, the ventriloquist dismissed him and that very same evening gave herself to a likely fellow with less complicated requirements and more reliable loins.
>
> (Huysmans 1998, pp 88-89.)

By the time that he is ensconced at Fontenay, Des Esseintes' practice has progressed, and he no longer needs this elaborate staging, or another person, in order to approach the Aesthetic experience through the diversion of the drives, though a *representation* would still seem at least nominally integral.[54] This is indicated by a reverie there, described as typical, that focuses on the mythical person of Hérodiade, approached through her representation in two works of art in different media; this reverie hovers on the border between hallucination and *contemplation*, the theological implications of which word are not entirely inappropriate here. It comes during a discussion of the fragments of Mallarmé's unfinished play, *Hérodiade*:[55]

> How many evenings, beneath the lamp that lit the silent room with its dim glow, had he not sensed the gossamer touch of that Hérodias who, in Gustave Moreau's painting—now sunk in shadow—was fading into something ever more faint, leaving only an indistinct glimpse of a white statue amid the dying embers of a brazier of jewels! The darkness hid the blood, deadened the colours and the gold, plunged the far reaches of the temple into shadow, engulfed the accomplices of the crime where they stood wrapped in their somber

---

[54] See the discussion of Anna Blume and her structural, rather than exclusively representational ~~existence~~ in order to elucidate this observation.

[55] It should be noted that it is this text which precipitated Mallarmé's crisis in which his 'personality' was annihilated in the void and from which he emerged considering himself not so much a person as a textual *function*, claiming that, 'the Stéphane you knew is dead'. This crisis, and *Hérodiade's* role in it, is discussed elsewhere in this book.

hues and, sparing only the pale tones of water-colour, drew out the woman from the sheath of her jewels, enhancing her nakedness.

He would turn his eyes compulsively toward her, picking her out by the well-remembered lines of her body, and she would live once more, evoking for him these strange, sweet verses that Mallarmé puts in her lips:

> ...O miroir!
> au froide par l'ennui dans ton cadre gelée
> Que de fois et pendant des heures, désolée
> Des songes et cherchant mes souvenirs qui sont
> Comme des feuilles sous ta glace au trou profond,
> Je m'apparus en toi comme une ombre lointaine,
> Mais, horreur! des soirs, dans ta sévère fontaine
> J'ai de mon rêve épars connu la nudité![56]

(Huysmans 1998, pp 159-160.)

Des Esseintes' Hérodiade here seems to occupy a space ambiguously between and partaking of Mallarmé's *Hérodiade*, *Hérodiade* of Moreau, and Hérodiade the mythic figure, in part composed *from*, but also *apprehended through* these two works, and his relationship to her hovers between the intellectual and the corporeal; one might compare this to the contemplation of religious icons.

Huysmans would, then, have been prepared to see the value in, and approach the practice of, Courrière's version of hallucinatory activity, and while her Spiritualist-Occult approach differed from his materialist one, the influence of less completely deviant religious influences, as well as their shared artistic influence, provided a discursive bridge. Of course, *La-Bâs* was published seven years after *Against Nature* had catalyzed the French Decadent community, so it is more than conceivable that Huysmans' practice as encoded there, and/or through conversation, had influenced the development of her own; and even in her letter of seven years later there is what might be read as a nod to the ambivalence between these two discourses permeating *La-Bâs*:

---

[56] Weinfield translates this passage as follows: 'Mirror, cold water frozen in your frame / Through ennui, how many times I came, / Desolate from dreams and seeking memories / Like leaves beneath your chill profundities, / A far-off shadow to appear in you: /But oh! Some evenings in your austere pool, /I've glimpsed the ideal in all its nakedness!' (Mallarmé 1996, pp 30-31.) Art (figured not as a product but as a *search*), the Ideal (the rejection of Nature), and a subtle eroticism; the significance of mirrors in the tradition of the Yellow Sign, and especially to Mallarmé, is discussed elsewhere in this book.

Analysts have demonstrated that miracles were hallucinations and that the wonderful was confined within a cerebral hemisphere.

But the philosophers have affirmed that the will was the magic lever and that the idea created the act.

(Jarry 1993, p 34.)

The way that Huysmans may have maneuvred his way through this discursive and conceptual dilemma may be reflected within *La-Bâs* (assuming as always that our entire argument is not merely a convincing chimera). Some time after the exchange in which Madame Chantelouve reveals her involvement with this odd brand of incubism, Durtal presents her with a notion that represents, as it were, an Aesthetic take on an Occult notion (or vice-versa)—speaking of it through the lens of Catholic demonology and Satanism though taking as his own model the pagan story of Pygmalion and Galatea. After opening by comparing the proposed practice he is about to reveal to bestiality, demonality, incest, and sacrilege, he proceeds to describe what, in itself, is a logical extension of the Aesthetic emphasis on artifice and its fetish of the art-object; moreover, he implicitly links it with the earlier practice surrounding the figure of *Hérodiade* described in *Against Nature*:

Gustave Moreau, *The Apparition (Hérodias)* (1874-76). (Moreau 1999, p 168.)

> 'Imagine, if you will, an artist who has fallen in love with his own creation—an Hérodiade, a Judith, a Helen, a Jeanne d'Arc—whom he has either described in writing or painted; and as a result of this very act of evocation, let us imagine that this same artist later possesses his creation in a dream. Well, this is a crime of love which is distinctly worse than ordinary incest... In Pygmalionism, however, the father violates his own spiritual child, the only one which is totally and truly his... The act is a crime against nature, that is to say against God, since the victim is not, as would be the case even with regard to bestiality, a palpable and living creature, but an unreal being created by the use of a talent which is itself being desecrated, a being almost celestial, for is not the aim of art to produce, whether by genius or by artifice, works which will be immortal?
>
> (Huysmans 2001, pp 155-156.)

But however logical the extension of the practices described in *Against Nature* to that suggested here might be, it is couched in distinctly different terms through which Durtal is attempting to articulate it to Madame Chantelouve, and which possibly reflect the way in which, in the midst of his gradual conversion to Catholicism, Huysmans himself was beginning to recontextualize his practice. This is particularly evident in what might almost be read as a kind of slip, when Durtal frames the practice as, 'against nature, that is to say against God' (and the title of *La-Bâs* can translate to 'The Damned' as well as 'Down There', so that this short phrase very nearly juxtaposes the titles of those two books, like two sides of the same coin, though one might still hope for a certain one to come out on top when it is flipped).[57] When the idea is told to Madame Chantelouve's husband, he answers that, 'it is simply a refined form of succubacy.' (*ibid*, p 156.)

But while Huysmans may have been well-prepared to take on the modalities of hallucinatory practice (probably) put forward by Courrière, He had something to learn from her in developing it. The relative underdevelopment, in his practice as encoded in *A rebours*, of the *psychological* potential of hallucinatory practice is evident even in that book's most complex and successful example of the evocation of individual *people*, the scene in the 'English pub' in Paris, where Des Esseintes peoples the interior with characters from Dickens. (Huysmans 1998, pp 109-114.) The evocation of quasi-incubi described by Madame Chantelouve in *La-Bâs* goes much farther in manipulating the way that the hallucinatory subject's psychology is being modulated. In the English pub, the hallucination remains a spectacle; Des Esseintes is essentially removed from it, *watching* it; he does not interact with it. There is a sense in which, through projecting his hallucinated people *into* the scene, he removes himself *from* it. These evocations therefore retain the nature of *characters* in a novel, they are observed from a distance, and are still effectively in their own world—even if their own world happens also to be Des Esseintes' own.

In Courrière's practice, however, this division is not so simple. She exists on the same plane as her hallucinated people, and interacts with them *as* people. Whether tyrannizing over them or making love to them, whether in a fantastic dream-world or in her own bedroom with her husband next to her, she is emphatically,

---

[57] In this way, this passage reflects the course that Huysmans' apostasy took. While the occultism portrayed in *La-Bâs* (and it should be noted that Huysmans' eventual conversion was not entirely orthodox, but was very far from occult) represents an anti-social stance and reacts against many of the same aspects of Bourgeois culture as the materialist Aestheticism articulated in *Against Nature*, the model of its dissenting gesture was ultimately less radical. Like the Aesthetic project, Satanism, especially as portrayed in *La-Bâs*, operated largely through a system of détournement, a willful mis-reading or mis-use of dominant cultural artifacts and forms. Unlike the former however, it did not devalue the dominant in doing so, in fact the Satanist's experience is dependant upon, and therefore ultimately reinforces the claims of power of the institution itself, as for instance Courrière's lover Gourmont has pointed out. (Huysmans 2001, pp xxiii-xxiv.) It is difficult, for example, to imagine the Huysmans of *Against the Grain* appealing to the simplistic Classical notion, adopted so wholeheartedly by the Bourgeois order, of 'the aim of art to produce, whether by genius or by artifice, works which will be immortal,' *even* (or *merely*) in order to heighten the perverse shock of his proposition.

psychologically *with* them, they are not mere images floating on the screen of her perception. Especially in the form of practice described in *La-Bâs,* she is in no way detached. The sexual nature of the practice presented here (and its sexual aspect might not, of course, represent the entirety *of* the practice) is particularly revealing, focusing as it does upon desire for the *other;* the hallucination represents *a lack* in the hallucinating subject (Fink 1997, p 44 *passim*.). It must on the one hand function as a manifestation of the hallucinating subject's object (which is to say, cause) of desire (*ibid,* pp 50-52.)—that is to say, as a condensation and representation of a certain palimpsest or orientation of the subject's psychology. It must on the other hand be experienced by the subject not merely as an *image*, but as a *person* (or anti-person) capable of its own volition—that is, as emphatically *outside* the hallucinating subject not only perceptually, but as an unknowable *intelligence,* at least within the brackets of the hallucination itself.[58] Such a practice therefore entails a complex *psychological* maneuvre co-ordinated with the cognitive maneuvres Huysmans had been exploring for a number of years; moreover, it entails *within* the subject the figuration of that lack, a figuration with which the subject as a whole then interacts—an interaction with the negation integral to the structuration of the human subject.

To reroute desire, to reroute the way in which the drives operate, is to rearrange the structuration of the subject herself. The creation of a ~~person~~ in whom energies are bound up provides a focal point for this *conscious* sublimating action; by investing them in the hallucinated ~~object~~, they can be explored and then dealt *with*, rearticulated; the image that is their avatar becomes a kind of handle by which the subject can take hold of a certain configuration of himself; through this avatar the energies and drives invested in it can begin to be *trained*.

The conceptualizing of this 'object' as an 'other' (that is to say, an 'other subject') prevents its simple and immediate re-integration into the subject; the unknowability *attributed to* it does not allow it to act as a simple 'symbol' and therefore necessitates that—these drives, complexes, and psychological coordinates having been 'cut out'—something must now 'be done with' them. At the same time, the subject's awareness of the hallucinatory character of this projected ~~person~~—and the importance of this awareness has been remarked in an earlier footnote[59]—also productively complicates the process of transference that is implicit in the process upon which I am speculating, for the unknowability of this (anti-)person is emphatically *attributed to*, in order to constitute it as 'other' (especially in sexual fantasy); this bracketed or provisional unknowability, comparable to the 'suspension of disbelief' which some readers prefer, for whatever reason, to adopt while reading fiction,

---

[58] This 'otherness' is confirmed by the specificity of Chantelouve's evocations—specific writers, chosen on the basis of a decidedly *sublimated* desire, thoroughly run through her own psychological coordinates, rather than more-or-less anonymous or stock 'males' (etc.) to satisfy a basic *need*. (Fink 1997, pp 235-236, n. 4.)

[59] This dynamic of knowability/unknowability will be further developed in relation to other possible examples of hallucinatory practice.

history, psychoanalysis, physics, etc., is balanced in this practice by a parallel awareness *of* that suspension, that in fact this ~~person~~ could 'be' anything the subject 'wants', and that therefore what this ~~person~~ 'is' is necessarily what the subject 'wants'; transference then must be *read* by the subject *as* transference, its character *as* transference announces itself in definite terms.[60]

As the *act* of transference unmasks itself and offers itself to reading by the subject, the *object* of transference is removed from the 'outside' and is placed *within* the subjective economy. If the object of transference—lover, analyst, father, etc. etc. etc.—represents the register on which, and the figure *through* which the subject articulates her desire and plays out her relationship to the Other, then the operation just described, by locating that object of transference *within* the subject, has effectively *transgressed the exteriority of the Other*. The subject now plays out that relationship to the Other through this internalized figure who is *recognised in practice* as being *of the subject herself*—that is to say, *not the Other*,

> To invent not this or that, some *tekhne* or some fable, but to invent the world—a world, not America, the New World, but a novel world, a new habitat, another person, another desire even.
>
> -Jacques Derrida, *Psyche: Inventions of the Other* (1987).
> (Derrida 1991, p 218.)

though partaking of the ~~Other~~ structuring the subject from ~~within~~. Within the brackets of this hallucinatory 'suspension of disbelief', and to the extent to which that suspension remains in play, castration has been provisionally reversed.[61] Whereas the 'actual' object of transference will continuously frustrate the desire of the

---

[60] To attempt to specifically 'cite' the (mostly psychoanalytic) ideas being manipulated here would result in a text absurdly peppered with the word '*passim*'. While this would have a certain charm to it, I have decided to spare you. It will be evident to readers familiar with him that this part of my discussion draws primarily from Lacan, though some simplification has been necessary for the sake of the brevity which I shall never tire of proclaiming as my most salient strength; my primary source has been Bruce Fink's *Clinical Introduction to Lacanian Psychoanalysis*, which is remarkably straightforward considering its subject-matter. In that book Lacan is quoted as defining the goal of analysis as, 'no other than bringing to the light of day manifestations of the subject's desire,' and the development of a 'decided desire' or 'determined desire'. (Fink 1997, p 206), a definition which one will see corresponds quite closely to what I am speculating upon here; however my unorthodox torturing of these psychoanalytic ideas suggest a practice moving beyond the practical goals of psychoanalysis, which generally involve a 'return' to normativity and a continued orientation in relation to the Oedipal drama (indeed, Fink essentially insists upon this, pp 110-111.). In this sense, my speculations here are inspired largely by Kristeva's *Revolution in Poetic Language* and Reed's critique of her text in turn in his *Imagining Revolt*, though this torturing does not precisely follow the directions sketched out in those texts, is doubtless less responsible than either.

[61] It is important here to make a distinction between an imagined *reversed castration* and the *failure of castration* characterizing psychosis in the Lacanian schema. (*ibid*, pp 89, 96-97.) In the latter case, the distinction between subject and object, already weak, would disappear and the subject would cease to operate as such. (*ibid*, pp 88-90.) The operation upon which we are speculating is not the creation of a psychotic state, but rather the re-inscription of certain of its elements *within* a subjective structure that, while continually and radically re-structuring itself, nonetheless remains *a subject*, meaning that some integral recognition of this division still remains. The subject/object split however (which can be recast as 'real'/ 'imagined', 'self'/ 'Other', etc.) is recognised as an element of the *rhetoric* of subjectivity, rather than as an originary logic prior to it. Lacan asserts that psychosis cannot be 'developed'; after the critical stage in childhood, one cannot 'become' psychotic later in life. (*ibid*, p 82.) The subjective state implied by our speculations would then, in some respects, be a *parasitic* subjective state, necessitating neurotic or perverted subjective structures as a *base* (as one might name a *base* metal for an alchemical operation) which is then gradually sublimated and transformed to a subjective structure which defies all of psychoanalysis' categorizations, at which point this discourses loses its hold upon it; Kristeva's notion of the textual process of subjectivity in *Revolution in Poetic Language* suggests what *one* such possible subjective configuration might look like, and that model is

subject, due to its inherent unknowability and inevitable refusal to map to the subject's desire, the hallucinated object of transference *is itself a palimpsest of the subject's desire*. Desire is no longer thwarted, and is free to be directed elsewhere, to reconstitute itself and with it, the subject herself. This is similar to the goal of Lacanian psychoanalysis, 'a new configuration of the subject's fundamental fantasy, and thus to a new relation…to the Other' (*ibid*, p 70.), but the means by which the has reached this point create other implications.[62] For the methods of psychoanalysis, describing an ever-widening compass of awareness and acceptance regarding a-logical and unconscious elements of the subjective economy, nonetheless operates from a centre of normative human relations and communication; whereas (as the absurdly exhaustive investigation we have carried out so far regarding hallucinatory modalities has hopefully demonstrated) in such a practice suggested by this hybrid of Huysmans' and Courrière's, this goal is approached through a progressive, and progressively radical, restructuring of not only psychological processes but the cognitive and physiological structures which interact with and to a large extent underlie them. The subject is therefore prepared to direct this desire *not*, as traditional psychoanalysis would have it, back into the normative modes of existing characterized by the prevailing models of thought, centred around the logos of Oedipus, which have already shown themselves to be utterly bankrupt; but rather to move *with* that desire, we might even say, personified as it can be (though need not be), *beside it*, into new modes, where even the supposed split between the subject and the object, the self and the Other, the 'real' and the 'artificial' is experienced as no more than a crease.

---

central to our speculations here. She continues, as Reed points out, to connect this model to Oedipus, though this might be read merely a practical way in which a textual subjectivity might attach itself to and grow *out of* this Oedipal model into a subjective process free from it; she does not however make this manifest.

[62] This is not to suggest that these methods would be mutually exclusive.

-Gustave Moreau, *Hesiod and the Muse* (1858). (Moreau 1999, p 60.)

The Immaculate Conception will be the experimental source to which one will have to return in order to recognise the power thought has of adopting successively all the modes of madness; to recognise this power is equivalent to admitting the reality of this madness and affirming its latent existence in the human mind.

-Paul Éluard and André Breton, insert to *The Immaculate Conception* (1930). (Breton et. al. 1997, p 160.)

With a royal gesture [the Baroness Else von Freytag-Loringhoven] swept apart the folds of a scarlet raincoat. She stood before me quite naked—or nearly so. Over the nipples of her breasts were two tin tomato cans, fastened with a green string about her back. Between the tomato cans hung a very small bird-cage and within it a crestfallen canary. One arm was covered from wrist to shoulder with curtain rings, which later she admitted to having pilfered from a furniture display in Wanamaker's. She removed her hat, which had been tastefully but inconspicuously trimmed with golden carrots, beets, and other vegetables. Her hair was close cropped and died vermilion.

-George Biddle, *An American Artist's Story* (1939)   (Gammel 2002, pp 200-201.)

Leaving his almost monastic isolation, [Marcel Duchamp] flung himself into orgies of drunkenness and every other excess. But in a life of license as in a life of asceticism, he preserved his consciousness of purpose: extravagant as his gestures sometimes seemed, they were perfectly adequate to his experimental study of a personality disengaged from the normal contingencies of human life. He later recognized, in an interview with James Johnson Sweeny, that in this fabrication of his personality he was very much influenced by the manner of Jacques Vaché, whom he had met through Apollinaire.

-Gabrielle Buffet, *Some Memories of Pre-Dada: Picabia and Duchamp* (1949).   (Motherwell 1981, p 260.)

The Art of Madness I

"In the case of Else von Freytag-Loringhoven I am not talking of mania and disease, of numbed sensibilities . . . . hers is a willed state," says "jh". I concede it to be true that in no effort in which self-consciousness of any sort persists is the will absolutely in abeyance, and the beginning of madness is rarely an absolute state. To express life in words is to juggle with the poison that lies in the very medium... The artist often courts the speech of the madman because he desires the emotion he has ensnared to escape the petrification of intellectualization, but there is a point at which the will weakens beneath the onrush of forces it has itself loosed. Amidst flashes of insight like fire in the rain perception dims and is finally extinguished in the blindness of pure sensation. Else von Freytag-Loringhoven, in my opinion, has walked perilously near (if she has not passed over the edge) beyond which the vision of delirium melts into the blank self-enwrapped exaltation of trance.

Margaret Anderson is good enough to inform me that through the carelessness of the printer "jh" was misquoted in her reply to me in the last issue, so that "working" should be supplemented for "evoking", in which case I quote "jh" as follows:

"The artist working his consciousness at a high power on some piece of difficult work appears to have become callous and stupid or a wild man to the layman." For the sake of "jh" I am sorry that the correction must be made, as by this alteration in her statement a word of vague applicability is supplemented for one of clear connotation. One must now inquire in what manner and under what circumstances the artist is able to "work" his consciousness.

A man may be working a sewing machine or a plow or, in the vernacular of the day, he may be working a woman. In each case an initiation of will is required. The point at issue is to decide wherein lies the difference in the relation which the man holds to the sewing machine and the plow, and to the woman. In one case we have the will acting without limitations other than those which inhere in the quality of metal. The man may mar the machine and destroy the plow and even then he can collect the mutilated parts and reconstruct them to their original use. But over the woman he has not an equal sphere of dominance. By suggestions of fear or benevolence he may temporarily put one or more of her powers at his disposal, but she will continue to exist under her own condition which he has not created and cannot re-create. It would seem that only in this sense can the consciousness be "worked", for it is distinguishable from the will while existing on unalterable terms. One bends to one's uses the thing one can not break and the most literal word to express this act is the word which "jh", unfortunately, did not use,—evocation.

I did not anywhere make a statement which would contradict the supposition that the madness of the artist in question was evoked as is often the madness of the religious ecstatic, only that the features of madness were in her work. Synthesis looses the will. One may evoke a god, a muse, or a madness, but to speak of conditioned disorder would be to contradict oneself, and I certainly believe that Else von Freytag-Loringhoven is powerless to condition the disorder she has evoked.

-Evelyn Scott, *The Little Review 6* (Dec., 1919.)   (Lane 1998.)

In February 1915, German zeppelins had begun bombing Britain, focusing mostly on London; in March, Britain began to bomb German trains carrying soldiers to the front. The Baroness echoed these events on her body, parading in an aviator hat in 1915. When the young French American painter Louis Bouché first met her at a Broadway subway station, she was "wearing a French Poilu's blue trench helmet."

    -Irene Gammel, *Baroness Elsa* (2002).   (Gammel 2002, p 165.)

"I almost bought it," says Vaché, "—in our last retreat. But I object to being killed in wartime." He killed himself shortly after the Armistice. "I was just finishing this article," writes Marc-Adolphe Guégan in *La Ligne du Coeur* (January 1927), "when a trustworthy source sent me a horrifying revelation. Apparently Jacques Vaché said a few hours before the tragedy: 'I will die when I want to die… But then I'll die with someone else. Dying alone is too boring… Preferably one of my very best friends…' Such statements," adds M. Guégan, "casts doubts on the hypothesis of an accident, especially if we recall that Jacques Vaché *did not die alone*. One of his friends fell victim to the same poison, on the same evening. They seemed to be sleeping side by side, until it was discovered they were no longer alive. But to admit that this double death was the consequence of a sinister plan is to make someone's memory horribly responsible." To provoke the denunciation of that "horrible responsibility" was, without a doubt, the supreme ambition of Jacques Vaché.

    -Andre Breton, quoting M.-A. Guégan, *Anthology of Black Humor* (1945)   (Breton 1997, pp 294-295.)

On that fatal night of 14 December [1927], as she prepared for bed, her little dog Pinky was by her side. Somehow the gas jets were left on that night, with the deadly fumes slowly seeping out and spreading through the apartment.… She left no suicide note, a strange silence for someone so compulsively voluble. "I have just discovered that I am not, and why I am not made for suicide—unless it could be done gaily—victoriously—with flourish," she had written from Berlin. The dada flourish was missing from her death, leaving a baffling question mark.

    -Irene Gammel, *Baroness Elsa.*   (Gammel 2002, p 383.)

The Art of Madness II

But now let us see who is talking about what? It all started from a statement of mine: "No one has yet done much about the Art of Madness." Then Miss Scott jumped in and talked about the madness in the Art of von Freytag—not the Art in her Madness. I never thought of discussing those psychological peculiarities in the artist which are beyond the reach of the will. Haven't those things been recognized and summed up even by laymen in "artists are born not made?"

Odilon Redon, *Madness* (1883).
(Redon 1996. p 52.)

Words do not mean so many things to me as they do to Miss Scott. Consciousness does not mean the sum of ungovernable, dispersed faculties. Consciousness means complete *being*. So I am not talking of a state in which the consciousness is only kept from being nothing by a weak and tottering will, but of one in which the will is so powerful that it creates the being—the state of consciousness it desires. When I speak of disease I mean disorder. When a person has created a state of consciousness which is madness and adjusts (designs and executes) every form and aspect of her life to fit this state there is no disorder anywhere: there is therefore no disease. There can be no legitimate standard for valuing the order of sanity higher than the order of madness, except a moral one.

Now I will try to answer Miss Scott's problem of working and evoking. I did not use the word evoke because it is an unknown and unnecessary word to me. Evoking comes in the class with rain-making, etc. If one has the power to evoke he has more power than the evoked.

It is perhaps not necessary for the artist to make any outward sign that he has had his specialized creative experience, but it is customary and human and we are speaking of these signs (works of art). After the æsthetic intuition of Beauty there is a simultaneous mental and emotional conception,——the complete vision and creation of this beauty : the internal expression : the experience of the creative impulse…

Miss Scott has information, knowledge and words. All that she says is true but it does not make sense because it does not fit this discussion. Unless I had tried to begin my discussion far beyond the cause which may be pathological and the effect which is not . . . beyond the support of knowledge and evidence and academic definition. . . I should feel that I had offered an affront and an insult to Else von Freytag-Loringhoven.

-Jane Heap, *The Little Review 6* (Dec., 1919.) (Lane 1998.)

Entirely out of balance you!
Does art affect thus?
Result: *balance.*
Not must leave bad memory—*carry such!*
Feeling of something exquisite—extraordinary—great—joyful—to be proud of—carry into age—no matter what happened—no matter what subject—will linger—must! *or individual unfit to indulge!*
Art—strength—joy conveys joy—to strong.
[. . .]
Never losing balance—in deepest abandon—highest excitement—breeding of artist in blood—subconsciously tells how far to go—we becoming sober to criticize in cold blood.
Retires when becomes inexpressive—inarticulate—
silence—
death.

-The Baroness Else von Freytag-Loringhoven,
  Thee I Call 'Hamlet of the Wedding Ring' (1921). (Lane 1998.)

"[Vaché's] triumph was his death at Nantes, some time before the Armistice. He not only committed suicide in a formidable and humorous fashion, by taking, *and forcing two of his comrades to take,* a large over-dose of opium, although he knew very well what the proper method of employing the drug was..." (Bouvier: *in* Putman: *op. cit.*).

-Quoted by Robert Motherwell, *The Dada Painters and Poets* (1951), (Motherwell 1981, p xxx.)

Her head: shaved and occasionally shellacked in striking colours like vermillion red. Her makeup: yellow face powder, black lipstick, and an American stamp on her cheek. Her jewels: utilitarian, mass-produced objects like teaspoons as earrings or large buttons as finger rings. Her accessories: tomato cans and celluloid rings adorning her body; the hem of her skirt decorated with horse blanket pins.

An electric battery taillight decorates the bustle of her black dress in imitation of a car or bicycle… She also used live animals… a wooden birdcage round her neck housing a live canary; five dogs on her gilded leash as she promenaded up Fifth Avenue… With each new day, she added new twists to her repertoire of makeup, headdresses, and costumes that were frequently made from junk objects collected in the streets.

    -Irene Gammel, *Baroness Elsa* (2002).   (Gammel 2002, p 182.)

The western world follows us everywhere.

I am never close to it—
        because it is there all of the time.

I hear the narrative of hunters.

It is not a coincidence—
        the patterns and the option of madness—

    -Imogene Engine, *The Iuk Kide* (2007).   (Engine 2007, p 7.)

The Art of Madness III, by Else von Freytag-Loringhoven

The Little Review, 6 (December 1919)

"jh" understands me wonderfully—perfectly. Don't I say in "The Cast-Iron Lover": "look full of laughter—look full of motion—look full of dizziness—insanity!—which makes steady and sane!—maketh steady and sane thine body!"

Is it not necessary for emotions to come out—is it not necessary for emotional people to be like insane sometimes?—to be more sane and steady and strong than other, weaker people, after that? Is it not wonderful to be able to control that then, that emotion, which otherwise would throttle you?—but take it by the neck and make Art out of it? and be free?—that is, the *master*? Only *such things*—done *that* way are Art! It is Goethe's art! *He knew that too!*—he too had to do it: "Nur wer die Sehnsucht kennt—weiss was ich leide" . . . That is just as insane as my "Cast-Iron Lover" (and would have been too sentimental if Goethe had not been such a strong artist); and my "Cast-Iron Lover" is not an iota more insane nor less art!

Perhaps the America people need to be told it—Europeans wouldn't; not people who read books like the *Little Review*.

[. . .]

—tell the Americans that in nations of high culture it even was a public custom, as it is still—for instance in the mardi gras—or "Fasching"—and in old Greece in the feast of Dionysus ("die Dionysien" as we learned it in Germany), and always will be—because it has to be—

-The Baroness Else von Freytag-Loringhoven, *The Little Review 6* (Dec., 1919.)   (Lane 1998.)

On my funeral you can save—I am not interested in junk—unless I could be embalmed as a beautiful shell of rare queen—and you wouldn't care enough for me to do that—so you'd better sell me to a medical college and present Djuna Barnes with the proceeds—

-The Baroness Else von Freytag-Loringhoven, Letter to George Biddle, 1927. (Gammel 2002, p 382.)

I've been successively a crowned man of letters, a well-known pornographic artist, and a scandalous cubist painter—Now, I stay at home and leave the task of explaining and discussing my personality to others… and I ask you to believe in my memory.

    -Jacques Vaché, Letter to André Breton, 16 Oct., 1916.   (Cravan et. al. 205, p 192-193.)

I went to the consulate with a large—sugarcoated birthday cake upon my head with 50 flaming candles lit—I felt so *spunky and affluent*—! In my ears I wore sugar plumes or matchboxes—I forgot which. Also I had put several stamps as beauty spots on my emerald painted cheeks and my eyelashes were made of guilded [sic] porcupine quills—rustling coquettishly—at the consul—with several ropes of dried figs dangling around my neck to give him a suck once and again.—to entrance him. I should have liked to wear gaudy coloured rubber boots up to my hips with a ballet skirt of genuine goldpaper white lacepaper covering it but I couldn't afford *that*. I guess—that inconsistency in my costume is to blame for my failure to please the officials?

    -The Baroness Else von Freytag-Loringhoven, Letter to Djuna Barnes, c. 1924.

    (Gammel 2002, p 182.)

"to aim so purposely to miss your mark"—naturally, written irony is unbearable—but naturally you also know very well that 'umour isn't irony, naturally—*Like that*—what do you want? It's like that and not otherwise—Everything's so funny, very funny, it's a fact—Everything is so funny!—(and if we killed ourselves as well, instead of merely going away?)

    -Jacques Vaché, Letter to André Breton, 9 May, 1818.   (Cravan et. al. 2005, p 207.)

Sure—suicide is but simple witted relative effectively shrouded practical joke—but—but—but—all buts I conjure up against that spectral pageant.

-The Baroness Else von Freytag-Loringhoven, Letter to Peggy Guggenheim, 1927.

(Gammel 2002, p 382.)

-The Baroness Else von Freytag-Loringhoven, c. 1915. (Gammel 2002, p 7.)

In his text (you shall discover why I hesitate to call it 'fiction') *The Signpost,* Paul Verlaine opens with a discussion between himself and Poe; and the a-temporality of the discourse of the Yellow Sign is hinted at when we note that Verlaine's conversation with his dead, mythic predecessor is emphatically two-sided: 'While doing justice to the considerable measure of obvious truth contained in [Poe's] proposition, I could not forbear to contest the axiomatic form in which it was cast... Edgar Poe seemed to be listening to me with interest and, the conversation continuing on that subject, I went on to tell him a story about my youth'. (Gourmont 1994, p 207.) The following account is thus, both from within and from without the narrative framework of the story, a response to Poe, one in the course of which Verlaine himself becomes American, and, in the story he is currently telling to Poe, inserts himself into the history *of* Poe his intralocutor (yes, the choice of this word is intentional):

> In Charleston, where I was a penny-a-line scribbler, I was for a long time Edgar Poe's opium-companion and, to a degree, his collaborator. Later, in my capacity as slave-owner, I joined the Confederate army, in which I became a colonel. Proscribed after the capture of Davis, and to some extent involved in the Booth-Lincoln case, I made my way to Mexico at the height of the Second War of Independence during which, not without taking any side, I placed myself at the head of a gang whose exploits still, at this moment, arouse fear and trembling in Matamoros, Oaxaca and Queranto.

(*ibid*, p 209.)

We can see here that Verlaine inhabits Poe autobiographically and creatively in the first sentence of this passage, their figures merge. But whereas Poe dies in 1849 Verlaine, through this merging of figures, carries him forward, providing him with an alternate life extending beyond his early death; an action which is itself a figuration of the cross-generational project of the Yellow Sign. (There is perhaps a trace of Rimbaud, who became a slave-trader after his renunciation of literature, here as well.) But whereas, during his 'actual' life in the first sentence Poe is restricted to his biographical life of banality and indigence (much like the Verlaine of this writing), after his death frees him from this biographical (*subjective*) imperative Verlaine provides him (or them both) with a dynamic and adventurous life more befitting the texts he produced—eventually making his way, appropriately, to revolutionary Mexico, where the closest we can find in American writing to Poe's literary descendant, Ambrose Bierce, would himself disappear some years later in the chaos of Pancho Villa's own revolt. In *The Book of Masks,* Remy de Gourmont suggests that Verlaine, in a role representative of the generational transmission-through-refiguration of the Yellow Sign, had performed a similar operation on the Romantic impulse itself: 'he accomplished the disjoining of Romantic verse... having rendered it shapeless, having bored into it and unstitched it in order that he might allow entrance to a greater variety of things'.) (*ibid*, p 206.)

-Olchar E. Lindsann, *The Yellow Sign.*

[The accused pirate] Eugène Degraeve is neither innocent nor guilty: *Eugène Degraeve* is ARTHUR GORDON PYM. Let anyone take up Degraeve's memoirs, *Le Bagne,* and Edgar Allan Poe's *Narrative of Arthur Gordon Pym*: we defy him to discover a single fact in the one that does not have its counterpart, and more often than not its exact copy, in the other.

The pivotal character of the two tragedies, or rather of the single tragedy lived twice, is the black cook, Mirey/Seymore, "who in all respects was a perfect demon," according to the *Gordon Pym* version (ch. 4), and the man "who was to become the abominable accuser" and "who had an evil glint in his eye", according to the Degraeve version (pp.32-33). The mutiny on board breaks out under the same nautical conditions in each: "We were on the starboard tack, that's to say the wind was blowing from the right-hand side" (Degraeve, p.40); "I was entirely satisfied, from her continual inclination larboard, that she had been sailing all along with a steady breeze on her starboard quarter" (*Gordon Pym,* ch. 2).

[…]

It would be tiresome to go on multiplying the quotations… The coincidence of the two accounts is complete, bar a few embellishments absent from Poe's original text and which go to confirm the impression that Degraeve's memoirs are a new revised edition of *The Narrative of Arthur Gordon Pym*, with but few additions.

[…]

There is no departure from Poe's original conception until the death of [Eugène's brother] Léonce Degraeve, that sorrowful accident which is all too real: "The following day my brother was thrown to the sharks," says Eugene Degraeve, "fifty metres away from the side of the ship. And must I say it? Must I relate once more that sorrowful thing? Must I write that I saw his limbs torn off and his body mutilated till it became a plaything for the sharks? Alas yes… my whole being trembled before this spectacle of indescribable horror; I saw these monsters tearing at the last remains of his flesh!" (p.290). How much more tragic the simplicity of the original: "we lay motionless by the corpse during the whole day, without exchanging a word; it was not until some time after dark that we took courage to get up and throw the body overboard. … As the mass of putrefaction slipped over the vessel's side into the water, the glare of phosphoric light with which it was suddenly surrounded plainly discovered to us seven or eight large sharks, the clashing of whose horrible teeth, as their prey was torn to pieces among them, might have been heard at the distance of a mile." (*Gordon Pym,* ch. 13)

-Alfred Jarry, *Edgar Allan Poe in Action* (1901). (Jarry 2001, pp 229-231.)

Allow us to examine Mallarmé's sonnet, *The Tomb of Edgar Poe:*

> As to Himself at last eternity changes him
> The Poet reawakens with a naked sword
> His century appalled at never having heard
> That in this voice triumphant death had sung its hymn.
>
> They, like a writhing hydra, hearing seraphim
> Bestow a purer sense on the language of the horde,
> Loudly proclaimed that the magic potion had been poured
> From the dregs of some dishonored mixture of foul slime.
>
> From the war between earth and heaven, what grief!
> If understanding cannot sculpt a bas-relief
> To ornament the dazzling tomb of Poe:
>
> Calm block here fallen from obscure disaster,
> Let this granite at least mark the boundaries evermore
> To the dark flights of Blasphemy hurled to the future.

And now, allow me to begin by remarking that in the first line Poe, through his death (the tangible term in the metaphor for the Artesian withdrawal of his 'authority' from the text) is paradoxically transformed into the capitalized, ideational manifestation of 'Himself': the (or a) Poe of legend, who, as I have discussed, was quickly established as a seminal figure of the Yellow Sign by Baudelaire, whose myth-making legacy Mallarmé is implicitly taking up. And Mallarmé's Poe retains the essential dynamic established by Baudelaire: the persecuted Poet at war with the materialist society in which he was enmeshed. It is at this point—when he has passed into myth, passed into the text of the social structures of the Yellow Sign—that Poe becomes potently dangerous to the society he has combated, 'reawakens with a naked sword', his 'dark flights of Blasphemy hurled to the future.' Like Baudelaire—albeit in a typical verbally-indirect manner that requires some parsing, Poe is caught up in the theme of Addiction, which as it so often does, intersects with this struggle with society. After this, however, we can see Mallarmé's treatment of the Poe myth inflected in a different direction than that of Baudelaire, perpetuating the necessary mythic multivalency of the figure.

Baudelaire's Poe is a figure of a twisted kind of social strength; like the marginalized yet defiant Romantic impulse that the Yellow Sign represented for Baudelaire, Poe could not make practical headway against the positivism of his society, but he lived his life as a form of defiance against every imperative of that society, including success and respectability themselves; Poe was not, ultimately, destroyed by this society, he destroyed *himself* as a conscious act of immolatory revolt: In *Edgar Poe: His Life and Works*, Baudelaire argues that, 'Poe's death is almost a suicide—a suicide a long time in preparation.' (Poe 1980, p 82.) On the following page he expands:

> we might say that, under the pressure of certain circumstances, given serious examination of certain incompatibilities, with firm belief in certain dogmas and metempsychoses, we might say without bombast or fanciful words, that suicide is sometimes the most reasonable act in life.
> (Poe 1980, p 83.)

He goes on to foreshadow Mallarmé's intimation of Poe's death passing him into the Yellow Sign, as it were, transforming him into a kind of literary and philosophical virus, or martyr:

> And thus is formed a fraternity of already innumerable phantoms, which haunts us intimately, each member of which comes to praise his present repose, and convert us with his beliefs.
> (*ibid.*)

Poe's alcoholism is equally a conscious, aggressive, anti-social act:

> I am told that he did not drink as a gourmand but as a barbarian, with a briskness and economy altogether American, as if to commit an act of murder, as if *something* in him had to be killed, *a worm that would not die*.
> (*ibid*, p 88.)

Baudelaire then, on the following page, connects Poe with the more specific figure of the *Inspired* Addict, the artist for whom addiction is a Faustian pact which forms an essential aspect of his methodology of both artistic creation and life itself, a way of apprehending the ~~presence~~ and the action of the Yellow Sign—a tradition which we can trace back through Poe to De Quincey, then to Coleridge, and one into which Baudelaire quite consciously inserted himself. He connects Poe to this tradition in the following three sentences:

> Now, it is incontestable that—(like those striking and fugitive impressions, most striking in their repetition when they are most fugitive, sometimes following some exterior sign, a kind of warning like the tolling of a bell, a musical note, a forgotten perfume, and which themselves follow events similar to others already known, occupying the same place in a previous chain of thoughts, just as strange repetitive dreams arise in our sleep)—there exists in drunkenness not solely the enchantment of dreams, but a rational sequence that, to recur again, would necessitate the milieu which inspired it. If by now the reader has not been repulsed, he may have already divined my conclusion: I believe that very often, though certainly not always, Poe's inebriation was a mnemonic means, a method of work, a method drastic and deadly, yet appropriate to his own passionate nature. The poet had learned to drink, just as a careful writer takes pains to keep notes.
> (*ibid*, p 89.)

We can see then how Baudelaire's construction of the Poe figure was heavily inflected—as indeed it ought to be—toward those aspects of the Yellow Sign which were the particular province of Baudelaire the myth-maker, and also toward one of the central themes of Baudelaire's version of the Baudelaire figure that he created and lived. Mallarmé, however, cast Poe, and the addictive theme with which he was infused, in a different role in relation to the society to which he was opposed.

While in Baudelaire, Poe's alcoholism is an act perpetrated by himself, and his death an unanswerable gesture of individualistic defiance, in Mallarmé Poe's death takes on the nature of a kind of sacrifice that, while inherently unjust and perhaps still culpable, registers firmly within, rather than against, the order of society; and his alcoholism is imposed upon him by that society as a kind of ritual wound.

It is society itself, 'His century', that, in response to the threat posed by Poe—represented as a Seraph (the addition of a single letter would render Poe the capitalized, Ideational Poet in his native language)—to the 'language of the horde,' has bestowed the wound of addiction upon him, rendering him a ceremonial Other: 'proclaimed that the magic potion had been poured / From the dregs of some dishonored mixture of foul slime.' In Mallarmé's version, Poe suffers two deaths: one which sublimates him, takes him up into the play of mythic textuality, and another which casts him out from the society whose language he attempts to vitalize, his creative action obscured and humiliated by the addiction he has been caused, or proclaimed, to bear. Mallarmé's Poe is a victim of society, but there is a sense that this very victimization is representative of a certain cultural necessity, of the role of the Poet within the positivist society of Modernity. Mallarmé's Poe has become the Pharmakon.

-Olchar E. Lindsann, *The Yellow Sign*.

I remembered how once, when looking at myself in it, I had experienced the strange sensation of sinking into that mirror up to the neck, as if into some muddy lake.
    -Rachilde, *L'Araignée de crystal* (1894).   (Pierrot 1981, p 212.)

I recoil before mirrors, seeing my face debased and dull
    -Stéphane Mallarmé, Letter to Henri Cazalis, c. Jan. 1865.   (Mallarmé 1988, p 44.)

This strophe should begin with mirrors. I wish to watch you asking me: what is it that makes a mirror, from certain perspectives (you can guess some that I have in mind), so like a text? Perhaps this: it cannot be seen. For very few of us can be certain, strictly speaking, that mirrors exist; those who solve the problem are often terrified. Certainly, this was true of Mallarmé. I myself have never seen a mirror, any more than I have ever seen a text. I have spent hours staring until my eyelids clatter against their spherical children, desperately attempting to catch a glimpse of the mirror—but alas, I have never been entirely certain of seeing anything but the image obscuring its surface. I should also mention this: I used to fatigue myself unimaginably when reading, because I was in the habit of attempting to force all of my focus onto the argument, the rich sensuousness of the things and the ideas described; but it was futile, and I could never entirely see past the marks on the surface of the paper. When I was quite young—younger than I can remember—I believed that there was a world of space inside the mirror; but I was wrong. I will never forget my disappointment. I have attempted to convince myself that by removing a mirror from the wall or the countertop or the automobile or the hedgerow-corner or the periscope or the small case containing make-up or the interrogation room or the kaleidoscope or the funhouse or the laser or the camera or the telescope or the optometrist's office or the microscope or the mechanism of a photocopier, and by peering at it from the side, top, back, or some other angle, I could claim to have seen the mirror itself. I once did the same with a text- excitedly throwing open a book, latching my eyes without hesitation onto the page, the black and white marks that I saw there; in my enthusiasm, I even tore a page from the book, examined it from every angle; but this was not the *text*, I soon realized; the text itself both exceeded and eluded it. Likewise, it was merely some combination of metal, plastic, wood and glass. It certainly was not a mirror, for a mirror is something that consistently seems to be what it is not; and this, seen from the side, top, back, or some other angle, both seemed and was merely some combination of metal, plastic, wood and glass. Upon several occasions I have thought that I saw myself in a mirror; but further examination has always proven me mistaken. I have written about these incidents; later I have read them. I am uncertain which of the preceding clauses contain an accurate statement; perhaps they both do. I could tell that the figure I saw there was not myself; for I myself could move my eyes, while he or she would not. The text is always staring, it interrogates me. Perhaps you too, reader, have

> The silvering *(tain)*, which excludes transparency, and authorizes the invention of the mirror, is a trace of language
>
> -Jacques Derrida, *Psyche: Inventions of the Other* (1987). (Derrida 1991, p 214.)

> The single diagonal cut on his forehead is not enough; one cannot traverse a mirror with impunity, it is not possible; everyone would have felt more reassured if they had been able to count numerous bloody injuries.
>
> [. . .]
>
> Why did Simon pick up the debris of the broken mirror and place it splinter by splinter on a large tea tray? Why, when he had done this, did he carry this, his work, with a gravity which already marked the face of Lord Patchogue more visibly than his own, this little pile of crystals and fragments into the bedroom of Muriel, who was already laid out barefoot, and place it on the bed?
>
> Why did Muriel begin to trample on the splinters of glass as if dancing, as if making a sacrifice, and, above all, despite the violence of her actions, why did her feet remain unscathed of any cuts?
>
> Only Lord Patchogue's forehead bled imperceptibly.
>
> Douglas went out in order to vomit. The others prayed.
>
> -Jacques Rigaut, *Lord Patchogue* (1934).
>
> (Cravan et. al. 2005, p. 93.)

had a similar experience, with a mirror. Furthermore, let us pose this question: does the image obscure the mirror itself from our sight? Yet without that image, the text would not be a text, merely some combination of metal, plastic, wood and glass. Does the image reside *in* the mirror? But the text is nothing *but* a surface. The image on the mirror *is* the text, and that image is impossible without it. A mirror, like a text, is something you can only feel. On the twenty-fourth of July, 1924, in the home of Cecil Stewart, the Dada Jacques Rigaut passed briefly into the other side of the mirror—became a reflection. You can see why this alone should give him an eminent place in the canon of the Yellow Sign; especially if we see this mirror as a present (I use this word to distinguish it from *absent*) metaphor. In passing into the mirror, Rigaut passed into text; or at least, passed into the passing into text, metonymically.

Furthermore, you will note that if one accepts the above hypothesis, in parentheses as it were, then the 'real' mirror was in fact being rendered a metaphor that was a surrogate for an *abstract* (or provisional) textuality, which does not 'exist', reversing the habitual direction of the metaphoric process on a phenomenological level; the tangible exists merely in order to point toward the linguistic. Here again is one trace of the Yellow Sign, one which is at play in the explosion of the Yellow Sign out of literary technique or poetics and into the *inscription* of life on the world. Rigaut describes the act of passing through the mirror, of becoming the reflection—that substanceless, depthless thing—in *Lord Patchogue*:

> Lord Patchogue and his reflection slowly advance toward each other. They consider each other in silence, they come to a halt, they bow.
> A great dizziness seizes hold of Lord Patchogue. It was brief, easily done, and magical: forehead first, he suddenly springs forwards. He strikes the glass, which shatters, but there he is on the other side. Everyone had stood up.
> The marvelous is not rare, incredulity is stronger than miracles. Miracles have difficulty in recruiting witnesses amongst the small number of people prepared to subscribe to the supernatural. Lord Patchogue was the first to be unsure that he had crossed the threshold.
> (Cravan et al 2005, p 92.)

In penetrating the surface of the mirror—which is to say (as borne out in *Lord Patchogue*), in inhabiting it—Rigaut was participating in several prominent motifs within the *social* literature of the Yellow Sign. (You will note, too, that the unstable tense of the events described—past, past perfect, present—not only mirrors *Maldoror*, but in a subtle way also re-injected into this potentially naturalized narrative the a-temporal logic of play that, in microcosm, was involved in the (from a Realist perspective) extra-textual act that he 'himself' carries out.) (I beg you to note, at the same time, that the 'fictionalization', the bracketing of this experience (or its articulation) as an artistic creation, represents another process—metonymic again—that enacts a passage from the 'real' world of the subject into the 'fictional' world of the text.) In fact, it might not be mere

> Touch my forehead. Good! Now look at your fingers, they are stained with my blood.
>
> It is the conventions of language which make me say my *forehead* and my *blood*. If I doubt *my* existence, it is not existence I wish to contest, only that it should be mine. The usage of possessive pronouns is forbidden me.
>
> -Jacques Rigaut, *Lord Patchogue* (1934).
> (Cravan et. al. 2005, p. 87.)

Max Klinger, *On Death, Part II: Philosopher* (1898-1909). (Klinger 1977, p 72.)

chance, but rather Objective Chance, that the Dada movement itself, in which Rigaut was a participant, was born at the Cabaret Voltaire, which was located, as we all know, at 1 Spiegelgasse—which translates, of course, as 'Mirror Lane'. By the time of Rigaut's writing, mirrors had also become a prominent motif within the *inscribed* literature of the Yellow Sign. For instance, Jarry, on the forty-fifth page of Atlas Press' edition of *Days and Nights*, refers to his own literary self-projection, Sengle, as 'He who was scared of mirrors'.

Lautréamont too had written on the mirror; and furthermore, his treatment serves me with another example (I have bypassed so many!) of an inscribed codification, or perhaps I might venture to say treatment, of a mythic theme. In the Fourth Canto, Fifth Strophe of *Maldoror*, we find a first-person harangue against the reader, who may or may not (the question is discussed at some length) have been scalped at some earlier date. The first-person, *Maldoror*, does not recognize the second-person, the reader. But he warns: 'Whoever you are, defend yourself; for I am going to hurl at you the sling of a terrible accusation: those eyes are not yours...' He speculates:

> Who then has scalped you? If it was a human being—because you incarcerated him for twenty years in a prison—and who escaped so as to prepare a revenge worthy of his reprisals, he has done as he should, and I applaud him; but—and there is a but—he was not harsh enough.

Two pages later however, in continuing this dialogue with you, *Maldoror* recognizes you at last:

> Let us seek this undiscoverable body, which, however, my eyes perceive; from me it deserves innumerable signs of my sincere admiration. The phantom mocks me: he helps me search for his own body. If I motion him to stay where he is, he makes the identical sign back... The secret is out. But not, I must frankly add, to my greatest satisfaction.

Here we can see Lautréamont describing in the mirror the *tangible absence* which, I have suggested, characterizes the text; for he does not look *at* the body in the mirror, he looks *for* it (as you, my reader, are doing now). And through his unsatisfying (and thus desire-ridden) realisation that the object of his scorn ('I am not as evil as you: that is why your genius bows down before mine... Really, I am not as evil as you.') is in fact the reader yourself (the mirror-image of himself, the writer)—that you and I coincide—he confirms, through the trope of the mirror, the annihilation of the subject that lies latent in the text. Furthermore, *Maldoror* goes on to read:

> What's left for me to do is to smash that mirror into smithereens with the help of a rock...
> This is not the first time that the nightmare of temporary loss of memory took residence in
> my imagination when, by the inflexible laws of optics, I happen to be confronted with the
> failure to recognise my own reflection!

I believe I have explained already the a-temporality inherent in the text, to which the passage above can be seen to refer. Let us also remember that Lord Patchogue (he who is ~~not~~ Jacques Rigaut) passed into the mirror (as Lautréamont, I have argued, passed virtually into text) *by smashing it to pieces*. The shattering that *Maldoror* describes here might then be an act calculated not to *regain* memory, but to fulfill the promise of complete temporal annihilation. And let me now remind you that we have been told that Baudelaire often donned a wig, as Lautréamont discusses the possibility of his interlocutor (or intralocutor) doing; and let me remind you too that in his final days he was often seen to greet his own unrecognisable image in the mirror, he converses with it, he is cannier than many of us. How much of Baudelaire is here in *Maldoror*? And in light of the most recent passage I have imported from the strophe in question into my own text, it is important to take note that it is the mirror that serves as the active agent of this annihilation of both memory and subjectivity; it does not *reflect* a loss of memory, it *induces* it. Reflection is a state of a-causal *induction*. The loss of memory, the dissemination of self, is merely the reflection of the text of the mirror. Rigaut practiced mythically, that is *actually*, what Lautréamont and so many others and so many others had, and would, practice in writing, that is *literally*.

-Olchar E. Lindsann, *The Yellow Sign*.

           gazed at mirror and said the
rorrim sucol .ohw now ?

-John M. Bennett, BACKWORDS (2007).
(Bennett 2007, p 37.)

Disheartened and dismayed, the prophet did indeed pull the magnifier from his pocket. A mirror, incidentally, which had the girth of the Ferris wheels that can be seen at fairs. The exquisitely polished glass was mounted in silver and elegantly affixed to a long wooden handle. He raised the mirror high above his head in a tragic pose, suddenly soared aloft, smashed the mirror, the shards clattered, and he vanished in the yellow seas of the evening.

But the splinters from the magic glass sliced through the houses, sliced through the people, the cattle, the tightroperies, the pit tunnels and all the unbelievers, so that the count of the gelded mounted from day to day.

-Hugo Ball, *Tenderenda the Fantast* (wr. 1914-20.)   (Ball et. al. 1995, p 94.)

Now as I consider the person who is about to be my son, as the mirror in which he is to view himself from morning to night, and by which he is to adjust his looks, his carriage, and perhaps the innermost sentiments of his heart,—I would have one, Yorick, if possible, polished at all points, fit for my child to look into.—This is very good sense, quoth my uncle Toby to himself.

-Laurence Sterne, *Tristram Shandy* (1760-67).   (Sterne 1996, p 290.)

-Gustave Moreau, *Hesiod and the Muse* (1857). (Moreau 1999, p 59.)

In the course of his peregrinations around London, the young De Quincey, who made it a philosophical policy to converse familiarly with anyone—man, woman, or child—that he might meet, fell into a platonic romance with a sixteen-year-old prostitute, Ann,[63] an adorable creature full of tenderness and innocence. Baudelaire dreamed of plucking 'a feather from an angel's wing' with which to describe all the love and desperation that bound those two together. 'Poor Ann,' recounted Marcel Schwob, 'ran to Thomas De Quincey… as he stumbled in wide Oxford Street under the hefty street lamps. Her eyes brimming with tears, she held a glass of port wine to his lips, kissed and caressed him; then she disappeared once more into the night. She might have died not long afterward. "She was coughing," said De Quincey, "the last time I saw her." Perhaps she was still wandering the streets. But although he looked high and low, although he was ridiculed by all he approached, Ann was lost forever. When later he had a warm house to live in, he often thought with tears in his eyes that poor Ann should have been living there, with him, instead of (as he imagined her) being ill, or dying, or desperate, in the central darkness of a London brothel. She had taken with her all the pitiful love that was in his heart.'

Lost forever? No, for at least she returned seventeen years later to haunt his opium-eater's dreams (it was only in 1812 that he began using drugs, to overcome the suffering caused by his long earlier experience of hunger). Her luminous apparition again calmed the torments of utter perdition that are, in De Quincey, the terrible underside of 'the most astonishing, the most complicated, the most splendid vision.'

-André Breton, *Anthology of Black Humor* (1945), pp 54-55.

Note that above, Breton incorporates into his *own* treatment of De Quincey a part of the version encoded by Marcel Schwob in his *The Book of Monelle*. While for Breton, this is a straightforward engagement with the myth of another figure, in Schwob's case the treatment of the De Quincey mythos is more complex, for Schwob is *himself* actively engaged in expanding the motif that De Quincey has founded. Baudelaire had begun quite early to expand upon the motif suggested by De Quincey's urban muse in a relatively diffused manner. Schwob, however, was returning to a more traditional and centralized treatment of the motif in his own relationship with a young consumptive prostitute whose given name was Louise, but whom he figured as Monelle in the book dedicated to her, published after her death, from which Breton's excision is taken. (Gourmont 1994, p 282.) Therefore, Schwob was not only presenting one version of the De Quincey—Ann legend, he was also

---

[63] Please note: Poe's *For Annie* ⇒ Anna Blume of Schwitters ⇒ Antonia of Dujardin ⇒ Ann of De Quincey ⇒ St. Anne of Jarry.

constructing a carefully inflected context through which his own engagement with this particular mythic tradition could take form and through which it might be viewed. In re-writing De Quincey he was, in part, re-writing himself as well, and also Baudelaire and all others who had participated in this tradition inscribed in life, or would—whether leaving traces and impressions in books (like he and Baudelaire) or allowing their writing to withdraw *entirely* with the dissolutions of their personalities and immediate social circles.

All of these figures merge, caught midway between unity and multiplicity.

Mallarmé's sonnet *Tomb* was written in commemoration of the first anniversary of Verlaine's death, in 1897, and may be the last poem that Mallarmé ever completed (Mallarmé 1996, p 226); in it we find Mallarmé making an immediate intervention in the myth-making process while it is still in its nascent stage; in contrast to his re-working of established themes in his treatment of the established figure of Baudelaire, he is attempting to *set* the themic complex of the Verlaine figure, to rescue it from the threat of insensitive and irresponsible interpretations that might mar the future development of the Verlaine myth:

Anniversary—January 1897

The black rock raging that the wind has rolled
It won't be stayed even for pious hands
Feeling its likeness to the woes of man
As if to bless in it some fatal mould.

Here often if the ringdove's tale be told
This cloudy grief in nubile folds descends
Upon the ripened star the future sends
Whose scintillations silvercoat the crowd.

Who seeks, pursuing the reclusive bound
Till now exclusive of our vagabond—
Verlaine? He's hidden in the wooly sward

Only to find naively in accord
His lip not drinking there or bating breath
A shallow stream calumniated death.

Mallarmé has recognized that Verlaine's alcoholism will inevitably come into play in the construction of his myth. And the vision of Verlaine as a once-promising poet degenerated into a weak-willed, unstable reprobate is indeed one—though thanks partly to Mallarmé not the *only* one—that has persisted; this version of the Verlaine myth typically places narrative emphasis on his fabled relationship with the equally volatile but dominant (and dominating) Rimbaud, which ended with Verlaine putting a bullet through his arm (one of the earliest appearances of the Pistol motif that would continue to grow in prominence at least until the Surrealist period, and which would be internalized in one sense by the Situationists). Mallarmé, however, could not be expected to show a great deal of interest in relegating the Verlaine figure to that of hapless straightman in the Rimbaud mythos. The incidents upon which the Rimbaud cycle hinge operate, for the most part, without detailed or specific reference to the creative register; while Rimbaud was writing a social myth at the same time that he was inscribing written texts, the social myth largely excluded the involvement of textuality, the drive to poetic inscription was not *itself* inscribed within the social myth; Rimbaud need not have been an artist at all to have acted as he did. Rimbaud, in the standard presentations of his myth (which were already well under formation by the end of the century), displayed neither the Anti-heroic, degenerate *stoicism*, the systematic exploration of self-destructive revolt epitomized by Baudelaire; nor the sustained theological hermeticism of Mallarmé himself; his mythmaking, from a Mallarméan perspective, was insensitive and irresponsible. One can imagine little sympathy on Mallarmé's part toward a poet who had abandoned the vocation of poetry, shirking its responsibility and letting his potential for that vital process go to waste in a spurt of adolescent rebellion; and he would be little content to allow Verlaine, a personal friend whose dedication to the Yellow Sign had been consistently demonstrated, to become what he is in these versions of the Rimbaud myth—a sad reflection of Rimbaud's apostasy, stripped of the latter's dynamism, youthful force, and unflinching dedication to that apostasy itself.

This attitude toward Rimbaud was certainly at play with certain inductees who were particularly interested in the responsible transmission of the Yellow Sign. In *The Book of Masks* (published within a year of Mallarmé's sonnet), Gourmont, while recognizing through his very inclusion of Rimbaud that his myth is too prominent to be ignored, reprimands him thoroughly, discussing him as if it is an unpleasant duty, devoting the required measure of text to an attack upon that very duty, saying that 'Rimbaud had that sort of talent that interests us without pleasing us.' (Gourmont 1994, p 122.) Like Mallarmé, he downplays the story of his relationship to Verlaine, calling it dryly 'the little misunderstanding that separated them.' He goes on to suggest that his myth, unlike that even more mysterious writer Lautréamont, whom Gourmont himself had discovered, is in fact worse than obscurity—closing with a thinly veiled judgment regarding his relationship with Verlaine:

> It is unfortunate that his life, so imperfectly understood, could not be a true *vita abscondita*; what there is of it that can be understood, disgusts us. Rimbaud was like one of those women who fail to surprise us by announcing in a brothel that they will embrace religion; but what is still more revolting to us, he seems to have been a jealous and a passionate mistress: here the aberration becomes debauched, because sentimental.
> (*ibid.*)

Almost fifty years later, in his *Anthology of Black Humor* (a successor to Gourmont's anthology), Breton would also criticize Rimbaud's apostasy: 'We shall ignore his later years, in which the puppet gained the upper hand, in which a pathetic buffoon waved his golden sash every other minute, and consider only the Rimbaud of

1871-72, a veritable god of puberty such as no mythology had ever seen.' (Breton 1997, p 164.) He adds on the following page that Jacques Vaché too found Rimbaud 'childish and disappointing'.

It is not surprising then that in this sonnet Mallarmé has chosen the theme of Addiction—which does at least have a respectable heritage—to treat, without reference to the Rimbaudian cycle. But while Mallarmé recognized this thematic correspondence between Poe and Verlaine, he also recognized that, due to the very familiarity of the person of Verlaine himself to the young artists who would carry on the Yellow Sign, it could not be treated in the same way it had been in the sonnet to Poe. Unlike Poe, who within the social networks then constituting the nervous system of the Yellow Sign had never existed *except* as a myth and who could therefore be unproblematically grasped as one, Verlaine would have to be *ushered* into his mythic status, at least if one was to avoid as the dominating aspect his tumultuous relationship with Rimbaud and the consequent positioning of his later degeneracy as a *falling out* from myth.

Indeed, this might explain in part the predominance of the latter version, since very few if any of the young generation Mallarmé was transmitting the mythology to had met Rimbaud or had known Verlaine in his youth; unlike Verlaine's projected self/Poe, he had in this sense grown *out* of myth and *into* life. The artists to whom, in its role as social document, the sonnet was addressed, were accustomed to a Verlaine not yet passed through the alembic of the mythologizing process; theirs was a Verlaine of *gossip,* and his alcoholism was thus firmly situated, when Mallarmé sat down to this poem, as a sordid failure of will, little different from the other drunks populating their habitual meeting-places; the only difference was that this drunk *used* to be Verlaine. It was Mallarmé's task, as mythologizing psychopomp, to make him Verlaine again; and, not surprisingly, he did this by passing Verlaine, quite literally, into text, by discovering Verlaine *in himself.*

Mallarmé, in the penultimate tercet, recognizes this sense of Verlaine—the mythic Verlaine—having disappeared, replaced by the man his inducted readers remember from the pubs:

> Who seeks, pursuing the reclusive bound
> Till now external of our vagabond—
> Verlaine?

Even within this recognition, however, he re-figures Verlaine's position in relation to that social group; he is 'our' vagabond, 'Till now external'. Where is he then? As Mallarmé's translator Weinfield explains in the notes to his translation on page 226, 'Verlaine has disappeared into his *name* and has become his name: *verte, laine,* green wool'.

In order to make this homophonic association manifest in the English, Weinfield has, as you can see, rendered the phrase as 'wooly sward', but in the original Verlaine does indeed vanish literally into his name, as one might vanish into one's reflection in a mirror. Verlaine the subject, as manifested in his Sign, has *become* his Sign. In fact the line in which this transference itself is played out—a subtle, perhaps indistinguishable, but nonetheless hugely consequential *disappearance,* as I hope Lautréamont, Rigaut, and Mallarmé have convinced you—places Verlaine (Verlaine the projected subject and Verlaine the amalgamation of letters) on either end of the line, facing each other, each bracketed off from the words separating them by marks of punctuation, thus:

Verlaine? Il est caché parmi l'herbe, Verlaine

Through Mallarmé, Verlaine has undergone the same annihilation that Mallarmé himself underwent, like so many others and so many others, before a mirror. And on the other side (both sides), having internalized the 'reclusive bound', having passed beyond, questioned and transformed it, we find Verlaine, now passed into myth in the final tercet, 'His lip not drinking there'. Of course, the Verlaine of myth, at least in every version I myself have heard, dear reader, *does* indeed drink. Nonetheless this statement marks an important difference in the way that the Addiction theme has been situated previously, by both Mallarmé and Baudelaire, both of them treating a figure who came to them already inescapably mythologized. Baudelaire's Addict bears his addiction as a mark of pride, carries it next to his breast up to the moment of death as he marches into the withering blast of ennui in his struggle against his society; Mallarmé's Poe bears his wound of Addiction stoically, it is paradoxically the Sign of his position within and without the society from which he is excluded. But for Verlaine this Addiction is a thing *to escape*. In this sense, Mallarmé's Verlaine is humanized to a much greater degree than Poe, he is positioned in a space midway between the abstracted, thoroughly Symbolic Poe/t and the grimy old man of the pubs. Mallarmé is meeting his audience half-way, presenting for them not a mythologized Verlaine fully formed in opposition to another mythologized Verlaine with which they are already familiar; rather, he is presenting them with a cipher for the *mythologizing process itself*. The entire poem in fact underscores the immediacy of its subject, and its position within a community for whom Verlaine was in fact a *subject* as well as a *figure*; this is first signaled by it's heading, which contrasts the relative timelessness of the sonnet on Poe by situating the poem at the historical moment of its application. And throughout the poem the mourners of Verlaine, their 'pious hands', are active participants, the community itself is heavily inscribed within the poem itself, as 'This cloudy grief in nubile folds descends / Upon the ripened star the future sends / Whose scintillations silvercoat the crowd' of initiates who will, in their turn, create that very future. This community is inseparable, ultimately, from Verlaine himself.

In this way we can see Mallarmé not only engaging with the Verlaine figure early in its most crucial phase of development—immediately following the death of Verlaine the subject—he is also, and more importantly, offering to younger generations of the Yellow Sign a *lesson*, a lesson he had learned decades earlier, when he forgot himself for several months before the mirror: that the subject and the myth are not two distinct terms to be exchanged, but two poles of a space to be traversed, navigated, inhering in one another.

-Olchar E. Lindsann, *The Yellow Sign*.

-Max Ernst, from *Une Semaine de Bonté* (1934). (Ernst 1976, p 95.)

The man who is unable to people his solitude is equally unable to be alone in a bustling crowd.

    -Charles Baudelaire, *Paris Spleen* (1869).   (Baudelaire 1970, p 20.)

I know not whether my reader is aware that many children, perhaps most, have a power of painting, as it were, upon the darkness, all sorts of phantoms; in some, that power is simply a mechanic affection of the eye; others have a voluntary, or semi-voluntary power to dismiss or to summon them; or, as a child once said to me when I questioned him on this matter, "I can tell them to go, and they go; but sometimes they come when I don't tell them to come." Whereupon I told him that he had almost as unlimited command over apparitions, as a Roman centurion over his soldiers.

    -Thomas De Quincey, *Confessions of an English Opium-Eater* (1821).   (De Quincey 1995, p 60.)

I used to lay awake at night as a child and get more entertainment and terror out of blank walls and plain furniture than most children could find at a toy-store.

    -Charlotte Perkins Gilman, *The Yellow Wallpaper* (1892).   (Blair 2002, p 145.)

(1897)
First contact with hallucinations: measles. Fear of death and destructive forces. A fever vision, inspired by a panel of imitation mahogany opposite the foot of the bed. The grain of the wood gradually took on the appearance of an eye, a nose, a bird's head, a 'menacing nightingale', a spinning top, and so on. It is certain that little Max enjoyed being plagued by such visions. And later he voluntarily induced similar hallucinations by staring at wooden panels, clouds, wallpaper and unpainted walls in order to allow his imagination free play.

    -Max Ernst, *Autobiography*.   (Richter 1997, pp 157-158.)

The front pattern *does* move- and no wonder! That woman behind shakes it!

Sometimes I think there are a great may women behind, and sometimes only one, and she crawls around fast, and her crawling shakes it all over.

Then in the very bright spots she keeps still, and in the very shady spots she just takes hold of the bars and shakes them hard.

And she is all the time trying to climb through. But nobody could climb through that pattern—it strangles so; I think that is why it has so many heads.

-Charlotte Perkins Gilman, *The Yellow Wallpaper* (1892). (Blair 2002, p 152.)

-Max Ernst, from *Une Semaine de Bonté* (1934). (Ernst 1976, p 119.)

even later Max identified himself with 'Loplop, the Superior of Birds'. This phantom remained inseparable from another, called *Perterbation ma soeur, la femme 100 têtes*.

-Max Ernst, *Autobiography*. (Richter 1997, pp 158.)

BEUYS:

There is this experience, a kind of waking dream, which keeps recurring for two years. An experience where… I'm sitting on the roof, on the ridge of the roof. And… I'm repeatedly being told by this figure, coming from outside, I don't know how you'd describe it today, well, naively put, one could describe it as a kind of angel, which said to me over and over: you're the Prince of the Roof. So, quite simply, this sentence came to me stereotypically again and again, until the moment when its meaning became clear to me—that the roof is the head. That wasn't said, it came out of this hallucination or daydream, that happened while playing; I was still very small.

[. . .]

[A hallucination] always in a stereotypical form, repeated over the course of an entire period. I am running across a meadow, in Cleves, an image, and there the train passes [. . .] A completely empty meadow, with only the train on the horizon, actually not so far away, but at that moment forming a horizon, as a line. The train stops, a man gets out, dressed completely in black, with a top hat on, approaches me—and says, "I tried with my means, now you try with your means—alone!"

JAPPE:

How old were you?

BEUYS:

Oh, about seven or so, perhaps a little older.

-Joseph Beuys, 1976. (Ray 2001, p 192.)

It took me awhile to explain. It wasn't easy to put into words. The best I could do was liken my father's presence there in the kitchen to a kind of ghostly illusion. At that age, 16, I had not yet encountered the term for *autonomous psychic projection*, hadn't yet learned that the word for such a phenomena was "tulpa".

"I don't think he's really there," I told Carol in a low voice.

"Why do you say that? He looks, right now, there enough to me."

"Yes, but I happen to know that, right now, he's really three hundred miles away. He's a patient at the Army Psychiatric Hospital, in Battle Creek, Michigan."

-Blaster Al Ackerman, Introduction to R. Wondolowski's *The Incredible Sleeping Man* (2006).

(Ackerman 2006, p 45.)

According to Schwitters (as recorded by Nill), "Else had been his favorite playmate until she became a teenager and then Schwitters was no longer able to play with her [. . .] One summer night in Isernhagen (the same place where he had his ill-fated garden), he woke up in the dark of night and saw Else hover in front of him in a long, white lace gown. The following day a death announcement appeared in the paper: Else had died suddenly at age 18 of blood poisoning.

-Elisabeth Burns Gamard, *Kurt Schwitters' Merzbau: The Cathedral of Erotic Misery* (2000).

(Gamard 2000, p 80.)

a single character may move about in an atmosphere deformed by his own hallucinations, his temperament: the only *reality* resides in this deformation.

-Jean Moréas, *The Symbolist Manifesto* (1886). (Caws 2001, p 51.)

In the earliest of these visitations, when [William Blake] was four years old, God looked through the window at him and set him screaming. When he was eight or ten he saw a tree filled with angels, bright wings shining from every bough. He naturally reported this to his father, and the honest hosier threatened to spank him for lying.

-David Perkins, *English Romantic Writers* (1967). (Perkins 1967, p 37.)

(1909)

Excursions into the world of prodigies, chimaeras, phantoms, poets, monsters, mountains, poisons, mathematics, etc. A book he wrote at this time was never published. His father found it and burned it. Its title: *Diverse Tagebuchblätter* ('Diverse Pages from my Journal').

-Max Ernst, *Autobiography* (Richter 1997, p 158.)

One can go so far as to believe that there exists above him, on the animal scale, beings whose behavior is as strange to him as his may be to the mayfly or the whale. Nothing necessarily stands in the way of these creatures' being able to completely escape man's sensory system of references through a camouflage of whatever sort one cares to imagine, though the possibility of such camouflage is posited only by the *theory of forms* and the study of mimetic animals. There is no doubt that there is ample room for speculation here, even though this idea ends to place man in the same modest conditions of interpretation of his own universe as the child who is pleased to form his conception of an ant from its underside just after he's kicked over an anthill… it would not be impossible, in the course of a vast work over which the most daring sort of induction should never cease to preside, to approximate the structure and constitution of such hypothetical beings (which mysteriously reveal themselves to us when we are afraid and when we are conscious of the workings of chance) to the point where they become credible.

-André Breton, *Prolegomena to a Third Surrealist Manifesto or Not* (1942). (Breton 1972, p 293.)

Reading or dreaming, he would soak himself in solitude until nightfall; by dint of always mulling over the same thoughts his mind became more concentrated and his as yet indeterminate ideas matured.

-J.-K. Huysmans, *A Rebours* (1884). (Huysmans 1998, p 5.)

I had been in my youth, and even since, for occasional amusement, a great reader of Livy, whom, I confess, I prefer, both for style and for matter, to any other of the Roman historians; and I had often felt as solemn and appalling sounds, and most emphatically representative of the majesty of the Roman people, the two words so often occurring in Livy, *Consul Romanus*; especially when the consul is introduced in his military character. I mean to say, that the words king—sultan—regent, &c. or any other titles of those whom embody in their own persons the collective majesty of a great people, had less power over my reverential feelings. I had also, though no great reader of history, made myself minutely and critically familiar with one period of English history, viz. the period of the Parliamentary War, having been attracted by the moral grandeur of some who figured in that day, and by the many interesting memoirs which survive those unquiet times. Both these parts of my lighter reading, having furnished me often with matter of reflection, now furnished me with matter for my dreams. Often I used to see, after painting upon the blank darkness a sort of rehearsal whilst waking, a crowd of ladies, and perhaps a festival, and dances. And I heard it said, or I said to myself, "these are English ladies from the unhappy times of Charles I. These are the wives and the daughters of those who met in peace, and sate at the same tables, and were allied by marriage or by blood; and yet, after a certain day in August, 1642, never smiled upon each other again, nor met but in the field of battle; and at Marston Moor, at Newbury, or at Naseby, cut asunder all ties of love by the cruel sabre, and washed away in blood the memory of ancient friendship."—The ladies danced, and looked as lovely as the court of George IV. Yet I knew, even in my dream, that they had been in the grave for nearly two centuries.—This pageant would suddenly dissolve; and, at a clapping of hands, would be heard the heart-quaking sound of *Consul Romanus*: and immediately came 'sweeping by,' in gorgeous paludiments, Paullus and Marius, girt around by a company of centurions, with the crimson tunic hoisted on a spear, and followed by the *alalagmos* of the Roman legions.

-Thomas De Quincey, *Confessions of an English Opium-Eater* (1821.) (De Quincey 1995, pp 61-62.)

"You see, I shall assist the drug. Before I swallow this pellet I shall give my undivided attention to the geometric and algebraic symbols that I have traced on this paper." He raised the mathematical chart that rested on his knee. "I shall prepare my mind for an excursion into time. . . This mathematical knowledge, this conscious approach to an actual apprehension of the fourth dimension of time will supplement the work of the drug. The drug will open up stupendous new vistas—the mathematical preparation will enable me to grasp them intellectually. I have often grasped the fourth dimension in dreams, emotionally, intuitively, but I have never been able to recall, in waking life, the occult splendors that were momentarily revealed to me."

-Frank Belknap Long, *The Hounds of Tindalos* (1929).   (Carter1971, p 218.)

Detectives are our cockades, and we say the "gadji beri bimba" as our bedtime prayer.

-Hugo Ball, *Tenderenda the Fantast* (wr. 1915-1920).   (Ball et. al. 1995, p 144.)

> I'll lock up all the doors and shutters neat and tight,
> And build a fairy palace for myself at night.
> So I will dream of bright horizons in the blue
> Where fountains weep in pools of alabaster hue,
> Of kisses in the glades, where the birds sing night and day,
> Of all to make an idyll in a childish way.
> Riot, that rages vainly at my window glass,
> Will never make me raise my forehead from the task,
> Since I am plunged in this voluptuous delight—
> Of conjuring the spring with all the poet's might,
> Of hauling forth a sun out of my heart, with care
> Transmuting furious thoughts to gently breathing air.

-Charles Baudelaire, *Landscape* (1857).

(Baudelaire 1993, p 167.)

Helpful suggestion: before falling asleep imagine with the greatest clarity the terminal state of a suicide who at last wishes to plumb the depths of self-awareness with a bullet. But you will only succeed if you have first made yourself ridiculous. Highly ridiculous. Terribly ridiculous. Ridiculous beyond all measure. So appallingly ridiculous that everything becomes equally ridiculous.

-Walter Serner, *Last Loosening Manifesto* (1917). (Ball et. al. 1995, p 159.)

After the premier of *Ubu Roi*, we are told, Jarry tried to merge with his creation come what may—but what creation *was* that?

-André Breton, *Anthology of Black Humor* (1945). (Breton 1997, p 212.)

Jarry, confusing in a perpetual hallucination his own existence with that of Père Ubu, identifying himself with his creation in every detail, to the point of forgetting his civil status, signifies the eruption of life into humour, the supreme value of 'those who know': that humour which he managed to exude with his last breath.

-Maurice Nadeau, *The History of Surrealism* (1964). (Nadeau 1973, p 77.)

As [Blake] walked through the streets of the city or the green fields around he saw angels and talked with spirits, and in later years he always spoke of his paintings as "copied" from the visionary world and of his poetry as having been "dictated" to him.

-David Perkins, *English Romantic Writers* (1967). (Perkins 1967, p 37.)

Ernst claimed to have a bird-headed visitant named Loplop (often portrayed in his work) who made revelations to him.

-Publisher's Note to re-print of *Une Semaine de Bonté*, first published 1934.   (Ernst 1976, p vii.)

A new myth? Must these beings be convinced that they result from a mirage or must they be given the chance to show themselves?

-André Breton, *Prolegomena to a Third Surrealist Manifesto or Not* (1942).   (Breton 1972, p 294.)

For several successive days his brain teemed with paradoxes, with fine distinctions, with a mass of petty quibbles, a tangle of rules as complicated as articles in a legal code, open to every interpretation, to every play upon words, resulting in a kind of celestial law of the most subtle and most elaborate kind; then in their turn the abstractions faded away, giving place to the visual, under the influence of the Gustave Moreaus hanging on his walls.

He saw a whole procession of prelates walking past: archimandrites and patriarchs raising their golden arms to bless the kneeling crowds, their white beards moving up and down as they read or prayed; he saw silent columns of penitents descending into gloomy crypts; he saw vast cathedrals rising up, where white-robed monks thundered from the pulpit. Just as De Quincey, after smoking a little opium, would, on hearing the words 'Consul Romanus', conjure up entire passages from Livy, would watch the consuls solemnly processing and the stately array of the Roman armies beginning their march, he, upon hearing some theological expression, would be left gasping, seeing surging crowds, and priestly presences silhouetted against a background of golden basilicas; these visions held him spellbound, extending through the ages right up to the present-day religious ceremonies, cocooning him in infinite swathes of mournful, tender music.

-J.-K. Huysmans, *Against Nature* (1884).   (Huysmans 1998, pp 67-68.)

CONSUL ROMANUS! enthused De Quincey; the brains, purples, and laticlaves! Valens remains handsome as the upright of the imperatorial toga; his curls uncoil their springy ringlets like nocturnal serpents; and, with kepi flung down in the mud, his face glows with the pale gold from an electric sun or a ball of lightning.

-Alfred Jarry, *Days & Nights* (1897.) (Jarry 1989, pp73-74.)

For since Maury proved that dreams can be tamed, guided by the will, since De Quincey the opium eater and Poe analyzed the sensations of the drug addict and the alcoholic, it has been proved that for any observer sufficiently master of himself to watch himself think there is a deep and inexhaustible mine to be exploited... these infinitesimal shifts in cerebral conception are what is interesting to record.

-Jules Lermina, *Histoires incroyables* (1885). (Pierrot 1981, p. 163.)

We can say that after Jarry, much more than after Wilde, the distinction between art and life, long considered necessary, found itself challenged and wound up being annihilated in principle.

André Breton, *Anthology of Black Humor* (1945). (Breton 1997, p 212.)

'Then there is this whole matter of incubacy. She admits quite freely to cohabiting, in her dreams, with the living and the dead.

-J.-K. Huysmans, *Là-Bas* (1891). (Huysmans 2001, pp 136-137.)

For what is mind but motion in the intellectual sphere? The essence of thought, as the essence of life, is growth. You must not be frightened by my words, Ernest. What people call insincerity is simply a method by which we can multiply our personalities.

-Oscar Wilde, *The Critic as Artist* (1890). (Wilde 1999, pp 228-229.)

Jarry's first published novel, *Days and Nights*, is generally considered an autobiographical account of his 13-months as an army conscript. It is less universally recognised as a codification of his initiation into the practice, or subjective position, or what we might in this case term the *Pataphysical state* toward which we are speculating.

The character Sengle is generally recognised as Jarry's literary self-projection in this work.[64] As Alastair Brotchie notes however, 'the identification of Valens with the poet Léon-Paul Fargue is more problematical.' (Jarry 1989, p 8.)

While Jarry's ex-lover is certainly at play in the character Valens, there is an evident unknown term—Brotchie and others conclude that other (unknown) partners are also present in the character of Valens; we would speculate, however, that the matter is much more complex. Valens may, while indeed encompassing the *influence* of a number of people, also be in fact a literal presentation of an individual who lived outside of that text; and who, furthermore, may not have existed at all.

Let me explain; please, bear with us.

This apparently impossible duality—identity and non-existence—is present in Jarry's ~~description~~ of Valens:

> he could not recollect Valens' face at all. Despite three or four photographs, one taken on his departure.[65] The eyes avoided him and the dumb mouth was as monstrous as the taxidermy of a bird.

---

64 As we shall show you, there are other, less recognised projections as well.

65 Is Sengle unable to perceive the faithful reproductions of Valens' features in these photographs? Or do these photographs inadequately re-present the features that Valens has? Or do they accurately present the lack of features that characterizes Valens?

> *In my immense grief-stricken solitude*
> *I sense my brother has forgotten me.*[66]
> *His dear face pales, his features all elude*
> *My grasp—and falsehood clouds my memory.*[67]
>
> *His portrait lies before me as I write.*
> *It's handsome—maybe ugly—who can tell?*
> *The simulacrum holds the grave's vain knell.*
> *His voice, once loved, no more rings clear and bright.*
>
> *That voice was generous—these posthumous*[68]
> *Unknown inflections add a rich new thrill:*
> *Unrecognised, but not anonymous,*
> *The broken touch of comfort's friendly quill.*
>
> He rediscovered a less elusive look and a mouth that for want of words brought a breathing likeness to an older picture of Valens taken five years earlier, almost a child still, in a black sailor suit, amid foliage.[69] And then he saw that he was perhaps mistaken and was looking at himself seven and a half years ago,[70] and that he must have murmured these verses before a mirror[71] which must have held his face without its aging.[72]
>
> (*ibid*, p 65-66.)

> children just don't exist. Children are only a transitory state before we become adults—an intermediary state which is consequently almost virtual. And so the photograph of me [as a child] that was published, sitting totally naked in a little wicker armchair, is a photo of a virtual object since it ceased to exist many years ago. If you prefer, it's a photo of an illusion—and a photo of an Illusion couldn't possibly shock anybody.
>
> -Boris Vian, 'Pataphysics? What's That? (1959.)
>
> (Vian 2006, p 16.)

Valens would seem to be simultaneously remembered and forgotten; real and abstract; to be himself and to be Sengle.

Jarry goes on:

> Sengle was discovering the true metaphysical cause of the happiness of loving: not the communion of two beings become one, like the two halves of man's heart which, in the foetus, is both double and separate; but more that enjoyment of anachronism and of communing with his[73] own past (Valens was doubtless in love with his own future, and

---

66 Is it not Sengle who has forgotten? Who is speaking or writing this poem? Is Sengle speaking Valens' voice?

67 Or is it Sengle after all? Might it be *both* simultaneously, speaking through each other?

68 Is Valens dead? He is *usually* treated as alive in the novel.

69 The clothing and the surroundings are described; Valens himself is not.

70 Once again, Valens and Sengle simultaneously.

71 This poem is an incantation.

72 Is this not what a camera is? But it is still a mirror…

73 not 'their'?

> perhaps that was why he loved with a more tentative violence, not yet having lived his future nor being able to understand it fully).
>
> (*ibid, p 66.*)

Sengle and Valens' love is now posited as the intersection of the temporal trajectories of their desire. But temporality itself is, in some unspecified way, disrupted or even negated in the course of the relationship between the two:

> It is admirable to live two moments of time simultaneously; this experience allows you to live out authentically one moment of eternity—or rather, all eternity, since it has no moments.[74]
>
> (*ibid.*)

Is it not clear that, *at the very least,* Valens is not so much a person as an *idea* of a person? To put it another way, that even within that framework of the story[75] which would render Sengle an 'actual' *person* rather than a *character,* Valens still retains the nature of a *character*—but one with whom Sengle interacts (or has interacted) *as* a person? And yet, one whom Sengle can also *be*, in a sense:

> Like his brother Valens,[76] whom he knows will be far away for ten months, Sengle the free distances himself from the soldier [that he is forced to become] and relives his past as Valens' present,[77] as impressions pleasing to him and hence the only ones true to his spirit.
>
> (*ibid, p 40.*)

Sengle, then, experiences life *as Valens* simultaneously with experiencing it as Sengle; he *is* Valens while also being Sengle. What is suggested here is a practice that goes beyond Huysmans' 'picturing' of other humans, and even beyond the practice of 'succubism' proposed by Courrière and possibly developed by the former; although in that practice the projected ~~person~~ is given individuality and an assumed 'interiority' constituting

---

74 Compare this statement to Bergson's conception of Time; Jarry regularly attended lectures by Bergson during the time that the latter was preparing that book, published one year prior to *Days and Nights.* (Jarry 2001, p 12.)

75 Assuming, *as we should not,* that we are expected to suspend our disbelief in relation to this story in a way different than in relation to our own lives…

76 Reading ahead to complete this passage, Valens relives Sengle's past as his own present within the same movement as Sengle reliving his own past through Valens' present.

77 To *live* the past as the *present* is of course they way we have conceptualised Huysmans' possible hallucinatory practice via Bergson's theory of memory. Moreover, if Valens can, as this statement would suggest, be the manifestation of Jarry's past *experienced as* present, than Jarry would represent Valens' future, thus further explicating why Jarry's 'lover' Valens is, 'doubtless in love with his own future'.

them not as image but as other, in Jarry's case we seem to find evidence that the *position of the subject* is itself mobile.

In the sense that Valens can be said to exist, he exists simultaneously in several places. Co-incidentally, Sengle 'learned that Valens had left France and was vegetating in fever-ridden India, about the same time as Sengle was cloistered inside the convict-hulk of the military snail.' (p. 65.) Twelve pages later, Sengle is confined to hospital; yet we find him 'going out yet again on his own time—although confined to barracks like all those reporting sick.' Soon, 'Sengle's prisoner's bed was borne away on the current down the irrigation ditch and swallowed by the little arch of the field's bridge, and he walked along the gilded road with Valens'—regardless of the former's confinement in hospital and the latter's present confinement in India—for a refreshing swim. (p. 78.)

This adventure takes place in the chapter titled 'Consul Romanus', a reference to the most deeply canonical passage in this possible tradition. The phrase itself is of course the one that served as a key for De Quincey, for whom:

> would be heard the heart-quaking sound of *Consul Romanus*: and immediately came 'sweeping by,' in gorgeous paludiments, Paullus and Marius, girt around by a company of centurions, with the crimson tunic hoisted on a spear, and followed by the *alalagmos* of the Roman legions.
>
> (De Quincey 1995, pp 61-62.)

Through this reference, within which (as the title) the entire swimming-trip with Valens is inscribed, this outing is brought into conjunction not only with De Quincey's hallucinatory practice—the conjuring of the imagined placed before the physical senses—but also with the entire tradition, through Baudelaire and Huysmans up to and including, most likely, this present of *our* writing, of the more-or-less systematic ~~literary~~ practice of such evocations, if of course such a tradition were to be posited.

It is, however, no mere literary conceit that that this hallucinatory practice (assuming of course that this is in fact what is being inscribed) is made much more difficult to identify or delineate, is more caught up with what we must accept as Sengle's experience of the *world*, than is the case with De Quincey, Baudelaire, or even Huysmans/Des Esseintes, where the artificiality of the vision, its difference from the banal 'real' world from which it is an escape, is privileged both in the terms of its discussion, and in the narrative structure of their representations of their lives—i.e. time is taken 'out' of their extra-hallucinatory lives to be devoted to this practice, it is not fully integrated *into* their lives. In the chapter entitled 'Pataphysics', Jarry explains that:

> I got used to elementary hallucination. I could very precisely see a mosque where there was a mere factory, a corps of drummer-boys made up of angels, ponycoaches on the highways of heavens, a living-room at the bottom of a lake— monsters, mysteries—the title of a vaudeville show set up real horrors before me.
>
> Then I'd justify my magic sophistries with the hallucinations of words!
>
> I ended up viewing the disorder of my mind as sacred.
>
> -Arthur Rimbaud, A Season in Hell (1873.) (Rimbaud 1991, p 37.)

he no longer made any distinction at all between his thoughts and actions nor between his dreaming and waking; and perfecting Leibnitz' definition, that perception is a hallucination which is true, he saw no reason not to say: hallucination is a perception which is false, or more exactly: *faint*, or better still: *foreseen* (*remembered* sometimes, which is the same thing).[78] [79] And he believed that above all there are neither nights nor days (despite this book's title, which is why it has been chosen), and that life is continuous; yet that life would never be aware of its continuity, nor even that life exists, without these pendulum movements; and life is primarily a beating of the heart. It is very important that there are heartbeats; but that the diastole is a rest for the systole, and that these little deaths support life, is merely a routine statement not an explanation, and Sengle did not give a damn for it and its formulator, some pedant or other.[80]

(Jarry 1989, p. 103.)

What we are proposing is as simple as this: perhaps Jarry meant and practiced *fully* and *routinely* what he wrote here. Perhaps any possible biography of Jarry could only ever touch *knowingly* upon *one* of his lives. Allow me to remind you that Jarry elsewhere stated that Pataphysics 'will explain the universe supplementary to this one; or, less ambitiously, will describe a universe which can be—and perhaps should be—envisaged in the place of a traditional one.' Or, we might hypothesize, simultaneous with or (to use a favourite term of Jarry's) *superinduced over* the traditional one.

You may see where I am heading here: does Valens represent a *'Pataphysical Subject'*? Is it possible that the character of Valens is not the condensation of several of Jarry's partners who are to be figured in the novel, but rather the literary projection of *a single individual*, existing 'Pataphysically', in the same sense as Sengle is a literary projection of Jarry himself—and that Jarry's memories of Fargue and the others were merely *material* out of which that ~~hallucinatory~~ individual emerged *as a discreet subject in Jarry's own life?* Is it possible even that

---

78 Note the way that the colons function in Jarry's sentence—as the reader (and the writer) passes through each one, Leibnitz' assertion is mirrored with a slight inflection or clinamen, restated in a different verbal form which, despite the modulation ostensibly playing purely on the *form* of the statement, brings the reader (and the writer) to a new understanding of the *import* of that assertion: by degrees, one is brought, by means of this system of reflected reflections, but also in stages as if through an alchemical act of purification, to a distinctly more radical appreciation of the statement: the mechanisms of a subtle and intelligent sophistry, which—when reflected yet deeper and enacted on the level of cognitive structures themselves—becomes a kind of mental or spiritual exercise.

79 Also see Bergson's *Matter and Memory*: 'This is as much as to say that there is for images merely a difference of degree, and not of kind, between *being* and *being consciously perceived*. (Bergson 2004, p 30.) Since for Bergson (as expressed in the paragraph preceding the sentence quoted) perception is not *projected out* from the subject or body but originates *in the object*, it follows that *to be perceived* is in fact *to be*.

80 The import of all this, and the reason that the seams between hallucination and that which lies outside of it are so much less explicit in Jarry than in Baudelaire, De Quincey, and Huysmans, is that 'Hallucination' as such, as Jarry discovered, is merely a stage in the process; one eventually passes through the final (or perhaps not final) colon of the sentence one is living (see the note above) and the hallucination ceases to be such; the seams disappear, or become merely the evidence of a pulse-like *function* in a process of living which recognizes no essential distinction, but merely a kind of rhythmic movement, between hallucination and its other. 'Reality' is revealed, or determined, to be the *excess* of hallucination, not the other way around; and the phenomenon ceases to be remarkable in the way it has been for so many in the tradition. It is simply and fully *the way one lives*. This practice ceases to be an *escape*, and becomes a *transformatory structure of thought*.

Jarry's closest friend, or even lover, who is figured in this novel, was entirely unknown to anyone else, was—to borrow a phrase by Mallarmé that *might* relate to this practice—*evoked* by him? (We are, of course, merely speculating.)

> Dujardin did not forget about himself: he wrote stories, poems, a novel and a dramatic trilogy, The Legend of Antonia…
>
> 'One day, as I viewed the faded portrait of a young girl in an album, someone passed who spoke a name…
>
> 'And so I knew you; having heard your name, you, I shall dream of you.'
>
> Thus begins a poem to the glory of this woman of dream whom one recognises, memory or vision, 'adorable face,' in many of the other pages in which she is the symbol of the ideal, the inaccessible.
>
> -Gourmont quoting and writing on Edouard Dujardin (1898.) (Gourmont 1994, p 196.)

If, for the sake of argument, you allow us this possibility, the question arises: if Jarry was introduced to this practice through the evocation of the *images* of 'real' people (as there are indications that Nerval, Dujardin, Mallarmé, Huysmans, Freytag-Loringhoven, and others may have been, and which *Days and Nights* certainly suggests), why take another step and create a new *subject*?

Before speculating upon this point[81], we might initially note, first, that even if this speculation is apt (and even in the almost purely speculative, abstract critical world in which we are now operating the evidence is, admittedly, wildly circumstantial; but we must delve into these dangerous waters at least once in this text), the transition may have been gradual, or we might be oversimplifying the matter (or, Jarry might argue, overcomplicating it) by even speaking of a transition. Sengle's confusion over the distinction between his own identity and Valens', while supporting the notion of Valens as a heavily-mediated or modulated evocation of *himself* rather than Fargue or any number of others, also ties in with his more willful refusal of unitary notions of time or space. To pendulum between identity and plurality, presence and absence, might have been key to the very identity of the figure orand subject figured by Valens.

This hypothesis in itself provides one possible answer to our hypothetical question: Valens (or the ~~subject~~ figured as Valens in *Days and Nights*) might have ~~embodied~~ a unique *mode* of subjectivity accessible only to a projected or evoked subject[82]; and the radical fluidity between this figure and Jarry himself would *allow*

---

[81] You will note that our argument moves farther away from any possible verification from the artifacts of 'reality': it moves by stages into more abstract and tenuous grounds: if we are not careful it will be pure fantasy: read on.

[82] obviously, the term 'subject' in its habitual philosophic andor psychological sense cannot be *quite* apt; I employ it in order to distinguish it from a mere 'figure' or image lacking the interiority or distinct (even if projected) *psychological* economy characterizing the experience of Modern consciousness, and from a projected 'person' such as that in Courrière's suggested practice, in which that interiority is projected 'onto' the image but is not, in its relationship to the subject, *operational* as such; it remains a symbolic 'Otherness'. The fluidity and confusion between Sengle and Valens, together with a great many statements, observations, and inferences in this and other work by Jarry, might be seen to imply that a figure such as Valens might be experienced simultaneously as a figure capable of being conceived and directed, in a vaguely literary sense at least, by Senglejarry *and* as capable of independent cognition orand volition. Valens is *an* other, but not *the* Other.

Jarry himself, through the subjective transference referred to throughout the book, to experience this mode as well—to experience it *vicariously* through 'himself'[83].

Valens, then, would inhabit a modulated form of subjectivity that contained its own negation—not merely an (imagined) object, but at the same time not estranged from Senglejarry's consciousness, from the interiority characteristic of subjectivity. If he is not an *other* who has been recalled to Jarry as a Bergsonian *image*[84] but is, in a sense, an *alternate subject* whom Sengle can both experience as a *self* and interact with as an *other*, it is due to his being a subject evoked from nothing—a void to be resolved[85]. It is essential to this process that 'Sengle was not sure whether his brother Valens had ever existed.' (p 65.)

The non-existent plays a privileged role in the novel, as it does in the writings and thought of Mallarmé, Huysmans, and so many others in the tradition. Jarry describes a childhood visit to St. Anne d'Auray, where:

> [Sengle] would remember a host of things he had seen at St. Anne[86] and which had never been there, such as one of the figures of Death amid the Holy Innocents, head shaped like a savage's club, with whom he had lengthy boxing-bouts in a dream, in a non-existent vault inside the basilica.
> And St. Anne was all that was pleasant, to the senses and to the soul, in Sengle's distant past.
>
> Sengle therefore chose St. Anne as his intercessor with the External and synthesis of all his strength strewn like saxifrage in the interstices of the military stones. And he composed this synthesis through a perpetual invocation according to his own lights and rites.
>
> (*ibid*, p. 109.)

Jarry has left us with an indication of these 'rites' in the most explicit description of Valens' evocation, using a blank white mask as a starting-point, in the penultimate chapter of *Days & Nights*, entitled 'En Route to Dulcinea' (the obvious implications of this title we leave to the reader):

---

83 Though of course it is questionable whether, at this point, we could say without complication 'himself'.

84 If we relate this speculation to a Bergsonian schema, Valens would, even in this otherness from Sengle, maintain the characteristics of the privileged image of Sengle's *body*. (Bergson 2005, pp1-13.) It is worth noting that Jarry, in his theoretical formulations quoted here, consistently calls upon Memory and Perception, both words which are key to Bergson's writing on *Matter and Memory* of 1896; a reading of Bergson's text in the light of Jarry's hypothetical practice is as illuminating as it is compared to Huysmans'.

85 Even if Valens were a straightforward evocation of Fargue, he could exist in this relation to Jarrysengle only after Fargue's unknowable interiority—and consequent potential for *volition*—in relation to Jarry was re-created as a knowable—if yet *unknown*—refiguration of Jarry's own, *un-*known interiority.

86 Please note: Poe's *For Annie* ⇒ the Ann of De Quincey ⇒ Anna Blume of Schwitters ⇒ Antonia of Dujardin ⇒ St. Anne of Jarry.

The lamp burned upon the red table and breathed its cricket's chirp. The walls were papered yellowish-green, and it might just as well have been the song of the insects' elytra as the intimate tearing of the trunk of sulphur with its crystalline heart.

Bronzed darkness speckled the white mask looking out from the wall,[87] and beneath the moulding[88] Valens began to appear and take on life. He slightly raised his eyebrows towards their outer corners, kept his eyes lowered and wept a little of his soul, like a wraith of smoke, from his eyelashes through his hairless lips and chin, towards Sengle. And his mouth mused.[89]

The mouth alone, like a leaf from a tree, is different on every face, and is the only feature one can draw without knowing how to draw, since one will invariable imitate with lines curved at random, lips and movements of lips that actually exist. And even when their voices are similar, two speakers have different mouths. Because there are moments when they do not talk and the mouths remain themselves.[90] It was mouths militarily tamed for the conventions of language that the little deaf-mute girls at Auray would watch closely before answering them with the geometry of a uniform gymnastics. Valens was silent and this indeed was the voice of the Silence of Valens free.[91]

-Fernand Knopff, *Secret* (1902).   (Gibson 1999, p 89.)

---

87 One might relate the function of Senglejarry's white mask to that of Mallarmé's *blanc*, his white page.

88 The implication here is that the sensory or perceptible form of Valens begins to resolve itself through a concentration on the abstract shapes found in the moulding and the 'speckled' mask; compare this to the technique Ernst later employs in his evocation of Lop-lop (Richter 1997, pp 157-158.), and to the process described by Huysmans and elucidated through Bergson of beginning with a perceptual object around which images can begin to proliferate, and then molding, as it were, the progressive condensation of images until the initial object (such as Des Esseintes' astrolabe) is no longer needed.

89 Here we follow Sengle's attention as he focuses on one detail after another—eyebrow, eye, tear-duct, eyelash, lips, chin—as his face is resolved, becomes perceptually concrete detail by detail. This follows Huysmans' advice in *A Rebours*: 'The secret is to know how to go about it, to know how to concentrate the mind on one single detail, to know how to dissociate oneself sufficiently to produce the hallucination and thus substitute the vision of reality for reality itself.' (Huysmans 1998, pp 19-20.)

90 Jarry provides us through example with further advice concerning the concentration of attention to the detailed modes and mechanisms by which human features or traits are individuated and thus de-idealized, brought nearer to a sensation of corporeal *presence*.

91 Valens' silence no longer indicates a *lack* of voice or its underlying intention, but is in fact his *expression*, a withholding-from-speech that presupposes a cognition capable of *withholding*.

And it is physically proven that lips cast in plaster are more eloquent than red lips: the latter drink the light and are black really; the mask's mouth returned to Sengle the kiss of all the suns sucked up together and of all the lamps expired on the table where they'd read.

And Sengle believed that at that very moment (without his wondering if the dreamed-of morbid inoculation were possible or whether the tins with the Japanese paper burning inside were enough to conserve life through minute imitations of its loss) his brother was awakening to freedom and escaping, as he had done two and a half years before, upon mounts of grey smoke.[92]

And to relive this past he raised himself up towards this mask; and the head was no longer the visit of a body that could not get through the spy-hole in the wall, but Sengle had upon *their* table and under *their* lamp the brain and soul of his brother.[93]

The white countenance was absolutely that of a hospital ward, embossed with candid beds, the nostrils seemed the rising of hunched knees, and the forehead was drawn over the spirit like a white coverlet.[94]

Valens still returned to Sengle's eyes the lamp's kiss;[95] the sizzle of elytra persisted still, and this was the reviviscence of the two brothers' last outing, the humming atoms like the tiny yellow crickets which inhabit the polyhedric galleries of sulphur; and once again it was absolutely similar to the music of the spheres.

The head was wholly alone and bare, and it was the intellect of Valens that Sengle covered and raised aloft between his hands, out of the red and blue of the disciplinarian chrysalis.[96]

The head was too alone even and too bare; the soul of Valens (Sengle still recognized the life or soul only by movements analogous to heart-beats)[97] was simply leaking, streaming through the lips, like a vase overflowing. When Valens was totally present in the room his soul was a great blue-brown butterfly, its wings raised highest

---

92 The second mention in this passage of smoke emanating from Valens' evoked body, which might be a way for Jarrysengle to fix visually (and possibly through touch, etc.) that inherently mercurial aspect of Valens escaping even a projected corporeality.

93 It is by now emphatically Valens *the subject*, not merely Valens the remembered *image* that is *present* in the material *space* of the room.

94 The physical perception that continues to underlie Senglejarry's projected ~~perception~~ is integrated into the hallucination, despite the apparent disjunction between them; we can see here how the development of literary manipulation of images has prepared him for a more radical cognitive practice.

95 Jarry mentions lamplight in conjunction with Valens at several points in the book; we might speculate that this too relates to issues of perceptual *technique* and anchoring detail.

96 See note 29

97 Here again Jarry implies that subjectivity is not so much a definitive presence or positive quality as one term of a dialectical movement, something which is alternately interior and other, and by virtue of that very fact simultaneously *both*.

towards the outer corners, which palpitated from the twinned flight of his eyebrows and eyelashes, uncovering and re-covering the miraculous ocelli of his eyes that were two black ponds.[98]

Sengle loved pools and the creatures that fly over pools; one never knows, he thought *en route* to Sainte-Anne, whether one will find the pools, or the same pools again.

A curl had remained crimped into the plaster on the side of the forehead; under Sengle's caress, the marvelous butterfly uncoiled towards him its spritespiral which was a dark crinkled feather, like the old trees in the first dreamed of desertion; and, alive, he crumpled it as one bending an index finger to beckon someone.

The Chinese ethnography of a people foreign to China… a certain wind must not blow…

The lamp elytra stridulated swifter still, and the din became more continuous, like a last trill.

Sengle leaned towards his brother whom, by now, across the distance, he could tell was free, so as to give him back all the affection of the good kiss of sonorous light.

The plaster mouth became flesh and red to drink the libation of Sengle's soul.[99] The lamp had turned red, then black, the metal died out in the eye and the air poised a mist of tears.

And after the momentary redness, the lips were green and adhered all chill to Sengle's blackened lips. These were too many complimentaries.[100]

The table rocked and Sengle was on the ground in a wake of the pile of crumbling snow, this time with a recollection of the caffeine rustling across his tongue, in the bed of the mixed hospital.[101] He buried his face amid the tiny scales, several of which stuck.

"Why did the mouth turn red to drink my soul, which escaped through the occiput when my face entered the flesh of the mask?"

And Sengle was fumbling in the night towards his Self vanished like the heart of a bomb, his mouth upon his murder.

(*ibid*, pp 152-154.)

---

98 As Valens' evocation is consummated and he becomes fully ~~present~~, the literary principle of metaphor itself achieves a kind of perceptual materiality or perceptive form, just as the act of *writing* itself is inscribed in Sengle's experience as a perceptual phenomenon.

99 While Valens' soul has been literally pouring from his mouth, Senglejarry now pours a religious offering of *his own* soul into that same orifice. There is a sense in which it is Sengle, as Valens, who has been draining for the past few paragraphs, that the soul 'simply leaking, streaming from the lips,' was itself this libation Jarrysengle offers to the subjective position that is Valens; there is another sense in which each of these subjective positions, Valens and Sengle, are now emptying themselves (one might note similar language in Mallarmé's confrontation with 'the Void') to fill each-other with themselves.

100 Even the colours of Valens' (only provisionally existent) lips are becoming their complimentary opposites.

101 This evocation itself, then, is in fact a hallucination, or (having been lived twice and therefore all points at once) has been temporally recontextualized—which, by the logic provided by Jarry above, come to the same thing. Note furthermore that this nesting of one evocation within another shows that Sengle does not merely 'resurrect' Valens as an other with full plentitude *as an object*, but also as *a provisional subject-in-flux*; that is to say that his quality *as* evocation is considered by Sengle an essential aspect of his ~~existence~~ and of their relationship. The same argument might be applied to Jarry's nesting of autobiographical experience *within this text itself*.

What you love is this *shadow* alone; it's for the shadow that you want to die. That and that alone is what you recognize as unconditionally REAL. In short, it's this objectified projection of your own soul that you call on, you perceive, that you CREATE in your living woman, and *which is nothing but your own soul reduplicated in her.*

[. . .]

Give it a try, then, if some last hope still stirs within you. And then you shall be the judge in your own intimate conscience whether this auxiliary Creature-Phantom that leads you back to the love of life doesn't really merit the name of HUMAN more than the living specter whose sorry so-called reality was never able to inspire you with anything but the desire for death.

 -Villiers de l'Isle-Adam, *The Future Eve* (1886).   (Hustvedt 1998, pp 590-591.)

'The more I think about it, the more determined I am to implore you not to destroy our dream. And then... May I be frank with you, so frank that I shall doubtless appear a monster of egotism to you? Speaking personally, I have no intention of spoiling my, for want of a better word, happiness. Yes, the happiness that our relationship has given me. I know that I have explained matters badly, that I must sound terribly confused. But what I want is to posses you when and how I please, just as for years I have possessed Byron, Baudelaire, Gérard de Nerval, all those whom I love.'

 'What do you mean?'

 'I mean I have only to desire them, as I only have to desire you, before I go to sleep and...'

 'And?'

 -J.-K. Huysmans, *Là-Bas* (1891).   (Huysmans 2001, pp 134-135.)

A vision on his sleep
There came, a dream of hopes that never yet
Had flushed his cheek. He dreamed a veiled maid
Sate near him, talking in low solemn tones.
Her voice was like the voice of his own soul
Heard in the calm of thought; its music long,
Like woven sounds of streams and breezes, held
His inmost sense suspended in its web
Of many-coloured woof and shifting hues.
[. . .]
Sudden she rose,
As if her heart impatiently endured
Its bursting burthen: at the sound he turned,
And saw by the warm light of their own life
Her glowing limbs beneath the sinuous veil
Of woven wind, her outspread arms now bare,
Her dark locks floating in the breath of night,
Her beamy bending eyes, her parted lips
Outstretched, and pale, and quivering eagerly.
His strong heart sunk and sickened with excess
Of love. He reared his shuddering limbs and quelled
His gasping breath, and spread his arms to meet
Her panting bosom:… she drew back a while,
Then, yielding to the irresistible joy,
With frantic gesture and short breathless cry
Folded his frame in her dissolving arms.
Now blackness veiled his dizzy eyes, and night
Involved and swallowed up the vision; sleep,
Like a dark flood suspended in its course,
Rolled back its impulse on his vacant brain.

-Percy Shelley, *Alastor; or, The Spirit of Solitude* (1816).

(Shelley 2002, pp 77-78.)

To paraphrase the phrase, without nibbling the words, of Don Quixote on the subject of the lack of importance of whether Dulcinea really existed: "if she did not exist I would not love her any the less", I can say and I will say, here and now, that even if Jarry had not been born 99 years ago, or even if he had not been born at all, WE WOULD NONETHELESS HAVE INVENTED 'PATAPHYSICS BECAUSE WE ARE PATAPHYSICIANS.

-Opach, *Ce pain-là*, message addressed to the College of 'Pataphysics (P.E. 100, 1972 Vulgar).
(LIP Dept. of Dogma & Theory 2003 Vulg., pp 43-44)

Heart (Dance of Shiva)

Around me hovers the presence that thou art,
secretly atmosphere draws cloudy—dense—
perfume athwart mine cheekbone swings intense—
smile on mine lip—
I kiss thee—
with mine heart !

Ja—with mine heart—
that can perform fine tricks
since it's housed in wizardry and art—!
soul—how enchanted art thou—
by such heart ! !

Ho !—lover far—

-the Baroness Elsa von Freytag-Loringhoven (1920.)   (Lane 1998.)

If you wish, if you wish, I will make you the master of living matter, as the sculptor is of clay, but an incomparably better master; and you shall know the pleasure, constantly renewed, of escaping from yourself to forget yourself in another being.
-Charles Baudelaire, *Paris Spleen* (1869).   (Baudelaire 1970, p 41.)

it first took a year for [Larry] Miller to find a willing and capable hypnotist. He first approached a psychiatrist well-known for his therapeutic use of hypnosis. But this doctor refused to participate... Miller persisted and found a hypnotherapist who would work with him. They had six sessions together, five of which were audiotaped and the sixth and last of which was videotaped. Miller believes that in the last session he assumed his mother's identity.

As this videotape begins, Miller explains in a voice-over why he is being hypnotized:

I wanted to know what it would feel like to become my mother, to lose consciousness of my own identity through hypnosis and to believe for a while that I was Mom.

-Kristine Stiles, *Anomaly, Sky, Sex, and Psi in Fluxus*.　　　　　　(Hendricks 2003, pp 78-79.)

For instance, one can see, or persuade others to see, all sorts of shapes in a cloud: a horse, a human body, a dragon, a face, a palace, and so on. Any prospect or object of the physical world can be treated in this manner, from which the proposed conclusion is that it is impossible to concede any value whatsoever to immediate reality, since it may represent or mean anything at all.

-Marcel Jean　　　　　　　　　　　　　　　　　　　　　　　(Brotchie 1995, p 70.)

A vice-queen IS an armchair. World views are word mixtures. A dog IS a hammock. *L'art est mort*. Viva Dada!

-Walter Serner, *Last Loosening Manifesto* (1917).　　　　　　(Ball et. al. 1995, p 160.)

The truth was, his road lay so very far on one side, from that wherein most me traveled,—that every object before him presented a face and section of itself to his eye, altogether different from the plan and elevation of it seen by the rest of mankind.—In other words, 'twas a different object, and in course was differently considered.

-Laurence Sterne, *Tristram Shandy* (1760-67).　　　　　　(Sterne 1996, p 269.)

At some point I realized that my backwardness, at least some of it, was starting to wear off. I could tell it was starting to wear off by the way I gradually found myself walking sideways. I was walking sideways just like a crab does. Scuttling, really. In this manner I quickly left the road altogether, and crossed several fields. And, I don't know, but somehow, when you're moving sideways at a rapid clip it's a lot different from moving forwards, or even backwards. It puts you in a much stranger frame of reference. It's hard to explain, except to say that in moving continuously sideways I began to see things I'd never noticed before. For one thing, I was seeing everything at right angles. I became aware of the odd intervals that separate everything when you view the world from the sidelines, so to speak, rather than meet it head-on, and as I looked more closely into the shadowy intervals that lie between things, I perceived a multitude of hidden wires and pulleys, busily at work. A wave of sick vertigo overcame me at the sight of all this mechanistic contrivance going on behind the scenes and in the interstices—and I lost consciousness.

    -Blaster Al Ackerman, *Corn & Smoke* (2006).   (Ackerman 2006, p 29.)

I have always been struck by the obstinacy of the mind in insisting on thinking in terms of dimensions and intervals, in adhering to arbitrary states of things in order to think, in thinking in segments, in crystalloids, in thinking that every mode of being solidifies a starting-point, that thought not be in instant and uninterrupted contact with things, but that this fixation and this immobilization, this kind of erection of the soul into monuments, arises into being, so to speak, BEFORE THOUGHT.

    -Antonin Artaud, *I Really Felt...* (c. 1930?)   (Artaud 1965 pp 32-33.)

The hallucinatory tradition upon which we have speculated has itself been transmitted (if at all) primarily through processes that are in themselves structurally hallucinatory—a tradition that even in its continuation could only tenuously be said to have 'existed' or to 'exist'. For it is, paradoxically, primarily through books that it has been (may have been) encoded and decoded across generations; the continual evocation of De Quincey's CONSUL ROMANUS over generations most explicitly underlines this observation.

It would seem initially that books would be the least likely transmitters of such a tradition, since it is (if anything) the tradition of a practice that in itself *cannot be recorded*, it is a writing on and through the human subject itself, which is precisely what the *text*, as such, annihilates and renders ultimately incommunicable. All that can be 'recorded' in print are relics and fragments without the presence of the 'life' which produced them, which is always already withdrawn. A 'literary' tradition can withstand this, for its focus is on the text itself, the *object* of the writing as always already divorced from its production: in a literary tradition, the poem, the story, the *writing* is in some sense *itself*; in a hallucinatory tradition—and there is no reason to think that the tradition *of* hallucination is the *only* hallucinatory tradition—the writing is merely an index toward something that cannot possibly be indexed. Such a tradition cannot be *known*.

To participate in such a tradition, then, is to offer oneself up to the logic of the hallucination before the practice itself has even begun, it is to place oneself *within* the hallucination before one has even conceived it. The tradition itself can only *be* hallucinated, its 'reality' always in question; and the more one delves into its coordinates, the more fully hallucinatory it becomes. This is what binds its practitioners so closely together—if indeed they are bound at all. Their communication across generations would take on a strange intimacy, linked as it would be to the most secret—and yet most unsharable in their essence—parts of their lives, their very structuration *as* human subjects; or else, that communication would not exist at all, would be a 'mere' chimera for the individual who, thinking he is in the most intimate company, is in fact all alone. The initiates would never 'know'; and so they themselves, the subjective modes through which they have (re)constituted themselves (if indeed they have), would in fact 'be' hallucinations. In this way the indexes scattered in printed books, pointing toward an unknowability, are also initiatory texts, for they propel the initiate into the space of hallucination itself; yet it is the hallucination *itself* through which these texts have been read, *constituting* them as initiatory; and this is the aporia at the heart of *reading*.

It is no wonder then that the evidences of this practice, if they are indeed evidence, are *generally* scattered, discontinuous, and subject to a multitude of readings and interpretations, of which the one we are concerned with is usually (though not always) far from the most obvious. It is only through an emphatic *act* of reading that these scattered artifacts can be drawn together, read in a certain way, while still refusing to fully *exist* as such, constituting themselves only as a system of *projected* readings, a cycle out of the subject, through the object, and back to the subject, never existing as a definite *corpus*, unitary and complete. And no doubt the various developers of this tradition—and we have seen that if it does in fact exist, it has been *developed* and not simply re-discovered each generation, though certain practitioners (or all of them—if there are any) may have developed these practices on their own—were always uncertain as to whether these hints would be read in a way which would open them up, their readers were also always in doubt.

And yet, from the standpoint of a tradition, even one that cannot be said to precisely exist, this carries great dangers. One might speculate that those who have created in themselves a keen awareness of this practice *as* tradition might ask themselves how to ensure its survival; and it might be from these considerations that the occasional texts emerge which are explicit and condensed. One might conceptualise Swedenborg in this connection, and see his success in Blake; in relation to the modern practice we have had in hand, we must surely look to Huysmans.

These efforts—if they are indeed efforts—are never direct. We have looked at how *Against the Grain* mixes autobiography, social observation, and fiction in such a way that while practices of evocation are discussed explicitly and often, it is impossible to say at what point rigour ceases and 'fiction' or hyperbole begins; we see the same strategy in Jarry (whether or not it is there to see), while Breton (if indeed he is pertinent to this matter) obscures the points where his discussions of these practices merge into fiction, into theoretical speculation, into rhetoric, into *other* practices such a automatic writing. Huysmans, in particular, found a way in which, on the one hand, to treat the practice explicitly, in detail, to suggest the rigour with which it might be approached conceptually, discursively, and technically, and to save it from dying out (if indeed it had ever lived) or from failing to live up to its full potential as a way of radically transforming *thought* itself; while on the other hand refusing to strip it of its hallucinatory quality, to trap it—as we assume the initiate of such a practice would not want to do—within the confines of an 'existent' practice that could be approached and tritely *consumed*. No doubt other ways of achieving this are possible as well:

That would be a nice story, wouldn't it? And yet—only a nice story, and a rather far-fetched one at that. And yet perhaps we are giving *writing* too little credit; for it is possible to use words and ideas in such a way as to create the *illusion*—which is to say, in a slightly different sense, the hallucination—of an index pointing toward what has disappeared; the fact is however, that *anything* could be slipped into that empty space prior to the text, that origin that has been effaced, so long as it does not directly contradict the text itself. There are any number of hypothetic traditions we might speculate as lying behind those texts, and if one looks hard enough, as conventional wisdom tells us, we can find evidence for anything everywhere. Perhaps there *is* no practice that these indexes point toward; perhaps they are in fact merely a literary *effect*.

Huysmans himself called the hallucinatory practice described in *Against the Grain* as 'this kind of devious sophistry'; is it not just as likely that the phrase refers in fact to the whole fictitious practice that he has created for his eccentric character, who after all does not anywhere refer to the Decadent community which he represents only as a hyperbole? It may be true as they say that 'the greatest trick the devil ever pulled was convincing the world he didn't exist;' but it is equally possible that his greatest trick was convincing the world that he *did*. And while the people identified in this book as 'practitioners' *might* indeed have been perpetuating a radical way of living whose relics in print disguised themselves as a 'literary' tradition, it is *at least* as likely that they were, in fact, perpetuating a literary tradition *disguised* as an extra-literary practice. Most of these people, after all, were more-or-less closely related to a well-established literary tradition, and one in which visions and fantasy—not necessarily hallucinated—were stock in trade and developed to a high degree of subtlety and artistic awareness. Nor is this necessarily *much* less radical; especially if one looks, for instance, at the repetition of De Quincey's CONSUL ROMANUS incident mentioned above. For looking at it in this light, we have a literary tradition—or sub-tradition, or strain—that has been little remarked, and which is not content with reworking and developing themes and motifs, but deals specifically with their sites and modes of deployment. The government clerk and writer Joris-Karl Huysmans, for instance, need not have 'actually' trained his senses and nervous system over years in order to be able to induce especially vivid hallucinations; without any such engagement, he could still have written about such an imaginary practice with a good deal of detail—such things are regularly done, for instance, in Science Fiction—and, very keenly, he would have done so in a work which, *because* it straddled the lines between biography and fiction, would have a very different effect than it would in, for instance, a work of Science Fiction.

This hypothesis (probably more likely than the idea of a quasi-secret practice openly carried out and discussed in semi-disguised form through codification in texts) becomes more interesting when one considers that this literary theme—self-induced hallucination—came to be worked out within this literary tradition primarily in works that were ambiguous as to their truth-status, as opposed to those that were openly and fully fictional; though there have always been plenty of the latter as well (Villiers', for instance). In this way, the theme itself came to include this ambivalence, became particular to quasi-non-fictional forms; a notion that would fascinate any fully engaged writer—and most of the people engaged with the *manifestation* of this practice (which need not to have actually existed) were remarkably engaged with writing in its deepest implications.

It would, of course, be a short leap from here into these themes being confused—possibly even with these writers' encouragement—with some fictitious actual 'practice', as indeed may well have happened after the publication of *A rebours*. It has been remarked, after all, how that book served as a model for the Decadent Aesthetic community (Deak 1993, p 253.), so it is even possible that certain individuals, mistaking this fiction for an actual practice, may in fact have tried it, thinking they were engaging in a pre-existing practice when in fact they were the first to attempt it in anything but a deft writerly maneuvre; if so, it is impossible to say how much success they may or may not have had.

In this way, the writers engaging in this literary practice, through a combination of chance and manipulation, may have watched this fictional practice become, in effect, a meme. A literary *idea* which, while not practiced, was *thought* to be practiced. This would represent a radical invasion of writing, including its fictionality, into the social register usually mediated through the agents of Truth, and would therefore present these writers with an opportunity to carry their project into new realms, to write *not* through the individual mind as they would *seem*, without *quite* claiming, to claim; but rather to write into the social body itself the *myth* of such a practice. They created in a writing a kind of detective-game for readers to play, which yielded nothing but produced much; and at this point, of course, writing is no longer restricted to the printed text.

Most of the authors who were heavily involved with this theme were connected to Dandyism, Aestheticism, or their heterogenous descendants, and to the mythic manipulation that had been a part of Avant-Garde and proto-Avant-Garde communities for generations, so that the transference of this literary theme from exclusively published writing to the social register would seem natural, especially after the success of *A rebours* in convincing a whole community that this was something *other* than a sophisticated textual deployment. A project—in 'actuality' much more secret and 'duplicitous' than the fictional 'hallucinatory practice' that was merely its mask—may well have evolved to perpetuate this theme on the social register as well—in conversation, in correspondence, in oral story or rumour.

And if, as has been posited elsewhere, it would be possible to pick out the 'evidence' of this 'practice' and reconstruct it as a tradition, would it not be at least equally possible to pick out the *fact* of the trope *of* such a practice, regardless of that practice's 'reality', and to perpetuate the deployment of this trope, of this literary deployment that occasionally explodes the boundaries of the literary, infects the microsocieties around it? To do so would be to identify and perpetuate a collective myth which was also a giant, complex literary hoax.[102] The real object would not be the reorganization of human thought *coded through* writing, but the utilization of the revolutionary potential of writing itself to implant in society the *notion*, the myth, of such a potential.

This hoax (if it was a hoax, we cannot know—the possibility remains that it has been an 'actual' practice) would then have been transmitted, would have effectively formed a tradition—a tradition of creating the convincing *illusion* of a hallucinatory practice; and this transmission would presumably have occurred, just as the hoax was perpetuated, both in writing and in society; and, no doubt, in that form where the two meet, the letter.

One of the most explicit letters dealing with this hoax, or this practice—whichever you prefer, since we cannot know which, if either, it is—is also the most explicit evidence we have of the *direct* transmission of this practice, through personal association rather than through the annihilating medium of the text. Its writer is Berthe de Courrière, who was deeply involved in this practice—let us call it this again, whether it was the practice of fooling the perceptions or of fooling the Other, of personal or of social hallucination. Courrière had been the primary model for Madame Chantelouve, the invoker of incubi in *La-Bâs* and a friend of Huysmans, who was, as we have just discussed, central to the manifestation of this tradition; the letter was written to Alfred Jarry, who has left us the most detailed descriptions of evocation since Huysmans; and it discusses this practice itself.

---

[102] It is worth noting that such an argument could equally be made for the tradition of Surrealist automatic writing, the veracity of which is in its nature untestable as such; which has a tradition that can be traced at least as far back as Walpole, even if we remain within the bounds of 'literary' activity; and which would fulfill the Surrealist longing for a collective myth. In fact, Breton and Aragon, as noted elsewhere in this book, both connected automatic writing explicitly with hallucination, and claimed Rimbaud and Lautréamont—on rather shaky ground—as predecessors.

In it, Courrière describes her own practice as highly advanced, involving a fully articulated fantasy world, peopled with whole nations, and capable of being (effectively at least) perceptually shared.[103] She invites Jarry to share it with her, promising to initiate him into the mysteries of its creation. There is a sense that she is aware that Jarry had been exploring similar territory on his own, and indeed his autobiographical novel *Days & Nights*, which seems to describe a hallucinatory practice derived from De Quincey, had just been published; Jarry was also—for a short time longer—good friends with Courrière's long-time lover, Remy de Gourmont.

This letter was ill-fated; Jarry was utterly contemptuous of it, and included it nearly verbatim in his next novel, *Visits of Love*, put out by a pornographic publisher, along with a scathing depiction of Courrière. (Jarry 1993, p 7.) This caused a permanent rift between Jarry and Gourmont (Jarry and Courrière, despite what the content of the letter might seem to imply, had always hated each other),[104] who threatened a lawsuit. (*ibid*, p 10.)

On one hand, it is easy to understand Jarry's reaction; as we have already discussed, his own practice, or at least his *representation* of it in *Days and Nights*, was already farther advanced, and more thoroughly situated, than that described by Courrière; though she makes great claims concerning what can be imagined, the 'what' of the hallucination is hardly the greatest challenge, and the hallucinations she describes seem not to penetrate her psychological economy deeply enough to transform it in the way that Jarry's own practice was already doing, or was being portrayed as doing in his writing and in his social behaviour. Moreover, the terms in which her proposal is couched all but obscure the potential of her endeavour; indeed, the letter is difficult even to read without embarrassment, permeated as it is with clumsy quasi-archaic language, ridiculously flowery and grandiloquent hyperbole, and a fuzzy and confused occultist rhetoric that Jarry was bound to find laughable and intolerable.

At the same time, we should not be too quick to dismiss Courrière's practice in its entirety, as Jarry seemed to do. First we must recall Jarry's dogmatic misogyny (Rachilde was the only woman he considered his equal), added to which was his long-standing personal dislike of Courrière herself. Moreover, the letter obviously represents an attempt at a literary style, essentially a prose poem, and Courrière was not a poet, and did not claim to be one. We can detect a good deal of insecurity and awkwardness behind the absurd pomposity of this failed attempt by a woman past her prime to live up to the expectations of the most virtuosic and profound stylist of his generation, and to belittle her contribution to the development of this practice (if indeed it *is* a practice) on that account is to perpetuate, in a more silent manner, Jarry's own misogyny.

---

[103] The evocation of a 'large' landscape or of thousands people does not, of course, necessarily imply any particular stage of development in itself, as Jarry, if we choose to read this letter as evidence of an 'actual' practice, would no doubt have realised.

[104] The letter is the result of a practical joke spun out of control by their mutual friend Rachilde; knowing their hatred for each other, she had convinced Courrière that Jarry's virulent antipathy could not be construed as anything but an over-reaction against an ardent attraction. This illusion was soon dispelled.

It is more productive to view this letter, for instance, as an indication of the inadequacy of Spiritualist discourse, as it is situated within modern culture (before the onset of Modernity it might well have served far better), for the discussion of such radical practices. While I have noted serious reservations as to the uses Courrière ascribes to the practice here—which do not appear to go farther than simple 'wish fulfillment'—one must also recall, as discussed earlier in this book, that it may well have been Courrière who, through her use of evoked 'incubi', first introduced into the disembodied discourse of this tradition (if tradition it is) the prototype of the hallucinatory ~~subject~~ of which Sengle, Anna Blume, and others might be examples. The fact that the psychological operations introduced by her into the practice as reflected in *La-Bâs* seven years earlier seem not to have progressed, might be seen to reflect the limitations of the occult, spiritualist, and Satanist discourses through which she continued to approach it: the emphasis on self-fulfillment as fantasy-fulfillment rather than as a redirection of desire, an emphasis on ritual based in cultural models of the pre-modern age rather than the creation of new modalities or the radical re-conception of traditional ones, the continued recourse to logocentric dichotomies such as Good/Evil, God/Satan, Self/Other, etc. which restrained reformulation into new modes of thought, and the inadequacy of the language of these discourses to apply to the practice the rigour necessary to rescue its articulation from near-meaningless abstraction.[105]

This is, of course, if we take the viewpoint that all of this does in fact—as I have chosen to present it, however speculatively, in most of this book—relate to an 'actual' practice. Whatever our stance, this letter occupies an important place; either it represents the clearest, most explicit, and most reliable proof of the 'actuality' of the practice, and shows a direct transmissive link between three of the key developers of it; or it indicates the full extent of the duplicity of its presentation, the level to which the *illusion* of its actuality was perpetuated even in social gestures never intended for publication. Either way, we have just experienced a singular triumph of sophistry on a vital level.

The letter:

TUA RES AGITUR

Am I Cupid or Phoebus? Lusignan or Byron?[106]
My brow is still red from the kiss of the queen.

I posses a power, greater than all others, which contains them all, occult and unknown.

Do you want it?

---

[105] Breton deals quite cogently with this issue of the adequacy of Spiritualist discourse to articulate and conceptualise the potential radicality of its matter in his 1925 *Letter to Seers*. (Breton 1972, pp 195-204.)

[106] Note that Byron is one of the three poets evoked by Chantelouve in *La-Bâs;* though the Atlas edition of *Visits of Love* is unclear whether this epigraph was written by Jarry or by Courrière.

I posses the golden keys that open the ivory portals of the realm of dreams. Like Persephone, who weaves in a veil the lives of future humanities, I will cause every image that exists to pass before your eyes. Symbols will become embodied,[107] they will multiply a marvelous population, inaccessible to men.[108]

Do you wish for them?

By my action upon you, ideas will hasten in a throng to your brain, forms will take on a life and furnish us with a cortege such as no dictator ever had.[109]

Come, we shall reign with an uncontested power over a people created by ourselves.[110]

All the powerful intelligences that have wrested a part of their secret from the causes of things have worked for us.

We shall be the wondrous culmination of all those enlighteners, and their stupendous children.[111]

It was for us that the Trojans perished to save Helen—beauty; that the Romans subdued the Barbarians—brute force; that the Hindus, by centuries of meditations, discovered Nirvana; that the ancient religions deified the planets.

It was for us that Assyria erected its monuments and its peoples clashed together in ardent conflicts—so that we might have the memory of martial cavalcades.[112]

It was for us that men pitted themselves against each other in memorable conflicts—to leave us the memory thereof.

It was for the safe-keeping of the future that beliefs fought against powers, and that John of Austria triumphed at Lepanto.

---

[107] Compare to the sensory embodiment (or *translation*) of ideas that forms the focus of Loyola's training of the senses.

[108] That is to say, this practice, through the *embodiment* of ideas, creates a relationship *to* them inaccessible from normative modes of subjectivity.

[109] Again, before the emphasis of the letter shifts to the register of perceptual hallucination, its relationship to thought itself, in its abstraction, is reiterated.

[110] What is being described is a joint hallucination; one might recall the hallucination 'taught' by St. Benedict to his fellow monks discussed elsewhere in this book. (Carruthers 2000, p 188.)

[111] It is unclear—possibly deliberately—whether 'intelligences' is to be taken here in its sense of supernatural entities (deriving from the 'First Cause' etc.) or of human 'minds'; the following line, however, suggests the latter reading—rendering these 'enlighteners' as earlier practitioners (De Quincey, Huysmans, and others in addition to practitioners in mystic or occult traditions) and 'their children' as the hallucinatory ~~people~~ evoked by them.

[112] The emphasis on here on a variety of mythical models and mythologized ancient cultures betrays the debt of Courrière's version of this practice to the Sâr Péladan's kaloprosopia; the emphasis on the necessity of violence, and the implied preeminence of the 'Self' over the social, betrays its debt to Satanism. These themes, however, are tied together in their function as providing material for 'the memory of martial cavalcades'—such as that re-presented the most famous account of a composed hallucination in the tradition we are examining, the CONSUL ROMANUS of De Quincey.

Come, and see how the world is growing old and is preparing itself for sleep;[113] it has brought forth all the endeavours it had within it. The poets have exhausted all their comparisons and the scholars all their enquiries.[114]

Come, our time is drawing nigh. The hour of all earthly dominions is past. For the conquerors nothing is left, for we know that nothing human is worth the effort of its conquest.

Analysts have demonstrated that miracles were hallucinations and that the wonderful was confined within a cerebral hemisphere.

But the philosophers have affirmed that the will was the magic lever and that the idea created the act.[115]

Come then: by our sovereign will we shall be all-powerful in this world. All the works of the spirit will be our magnificent trophy; we shall realise them in ourselves.[116] We shall be the heroes sung by the poets, the dominant rulers treasured by history, the conquerors acclaimed by warriors. We shall be young and imperishable, we shall have all the flowers, all the fruits, all the perfumes, all the essences.

Come! The impetuosities of my being hasten toward you like ardent coursers the rider can barely restrain, and which will soon carry him

Edward Burne-Jones, *Pygmalion: The Godhead Fires* (1878). (Lucie-Smith 1972, p 129.)

---

[113] While this assertion aligns with the Decadent rhetoric with which Courrière was associated in her prime, it should also be noted that 'sleep' is where her hallucinations occur; there is a potential reading for the possibility of a differently-structured world inherent in its own 'sleep'.

[114] Is this not a kind of demand that new, more radical methods are called for?

[115] There is little to add, but these two lines might be read with italics. A hallucinatory practice, hallucinatory not only on the register of perception but of structure, language, society, and every other, denies both (and all) of these limitations and static frameworks for thought.

[116] This phrase can be read doubly: to make these 'works' 'real' within our own consciousnesses, or to bring to 'realization' these manifestations of 'spirit'. These readings are, of course, more parallel than divergent.

at a furious gallop across the river of desires.

Come, I hear the fanfares of triumphal marches approaching; living, we shall rise to Valhalla. In place of hydromel I shall pour out for you ecstasy, I shall grant you the joys of thought.

Come, there is none to equal me. I know the despair of Orpheus and the anguish of his plaints. The vulture will cease to devour Prometheus and Pygmalion will no more to animate a futile shade.[117]

Come, I shall give you time and eternity, I know the secret of the beyond, and you will not uselessly implore deaf gods and you will not shatter your dream on the limits of the possible.

Come, and you will prevail;[118] come, that I might carry you off to limitless space. I have won over all the Chimeras,[119] I shall give you an unending dream.

My arms are strong enough to carry you, my heart stout enough to sustain you, my spirit mighty enough to initiate you.

I have prepared for you an incomparable dwelling; but alone I cannot open its portal. In vain, to seize life's secrets, would you pore, like Faust,[120] over grimoires, it would remain impenetrable, you would seek in books for that which they do not contain. I shall give you the absolute by the supreme communion of

---

[117] Two myths which lie at the heart of this hallucinatory tradition, if it exists. Prometheus, who while not creating life itself created its *value* (and the very concept of value) through bestowing *thought*, is most explicitly linked to the creation of another subject, of course, in M.W. Shelley's *Frankenstein; or, the Modern Prometheus*. If the Visitation of God provides (quite explicitly) the mythic lens through which both Mystic and Occult approaches to practices of evocation are conceived, the hallucinatory tradition as articulated within Modern creative communities is much more subtly underlain and mapped out through the myth of Pygmalion and Galatea, though seldom referred to directly (with the exception, of course, of Huysmans). This model, as opposed to the other, is more closely aligned with the subjective and social modalities of Modernity: the socially-binding myth of God, his precise opposite Satan, and their avatars in demons or angels are replaced by the atomized myth of discreet and unique subjectivities, so that the vision of the religious *entity* conceived 'outside' the subject and imported from the social world is replaced in the more fully developed Modern practices by the unique hallucinated subject conceived 'within' the evoking subject and (in Jarry's practice and in many others) to some degree at least, projected *onto* the social order.

Of course, despite her realisation of the importance of this myth, the very self-aggrandizing practice described here by Courrière conceives of hallucinated 'people' merely as anonymous units of a large mass over which to rule, as components of a social mass to be dominated, and in so doing fails to fulfill the model provided by Galatea, the individual to be loved, while also failing to socially situate the more abstract nature of her evocations in the way that mystic and occult models do. This may be one large part of the reason why Jarry was uninterested in the manifestation of the practice she describes; he had in many ways progressed far past it.

[118] This phrase might seem to indicate a present struggle on Jarry's part which she is promising to end, and imply that she had detailed knowledge of Jarry's ongoing project, not an impossibility given her lover Gourmont's mutual friendship with Jarry, Huysmans, Mallarmé (who died the year this letter was published), and other probable or possible practitioners. This is nonetheless, of course, pure speculation.

[119] The same word used in *La-Bàs* by Madame Chantelouve to describe her hallucinatory lovers.

[120] A more apt model for Courrière than Pygmalion and Galatea.

intelligence. I shall cause you to conceive the immortal masterpiece that is knocking at the door of your understanding,[121] that you might let it penetrate within you.

Like the goddess that traverses the earth, I have sought to grant you the supreme hour, the thirteenth, that which I am myself, which does not exist for other humans.

Come, and add a new page to the book of the Spirit. I shall reawaken in your memory the recollection of everything that has lived, I shall give you the absolute awareness of the universe, I shall cause the divine soul to descend into you,[122] I shall cause you to surmount the abyss that separates it from mankind.[123]

Come, you will be the Conqueror, if you can understand and dare.

(Jarry 1993, pp 33-35.)

I've worked infinitely hard this summer, on myself first of all, creating, through the most beautiful synthesis, a world of which I am the God

-Stéphane Mallarmé, Letter to Armand Renaud, 20 Dec., 1866.   (Mallarmé 1988, p 72.)

I chat with you mentally so often in my room, which your dear presence fills even more than your portrait which hangs on the wall, that not only do I think it utterly unnecessary to write to you, but I'd even be afraid that by placing between us the reality of the post and the time it takes for a letter to reach you, I might make your ghost fade away.

-Stéphane Mallarmé, Letter to Armand Renaud, 20 Dec. 1866.   (Mallarmé 1988, p 46.)

---

[121] Another very interesting phrase, which might be read as being privy to 'inside information'. It suggests of course that this potential 'masterpiece' would take the form not of a publication but of a hallucinatory 'act' for lack of a better term, but also suggests that such a conception might possibly—we could speculate—have been working in Jarry already.

[122] While the hallucinatory modality of her practice once again contradicts her rhetoric here, the 'emptying' of self so that the Holy Spirit or 'divine soul' can descend into the body is the ultimate goal of Christian Mysticism. (Lash 1947, pp 51-52.)

[123] While this and the two previous paragraphs mark the climax of the hyperbole that permeates the letter, they also mark a return to an emphasis on the efficacy of hallucination as the catalyst for new forms of *thought*. Unfortunately the final line largely contradicts this.

From the letters of Mallarmé to Eugéne Lefébure & Henri Cazalis:

3 May, 1868 to Lefébure:

There is a very beautiful line, which constituted my entire life in the period when I was dead:
> They pass through the Infinite to create new places.

18 July 1868 to Cazalis:

And too, my dear old friend, we'll repeat a certain outing we went on at Fontainebleau! Everything began there, our friendship dates from then, and that's when your heart came alive, to be filled with a delicious child. Poor friend, I suffer greatly from the fact that your marriage has been delayed! But still, don't our souls know how to use the Dream to create happiness from bitterness, and you'll draw ecstasy from thinking of the future, whose entire charm you are perfectly able to evoke, and this time that charm will be supreme!

July 1868 to Cazalis:

But I'll return to Véve, to Marie, to the garden, which you inhabit, for your presence is entirely a product of summer:

14 Nov. 1869 to Cazalis:

I'll place this sheet of paper between us. Breaking the spell of your permanent presence, that sheet will at least initiate you into what the invisible do not see, the minute details of daily life.

20 March 1870 to Lefébure:

Then it would be the real [Lefé]Bour, who would see everything, and not the one who appears to me as an empty shadow of himself and which I've worn out by constantly evoking him.

(Mallarmé 1988, pp 85-92.)

I'm a little hungry to see you; and if you're occasionally absent from the shores of your beautiful lake, it's because you're no longer there but have popped up, unbeknownst to you, on the banks of the river here, amid the reeds, when I'm out wandering.

-Stéphane Mallarmé, letter to Méry Laurent, 29 Aug., 1890. (Mallarmé 1988, p 168.)

I want to begin an important scene of *Hérodiade*. Pity me.

-Stéphane Mallarmé, Letter to Henri Cazalis, Feb. 1865. (Mallarmé 1988, p. 50.)

As Stéphane Mallarmé was working on *Hérodiade* (whose 258 lines, simultaneous with *L'Après-Midi d'Un Faune*, took nearly two years to compose, and would continue to be revised throughout his life) in July 1866, he wrote:

> I have died and been born again with the gem-encrusted key to my final spiritual casket. It's up to me now to open it in the absence of all extraneous impressions and its mystery will emerge into a very beautiful sky. I'll need twenty years during which I'll remain cloistered within myself, renouncing all publicity other than readings to friends.
> (Mallarmé 1988, p 66.)

As he dedicated himself, through *Hérodiade,* to opening this casket, his engagement led him through a spiritual crisis and toward a unique form of atheism wherein Poetry becomes,

> not only the vehicle, but the locus of the sacred for Mallarmé, and in a sense, he remains a religious poet even though he loses his belief. The sacred exists for Mallarmé, but only insofar as it can be experienced phenomenologically; it exists only as an experience, through the concrete medium of language
> (Mallarmé 1996, pp xii-xiv)

Let me bring to your attention certain observations regarding the nature of this crisis, which relate to the Yellow Sign; and which, I emphasize (in several pages I shall use Kristeva to support my contention), emerged from Mallarmé's engagement with this text itself; and which, I may state with authority, can also emerge from the engagement of a *reader*. After all, as Lautréamont has reminded us, it is the mirror, the text, that is, or can be, the janus-faced agent of these hermetic realisations.

Ten months further along in the composition of *Hérodiade*, in May 1867, Mallarmé reported to his friend Henri Cazalis that,

> I've just spent a terrifying year: my Thought has thought itself and reached a pure Concept. All that my being has suffered as a result during that long death cannot be told, but, fortunately, I am utterly dead, and the least pure region where my Spirit can venture is Eternity. My Spirit, that recluse accustomed to dwelling in its own Purity, is no longer darkened even by the reflection of Time.
> (Mallarmé 1988, p 74.)

Like Maldoror (whose first volume would be published the following year), Mallarmé had engaged in a battle with God.

> But as that struggle had taken place on his bony wing which, in death throes more vigorous than I had thought him capable of, had carried me into the Shadows, I fell, victorious, desperately and infinitely—until at last I saw myself again in my Venetian mirror, such as I was when I forgot myself several months before.
> (*ibid.*)

> Gazes into chasm of knowledge—void—frightened—dizzy—lacking architecture. Unable to serenely—trustingly—knowingly: gaze into depths hallowed—shifts gaze… —bird giantesque—God.
>
> -Elsa von Freytag-Loringhoven,
> *Thee I Call 'Hamlet of the Wedding Ring'* (1921).
> (Lane 1998.)

Before I proceed by allowing Mallarmé to proceed—the text of this crisis of Mallarmé is so dense, I nearly despair of making explicit to you an acceptable number of the salient points—let me deal with these passages so far. We can infer from the last sentence I have quoted that it was before a mirror that Mallarmé 'forgot myself' and was precipitated into this struggle. We can only speculate as to what extent this mirror was the text, and to what extent it was ~~not~~ merely a tangible (but metonymic) combination of metal, plastic, wood and glass; in any event, this crisis takes place *within the mirror*. The very Shadows into which Mallarmé has been carried reside within Hérodiade's mirror:

> Mirror, cold water frozen in your frame
> Through ennui, how many times I came,
> [. . .]
> A far-off shadow to appear in you:
> (Mallarmé 1996, p 30.)

And even a cursory glance through the poem will reveal how densely it is populated with shadows and reflections.

It is hardly surprising then that we find Mallarmé speaking of so many of the themes that inhere in the mirror in the testimonies of (among others) Rigaut, Baudelaire, Lautréamont, and Schwob. For instance, the whole crisis is played out within a space of a-temporal Forgetting, and within this textual, mirroring space Mallarmé is free of 'the reflection of Time.' You will also note, no doubt, that it is from the beginning Mallarmé's 'being'—the very status of himself as subject—that has suffered and been put at risk. It is only natural, then, to find once again that it is death that has been found there; it is within this mirror that Mallarmé has found the casket for which, a paragraph before, he had been given the key. Like Hérodiade herself, despite the impure 'Eternity' he discovers there and through which he fell 'infinitely', it has been 'a terrifying year'. But he is not finished discussing this mirror:

> I confess, moreover, but to you alone, that the torments inflicted by my triumph were so great, I still need to look at myself in that mirror in order to think and that if it were not on the desk on which I'm writing to you, I would become the Void once again.
> (*ibid.*)

Mallarmé has become inextricable with the mirror, with the text, with the constantly annihilating mode of existence that is inherent in the logic of the text, of the reflection, and which is therefore not exactly subjectivity in its classic, Cartesian sense. Mallarmé the self-contained subject exists only as a self-contained image in the mirror, projected outside the space of thought; exists only as an *object* of sight. Only as such can he inhabit this personality. Like Lautréamont, like Rigaut, Mallarmé has dissolved, has become the reflection; or, more precisely, has become the mirror—the mediation, the *hymen* or the *tympanum*, as Derrida might say, that dissolves the logocentric distinction between the reflection and the 'reality' that mimes it. Mallarmé goes on:

> That will let you know that I am now impersonal and no longer the Stéphane that you knew—but a capacity possessed by the spiritual Universe to see itself and develop itself, through what was once me.
> (*ibid.*)

With this sentence Mallarmé confirms what we might have been suspecting: after this passage, or more precisely perhaps, this *immersion*, Mallarmé does not return. His sense of himself as subject is caught up, suspended; there is something that exceeds him—'the spiritual Universe'—of which he 'himself' has become an emanation, an evocation. It speaks 'through what was once me'; he has become a trace of himself, a subject in a state of perpetual disappearance and, consequently, perpetual emergence.

Subjectivity has not, in *every* sense, been annihilated; but it has been made, or shown, to be contingent; it is a textual *function*. The subjectivity that has been (to use Mallarmé's term) *voided* by the realisation (mark this term) of linguistic dissemination at play (this also) within the very constitution of the *thinking subject* still exists as a structural space. It is open (this also) as a position from which that 'capacity' exceeding subjectivity—Language, the Universe, or whatever amalgamation of letters one chooses to employ—can observe and develop itself; a space of extra-subjective psychosis, as it were. The subject becomes simultaneously the reader, a writer, and a structural device of the text/s of existence itself, and of existence's inherent negation.

> Take spoon—scalpel—
> Scrape brains clear from you—
> how it hurts to be void!
>
> -Elsa von Freytag-Loringhoven,
> *Blast* (1920). (Lane 1998.)

Julia Kristeva, 107 years later (chronologically speaking), describes in Leon S. Roudiez's criminally incomplete translation of her *Revolution in Poetic Language* (her extensive discussion regarding Lautréamont and

Mallarmé have been mostly excised) an analogous process within what she designates as the signifying practice of Narrative:

> The *matrix of enunciation* in narrative tends to center on an axial position that is explicitly or implicitly called "I"
> [...]
> We could say that the matrix of enunciation structures a subjectal space in which, strictly speaking, there is no unique and fixed subject; but in this space, the signifying process is organized, that is, provided with meaning, as soon as it encounters the two ends of this signifying chain and, in between, the various crystallizations of "masks" or "protagonists" corresponding to the signifying process' abutments against parental and social structures. The subjectal structure thus appears as a series of entities, which are infinite to the extent that material discontinuity is projected there, but locked in place to the extent that the parental and social network is applied to it. Within this framework, One is all, and all (multiple addressees, the crowd, the community) are a structure of entities.
> (Kristeva 1984, p 91.)

> For a long time now I have felt the Void, but have refused to throw myself into the Void.
>
> I have been as cowardly as all that I see.
>
> When I believed I was refusing the world, I know now I was refusing the Void.
>
> For I know that this world does not exist, and I know how and why it does not exist.
>
> My sufferings until now consisted in refusing the Void.
>
> The Void that was already in me.
>
> I know there has been a wish to enlighten me by the Void and I have refused to allow myself to be enlightened.
>
> If I was made into a pyre, it was intended to cure me of being in this world.
>
> And the world took from me all I had.
>
> I struggled in my attempt to exist, in my attempt to consent to the forms (all the forms) with which the delirious illusion of being in the world has clothed reality.
>
> I no longer wish to be a Believer in Illusions.
>
> Dead to the world; dead to that which is for everyone else the world, fallen at last, uplifted in this void that I once refused, I have a body that submits to the world, and disgorges reality.
>
> -Antonin Artaud, *The New Revelations of Being* (1925).
> (Artaud 1965, p 85.)

---

107 years earlier (chronologically speaking), Mallarmé (and, almost simultaneously, Lautréamont) had radically realized the implications of this structure on life as it is lived; and rather than disintegrating the *structural* integrity of the subject thus shown to be contingent and emanative, the realization propelled him into a radical internalization of what Kristeva designate the *textual* process of subjectivity:

> The process' matrix of enunciation is in fact *anaphoric* since it designates an elsewhere: the *chora* that generates what it signifies. To have access to the process would therefore be to break with any given *sign* for the subject, and reconstitute the heterogenous space of its formation.   [...]
> That this practice assumes laws implies that it safeguards boundaries, that it seeks out theses, and that in the process of this search it transforms the law, boundaries, and constraints it meets. In this way such a practice takes on meanings that come under laws and subjects capable of thinking them; it passes beyond, questioning and transforming them. The subject and meaning are only phases of such a practice, which does not reject narrative, metalanguage, or theory. It adopts them but then pushes them aside as the mere scaffolds of the process, exposing their productive eruption within the heterogenous field of social practice.
> (*ibid*, pp 100-101.)

I would ask you to imagine the laws and boundaries Kristeva refers to, in the present situation, as the notion of the autonomous or discreet subject as imagined in the narrative mode of subjectivity; or, more radically, as the notion of an extra-textual 'reality' itself. I would further posit that the last two sentences, so construed, suggest the orientation of Mallarmé's new relationship with the ideas of the subject and of existence. It is in this sense that Mallarmé becomes 'a capacity possessed by the spiritual Universe'. Kristeva also suggests the terror expressed by Lautréamont, by Rigaut, and by Mallarmé upon their initiation, which is felt, there is little doubt, by all of us upon our introduction into this ~~new~~ structure of thought:

> This practice cannot be understood unless it is being carried out. To do so, the subject must abandon his "*meta-*" position, the series of masks or the semantic layer, and complete the path of signifiance.
> Such a practice has been carried out in texts that have been accepted in our culture since the late nineteenth century. In the case of texts by Lautréamont, Mallarmé, Joyce, and Artaud, *reading* means giving up the lexical, syntactic, and semantic operation of deciphering, and instead retracing the path of their production. How many readers can do this? We read signifiers, weave traces, reproduce narratives, systems, and driftings, but never the dangerous and violent crucible of which these texts are only the evidence.
> Going through this crucible exposes the subject to impossible dangers: relinquishing his identity in rhythm, dissolving the buffer of reality in a mobile discontinuity, leaving the shelter of the family, the state, the religion. The commotion the practice creates spares nothing: it destroys all constancy to produce another and then destroys that one as well.
> (*ibid, pp 103-104.*)

In all of this, my dearest reader, there is far more than a little of the Yellow Sign. And it will not have escaped you that Kristeva here touches upon the role of written texts as an integral and simultaneous codification of this subjective process; while they may reflect within themselves the lived, subjective process of their authors, this process does not precede them, any more than Jacques Rigaut precedes his reflection as he inhabits it ('This process cannot be understood unless it is being carried out'). It is *through* the writing of these texts (and consequently, through their *reading*) that this textual subjectivity comes into operation; and it is in this sense that these texts—and to whatever degree, all of the written texts touched with the Yellow Sign—are, or can become, spells, transformatory texts, as I have already insisted. We might recall, briefly, the discovery encoded in Lautréamont's passage on the mirror: that the reader, within this space where the mirror and the text merge, becomes the reflection of the writer. If, while keeping this thought firmly in our heads, we then recall the situation discovered by Lautréamont, Rigaut, and Mallarmé—that the mirror does not reflect a prior 'reality' but rather *creates both* of the terms that meet through its surface—then we can begin to see the mechanism by which the Yellow Sign, like a virus, is communicated across generations through these texts. It does not allow some kind of unproblematic access to something *written in* to the text prior to our reading; nor are we *reading in* to the text something definitively absent prior to our reading. Past and present are constantly emerging from these inherently a-temporal texts, in which our experience there has always already been at play.

-Olchar E. Lindsann, *The Yellow Sign.*

I have therefore lived a good deal with my poems. For nearly ten years they were for me an undertaking of infinite duration—an exercise rather than an act, a search rather than a deliverance, a maneuver of myself by myself rather than a preparation intended for a public.

-Paul Valéry, *Concerning 'Le Cimetiére Marin* (1933). (Valéry 1958, p 141.)

Psychoanalysis has detected the presence of an anonymous mannequin in the recesses of the mental attic, "without eyes, nose, or ears," not unlike the ones Giorgio de Chirico painted around 1916. This mannequin, once the cobwebs that concealed and paralyzed it were brushed away, has proven to be extremely mobile, "superhuman" (it was precisely from the need to give this mobility free rein that Surrealism was born). This strange character, freed from the deformities that mar Mary Shelley's admirable creature in *Frankenstein*, enjoys the faculty of moving about without the slightest friction, in time as well as in space; in a single bound, it eliminates the supposedly unbreachable gap separating reverie from action.

-André Breton, *Anthology of Black Humor* (1945). (Breton 1997, p 226.)

The difficulty was semantic rather than real. The 'fault' lies with language, and as language is the tool of thought, the fault lies with our way of thinking.
-Hans Richter, *Dada: Art and Anti-Art* (1964). (Richter 1997, p 60.)

The use of various drugs—opium, wine, hashish, caffeine, ether—in connection with hallucinatory practice was established early in the tradition with Fuseli, Coleridge, and De Quincey, and the theme has had a consistent presence ever since—it has been at play to some degree with Poe, Baudelaire, Jarry, Vaché, Ackerman, Jacob, Flaubert, Nerval, Artaud, Verlaine, and to a certain degree the Bouzingos, the Paris Dadas and early Surrealists, as well as the Lettrists, Gavin Twinge, Blaster Al Ackerman, David Zack, and others. It's role however has always been ambivalent; De Quincey himself, in his *Confessions,* seemed to extol and condemn their use in the same breath; and in the same book where he presented De Quincey's ideas to the Francophone world, 1860's *Artificial Paradises,* Baudelaire also condemned their use, after intense and detailed description of their effects, warning that, 'we must consider another inevitable and terrible danger, which is true of all habits: they all rapidly become dependencies. He who would resort to a poison in order to think would soon be incapable of thinking *without* the poison.' (Baudelaire 1996, p. 74.)

Baudelaire, however, had long been a leading member of the Club des Hachichins, a group including himself, Flaubert, Gautier, and Boissard de Boisdenier, which met weekly to experiment with hashish-inspired hallucination. The Hachichins entered the mythology and later generations, including certain Decadent and Symbolist circles, the Paris Surrealists, the Doodaa group, and Neoists would also meet to explore how drug-induced states, hallucinatory practices, and the group dynamic could be used to formulate alternative modes of communication and collective consciousness.

Jarry presents a transcription of one of his hashish-sessions in Book V, Chapt. 4 (Jarry 1989, p 138-146). Jarry and his comrades—tentatively identified as the philosopher Albert Haas, Jarry's cycling friend and writer Gaston de Pawlowski, and Maurice Dide—engage in an extended attempt to transform their own cognitive apparatus as individuals and as a social group, carrying on an elliptical conversation in which their thought and communication are based less on semantic than on homophonic, etymological, and other lateral associations. Communicable hallucinations also play a role, one individual's hallucination affecting the group dynamic as its effects play out on various registers. As the session moves on, subjectivity itself does in fact begin to show itself as something mobile: 'The old man of the woods, his crisis abating, again becomes the German philosopher Herreb.' (p 145). Jarry describes himself detached from the group, observing in detail the way that the group interacts within, and attempts to control and sustain, this state of perception and interaction:

> They no longer have a notion of distance, optical *accommodation* being no more than a cinematographic trembling, and need a periplus to land a hand upon the arm of a chair. There was a silence after Nosocome's conclusion, which was on a coined or archaic word, notoriously incomprehensible anyway. The four were still almost lucid; Sengle in his corner more screened from the scents was listening and taking notes, and they resorted to ruses for further hallucination.
>
> The flame under the burner was extinguished, the fire covered, and in the darkness Nosocome began rhythmically running on the spot, the floorboards creaking.
>
> (*ibid,* pp 140-141)

That Jarry coolly observes what is happening does not imply that he is not at the same time *experiencing* what is being observed; rather, despite (or beside) his own hallucinations, some of them shared by his friends, Jarry's textual surrogate Sengle is:

> the most lucid—for the hashish state most resembles his normal state, since it is a superior state—[and] by a simple reversal has become almost a normal man, and has taken notes.

(*ibid*, p 145)

This simply reinforces the fact that the use of drugs is, of course, not *necessary* for such a practice, consists largely in a use of language in which 'communication' is continually and fluidly shifting from one register to another of the language through which it works—from literal signification, to the correspondences of its materiality and sound, and to its lateral associations (personal, cultural, sub-cultural, auditive, visual, etc.), to literary or historical reference. The modality of thought at play in each individual is constantly unsettled, at the very brink of coherence or comprehensibility, and the communication becomes emphatically a space of *communal non-meeting*, through which previously un-thought forms of social activity and relationships begin to emerge; such conversations have been either explicitly described or implicitly hinted to have been a part of the lives of many groups associated with the Yellow Sign, including the Club de Hachichins, Jarry and his circle, the Russian Zaoum group, the Zurich and Paris Dada groups, the Paris Surrealists, and Deconstructionist circles.

Chance, in the form of more or less free association, began to play a part in our conversations. Coincidences of sound or form were the occasion of wide leaps that revealed connections between the most apparently unconnected ideas.

-Hans Richter, *Dada: Art and Anti-Art* (1964.)   (Richter 1997, p 52.)

NOSOCOME: This little morsel lives at the corner of the Boulevard Saint-Michel.

PYAST: And the Boulevard Haussman wants to get off with her, a nice free sampleton.

NOSOCOME: He gets simple like that, in his cups. Here's a free verse in the sample.

PYAST: He's no need of bottle, he cleans himself out with an arse-glass of free wurst.

NOSOCOME: That's crazy. I've not seen it, no…

PYAST: That crazy Jeanot.

NOSOCOME: And Hunyadi-Janos is no wet flannel.

PYAST: Flannel's like corn on your feet, no one wears it anymore.

NOSOCOME: As from tomorrow you all wear flannel.

PYAST: From tomorrow? We'll never get out of today.

NOSOCOME: You're linking cause and effect? You're taking your head in your hands.

    -transcribed by Alfred Jarry, *Days and Nights* (1897).   (Jarry 1989, pp 138-139.)

Here I am fond of the French word *piège,* meaning trap: it was, a few years ago, a favorite theme in elliptical and lighthearted discussions between Paul de Man and myself.

    -Jacques Derrida, *Psyche: Inventions of the Other* (1987).   (Derrida 1991, p 211.)

Olchar: I wonder where David Edwards went, he was in the waiting room for awhile
aaroneous: dead to the world
********** at 6:05 PM Airborn joined the room
Olchar: Apparently. Emily may show up, she's online.
aaroneous: emily a
Olchar: ANTI ANTI ANTI!
********** at 6:05 PM Airborn left the room
Olchar: emily b
aaroneous: burning churches
Olchar: burning churches.
Olchar: emily c
aaroneous: emily me
Olchar: emily si
aaroneous: emily p
Olchar: emily we
Olchar: burning churches.
aaroneous: indeed
Olchar: indeed indeed.
aaroneous: outdone
Olchar: indone
aaroneous: done in
********** at 6:08 PM David Beris Edwards joined the room
Olchar: done in a burning church

David Beris Edwards: Hullo.
Olchar: ANTI ANTI ANTI!
aaroneous: wwwwweeeeeeee
David Beris Edwards: VVVVVIM!
David Beris Edwards: VVVVVVOM!
David Beris Edwards: VVVVVVVVVVVVVVVVVIM!
aaroneous: burn any churches?
Olchar: vim vom vim vom VIM
Olchar: BURN ALL CHURCHES.
David Beris Edwards: Not since this afternoon
aaroneous: oh yeahh
Olchar: Indeed burning churches indeed.
aaroneous: not now no how
Olchar: well THAT'S a horse of a different colour:
David Beris Edwards: Slint.
********** at 6:10 PM Tomas *Fighting Falcon* joined the room
Olchar: purpley
Olchar: ANTI ANTI ANTI-!
********** at 6:10 PM Tomas *Fighting Falcon* left the room
David Beris Edwards: VIM VOM VIM!
aaroneous: striking a blow for the status quo
Olchar: BAR BAR BAR!
aaroneous: oi oi oi!
Olchar: VIM VOM VIM!

-Aaron Andrews, O. Lindsann, & D.B. Edwards, transcript of trans-continental Anti-conversation, A.Da. 9o.

NOSOCOME: You mentioned flame, I believe? You were in the water.

HERREB: Are you penetrating two things at once?

PYAST: In the middle, with two paper hoops.. I think… In the middle, with…

NOSOCOME: Suc-cess-ive-ly.

HERREB: He's found it.

PYAST: I dropped it. It was sitting along the lie of the fields, so it had its back to the road.

NOSOCOME: But if you were in the middle, you couldn't anticipate that.

PYAST: There are schemes which cannot be sinuous.

NOSOCOME: That's fifteen years you've been explaining something to me.

PYAST: Fifteen years?

NOSOCOME: You trying to prove shomething?

PYAST: Shun nothing.

NOSOCOME: Now then, in your smugglering, could you trim your words?

PYAST: Polish morale…

HERREB: Polish mural…

NOSOCOME: You all but said long live Poland…

-transcribed by Alfred Jarry, *Days and Nights* (1897). (Jarry 1989, pp 139-140.)

This giddy cheer, poignant or languid by turns, this uneasy joy, this insecurity, this permutation of the malady, generally lasts but a short time. Soon the links that bind your ideas become so frail, the thread that ties your conceptions so tenuous, that only your accomplices understand you. And here again you cannot be certain; perhaps they only think they understand you, and the illusion is reciprocal. These outbursts of loud cries and laughter, which resemble explosions, seem like true madness, or at least like the ravings of a madman, to all who are not similarly intoxicated.

-Charles Baudelaire, *Artificial Paradises* (1860). (Baudelaire 1996, p 29.)

********** at 2:32 PM tattooedmama joined the room
nicole: ANYONE WANNA CHAT
Warren: we
********** at 2:34 PM tattooedmama left the room
aaroneous: more of it
Meg: slip
********** at 2:34 PM deceptivedeath joined the room
Warren: into
aaroneous: we aren't chatting are we
Meg: our
bradley: chat about?
deceptivedeath: hey tattooedmama
nicole: ANYTHING
deceptivedeath: n evryone else
Warren: a word hebenon
bradley: I like peanutbutter
aaroneous: about what
nicole: SO DO I

Warren: flung
nicole: N JELLY
Meg: yes butter
deceptivedeath: damn, i'm a lil late
bradley: I like pumpkin in my underpants
Warren: barr barr barr
aaroneous: in a rape hole?
nicole: GROSS
Warren: too many philistines
bradley: yup
aaroneous: nope
deceptivedeath: hi
Warren: skin rope
bradley: hi
Warren: hello
aaroneous: skin tastic
Meg: love rope
deceptivedeath: how ya doin?
Warren: pink sock
Meg: lol
Warren: candy hotel
aaroneous: mutated member
Warren: brown train
bradley: oh shit pink sock!
bradley: pull it out!
Warren: stab bath
deceptivedeath: lol
aaroneous: cleveland
Warren: oh
aaroneous: steamer
Warren: oh
Meg: shitter
Warren: oh
bradley: dd i'm alright
Warren: oh

-Warren Fry, Aaron Andrews, Megan Blafas, Bradley Chriss, & strangers, transcript of Post-NeoAbsurdist Anti-Conversation.

Will my publisher reimburse me if they discover that the huge expense incurred on account of my mishap was in fact for mind-altering drugs? Thoughts rushed through my brain more speedily than usual. Funny—and come to think of it, how was I able to write down what Gavin just said, when I couldn't hear a single word? Had the Doodaa group discovered some secret elixir, and was I going to be allowed to leave once I had spoken with everyone and learned some of their secrets? Was the Doodaa group some strange religious sect? Do they induct innocent people like myself and use them as specimens for their dark practices? Is art a religion, and does it consume its practitioners and transform them into fiendish zombies with alien motives?

Do they realise they are possessed, if they are, and am I the only one who realises this, and therefore cannot be one of them? Gavin was standing in front of me performing a strange sign language and, even stranger, I can understand it!

    -Ralphael Steed, *Doodaaa: The Balletic Art of Gavin Twinge* (2002.) (Steadman 2002, p 194.)

HERREB, *knocking on the door*: Present, here's a surface one.

PYAST: Can't he say his name?

NOSOCOME: One should not demonstrate oneself in the street.

HERREB: Open up, Monsieur, here's the dead man.

PYAST: Why knock three times? Four and two make six, and half of six is three.

NOSOCOME: Metaphor.

PYAST: Felix, Felix!

NOSOCOME: What?

PYAST: My dear friend, there are three what, there are three what, there are three…? It's the way the duck speaks French, who's… Canal, what's passing in front of you. You're spilling.

NOSOCOME: I wasn't spilling out.

PYAST: It's a parallel with the canal. You're parallel to the canal. What a wretch, he's fathered your folly.

NOSOCOME: He's fathered me fully on the bicycle of your bollocks.

PYAST: *Ergo nominor leo*. [I am lion.]

NOSOCOME: Get on with you, Jules Simon. The condition for two parallels to be parallel is that they are in opposed directions.

PYAST: But speak for the resultant.

NOSOCOME: It's your paralleliresultant.

PYAST: What a bore! no result from it. Do you want a salad of spectacles?

    -transcribed by Alfred Jarry, *Days and Nights* (1897). (Jarry 1989, p 144.)

[Blaise Cendrars, Max Jacob, Guillaume Apollinaire, and Pablo Picasso] sometimes took hashish too. If Fernande Olivier's account is to be believed, it could produce strange effects. One night when they had smoked some at the home of [Maurice] Princet, a mathematician who was more or less an insurance agent in Montmartre (and in whom, surprisingly, some have seen the real theoretician of Cubism), Apollinaire was overcome by a sensation of ubiquity: he suddenly thought he was in a brothel. As for Picasso, he entered into a sort of painful trance, weeping and shouting, lamenting that since he had discovered photography, he had understood that his art was worth nothing, and the best thing to do was to kill himself.

-Dan Franck, *Bohemian Paris*. (Franck 2001, pp 62-63.)

aaroneous: cleaning my crevice with a tooth brush of twigs i found the offending corn
aaroneous: ruff and rigid
Olchar: banging against the little sack dangling over my chest
aaroneous: worms expanding into ribs making a mockery of a cage holding feral children cutting away layers of filth and ribbon
Olchar: until it is discovered to their consternation that there is nothing in the center, and the children, escaped, are chewing on the heads of rabbits
aaroneous: scraping the legs of giants hurling boulders toward an uneasy convenience store having a sale on krispy kreme (my dog has to pee)
Olchar: i have to pee. i have to pee. give me a creamy crisp lease
Olchar: David Beris Edwards is in purgatory
********** *at 6:01 PM Chris left the room*
Olchar: Superb.
aaroneous: jack jack is in the hall
aaroneous: noooo
Olchar: Jack is in the hall?
********** *at 6:01 PM My Love Is Toxic 4 Eever! joined the room*
aaroneous: no not that jack
My Love Is Toxic 4 Eever!: heyy
aaroneous: burning churches
aaroneous: weeeeeeeeeeeeeee
aaroneous: oioioi!
********** *at 6:01 PM Smooth™ joined the room*
Olchar: burning churches
Olchar: burning churches
aaroneous: burning churches
********** *at 6:02 PM My Love Is Toxic 4 Eever! left the room*
********** *at 6:02 PM Smooth™ left the room*
aaroneous: weeeeeeeeeeee
Olchar: Ha!
aaroneous: pussies
Olchar: pussies indeed.

-Aaron Andrews & O. Lindsann, transcript of trans-continental Anti-conversation, A.Da. 9o.

A REFINED ÆSTHETIC EXQUISITE.

"Been to the Old Masters, Mr. Millefleurs?"
"A—no—a—I—a—go in for High Art, you know!"
[*What does he mean? We don't know, no more does she, no more does he. Nobody knows*]

-from *Punch*, 16 March, 1878.

That strangely constituted mind of his harboured unexpected associations, correspondences, and contrasts of thought, as well as a peculiar procedure whereby the etymology of words became a springboard for new ideas which, albeit inspired at times by rather tenuous associations, were almost invariably ingenious and vivid.

-J.-K. Huysmans, *A Rebours* (1884) (Huysmans 1998, p 127.)

2. For this, and all other changes in my dreams, were accompanied by deep-seated anxiety and gloomy melancholy, such as are wholly incommunicable by words. I seemed every night to descend, not metaphorically, but literally to descend, into chasms and sunless abysses, depths below depths, from which it seemed hopeless that I could ever re-ascend. Nor did I, by waking, feel I *had* re-ascended. This I do not dwell upon; because the state of gloom which attended these gorgeous spectacles, amounting at last to utter darkness, as of some suicidal despondency, cannot be apprehended by words.

3. The sense of space, and in the end, the sense of time, were both powerfully affected. Buildings, landscapes, &c. were exhibited in proportions so vast as the bodily eye is not fitted to receive. Space swelled, and was amplified to an extent of unutterable infinity. This, however, did not disturb me so much as the vast expansion of time; I sometimes seemed to have lived for 70 or 100 years in one night; nay, sometimes had feelings representative of a millennium passed in that time, or, however, of a duration far beyond the limits of any human experience.

-Thomas De Quincy, *Confessions of an English Opium-Eater* (1821).

(De Quincey 1995, pp 60-61.)

I felt that the snatches of sight I experienced had a profound and terrible meaning, and a frightful connection with myself, but that some purposeful influence held me from grasping that meaning and that connection. Then came the queerness about the element of time, and with it desperate efforts to place the fragmentary dream glimpse in the chronological and spatial pattern.

-H.P. Lovecraft, *The Shadow Out of Time* (1936). (Lovecraft 1982, p 359.)

The glimpses themselves were at first merely strange rather than horrible. I would seem to be in an enormous vaulted chamber whose lofty stone groinings were well nigh lost in the shadows overhead. In whatever time or place the scene might be, the principle of the arch was known as fully and used as extensively as by the Romans.

-H.P. Lovecraft, *The Shadow Out of Time* (1936). (*ibid.*)

Mr. Coleridge, who was standing by, described to me a set of plates by [Piranesi], called his *Dreams*, and which record the scenery of his own visions during a delirium of fever... vast Gothic halls: on the floor of which stood all sorts of engines and machinery... Creeping along the sides of the walls, you perceived a staircase; and upon it, groping his way upwards, was Piranesi himself: follow the stairs a little further, and you perceive it to come to an abrupt termination, without any balustrade... but raise your eyes, and behold a second flight of stairs still higher: on which Piranesi is perceived, but this time standing on the very brink of the abyss. Again elevate your eyes, and a still more aerial flight of stairs is beheld: and again is poor Piranesi busy on his aspiring labours: and so on, until the unfinished stairs and Piranesi both are lost in the upper gloom of the hall.—With the same power of endless growth and self-reproduction did my architecture proceed in dreams. In the early stages of my malady, the splendours of my dreams were indeed chiefly architectural: and I beheld such pomp of cities and palaces as was never yet beheld by waking eye, unless in the clouds.

-Thomas De Quincey, *Confessions of an English Opium-Eater* (1821).
(De Quincey 1995, pp 62-63.)

I saw tremendous tessellated pools, and rooms of curious and inexplicable machinery whose outlines and purpose were wholly strange to me, and whose sound manifested itself only after years of dreaming.

-H.P. Lovecraft, *The Shadow Out of Time* (1936).
(Lovecraft 1982, p 370.)

Upon retiring, he had had an unprecedented dream of great Cyclopean cities of Titan blocks and sky-flung monoliths, all dripping with green ooze and sinister with latent horror. Hieroglyphics had covered the halls and pillars, and from some undetermined point below had come a voice that was not a voice; a chaotic sensation which only fancy could transmute into sound, but which he attempted to render by the almost unpronounceable jumble of letters, "*Cthulu fhtagn.*"

-H.P. Lovecraft, *The Call of Cthulu* (1928)
(Lovecraft 1985, pp 65-66.)

He was half lying on a high, fantastically balustraded terrace above a boundless jungle of outlandish, incredible peaks, balanced planes, domes, minarets, horizontal disks poised on pinnacles, and numberless forms of still greater wildness—some of stone and some of metal—which glittered gorgeously in the mixed, almost blistering glare from a polychromatic sky... Behind him tiers of higher terraces towered aloft as far as he could see. The city below stretched to the limits of vision, and he hoped that no sound would well up from it.

-H.P. Lovecraft, *The Dreams in the Witch-House* (1933)
(Lovecraft 1982, p 330.)

Project for a realistic urbanism: replace Piranesi's staircases with elevators, transform tombs into office buildings, line the sewers with plane trees, put trash cans in living rooms, stack up the hovels, and build all cities in the form of museums; make a profit out of everything, even out of nothing.

-Raoul Vaneigem, *Comments Against Urbanism* (1961).
(McDonough 2004, p 123.)

But through what I have learned, it is possible to know that Cthulu is one of the Water Beings, even as Hastur is of the beings that stalk the star-spaces; and it is possible to gather from vague hints in these forbidden books where some of these beings are. So I can believe that in this mythology, Great Cthulu was banished to a place beneath the seas of Earth, while Hastur was hurled into outer space, into *the place where the black stars hang*, which is indicated as Aldebaran of the Hyades, which is the place mentioned by Chambers, even as he repeats the *Carcossa* of Bierce.

-August Derleth, *The Return of Hastur* (1939). (Carter 1971, pp 142-143.)

Of course, as I have noted, perhaps *all* of these supposedly 'autobiographical' incidents are in fact fictions masquerading as evidence of life, part of a giant intertextual hoax. This possibility foregrounds what might be looked at as a kind of distorted mirror-image of the tradition which has been the focus of this book, or as its twin, a sibling that has manifested itself so differently that the two rarely meet any longer, and their family resemblance is easily missed: this is a certain tradition of Anglophone, largely American Gothic-Horror, deriving very largely from the High Gothic and from Poe as does the Francophone trajectory of the Yellow Sign, and including Brown, Hawthorne, Poe himself, Ambrose Bierce, Robert Chambers, Oliver Onions, Henry James, Algernon Blackwood, Arthur Machen, Clark Ashton Smith, H.P. Lovecraft, August Derleth, Ramsey Campbell, Harlan Ellison, and others.[1] This tradition—which has only a nominal presence in this book for reasons of relative focus and will be more fully treated, in more appropriate form, in other works—has of course taken a vastly different, and less critically self-interrogatory path due to its vernacular articulation (for which it has gained benefits as well), but it has pursued many of the same themes as its Continental counterpart, and perhaps due to its isolation has explored some much further.[2] The status of the Book as the transmitter of culturally subterranean micro-traditions, the personal transformation of the individual who is initiated through such acts of reading (*The King in Yellow*, the *Necronomicon*, the *Book of Hastur*, etc), is

---

[1] Since both traditions share a very similar traditional trajectory from Walpole through Poe, at which point they split, the Anglophone tradition might be looked at genealogically as the more 'natural' progression of the (primarily Anglophone) Gothic form, while the Francophone tradition would in effect be an idiosyncratic, heavily intellectualized off-shoot of that form with heavy influence from French 'High' literature. In effect, this positions most of the Avant-Garde tradition as a sub-genre or development of Horror. This may be worth thinking about.

[2] The American element of this tradition in particular has generally been aware of its estrangement from both the American culture in which it was situated and the European culture from which it derives and continues to draw a mythic sensibility, as evinced by the Francophilia of Chambers and the Anglophilia of Poe and Lovecraft especially.

indispensable to this tradition; and over several generations, from Bierce to the preset, writers in this tradition have developed complex systems of intertextual references into a shifting and vital mythos, interwoven with various 'real' mythologies, traditions, and practices, which eat away at the divisions between these 'actual' and 'fictional' worlds. It is no wonder that Chambers—who frequented Parisian artistic circles at the height of the Decadent movement as a student at the Ecole-de-Beaux-arts (Chambers 2000, p xi.) and shared with Jarry a fascination for the latter's home region of Brittany and the stories of Ys, the chimerical city with inhabitants experienced as hallucinations—was the first to identify and *name* the Yellow Sign itself (the initials of which are, of course, Ys). (*ibid*, pp 70-82.) The Cthulu Mythos is, then, a non-existent system of reading, and through it a non-existent practice that is more or less occult, *evoked* throughout an artistic community and across generations, developed through an extensive system of citations, quotations, and references, with the points of intersection *with* and separation *from* 'real' practices obscured through the modes of their deployment. Might the supposed 'hallucinatory practice' we are discussing be a Decadent/ Symbolist/ Avant-Garde manifestation of the same principle at work, taken farther and made more radical because the discourse though which it was articulated allowed it, because the mythologically structured modes of sociality developed there allowed this illusion to be cast around 'existent' people rather than eldritch gods, and because the less commercially-mediated structures surrounding its reading allowed it to more fully permeate the social structures themselves of the community? After all, the vernacular manifestation of this practice has not been without success; practitioners of chaos magic sometimes evoke Cthulic deities (wikipedia, 'Chaos Magic'), several versions of the *Necronomicon* have appeared, and the Sign at the heart of *The King in Yellow* has been discovered, in 'academic' language, to have always already been at play…

Derleth, especially, moves the Cthulic tradition in this direction in works such as *The Return of Hastur*, where we find the fictionality of the mythos called into question through its re-importation into itself as *ostensible* fiction, and an emphasis (reflecting that of Lovecraft in such pieces as *The Case of Charles Dexter Ward* and *The Picture in the House*) on practices of reading, of marginalia, of collation. What if, rather than in a *fantastic* fictional setting dealing with supernatural powers, such a work was composed in a fiction partaking of 'the real', and dealing with things that, while unlikely, were *possible*? What if this fiction utilized the language of 'truth' of empirical 'investigation', so that it scarcely resembled fiction at all, and was *read* as non-fiction, was in fact only fiction *from a certain reading*, even if it had the audacity to declare itself fictional in the very first paragraph? Would this not realign, to a great extent, these two twin traditions, and their various radical potentials? And would such a text even be easily recognizable as a continuation of both the mythos containing, and contained within, the Necronomicon and the King in Yellow, and also a continuation of the tradition of the Avant-Garde—those two divergent offspring of Poe?

"Among the few marginal notations made by my uncle, there are two or three especially remarkable ones in the *R'lyeh Text;* indeed, in the light of what is known or can be justifiably guessed, they are sinister and ominous notes."

[. . .]

"Observe the underscored line of text: *Ph'nglui mglw'nafh Cthulu R'lyeh wgah' nagl fhtagn,* and what follows it in my uncle's unmistakable hand: *His minions preparing the way, and he no longer dreaming? (WT: 2/28.)*... I turned my attention to the parenthetical notation, and within a short while solved its meaning as a reference to a popular magazine, *Weird Tales,* for February, 1928. I have it here."

He opened the magazine against the meaningless text, partially concealing the lines which had begun to take on an uncanny atmosphere of eldritch age beneath my eyes, and there beneath Paul Tuttle's hand lay the first page of a story so obviously belonging to this unbelievable mythology that I could not suppress a start of astonishment. The title, only partly covered by his hand, was *The Call of Cthulu,* by H.P. Lovecraft. But Tuttle did not linger over the first page; he turned well into the heart of the story before he paused and presented to my gaze the identical unreadable line that lay beside the crabbed script of Amos Tuttle in the incredibly rare *R'lyeh Text* upon which the magazine reposed. And there, only a paragraph below, appeared what purported to be a translation of the utterly unknown language of the *Text: In his house at R'lyeh great Cthulu lies dreaming.*

"There you have it," resumed Tuttle with some satisfaction. "Cthulu, too, waited for the time of his resurgence—how many eons, no one may know; but my uncle has questioned whether Cthulu still lies dreaming, and following this, he has written and doubly underscored an abbreviation which can only stand for *Innsmouth!* This, together with the ghastly things half hinted in this revealing story purporting to be only *fiction,* opens up a vista of undreamed horror, of age-old evil."

-August Derleth, *The Return of Hastur* (1939). (Carter 1971, pp 144-145.)

My tantalized spirit
    Here blandly reposes,
Forgetting, or never
    Regretting its roses—
Its old agitations
    Of myrtles and roses:

For now, while so quietly
    Lying, it fancies
A holier odor
    About it, of pansies—
With rue and the beautiful
    Puritan pansies.

And so it lies happily,
    Bathing in many
A dream of the truth
    And the beauty of Annie—
Drowned in a bath
    Of the tresses of Annie.

She tenderly kissed me,
    She fondly caressed,
And then I fell gently
    To sleep on her breast—
Deeply to sleep
    From the Heaven of her breast.

When the light was extinguished
    She covered me warm,
And she prayed to the angels
    To keep me from harm—
To the queen of the angels
    To shield me from harm.

And I lie so composedly,
    Now in my bed,
(Knowing her love,)
    That you fancy me dead—
And I rest so contentedly,
    Now in my bed,
(With her love at my breast,)
    That you fancy me dead—
That you shudder to look at me,
    Thinking me dead:—

But my heart is brighter
    Than all of the many
Stars in the sky,
    For it sparkles with Annie—
It glows with the light
    Of the love of my Annie—
With the thought of the light
    Of the eyes of my Annie.

-Edgar A. Poe, from *For Annie* (1845).   (Poe 1975, pp 973-975.)

Anna Blume is the feeling just before and after bed
Anna Blume is the woman there beside you
Anna Blume is the only kind of love you still can do
Anna Blume is really you.
To kill Anna Blume means to kill you off too
Have you ever been offed in your whole life?
To kill off Anna Blume means to off you too
Would you be willing to just let them off and kill you?
No! Kill Anna Blume, the feeling just before going to bed
Kill Anna Blume the woman there beside you
To kill Anna Blume is the only offing you still can do
If you wouldn't be, Merz help you, a person who can't do it through and through

-Kurt Schwitters, *Call It Killing You Off* (1919)   (Schwitters 2002, p 17.)

-Kurt Schwitters, *Anna Blume* (1921).   (Gamard 2000, fig. 19.)

In the web of ~~subjects~~ figured, evoked, recalled, or discovered that I have conjured up before you, it would be easy to confuse them all, to see them all as facets of a ~~single~~ identity; for so many share in their names a single syllable. Leaving aside the poem by Poe—that singular progenitor of so many aspects of the Yellow Sign—in which sleep, dream, death, presence, absence, thought, and form so subtly intertwine, which is entitled *for Annie,* let us survey a certain number of initiates we have connected with the practice, and some phonemes intimately involved: we find De Quincey and his young (and later, hallucinated) saviour *Ann*; Jarrysengle and his intercessor St. *Anne*, chosen for the nonexistent things his senses experienced there; Dujardin and the ~~subject~~ he conjured up in response to the over-heard name: *Antonia*;[3] and finally (blessed with a surname in order to reduce this confusion) the beloved of Kurt Schwitters' twenty-seven senses, *Anna* Blume, an other potential *Anti*-subject.

> At first the servant imagined that grief, to crushing, had unhinged his master's mind.
>
> [. . .]
>
> To continue to serve *them* without taking heed of death?
>
> [. . .]
>
> The suppressed thought was fading! Sometimes, experiencing a kind of dizziness, he felt compelled to assure himself that the countess was no more, positively was dead. He became adept in the melancholy pretence, and every moment he became more forgetful of reality. Before long he needed to reflect more than once to convince himself and pull himself together. He realized clearly that in the end he would surrender utterly to the terrifying magnetism wherewith the Count, little by little, was infusing the atmosphere around them.
>
> -Villiers de l'Isle-Adam, *Vera* (1883).

Schwitters' 1919 poem *Anna Blume* (re-written, revised, and variously translated by him throughout his life) has become a lynchpin of the Dada canon, such as it is. And while this may be quite appropriate, its canonical position may in fact help to conceal what may (I merely speculate) be its most radical elements; for its most radical implications might emerge *not* primarily from its status as an art-'object for contemplation' but as the relic of a vanished, lived *practice*. What is not often enough taken into account is the fact that this poem is far from alone, that Anna Blume—whether a name or a ~~subject~~—is a persistent force in Schwitters' creative life; and can we assume that Schwitters, of whom his fellow Dada Hans Richter recalled:

> The Trojan war cannot have been as full of incident as one day in Schwitters' life. When he was not writing poetry, he was pasting up collages. When he was not pasting, he was building his column, washing his feet in the same water as his guinea pigs, warming his

---

[3] The only reason that Dujardin and Antonia, who seem quite pertinent to our case, have not been treated more fully in this book is the practical fact that *The Legend of Antonia* does not appear to available in English translation; making it impossible for me to investigate the details. That Dujardin was keenly interested in the relationships between writing and modalities of thought is certain; he was the developer of the Interior Monologue.

paste-pot in the bed, feeding the tortoise[4] in the rarely-used bathtub, declaiming, drawing, printing, cutting up magazines [...]
and in the midst of all this he never forgot, wherever he went, to pick up discarded rubbish and stow it in his pockets.

(Richter 1997, pp 138-139.)

> Days, nights, weeks sped by. Neither one nor the other knew what they were bringing to pass. And strange things were now taking place, so that it became hard to distinguish how far the real and the imaginary coincided. A presence floated in the air. A form was struggling to become visible, to weave some pattern of its being upon the space no longer within its measure.
>
> -Villiers de l'Isle-Adam, *Vera* (1883).

had any *but* a *creative* life? The selections in the English translation of his work edited by Rothenberg and Joris alone include sixteen poems, plays, stories, and theoretical writings mentioning Anna by name or dedicated to her, in addition to others which, as we shall examine, seem to implicate her in various other ways; several drawings also share her name, and Schwitters named three volumes of his work after her. In her incisive full-length investigation of Schwitters' *Merzbau*, the constantly-evolving work of art into which he turned his home over a matter of decades (and which he also referred to as the Cathedral of Erotic Misery), Elizabeth Burns Gamard speculates that:

> [the poem/cycle] *An Anna Blume* appears to signal with even greater force Schwitters' deliberative search for the mystical sources and primal states underlying nature, art and life. For Schwitters, the character "Anna Blume" did not remain consigned to the pages of literature, but was to become Schwitters' idealized muse, the signature of "Manifeste Merz." In point of fact, "Anna" became the focus of a variety of Schwitters' inspirational episodes and was clearly the subject of his "desire": she was his Eve, his mistress, and his Madonna, among other "personages" and figures. In terms of the *Merzbau*, *An Anna Blume*, alone or coupled with subsequent revisions of the poem, provides the most significant insight into what may be viewed as the hermeneutic program and content of Schwitters' *Kathedrale*; "she" ("Anna/eve") is perhaps the *Merzbau's* chief resident. The fact that he not only recognized Anna Blume's "presence" in poetry, prose, and painting, but also dedicated many of these works to his "female mistress," suggests that the character of Anna Blume was Schwitters talismanic device in the fashioning of his private, highly esoteric magic kingdom.
>
> (Gamard 2000, pp 54-55.)

Kurt Schwitters, *Merzbau*, c. 1928.
(Gamard 2000, fig. 31.)

---

4 Compare this tortoise to that owned by Huysmans' proxy, Des Esseintes, in *A Rebours* and to that owned by Sandomir of the College of 'Pataphysics; and also, as Nathan Shaffer has pointed out, Jarry's chameleons, whose tails reputedly suggested the 'Pataphysical *gidouille*.

One translation of one version of *An Anna Blume*[5] follows:

> O Thou, beloved of my twenty seven senses,[6]
> I love thine!
> Thou thee thee thine I thine, thou mine.—we?[7]
> That belongs (by the side) not here![8]
> Who art Thou, uncounted[9] woman?
> Thou art—art Thou?[10]—
> People say, Thou werst,—
> Let them say, they don't know, how the churchtower stands.
> You wearest your head on your feet and wanderest on your hands,
> On thy hands wanderest Thou.
> Hallo thy red dress, clashed in white folds,
> Red I love Anna Blume, red I love Thine!
> Thou Thee Thee Thine, I Thine, Thou mine,—we?
> That belongs (by the side) in the cold glow.
> Red Bloom, red Anna Blume, how say the people?
>
> Price Question:
>   1. Anna Blume has wheels.
>   2. Anna Blume is red.
>   3. What colours are the wheels?
>
> Blue is the colour of thy yellow hair.
> Red is the whirl of thy green wheels.
> Thou simple maiden in everyday-dress,
> Thou dear green animal,
> I love Thine!
> Thou Thee The Thine, I Thine, Thou mine—we?

---

5 Note that the only mark distinguishing this *poem* from the *character/figure/subject* Anna Blume is a duplication, or *re*-inscription of the syllable (the significance of which is hinted at above): 'An'.

6 An entity not *present* in a *simplistically* phenomenological sense might well, according to Schwitters' Anti-logic, call for similarly multiplied Anti-sensory apparatuses.

7 In Schwitters' work as a whole, but *especially* in this and other work dealing with Anna, there is a kind of textual obsession with grammatical possessives. We might suggest that a certain *reciprocity* is built into the structure of the possessive, such that while 'you', for instance, might exist in the simple relation to 'me' of an *object*, 'yours' presupposes that I, too, might stand as an object in relation to *you*. In this sense, the possessive, and other permutations of basic pronouns, indicates not merely the existence of the speaking subject, but a truly *inter*subjective relationship. That is to say that through the possessive, or its internalization, Anna is not merely an *image* but a *subject,* or a Bergsonian *body* capable of acting (in some way) upon surrounding images; though in this case the *inter*subjective and *intra*subjective are both revealed as inadequate and clumsy notions.

8 Possibly belonging, instead, to 'the world in which Anna Blume lives, in which men walk on their heads, windmills turn, and locomotives run backward' described by Schwitters in *Merz* and drawn by him several times.

9 Uncounted because unknown, as such, to anyone but Schwitters himself?

10 'Thou art' could be read: 'You exist'. This is the same question we are in the midst of asking.

That belongs (by the side) in the glow box.
Anna Blume,
Anna,
A—N—N—A
I trickle your name.
Thy name drops like soft tallow.[11]
Dost thou know it, Anna,
Dost thou already know it?
One can also read thee from behind,
And thou, most glorious of all,
Thou art from the back, as from the front:
A—N—N—A [12]
Tallow trickles to strike over my back.
Anna Blume,
Thou drippes animal,
I
Love
Thine!

> I owe a lot to Anna Blume.
>
> -Kurt Schwitters, *The Artist's Right to Self-Determination* (1919).
>
> (Schwitters 2002, p 213.)

-Kurt Schwitters, *Anna Blume* (1942 version)   (Schwitters 2002, p 16.)

> So closely was the form of the young woman fused with his own that he could not but find her always with him. Now, on a garden seat on sunny days, he was reading aloud the poems that she loved. Now, in the evening, by the fireside, with two cups of tea on the little round table, he was chattering with the *Illusion*, who, for his eyes, sat smiling there in the other arm-chair.
>
> -Villiers de l'Isle-Adam, *Vera* (1883).

Looking at a wider range of poems in which Anna Blume appears, we can see several aspects of her multi-layered life, and even detect the relics of crises in their relationship. The poem *An Anna Blume* is, of course, quite forcefully a love lyric, and in it Anna Blume herself is consequently positioned as a personality outside or above banal 'reality', as even a 'real' beloved would be in such a poem. Other poems however seem to hint at a familiarity more down-to-earth, or at least figured as such, and at a conception of Anna as a terminal in a circuit of communication capable of linguistic *reception*: 'Today Ann received the following [communiqué] in Weimar-' (*Private Gentlemen,*

---

11 Compare the description of Anna's name trickling like candle-wax to Jarry's description of the evocation of Valens: 'the soul of Valens (Sengle still recognized the life or soul only by movements analogous to heart-beats) was simply leaking, streaming through the lips, like a vase overflowing.' (Jarry 1989, p 153.)

12 Schwitters gives at least one other hint as to the significance of Anna's name, also grounded in the Letter, but pointing in the same movement toward an artistic trajectory rife with the possibilities of similar evocations. In *Decay's Wake*, he notes that, 'Anna Blume and Arnold Böcklin have the same initials in their names: A.B.' (Schwitters 2002, p 26.) She is thus brought into conjunction with the painter of one of the most deeply canonical visual images in the tradition within which we have been investigating this potential practice: Böcklin's *Isle of the Dead*. Warren Fry has remarked that Anna also shares initials with André Breton; and looking at other initiates of the Yellow Sign, we might also note Decadent artist Aubrey Beardsley; Symbolist poet Alexander Blok; Ambrose Bierce, who took up Poe's mantle in America; Aloysius Bertrand, member of Borel, Gautier, and Nerval's Romantic *Petit Cénacle* group; and Alastair Brotchie, translator of Jarry and others.

Attention Please!) while others draw her projected personality back into a kernel of inscribed signs, or even *marks*, to be spatially deployed against the *language* of social control: 'K.A.P.D. = Kaiserliche ANNA BLUME Partei Deutschlands' (*The Secret Drawer*). In *The Prisoner* Anna moves through an atmosphere of words along with Apollinaire and Arp; in *Your Most Humble: Anna Blume* Hausmann delivers lectures on Dadadegy; and Anna accompanies Schwitters to the Funeral of Dada in *The Great Ardor of Dada: A Funeral March*.

In *Call it Killing You off*, which we shall presently examine more closely, Anna's ~~dual nature~~ as sensory ~~presence~~ after the possible model of Valens on the one hand and as intellectual and experiential *process* on the other is affirmed in the opening two lines: 'Anna Blume is the feeling just before and after bed / Anna Blume is the woman there beside you' (Schwitters 2002, p 17). She is emphatically both a feeling *within* you and a figure *beside* you (as reiterated in line 4 of *An Anna Blume*). This duality, which is indeed *not* so much a duality as a structural *fluidity* in the constitution of Anna as ~~subject~~, is central to Schwitters' conception of her. Schwitters describes 'the world in which Anna Blume lives, in which men walk on their heads, windmills turn, and locomotives run backward'. (*ibid, p. 215*.)

> this mode of life acquired a gloomy and persuasive magic. Raymond himself no longer felt any alarm, having become gradually used to these impressions.
>
> The glimpse of a black velvet robe at the end of a pathway; the call of a laughing voice in the drawing-room; a bell rung when he awoke in the morning, just as it used to be—all this had become familiar to him: the dead woman, one might have thought, was playing with the invisible, as a child might. So well beloved did she feel herself! It was altogether *natural*.
>
> -Villiers de l'Isle-Adam, *Vera* (1883).

In this way, Anna Blume, if we are to provisionally relate her to a potential practice we have speculated on in relation to other artists and figures, marks a radically different approach to those of De Quincey, who 'used to see, after painting upon the blank darkness a sort of rehearsal whilst waking, a crowd of ladies, and perhaps a festival, and dances,' preparing a detailed sensory panorama to experience passively afterward (De Quincey 1995, pp 61-62); from Huysmans, who (may have) taught himself to construct his hallucinations through rigorous attention to projected sensory detail, advising that 'The secret is to know how to go about it, to know how to concentrate the mind on one single detail, to know how to dissociate oneself sufficiently to produce the hallucination and thus substitute the *vision* of reality for reality itself' (Huysmans 1998, pp 19-20, my italics); and from those hallucinations of Jarrysengle in *Days And Nights* in which he accompanies the human *figure* of Valens on excursions within a naturalistic, if un- (or Anti-) 'real' world.[13] In these practices, the relationship with the

---

13 In Jarry, of course, a definite fluidity between form, 'essence', thought, memory, etc is certainly highlighted, especially in the penultimate chapter *En Route to Dulcinea,* in which while on one hand 'Valens was totally *present* in the room,' my italics, 'his soul was a great blue-brown butterfly', and 'the soul of Valens… was simply leaking, streaming through the lips…' (Jarry 1989, p 153) The (posited) evocation Valens, then, is not constrained, as those of De Quincey and Huysmans seem to be, by the conventions of sensory naturalism, and poetic metaphor and linguistic figures are part of the evocation; furthermore it is not merely his *image* that is present-ed, but his 'soul', his very subjectivity. Nonetheless, the aspects of Valens' projected subjectivity that fall in excess of physical form are still given sensory *representation*—his soul as a butterfly, for example—in order to affirm their independence and identity. In other words, the affirmation of Valens' 'soul', his identity as ~~distinct~~ from Jarrysengle's own, *must be translated into the sensory economy* in order to affirm itself. Whether the representation of Valens' evocation given in *Days and Nights* marks the terminal point of his (possible) development as a ~~subject~~/practice, or a comprehensive codification of the full extent or manifestation of it (assuming of course that it *is* even

projected subject is, to a greater or lesser extent, dependant upon a mimetic function; the ~~subject~~[14] is, so to speak, constructed from the outside in; beginning as an *ideational image* of an other; proceeding to a pictured or *sensory image* of an other (as with De Quincey), then to a (hallucinatory) *perception* of an other (as with Huysmans), thus acquiring (according to Idealist criteria at least) the status of an *object;* and finally, perhaps—with Courrière, and most explicitly and fully with Jarry—granted a certain *kind* of volition in excess of the primary subject's *conscious* control, either acting upon other images (in a Bergsonian sense) within the hallucinatory world and/or *on the primary subject itself*, as a secondary voice or will—thus infringing upon the hitherto sovereign realm of that *subjective experience.*[15] (In Jarry's case, these two forms of action may well have

---

an 'actual' practice) is, of course, impossible to say and difficult even to speculate upon; but in any event Schwitters' codification *in writing* of this dynamic as it inheres in his relationship with Anna Blume points toward a mode of (Anti-)subjectivity even more radical than, but clearly following the trajectory laid out by, that suggested in the textual relics Jarry *has* chosen to leave for us.

14 You will recall that I am attempting to resist the application of a single, author-itative term to apply to the practice or process under discussion.

15 This potential capacity of the secondary ~~subject~~ for independent action *upon* the primary subject, beyond its control—it should be kept in mind here that what we are, in such a case, discussing is a supplementary subjectivity or consciousness sharing with the primary or originating subject a single unconscious (and possibly sub-conscious) and *pre-*conscious in their various psychoanalytic formulations, or the same semiotic chora in a Kristevan schema (but with a modulated and multiplied thetic movement)—may explain Sengle's reaction of violation and terror in response to what might be interpreted as a kind of faltering of will or failure of concentration after the most explicit description of Valens' evocation, in the extremely thematically and linguistically dense conclusion of the chapter *En Route to Dulcinea*.

> The plaster mouth became flesh and red to drink the libation of Sengle's soul. The lamp had turned red, then black, the metal died out in the eye and the air poised a mist of tears.
>
> And after the momentary redness, the lips were green and adhered all chill to Sengle's blackened lips. These were too many complimentaries.
>
> The table rocked and Sengle was on the ground in the wake of a pile of crumbling snow, this time the recollection of the caffeine rustling across his tongue, in the bed of the mixed up hospital. He buried his face amid the tiny scales, several of which stuck.
>
> "Why did the mouth turn red to drink my soul, which escaped through the occiput when my face entered the flesh of the mask?"
>
> And Sengle was fumbling in the night towards his Self vanished like the heart of a bomb, his mouth upon his murder.
>
> (Jarry 1989, p 154)

gone hand in hand). In all of these cases, the Anti-subject is evoked *from* the position of both the *I* and the *eye*. To the extent that the ~~subject~~'s formation is grounded in the mimetic, the *mode* of its subjectivity is also thereby limited to a mimetic—and necessarily attenuated—re-production of the mode/s of subjectivity already at play in the primary subject. The secondary ~~subject~~ is, to the same extent, merely a *reduplication* of the primary subject in *structural* terms, not having undergone, or continually undergoing, an autonomous or semi-autonomous thetic moment.

Anna Blume's *mode* of subjectivity however, while necessarily finding its defining moment in the manifestations of re-jection (as formulated by Kristeva below) specific to Schwitters *as* subject, nonetheless can itself be seen to have developed *different* principles of structuration, intersecting with

> D'Althol lived a twofold life, like a visionary. The glimpse of a pale and gentle face, caught in a flash, within the twinkling of an eye; a faint chord struck on the piano, suddenly; a kiss that closed his lips at the instant of his speaking; the affinities of *feminine* thoughts which awoke within him in response to the words he uttered; a doubling of his own self which made him feel as if he were in some fluid mist; the perfume; the intoxicating, sweet perfume of his beloved by his side; and at night, betwixt waking and sleeping, words which he heard low-spoken—everything pointed to one thing: a negation of Death exalted finally into an unknown force!
>
> Once d'Althol felt and saw her so clearly beside him that he took her in his arms. But with that movement she vanished.
>
> -Villiers de l'Isle-Adam, *Vera* (1883).

notions of textuality and unicity in profoundly different ways. Thus for Anna Blume, the principle by which the unicity inherent in the notion of the subject operates is such that this unicity is not destroyed, or thrown so radically into question, when it is manifested as a (potentially sensory) figure one moment, and a series of ~~significant~~ marks on a page the next; when passing from a subject engaged with and constituted *through*, but not defined *by*, the Symbolic—i.e. a traditional model of the 'personality'—to a subject emerging from creative and/or poetic processes themselves. A kind of *speculative model* of subjectivity which can, at the same time, be *experienced* by Schwitters vicariously (though also, and no less importantly, by Anna Blume herself). And this vicarious nature of the experience is itself essential; for there is a sense in which Schwitters is *experiencing himself vicariously*—a

> It seems that true humour is nothing but a simple defense mechanism—especially a defense of the individual against outside forces, or even (for those of a metaphysical disposition) a defense of the circumscribed being who wishes to brave Everything.
>
> -Jean-Hugues Sainmont, *De minimis*' in the *Cahiers* of the College of 'Pataphysics. (P.E. 84, 1957 Anti-Vulgar)

speculative, alternative modulation of his own subjective process. This movement, by which the subject precipitates an internal rupture or, rather, *rejects* a part of 'itself' in order to create a kind of subjective stasis that can in turn be pushed aside, but which nonetheless inflects that movement in its passage, is a motif that Kristeva sees as inherent in material process as such, and at the same time as a precondition for the Symbolic function itself:

However, it must be remarked as well that this same autonomy—linked as it must inevitably be to the biological, historical, and psychological elements which are the material of subjectivity and from which the subject is gathered up and set into process—is in fact the inevitable mark of the transition of the evoked figure from an *image* to a ~~subject~~.

> By dint of accumulating ruptures, and through this heterogeneity, which uses the presignifying engram produced in the absence of any object isolated within itself, rejection becomes stabilized. Its tendency toward death is deferred by this symbolic heterogeneity: the body, as if to prevent its own destruction, re-inscribes [*re-marque*] rejection and, through a leap, *represents* it *in absentia* as a sign.
>
> This reinscription or mark is constitutive of rejection. The mark thwarts rejection in order to reactivate it and defers rejection so that it will return to divide and double the mark in turn. This mark is the "re" in re-jection and is the precondition of rejection's renewal. The quantitative accumulation of rejections nevertheless upsets the mark's stability: the mark becomes an unstable engram which ends up being rejected into a *qualitatively* new space, that of *representamen* or the sign. Rejection destroys the stasis of the mark, breaks up its own positivity and restraint, and, in the face of this "murder," sets up a qualitatively different thetic phase: the sign. The mark is thus a step in the development of the sign since it prefigures the sign's constancy and unity.
>
> (Kristeva 1984, pp 171-172)

That this movement is, as such, a precondition for the formation or continual emergence of the subject in process (the thetic phase) is reiterated farther down the page:

> Ah, Ideas are living beings! The count had hollowed out in the air the shape of his love, and necessity demanded that into this void should pour the only being that was homogenous to it, for otherwise the Universe would have crashed into chaos. And at that instant the impression came, final, simple, absolute, that *She must be there, there in the room!* Of this he was as calmly certain as of his own existence, and all the objects around him were saturated with this conviction. One saw it there! And now, *since nothing was lacking save only Vera herself,* outwardly and tangibly there, *it was inevitably ordained that she should be,* and that for an instant the great Dream of Life and Death should set its infinite gates ajar!
>
> [. . .]
>
> there at last the Countess Vera was gazing on him, and sleep still lingering within her eyes.
>
> 'Roger!' spoke the distant voice.
>
> 'He came over to her side. In joy, in divine, oblivious, deathless joy, their lips were united!
>
> And then they perceived, *then,* that they were in reality *but one single being.*
>
> -Villiers de l'Isle-Adam, *Vera* (1883).

Stasis (which material scission produces but also divides, jostles, and disrupts) tends to unify scission, mark One, and absorb it in the path of the desiring subject. Rejection generates the signifier and the desire adjoining it as a defense against the death that rejection brings about by carrying its logic of scission "to the end." But rejection is not simple destruction: it is re-jection. The prefix "re-" indicates not the repetition of a constant identity, but rather a renewal of division through a new unifying stoppage where something more than a mere mark—a *representamen* and an ego—will finally crystallize, and then be re-jected once again.

(*ibid.*)

The latter point relates, of course, to Kristeva's assertion that subjectivity, and most especially what she designates the subjective mode of textual practice (*ibid,* pp 88-106), constitutes a *practice* and a *process* rather than a structurally static 'personality' or 'awareness'; This in turn points again toward Anna's constant and radical re-invention of herself. The creation of Anna Blume as an Anti-subject differentiated from Schwitters' own subjective process positions her as a subjective scission or stasis which in turn modulates his *own* subjectivity through the very remove—vicariousness—through which his own subjective structure must pass in apprehending it. Yet in order for this scission to institute itself fully, it *must* be felt by him as something outside, other, *absent*—whatever his intellectual *understanding* of the rational 'fictiveness' of the *inter*-personal nature of the situation, Anna must be *experienced* not as an image *within* his subjective economy, but as an other subject heterogenous to himself.[16]

In this way, while many anti-subjects that we have speculated upon are, to a great extent at least, *products* of creative practice, of Symbolic and Semiotic re-formulation, Anna Blume can be seen to be radically *immersed in,* and always already *emerging from,* the modalities and subjective intersections and re-formulations inherent in creative *practice itself.* If there is mimesis at play, it is not so much a mimesis of form as a mimesis of structuration and subjective process. Because the locus, the defining mark of Anna Blume as ~~subject~~ is located at the point, or more precisely within the mechanisms of, the intersection of the thetic moment and its artistic re-formulation, she can move, so to speak, in any direction in the following through of her thetic process/es, as it/they are repeatedly re-jected.[17]

Kurt Schwitters, *Still Life with Chalice* (1909, detourned c. 1920?) (Richter 1997, fig. 71.)

It is therefore appropriate that the very name 'Anna Blume' refuses to rest comfortably in a single register; Anna Blume is the name of a character, possibly a subject, certainly with implications both within and without texts themselves; also the name of a poem, likewise a poetic sequence, several drawings, and

---

16 It might be noted by the side that, if we posit Schwitters to have *experienced* Anna Blume in as 'full' or integral a way as De Quincey, Huysmans, Jarry, and others may have, that the notion of the 'phenomenological' itself is likewise radically restructured, Anna being not only as 'real' for ~~herself~~ in the form of a textual deployment or psychosomatic or physiological sensation as in the form of a sensorily perceived/perceptible figure, but as 'real' for *Schwitters* as well.

17 We can see the correlations, then, between the way that Schwitters re-formulates the potential practice he may have inherited, eschewing the mimetic or shifting it to the register of linguistic and subjective process; and the Dada poetic (such as it was) at large. While this rupture from (or re-registration of) the mimetic was not exclusive to or original to Dada, it is worth mention in that it is suggestive of the ways in which Dada radically deployed heretofore 'literary' principles in various registers of social, political, and phenomenological life, and moreover points to the way in which many motifs in the *lived* traditions of the Yellow Sign were taken up by Dada, but so radically and idiosyncratically modified, internalized, re-formulated, or re-registered as to take on the appearance of a rupture; and, indeed, one might compare the *rejection* of *all* tradition (including the Avant-Garde and the Yellow Sign) that Dada laid claim to in its *discourse,* if not in its *practice,* to Kristeva's notion of rejection now under discussion.

elements of the titles of several books;[18] and, at the same time, reads in German as 'Anna Flower'. As a result, Schwitters' translator is faced with rendering the second word of the phrase 'Anna Blume' either as a semantic, and thus conventionally translatable signifier, thus 'Anna Blossom', or as the surname of a subject, and thus conventionally retained: Anna Blume. Therefore: is Anna Blume to be treated primarily as a subject, or at least a character, retaining her full name; or primarily as a textual coding, thus 'Anna Blossom'; or rather, which aspect of Anna Blume—since the two are ultimately inextricable, as are the phonemes in the German—is to be privileged? Schwitters, probably in attempt to preserve the essential ambiguity of these two linguistic functions converging in Anna Blume, was inconsistent in his own translations and re-writings;[19] his translators Jerome Rothenberg and Pierre Joris have generally opted for 'Blossom' in favour of 'Blume'. In view of my present discussion, I have taken the liberty (one I have not taken elsewhere in the present volume) of altering the translations, retaining 'Blume' where Rothenberg and Joris (and even where Schwitters himself) have substituted 'Blossom'.

In his 1925 *Shadow Play*, Schwitters addresses the dynamic between sensory 'concreteness' and linguistic or cognitive diffusion in such a subjective projection or evocation, and suggests how too exclusive a focus on the sensory can result in the implosion or, paradoxically, the re-integration (and thus dissolution) of the secondary ~~subject~~. In it, we meet Laura, who informs us immediately that, 'I am a young man's fancy. I was born out of a young man's fancy.' She becomes embroiled in a short confrontation with the jealous Elena, who complains that she is, 'A genuine woman. Which means I'll scratch your eyes out, little witch. Why can't a guy like that end up with me instead? I yearn until my soul is black and blue, and Friedrich cooks a woman up out of his fancy. A Laura.' (Schwitters 2002, p 167.) She then attacks Laura physically; the latter is dis-embodied, and her disjointed limbs thrown over the side of the stage.

The following three scenes further complicate the situation. Elena, at first jealous of the evocation Laura, 'cooked' up by Friedrich whom she has not even met, then falls in love with Lime, who is the 'escaped'

---

18 These titles are: *Anna Blume Seals* of 1919; *Fundamental. The Flower [Blume] Anna, The New Anna Blume* of 1922; and also in 1922 *Anna Blume's Memoirs in Lead, an Easy-to-grasp Method of Madness for Everyone.* (Gamard 2000, p 57) This last title is particularly notable on two counts. The 'Method of Madness' explicitly relates the figure/process of Anna to a systematic de-normalizing of structures of thought, and might be compared to the 'Art of Madness' practiced by Freytag-Loringhoven and promulgated in *The Little Review* in 1919, the year of the original publication of *An Anna Blume* (Lane, 1998). A 'Memoir in Lead' is particularly suggestive, as lead is generally taken as the base material in the process of alchemical *sublimation* and purification. Gamard discusses Schwitters' engagement with alchemical and other esoteric and hermetic ideas (which he shared with Ernst, Breton, Courrière, Huysmans, Villiers de L'Isle-Adam, and many others engaged in similar practices) throughout her study on the Merzbau. (Gamard 2000.) As Mark Leahy has pointed out, the title could also refer to the lead of movable type used in the printing of a text, and to the 'madness' resulting from lead poisoning. The *Memoirs in Lead* in its entirety has not been translated.

19 Schwitters also occasionally substituted 'Eve', especially in his later re-writings (Gamard 2000, p 54). It might be noted that 'Eve', like 'Anna', is 'from the back, as from the front' E-V-E, and that the Eve of the Old Testament was, of course, famously conjured from Adam's own rib—deriving from his body, yet maintaining a discreet subjective structure. While the notions of sexual inequality that have become culturally inextricable with this legend and which are therefore brought into relation to Schwitters' practice remain problematic, Schwitters' primary association with Eve is less likely to be social or religious (in an orthodox sense at least) than alchemical.

shadow of Friedrich's friend Emil, whom she is also unfamiliar with. When asked about Emil, Lime replies that, 'He's looking around for me until his eyes go blind, because he misses me so much.' (*ibid*, p 168.) Soon Friedrich appears on the scene, helping Emil in his search; he recognises Lime, who takes flight. Elena is not left alone long, for soon Emil arrives. Elena comments that he is 'a thousand times more handsome than your shadow!' and in an aside her jealousy toward Laura is repeated, in more indirect fashion, toward Lime: 'THIS guy's only concern is for his shadow. Aw gee, I wish I was his shadow.' After Emil runs off to continue his search, Lime appears again, now chasing Laura in a fit of unrequited passion.

At this juncture of my palimpsest of the narrative, it is worth examining these two characters more closely. Lime of course resembles Laura in one very important respect—he is an independent but secondary ~~presence~~ defined in relation to a primary subject. But he is emphatically of a different quality:

ELENA: O, you sweetheart! Are you the product of a *woman's* fancy?
LIME: No way. I am an honest to goodness shadow. I am the shadow of a man.
   (*ibid*, p 168.)

Lime considers himself, in some sense, more *real* or more *full* or 'true' than a mere fancy; and this supposition seems to rest on his mimetic plentitude, his more direct correspondence to a specific prior model of his own existence—he is the shadow *of a man*. He is, in fact, not 'imagined' but is simply a re-organisation of an existent subject in his full plenitude. (It should be remembered that since this is a *shadow play*—and the stage directions confirm that this is not merely a title but indicates its intended model of performance—that Emil himself is in fact no less a shadow than his 'shadow' Lime).

Laura, on the other hand, while born *from* Friedrich's fancy, cannot be reduced *to* him, even in a re-organized form. While Lime's name is simply the reverse of Emil, Laura's name is her own. While Emil is caused pain by his separation from his shadow, Friedrich does not even mention Laura at his first appearance, so busy is he helping in his friend's search. Lime, the shadow (who, in a shadow play, and as the reversal of his name suggests, is almost more like a *reflection*), is still, ultimately, homogenous with Emil's subjective structure. To be without Lime is, for Emil, to be a *split* subject, an unsustainable condition, and in the end, Lime discovers that he too is dying from the separation. He is not so much a secondary ~~subject~~ as a re-organised *image* of Emil, one which, being ultimately homogenous with and situated structurally *within* Emil, *cannot* act as the kind of subjective scission or stasis that would allow Emil to engage with Lime vicariously, *as* an other. Though Lime is posited or imaged *as* outside Emil, that image itself remains homogenous and ultimately comprehensible to Emil, a part of his organized subjectivity.

Laura, conversely, while inseparable *from* Friedrich, remains heterogenous to him—an evocation, but not reducible to him as subject; there is always already something at play within Laura as ~~subject~~ that lies in excess of his own *conscious* structures, a negativity through which his engagement must pass; Laura has remained a mark of heterogenous process that disrupts and maintains Friedrich's subjective process within the same movement; and, up to this point in *Shadow Play*, this has allowed both terms of this pair, Friedrich and Laura, to act separately without the kind of unsustainable pathology that results for Emil at 'The spot where I [Lime] broke off.' (*ibid.*)

However, Friedrich is about to make a fatal mistake. He arrives on the scene, and at the sight of Laura exclaims, in a line highly reminiscent of *An Anna Blume*, 'Laura, you creature of my fancy, you my soul, you one and only woman whom I love, I love you!' Laura replies: 'O save me, I'm dying beneath his stronger gaze.'[20] (*ibid, p. 170.*) Unperturbed, Friedrich continues:

> FRIEDRICH: I love this dear head on its slender neck, this black hair like the sea at night. O were it only mine!
>
> LAURA: *During the following she slowly falls apart, the pieces disappearing into or in back of Friedrich.* O, my poor head! *Her head flies to the back of Friedrich's head.*
>
> (*ibid,* p 171.)

Friedrich continues to name the parts of Laura's body—hands, arms, feet, limbs—punctuated with 'o were they mine!' until at last Laura has been completely dis-embodied, leaving only a foot. Elena responds to Friedrich's expression of shock: 'Dummy! She's with you now! You wished her up into yourself!' Emil and Lime, who is himself dying from his separation from Emil, re-merge, and run off with the euphoric Elena, while Friedrich, dejected, wanders off with nothing but Laura's remaining foot.

Emil's and Lime's re-merging is not only facilitated, but necessitated by their ultimate homogeneity. Friedrich, on the other hand, has lost his beloved anti-subject through succumbing to that same homogenous impulse. Rather than maintain the scission, the stasis of Laura's otherness, his emphasis on the sensual *image* of Laura and the simultaneous repression of the subjective heterogeneity that she represented (that which allows Anna Blume to exist as a *textual-subjective logic* as well as a phenomenal presence) has resulted in fetishism, and a consequent re-instatement of a psychical homogeneity. In disembodying Laura in order to re-assemble her in a *comprehensible* way free of what lies in excess of his own subjective constitution (her textual nature, in Kristeva's terms her relationship to the semiotic), the stasis that retains her ~~otherness~~ is removed, she is reabsorbed 'up into yourself'.

Shadow Play can thus be viewed as a kind of warning, a

> Writing is the passageway, the entrance, the exit, the dwelling place of the other in me—the other that I am not, that I don't know how to be, but that I feel passing, that makes me live—that tears me apart, disturbs me, changes me, who?—a feminine one, a masculine one, some?—several, some unknown, which is indeed what gives me the desire to know and from which all life soars.
>
> -Hélène Cixous & Catharine Clément, *Sorties* (1975).
> (Caws 2001, p 627.)

---

20 Already, the preponderance of the optical—which might be taken as metonymic of the sensual in general—is related to the danger of ~~subjective~~ dissolution.

practical exposition of the mental processes and vigilances necessary in maintaining the practice we are speculating upon. It is worth noting that in a play presenting the spectacle of the death of an evoked figure, we also find (in the character of Elena) a consistent jealousy or antipathy toward that evoked figure, and specifically against its non-existent nature; for two poems of 1919 (the year that *An Anna Blume* was probably written, in which it was published, and when Anna moved beyond Schwitters interior economy to leave traces 'on the world') seem to refer to a particular crisis, both responding to an unspecified attempt or demand to 'execute Anna Blume'. Whether this injunction came from the public sphere—most likely denunciations of the poem from elements in Berlin Dada—or from the private sphere of Schwitters' family or domestic friends (or if demands from various sectors were seen as essentially contiguous) is unclear, though in both of these texts (refer again to the opening lines of *Call it Killing You Off*) Anna is treated less like a text or public embodiment of artistic conviction and more like someone/thing both *person* and embodied *experience*.

Call it Killing You Off is the more straightforward of the pair, and is, along with *An Anna Blume*, the most sustained and concentrated explicit treatment of Anna. In it Schwitters sets out Anna's dual nature, and her ultimate inextricability from him:

> Anna Blume is the feeling just before and after bed
> Anna Blume is the woman there beside you
> Anna Blume is the only kind of love you still can do
> Anna Blume is really you.
>
> (*ibid*, p 17.)

and reiterates that 'To kill off Anna Blume means to kill off you too,' asking angrily, 'Would you be willing to just let them off and kill you? / No!'

While *Call it Killing You Off* takes the form of a lyric—one of Schwitters' most grammatically and semantically 'coherent' poems in fact, with its end-stopped lines and spell-like repetitions, *Execution: Merz Poem 9* eschews verse and abandons grammatical cohesion early on. While the former operates in Schwitters' world, the world of sense where she is *referred to by* the text, the latter is a text in which she herself can be embedded, and within which she can contract and modulate her significance as she inscribes herself amongst other words and significations. Anna is immediately situated as a deity, and the call for her 'death' as a demand for sacrifice:

> Someone demanded Anna Blume's execution. Execution triggers crucifixion. Crucifying Anna Blume executes you all.
> (*ibid*, p 18.)

The semiotic violence that would attend her death is brought into alignment with that of the symbolic register, state warfare:

> Ring glows the knife gun turrets do trigger knives do swing. Ring glows the knife onto your headless heads. Ring to surge corpses headless frenzy, frenzy.
> (*ibid*)

In the following paragraph, we are met with a flurry of fractured phrases, themes, and repeated words: snatches of verse from *An Anna Blume*, birds, humans, brains (both human and bird), themes of blooming, growing, death and wilting. 'Human', repeated eight times in the poem, brings with it decidedly negative connotations; most under attack is human reason, 'human brains'. Schwitters' attitude toward conventional reason and 'common-sense' in his writing tends to be gently mocking; the following year, he writes that 'I prefer nonsense, but that is a purely personal matter.' Here however he gives vent to an uncharacteristic rage, and confirms Anna Blume's distinctness from the human race:

> Humans! Humans brain Humans. You humans with a human brain. (But really!) People are so wise, so Anna Blume has a bird's brain.
> (*ibid*)

However, Anna can change these structures of thought, 'Thou greens the human brain.' The word 'green' is loaded with significance in Schwitters' work, especially when employed as a verb; it appears most often, by a wide margin, in those poems in which Anna Blume also appears.[21] Like all of Schwitters' verbal employments, any reading is likely to be reductive and it has many associations, some of them doubtless known only to Schwitters himself; but it tends to imply a blossoming—a *blooming*—of significance, positioning the human

---

21 One exception is *Green Child* of around 1918, the year prior to *An Anna Blume's* publication. This poem—composed of short, cut-off snatches of exclamations, exhortations, and rhythmic recitations of colours in various series and permutations, suggests some intense but unrecoverable narrative of nightmarish pursuit involving the speaker and the interlocutor, the 'Green Child' herself, who takes on a number of roles and positions in relation to the speaker (though the possibility remains open that both characters speak, their utterances undifferentiated), one after the other: bride, mother, child; beloved of the speaker, disgusting him. This scene of psychic anxiety and scission, the violent multiplicity of the unnamed interlocutor, the shifting of subjective positions, and the importance of Green, later usually reserved for poems involving Anna, all suggest the *possibility*—though certainly beyond possible confirmation—that this poem may represent a stage in her formation or resolution.

psyche as a pastoral landscape. Again we have an indication that Anna as Anti-subject can go places that Schwitters, *as* himself, cannot; 'Anna Blume does live worlds.'

As in *Call It Killing You Off*, to kill Anna Bloom is kill the 'bloom', the 'green' of Schwitters' brain, that which saves him from numbering himself among the 'Humans with a human brain.' He says to her, 'Thou dies, I die a human.' There is no text to suggest the precise outcome of this crisis, though Anna Blume's continued appearance in his work confirms the resolution expressed in these two poems.

'Does thread wilt humans?' asks Schwitters; and concludes in the final line with his essential argument for his continuing engagement, his *relationship* with Anna both as 'the feeling before and after bed' *and* as 'the woman there beside him':

'Anna Blume greens the wilt.'

Today Ann received the following in Weimar: From the National Assembly of Piecemeal. As first formation of a serious situation weapon poisoned all. For he, who her, who here hear da da, goldens Glotea. (Dissolution of the family fathers.)

- Kurt Schwitters, from *Private Gentlemen, Attention Please!* (1919). (Schwitters 2002, p 25.)

Your future too is presently in the past! (K.A.P.D. = Kaiserliche ANNA BLUME Partei Deutschlands.) In his imagination the loaded wagons were already rolling along the railroad tracks. Until finally everything she knew was in one letter.

-Kurt Schwitters, *The Secret Drawer: A Novelette* (1922). (Schwitters 2002, p 130.)

Someone demanded Anna Blume's execution. Execution triggers crucifixion. Crucifying Anna Blume executes you all. Ring glows the knife gun turrets do trigger knives do swing. Ring glows the knife onto your headless heads. Ring to surge corpses headless frenzy, frenzy.
Humans! Humans brain Humans. You humans with a human brain. (But really!) People are so wise, so Anna Blume has a bird's brain. O Thou, beloved of my twenty seven senses, A—N—N—A, thou from the back as from, she that I love, thou thine thy thee, this may not be. Gardens do gobble world kiss. Gardens to bloom hands, meadows do dwell at teepees, sky wilts thread, the autumn cables times. But thou, thou noblest, thou greenest bird. Thou satiates to tint a knife the pastures. Does earth wilt? Do humans wander and must die? The crazy steel raised high sparkles thine limbs. Death inward hard whips inward door wine. Only now die, o thou wise one. Thou greens the human brain.

Thou greens to tremble human brains. Thou dies, I die a human, Anna Blume does live worlds. O thou, beloved, thou greens life thou wiltest leaf.
Does thread wilt humans?
Poor old legs drop limbs.
Anna Blum greens the wilt.

    -Kurt Schwitters, *Execution: Merzpoem 9* (c. 1919).   (Schwitters 2002, p 18.)

Also this climbing around under the name "the" isn't unpleasant.
The clock ungreens the creases, now does it preen in silk.
Trumpets do climb up Anna Blume elephant. (Radioactive.)
The seats with the backs are the expensive seats.
Thou.
This great procedure that I also can't withhold from thee.
The thou, there thou, this them.
N.B. Anna Blume and Arnold Böcklin have the same initials in their names: A.B.

    -Kurt Schwitters, *Decay's Way* (1919).   (Schwitters 2002, p 26.)

Blood boils in cracks of veins before Apollinaire with zigzags mountains hoof it right and left. Right and left. Left and right. One, two, one two, one two, one two one the sound the beam to churn inside the eye. Thine eye, Anna Blume, thine eye stays free of tears. Thou twittering overwhelms Apyl women can will get from the cloudpump. Hans arp roaming Anna Blume green pinetree pump left two left two left two one. Left two one. Left two one. Two one. One. Eight.

    -Kurt Schwitters, from *The Prisoner: poem 4* (c. 1920).   (Schwitters 2002, p 33.)

Ardor bleeds Ardors bleed blood. Merz greening tempest charge at the clock. The churchtower rises a pervert clawing of claws (it goes without saying). Claws on top claws, pervert, claws; smackeroo. Blamm. Do slosh fish rumble lama guck (it's a Kaiser's Day special!) fish do unleaf itself deep inside slowly sea zeppelins… Rages, rages, rages—sea raging fish, airs, zeppelin. The turtledove drops drops (where?), drops skim stash halfway up (O Anna Blume, my lovely miss, did you ever read anything like this?). My corpse is too large, in the night—crumbles, crumbles, crumbles—too large is my corpse.

    -Kurt Schwitters, from *The Great Ardor of Dada: A Funeral March* (1921).   (Schwitters 2002, p 38.)

To begin with one has to learn dadadegy from Mr. Hausmann, so as to know how to dadadize Dada dadadada. Beyond that be very careful (but let's not speak of it here). I have to tell you that the churchtower rises very rapidly. On top fish spiketh in whipair. Sparkling air spikes
the whip's fish. Thin the spike does fish. Whipped air in air (this can result in
decomposed knots). Joy thinly spikes to the whipstink. Sir, I believe, you are sick;
but that's not very interesting. And the churchtower sunken Merz branchlet to the
left. Ardor bleeds, ardors bleed blood.—Hey! Your red legs!

    -Kurt Schwitters, *Your Most Humble: Anna Blume: (but deep down the matter is much more complicated)* (1921-22)   (Schwitters 2002, p 41.)

in the world in which Anna Blume lives, in which men walk on their heads, windmills turn, and locomotives run backward, Dada also exists.

    -Kurt Schwitters, from *Merz* (1920).   (Schwitters 2002, p 215.)

Wire is the soul of electricity.
A woman does screech: "Wow o wow!"
"Baa" the sheep says.
See the maiden with an apron on.
Also her bare foot is the maiden's own.
And on her bumble bridle *Blume Anna* sits alone.

    -Kurt Schwitters, *Village Poem* (1922)   (Schwitters 2002, p 44.)

An airy silverspeckled green.
In the hands of 5 to 6 daredevil types,
a little rented boat
to blow Mary the Red out of the water.
And then
when no one can go on,
to gurgle "Anna Blume" from full throats.

    -Kurt Schwitters, *Simile* (1921)   (Schwitters 2002, p 41.)

[Nadja] tells me of my power over her, of my faculty of making her think and do whatever I desire, perhaps more than I think I desire…. A brief scene in dialogue at the end of my [automatic text] "Poisson Soluble," and which seems to be all she has read yet of the *Manifeste*, a scene whose precise meaning, moreover, I have never been able to determine and whose characters are as alien, their agitation as enigmatic as possible—as if they had been tendered and swept away again by a flood of sand—gives her the impression of having actually participated in it and even of having played the—if anything obscure—part of Hélène. The place, the atmosphere, the respective attitudes of the speakers were indeed what I had imagined.

    -André Breton, *Nadja* (1928).   (Breton 1960, pp 79-80.)

She uses a new image to make me understand how she lives: it's like the morning when she bathes and her body withdraws while she stares at the surface of the bathwater. "I am the thought on the bath in the room without mirrors."

    -André Breton, *Nadja* (1928).   (Breton 1960, p 101.)

how gracefully she conceals her face behind the heavy, nonexistent plume of her hat!

    -André Breton, *Nadja* (1928).   (Breton 1960, p 108.)

I have taken Nadja, from the first day to the last, for a free genius, as one of those spirits of the air which certain magical practices momentarily permit us to entertain but which we can never overcome.

    -André Breton, *Nadja* (1928).   (Breton 1960, p 111.)

"With the end of my breath, which is the beginning of yours."

-André Breton, *Nadja* (1928). (Breton 1960, p 115.)

"Who goes there? Is it you, Nadja? Is it true that the beyond, that everything beyond is here in this life? I can't hear you. Who goes there? Is it only me? Is it myself?"

-André Breton, *Nadja* (1928). (Breton 1960, p 144.)

I was driving a car along the road from Versailles to Paris, the woman sitting beside me (who was Nadja, but who might have been anyone else, after all, or even *someone else*) pressed her foot down on mine on the accelerator, tried to cover my eyes with her hands in the oblivion of an interminable kiss, desiring to extinguish us, doubtless forever, save to each other, so that we should collide at full speed with the splendid trees along the road.

-André Breton, *Nadja* (1928). (Breton 1960, pp 152-153.)

That is the story that I too yielded to the desire to tell *you*, when I scarcely knew you—you who can no longer remember but who, as if by chance, knowing the beginning of this book, have intervened so opportunely, so violently, and so effectively, doubtless to remind me that I wanted it to be "ajar, like a door"… You who, for all those who hear me must be not an entity but a woman, despite all that has been levied upon me and upon me in you to make into a Chimera.

-André Breton, *Nadja* (1928). (Breton 1960, pp 156-157.)

Without doing it on purpose, you have taken the place of the forms most familiar to me, as well as of several figures of my foreboding. Nadja was one of these last, and it is just that you should have hidden her from me.

All I know is that this substitution of persons stops with you, because nothing can be substituted for you, and because for me it was for all eternity that this succession of terrible or charming enigmas was to come to an end at your feet.

    -André Breton, *Nadja* (1928).   (Breton 1960, pp 157-158.)

Since you exist, as you alone know how to *exist*, it was perhaps not so necessary that this book should exist. I have decided to write it nevertheless, in memory of the conclusion I wanted to give it before knowing you and which your explosion into my life has not rendered vain. This conclusion has its true meaning and all its strength only through your intercession.

It smiles at me as sometimes you have smiled at me, behind great thickets of tears. "It's still love," you used to say, and more unjustly, you would also say: "All or nothing."

I shall never dispute this rule, with which passion has armed itself. At the most I might question it as to the nature of this "all"—whether, in this regard, it must be unable to hear me in order to be passion. As for its *various movements*, even insofar as I am their victim—and whether or not it can ever deprive me of speech, suppress my right to exist—how could they divorce me from the pride of knowing passion itself, from the absolute humility I should feel before it alone?

    -André Breton, *Nadja* (1928).   (Breton 1960, p 158.)

In every domain the mind appropriates certain rights which it does not possess.

    -André Breton, *Nadja* (1928).   (Breton 1960, p 160.)

Late in coming, it seems to me, is the true condition or the possibility not just of expressing oneself but of modulating oneself as one chooses.

    -Stéphane Mallarmé, *Crisis in Poetry* (1886).   (Caws 2001, p 24.)

    For Ducasse, the imagination is no longer that abstract little sister who skips rope in a square; you have seated her on your knees and you have read your perdition in her eyes. Listen to her. You will think at first that she doesn't know what she is saying; she knows nothing, and in a minute, with that little hand you kissed, she will caress in the darkness the hallucinations and troubles of the senses. No one knows what she wants, she makes you aware of several worlds at once, until soon you don't know how to behave in this one. Thus is instituted the trial of everything all over again.

    -André Breton, *Le Pas perdus* (1922).   (Nadeau 1973, p 81.)

It's in front of the paper that the artist *creates himself*.

    -Stéphane Mallarmé, Letter to Eugène Lefébure, Feb. 1865.   (Mallarmé 1988, p 48.)

    Lautréamont was possessed by Language; among many other things, he is an image of possession, in more than one of its senses. Lautréamont baptized himself in Writing. Lautréamont's single work, *Les Chants de Maldoror*, is not as amoral as many have charged—but it accedes to only one morality, that of the text. *Maldoror* is a hymn to Language, to Writing, and it is a hymn inscribed within the very flesh of the deity itself. Lautréamont was not merely attempting an idiosyncratic work, he was attempting to change the way that he interacted with Language itself on every level, as we can see in his letters. For even an irritated note to a businessman bears the stamp of his verbose and ironically elegant syntax and argot, regardless of the emotional or thematic pitch of the ideas signified there; of his constant, ingrained and/or obsessive grammatical obfuscations; and of his constant *self*-questioning of Language, of the act of engaging it, of writing and reading. Take, for example, the following single sentence from a note to his banker:

> You have enforced the deplorable system of distrust vaguely prescribed by my father's eccentricity; but you have guessed that my aching head does not prevent my considering attentively the difficult situation in which hitherto you have been placed by a sheet of writing paper from South America, its main shortcoming lack of clarity; for I am not taking into account the offensiveness of certain melancholy observations which one readily forgives an old man, and which appeared to me on first reading intended to impose upon you, in the future perhaps, the necessity of deviating from your clearly defined role as banker vis-à-vis a gentleman come to live in the capital…
> (Ducasse 1978, pp 119-121.)

It is highly unlikely that this was the type of communication the banker was used to receiving from destitute, unemployed young men asking him to mind his own business and simply do his job. Certainly, he is unlikely to have appreciated the elegance of its syntactical construction. The writer of this sentence loves Language too much to do other than render it, through various means—some syntactic, others through various manipulations in voice (a vague concept, which involves so many others and so many others that it is difficult, without, that is, devolving, to some extent, into a prescriptive or reductive third-rate structuralism, to render or quantify), and even through certain allusive images—such as, for example, that of South America, representing, as it does, both his birthplace, in a sense, and also, as you will find, a certain cluster, or set, of themes relating, quite closely, to the Yellow Sign, in addition to which, the significance, if we consider it, of this image, South America, in juxtaposition, in this letter, to the image of *paper*, is, potentially, great, on several registers—opaque; the sentence then becomes a thing that one experiences, in which an entire thought might grow, permute, dissolve and tighten again—the reader moves along through the sentence not knowing what will happen next, or knowing what will happen next, if the reader has read the sentence, or part of it, before, and the marks of punctuation become markers by which the reader comes to grips with the sentence spatially: backtracking, counting clauses (so many of which are split by so many means—parentheses, commas, semicolons, dashes—all of which mean essentially a single thing, 'pause,' but each of which is in fact endlessly nuanced, with endless subtlety) and finding the sentence a place in which one can, in a sense, live, a thing that must be learned slowly, gradually—and yet somehow, at the furthest reaches, it remains a thing grammatically self-contained, and may even have a certain balance, a structure, almost as if in chapters or in acts, its own unique symmetry; the very workings of the intense and agonizing exhilaration of crafting a sentence as if one is crafting one's own life—or vice-versa, and including both fine-tipped gestures such as the dispersion of hyphens or commas, and less purely introspective concerns such as the relationship of the sentence to those, if any, that lie around it, which can sometimes provide just the right ambiguity to suspend the import of nearly everything contained within the sentence (in the realm of semantics) between two or more irresolvable possibilities, as Mallarmé was also discovering—is a thing deeply ingrained in the writer of this sentence. Antonin Artaud insinuates in his Letter on Lautréamont that:

these letters are, of course, extravagant, with the strident extravagance of a man who walks around with his lyricism in his left or right side, like an avenging and shameless wound.

He cannot write a simple ordinary letter that does not make us feel the eliptoid trepidation of the Word which, no matter what the meaning, does not want to be used without trembling.

(Artaud 1965, p 120.)

> By this time, [Arthur] Cravan had already retired his natural name and his natural identity, Fabian Lloyd, in favour of a paraself, an *alter idem,* a new biographical reality. The person who existed as Fabian Avenarius Lloyd from 1887 to about 1912 became a person of precarious biographical status thereafter. This was not simply a change of driver's license, but a repersonification. If there was a suicide, it was not tropical, but tropological; and it was not Arthur Cravan's, but Fabian Lloyd's.
>
> -Roger Lloyd Conover, *Arthur Cravan* (2005).
>
> (Cravan et. al. 2005, p. 21.)

Lautréamont knew, no doubt, that this literary gesture would be lost upon its only intended reader, the banker. The message contained in the language of the letter is intended only for that person, the banker; the language itself of the letter is intended only for one person: Lautréamont.

Or perhaps two. Because this letter is signed most explicitly by Isidore Ducasse. Who was Isidore Ducasse? I can see the muscles of your lips and tongue struggling to form the movements and gestures which, aided by a burst of wind from your lungs, would produce sounds roughly correspondent to the marks which are appearing on the screen in front of me as I type this. It is a question that is difficult to answer.

On one register, Lautréamont is a pseudonym of Isidore Ducasse; I say 'a' pseudonym rather than 'the' pseudonym because, as we shall see, one might question whether 'Isidore Ducasse' is any less a pseudonym. Once we recognize (as the Yellow Sign impels us to do) the life of the text as anything but distinct from the life outside it, the name through which we sign our actions in the one becomes, potentially, no less *and* no more valid than the name through which we sign our actions in the other.

You can see where the danger in this lies. I have suggested that what we see in these letters is an immersion in language that amounts nearly to a ritual act; and what is it to immerse one's self in the nuances of Writing, if not to immerse one's self in the very terms of one's own disappearance? And on some level at least (and as we slip into the expanse of Language, the Symbolic is as dangerous as the real... the distinction dissolves...) does not every ritual involve a sacrifice? And we can speculate that this constant sacrifice of self, and

Poster for the Prize-fight between Arthur Cravan and world middle-weight champion Jack Johnson, 1916. (Motherwell 1981, p 2.)

the constant emergence that is its double, was also the prayer of Lautréamont—that every interaction with words became, or *would have become* if it were not in fact by its nature unachievable (ah, vagaries of desire!) a ritual dissemination into… what? What else but the Yellow Sign. It is a ritual with which we have all become familiar. And yet—you can see where the danger in this lies. The Yellow Sign is not passive—and this is why the network of vacuums which Language is, and why the Yellow Sign, is not merely an oblivion. It acts. And at times it speaks; for some rituals are oracular. This too is something we have learned, as we shall see later; generation upon generation, in some form or the other, have encountered what Mallarmé, and later Breton, would call *the voice*.

You can see where the danger in this lies; and we can extract from Artaud's letter the hypothesis that Lautréamont was the name which was signed by the syzygy of this voice and Isidore Ducasse: that whatever part of Ducasse delved too deep in this *petit mort* of Language and returned, like Lazarus, to place absurdly beside him an open inkstand and a sheet of vellum, signed itself Lautréamont. Artaud writes:

> And I say that there was in Isidore Ducasse a spirit which always wanted to drop Isidore Ducasse in favor of the unthinkable Lautréamont, a very beautiful name, a very great name. And I say that the invention of the name Lautréamont, although it may have provided Isidore Ducasse with a password to clothe and introduce the unusual magnificence of his product, I say that the invention of this literary patronym, like a suit of clothes one can't afford, brought about, by its rising above the man who produced it, one of those foul collective obscenities with which the history of letters abounds and which in the end caused the soul of Isidore Ducasse to flee from life. For it was certainly Isidore Ducasse who died, and not the Comte de Lautréamont, and it was Isidore Ducasse who gave the Comte de Lautréamont the means to survive, and it would take little, I would even say that it would take nothing to convince me that the impersonal unthinkable Count of heraldic Lautréamont was in relation to Isidore Ducasse a kind of indefinable assassin.
> [. . .]
> And he died in the early morning, at the edge of an impossible night.
> (*ibid.*)

And in his letter 'Coleridge the Traitor', which appears on page 128 of the same volume, he condenses: 'it was because he, I mean Isidore Ducasse, wanted to be the Comte de Lautréamont, that he died.' Allow me to follow up the implications of this assertion; because Ducasse died only *after* having composed the very different *Poésies*—and this volume was published under his own name. And it is true that there have been those who saw the *Poésies* as a renunciation of the transgression of conventional morality that *Maldoror* represents; but they have no better reason for this assertion than that the volume *claims* to repudiate morally transgressive literature. To equate a written truth-claim with an actuality is evidence of an utter misunderstanding of what, as I have attempted to imply, Lautréamont's—orand Ducasse's—relationship with Writing, with Language, is. There is no reason to assert that Lautréamont andor Ducasse believed the ideas expressed in *Maldoror* any more than those in the *Poésies*. I will go further: there is no reason to assert that they believed in anything—except in Language. One can note, in addition, that this repudiation is issued in the

> We are not content with the life we have in us. We want to live in he idea others have of an imaginary life. We do our utmost to appear as we are. We exert ourselves to preserve this imaginary being, which is none other than the real one.
>
> -Isidore Ducasse, corrected from Pascal; *Poésies* (1870). (Ducasse 1978, p 79.)

Poésies primarily through the corrupted spillage of the mouths of the moralists of several centuries—the ideas embodied performing a circuit out of Ducasse himself before being reintroduced into the text which he would sign—innumerable tiny pseudonyms all of which, however, remain unsigned except by his own name; or the pseudonym that his own name is. For the *Poésies* represents, as it were, another facet of the intensely personal engagement with Language for which 'Lautréamont' is, if we are to heed Artaud, at least in part a Sign. (We must not forget that Lautréamont, while as I have said this does not of necessity imply any 'actual' intention, claims on page 213 of Paul Knight's translation of *Maldoror* that, 'only later, when a few of my novels have appeared, will you be better able to understand the preface of the fuliginous renegade;' and that the *Poésies*, as we can see on page 91 of Lykiard's translation, is referred to as 'This continuing publication'.) If the *Poésies*—while most certainly in a different way, through a plagiaristic technique looking forward in obvious ways to later innovations on the part of the adepts of the Yellow Sign, such as Tzara's cut-ups and the Assisted Readymades of Freytag-Loringhoven, Schamburg, and Duchamp, not to mention the plagiarisms of the Lettrists, the Situationists, the Eternal Network, the Neoists, Art Strike, and others—in fact represents a different manifestation of the *conventionally a-moral* immersion in Language that 'Lautréamont' represents, then is it not, in fact, more appropriate to say that Isidore Ducasse, in this instance, is the pseudonym of the Comte de Lautréamont? And is it possible that it is *this* reversal that constitutes the death of Ducasse at the hands of Lautréamont? And—with all respect to Artaud—is it possible that this death of Ducasse (which after all represents the consummation of the very *petit mort* that the act of Writing represents) was, in fact, his *consummation*, in more than one sense of the term? Might Ducasse have offered himself for final sacrifice, with Lautréamont as the officiating priest?

> What soul disputes my body?
>
> -Arthur Cravan, *Hie!* (c. 1913?).
>   (Cravan et. al. 2005, p. 23.)

> My fatal plurality!
> [...]
> And while the moon,
> Beyond the chestnut trees,
> Harnesses the greyhounds,
> And, as if in a kalaidoscope,
> My abstractions
> Elaborate variations
> On my body's
> Harmonies,
> May my fingers,
> Stuck to my delighted keys,
> Imbibe fresh palpitations
> [...]
> The only place left, O my neuroses!
> Is the bright stabling
> Of the urinals.
> [...]
> Let my souls revive themselves!
>
> -*Arthur Cravan, Hie! (1913).*
>   (Cravan et. al. 2005, pp 42-43.)

I only speculate of course. And Artaud—who died alone in the early morning, edged bolt upright in his bed—may have a better notion than any of us whether, in those last moments, whenever they were, Ducasse signed with a firm or a shaking hand; and no one will ever know which name he signed.

-Olchar E. Lindsann, *The Yellow Sign*.

The statue of Lautréamont

Its plinth of quinine tabloids

In the open country

The author of the Poetical Works lies flat on his face

And near at hand the hiloderm a shady customer keeps vigil

His left ear is glued to the ground it is a glass case it contains

A prong of lightning the artist had not failed to figure aloft

In the form of a Turk's head the blue balloon

The swan of Montevideo with wings unfurled ready to flap at a moment's notice

Should the problem of luring the other swans from the horizon arise

Opens upon the false universe two eyes of different hues

The one of sulphate of iron on vines of the lashes the other of sparkling mire

He beholds the vast funneled hexagon where now in no time the machines

By man in dressings rabidly swaddled

Shall lie a-writhing

With his radium bougie he quickends the dregs of the human crucible

With his sex of feathers and his brain of bull-paper

He presides at the twice nocturnal ceremonies whose object due allowance for fire having been made is the intervention of the

       hearts of the bird and the man

Convulsionary in ordinary I have access to his side

The ravishing women who introduce me into the rose-padded compartment

Where a hammock that they have been at pains to contrive with their tresses for

Me is reserved for

Me for all eternity

Exhort me before taking their departure not to catch a chill in the perusal of the daily

It transpires that the statue in whose latitude the squitch of my nerve terminals

Weighs anchor is tuned each night like a piano

    André Breton, 'Lethal Relief' (1932.)   (Breton 2003, pp 98-99.)

There are a great many things that none of us will ever know about Lautréamont; but for a number of us—for Breton, for Éluard, for Jarry, for Artaud, for myself—one of the many potential existences of our

bodies of work can be looked at in this light: a continuing elegy for Lautréamont, one passed from each generation to the next; an elegy which, in the end, is not an elegy for Lautréamont at all but an ecstatic collective song (and we must remember the full title: the *Chants de Maldoror*) through which a certain understanding of Language, and of the ir/responsibility of Writing continually emerges; and since only the living can sing an elegy, Ducasse's death—his nearly utter disappearance—represents the failure, *our* failure to follow to that depth beyond the margin; and it is into *his* death that *we* constantly disappear.

> When Maurice Blanchot writes: "is man *capable* of a radical interrogation, that is to say, finally, is man *capable* of literature?" one could just as well say, on the basis of a certain conceptualization of life, "incapable" half the time. Except if one admits that pure literature is nonliterature, or death itself.
>
> -Jacques Derrida, *Edmond Jabès and the Question of the Book* (1967).
>
> (Derrida 2001, p 95.)

For not only within his texts, and not only *into* his texts, has Ducasse, has Lautréamont nearly disappeared. Five months after the publication of the *Poésies*, at the age of twenty-four, he was found dead by one of the staff in the hotel where he was living, and was thrown into an unmarked grave the next day; another shiftless student gone bad, accomplishing nothing, swallowed up, furthermore, by the furor of the Franco-Prussian War in a besieged Paris. Not until 1977 was a single photograph of him discovered.

In this way, Lautréamont dissolved into the mythic literature of the Yellow Sign as surely as into the inscribed literature; only a few dates are known, a few letters available to read. Everything else is floating. Through the circumstances of his death Ducasse, Lautréamont, ensured that it would be impossible for his figure to escape a mythic status, in the sense that I have put forward in this text. One cannot deceive one's self that one knows anything about the Comte de Lautréamont, and one is thus forced into a constant consciousness that in speaking of Lautréamont, of Ducasse, one is perpetuating, and altering, and embellishing a myth.

Thus, in quite nearly as many minds as there have been adepts of the Yellow Sign, the faceless, unthinkable Lautréamont has manifested himself: sometimes as a brilliant madman, scribbling out the grotesque vagaries of his agitated conscience; sometimes in the form of a tortured Romantic, living in a self-imposed seclusion, bent over his manuscript in the late hours, banging the rhythms of his sentences out on an ancient piano long out of tune; and sometimes as young man with few friends, scratching out a living from his parents, whose family friends are unaware they even have a son; who has failed to complete school and desperately hopes he will not be forced to abandon Paris. He is quiet, his habits are regular, his feet leave few groans behind them on the stairs. His clothing is worn and tattered, but clean. He excites little interest or curiosity; he seems quite studious but, well, he doesn't seem to be *doing* anything with himself. You know, every unambitious young foreigner calls himself a writer… But you are wrong, he is on to something. He has found a Sign…

And you can read his corpse.

-Olchar E. Lindsann, *The Yellow Sign*.

And so it is not our own life that we live but the lives of the dead and the soul within us is no single spiritual entity, making us personal and individual, created for our service, and entering into us for our joy. It is something that has dwelt in fearful places, and in ancient sepulchers made its abode. It is sick with many maladies, and has memories of curious sins. It is wiser than we are, and its wisdom is bitter. It fills us with impossible desires, and makes us follow what we cannot gain.

-Oscar Wilde, *The Critic as Artist* (1890).　　　　　　　　　　(Wilde 1999, pp 218-219.)

We could feel that he was alone, and truly at that moment we all existed more or less through him. The phenomenon that binds a man so strangely to what he loves cannot anyway exist without authority, exactingness: it is as much an abuse of strength as it is a force. and part of its role is to distract demons.

-Paul Éluard and André Breton, *The Immaculate Conception* (1930).　　　(Breton et. al. 1997, p 201.)

Once and for all, I am not telling you the story of my life, only a story which I remember.

-Jacques Rigaut, *Lord Patchogue* (1934).　　　　　　　　　　(Cravan et. al. 2005, p. 97.)

There are three figures, a man, a woman, and someone else, each named Arthur Cravan. They are, in no particular order, a missing poet, an itinerant boxer and an elusive forger. They have carried on a century-long *ménage-à-trois*. Although each maintains a distinct *vita*, there is often identity slippage between them. Their characters sometimes merge into a metaphysical phenomenon that has no biographical counterpoint.

-Roger Lloyd Conover, *Arthur Cravan* (2005).　　　　　　　　　　(Cravan et. al. 2005, p 13.)

Multiplies himself in the manner of his book's microbes notably by schizo-genesis the one which separates itself from him has wings

    -Phillippe Soupault and André Breton, *The Magnetic Fields* (1919).   (Breton et. al. 1997, p 127.)

I suppose that if I carried off the Skullhead here before me in the egg, at the rate of one stopover per year I could encounter myself at every stage of my life and end up with some twenty-plus versions of myself of various sizes all in the same room.

    -Jacques Rigaut, *A Brilliant Individual* (1922.)   (Cravan et. al. 2005, p 100-101.)

I took [Johannes] Baader to the fields of Sudende (where Jung then lived), and said to him: 'All this is yours if you do as I tell you. The Bishop of Brunswick has failed to recognize you as Jesus Christ, and you have retaliated by defiling the alter of his church. This is no compensation. From today, you will be the President of The Christ Society, Ltd, and recruit members. You must convince everyone that he to can be Christ, if he wants to, on payment of fifty marks to your society. Members of our society will no longer be subject to temporal authority and will automatically be unfit for military service.

    -Raoul Hausmann, *Courier Dada* (1958).   (Home 1991, p 74.)

    It would be specious at best (or perhaps at worst) to call Monty Cantsin, a mere pseudonym.[1] Monty Cantsin does not serve merely to confuse identity; he serves to change it and to displace it. One does not *take*

---

[1] Of course, Monty Cantsin and Karen Eliot are representative of a larger subset of the practice, including Luther Blissett, Rrose Sélavy, Klaos Oldanburg, and Bob Jones. Blissett represents another manifestation of this basic Anti-subjective type, existing more specifically within the discourse of mass media representations, a kind of poltergeist living both within and against the official media, in the form of pranks which use the mechanisms of mass representation to subvert or unsettle its claims of authority over truth. Rrose Sélavy, on the other hand, demonstrates yet another, quite different ~~subjective~~

on Monty Cantsin simply to hide one's identity, to designate a certain body of work, to create a dialectical discussion or communication betwithineen (a) body/ies of work, to expand numbers, or just generally to confuse everything, though these are all valid strategies, and Cantsin may indeed have a hand in any or all of them when he performs an action. But all of these strategies are oriented exclusively *outward*, to produce an *image*; and Monty Cantsin is not merely an image, but a *subject;* albeit, a subject radically construed, his structure so *thoroughly* infused with negativity and heterogeneity that it may indeed be impermissible, upon further consideration, to designate him a subject; but not for the simplistic reasons that one might at first suppose.

Known variously as an 'open pop star', 'open name,' 'open personality' etc., pseudonymity, indeed heteronymity, is obviously at play. 'Anybody can become Monty Cantsin.' As Cantsin himself says in Smile 6, Dec. 1984,[2] 'Monty Cantsin is a true individual in a world where real individuality is a crime. He has witnessed the dematerialisation of the art object and knows that the only art work still worth creating is his own life.' Yet his is a life with which other subjects can merge: 'Anyone can become Monty Cantsin but no one will become Monty Cantsin until they have developed sufficient strength of personality that they are able to function freely in the world of subjectivity away from the bondage of unreality.'

Cantsin represents a radical re-writing, indeed in some senses inversion, of the practice we have been speculating upon elsewhere; another representative, Karen Eliot, moves one step farther toward the notion of an unbodied Anti-Subject existing not, as is the case with Anna Blume, Valens, and others, as an interior projection/extension of an individual subject and psychology, but rather a *social position* within a certain discourse *into which* individual subjects, psychologies, and actions are drawn and re-organised. While Karen Eliot exists within a communal discourse and social mythology closely related to, and largely overlapping with, that which supports Cantsin, her subjective structure has been delineated publicly in such a way as to strengthen her position *as subject*, however radically constituted, as opposed to merely pseudonymic. Like Monty Cantsin, 'Anyone can become Karen Eliot simply by adopting the name,' but (which has become unclear in the case of Cantsin) 'they are only Karen Eliot for the period in which the name is used. ... When replying to letters generated by an action/text in which the context has been used then it makes sense to continue using the context, i.e. by replying as Karen Eliot. However in personal relationships, where one has a personal history

---

structuration than the other examples discussed here. Primarily inhabited by Marcel Duchamp and Robert Desnos, especially when the two were on different continents, Rrose spoke and wrote only in aphorisms, puns, homophonic riddles, and other linguistic forms that unsettled semantics; Desnos would become Rrose in dreams and in trance-states, sometimes claiming to be literally inhabited *by* her, taking dictation. At other times he claimed to be receiving messages *through* her from Duchamp. In this latter claim we can see a genesis of later Neoist mythic motifs of psychic communication; in Rrose's intensely linguistic nature, and in the fluctuating nature of the space of her subjectivity and of her relationships with her primary subjects, we can see correlations with Anna Blume.

[2] It should be obvious why no full citations are given in this discussion. A more interesting question would be why they *are* included in other discussions in this text, when they are.

other than the acts undertaken by a series of people using the name Karen Eliot, it does not make sense to use the context.' Karen Eliot is a ~~subject~~ who exists *only* within the register of *inter*personal relationships and discourse, as opposed to many of the Anti-subjects upon whom we have speculated, who exist primarily as *intra*-~~subjective~~ modes. Anna Blume or Valens approach the primary subject (who is positioned on, or rather *as*, the point at which the 'internal' and 'external' meet and efface each other) from opposite poles as do Karen Eliot or Monty Cantsin. Nonetheless, the latter still (if engaged with in a vital way) entail a similar re-organisation of subjective structures on the part of the primary subject: 'When one becomes Karen Eliot one's previous existence consists of the acts other people have undertaken using the name. When one becomes Karen Eliot one has no family, no parents, no birth. Karen Eliot was not born, s/he was materialised from social forces, constructed as a means of entering the shifting terrain that circumscribes the "individual" and society.' At the same time, precisely because of the extreme 'openness' of the personality, one can never *know* the entirety, the plenitude of the history of the subject into which one is provisionally dissolving. In an Anti-subject so constituted, history necessarily precedes subjective structure, and therefore the subjective structure one is inhabiting is also unknown; and this, if engaged with in a certain way at least, can provide the stasis of negativity, of re-jection, constitutive of the subject-in-process; however, in order for Karen Eliot the ~~subject~~ to experience this negativity, s/he must experience it *through* the primary subject's experience of Karen's unknowability; there is therefore a sense in which Karen Eliot becomes the primary subject, and the individual 'inhabiting' her is in fact playing the role in Karen's subjective process that, I have hypothesized, Anna may have played in Schwitters'. Karen can experience her own re-jection only vicariously, through the primary subject, who then becomes a *function* within Karen's own subjective process. Karen is the social subject, and society itself her choratic process; we, when we take her name, are as much her projection as she is ours.

It is not only in the case of Lautréamont that pseudonymity factors strategically in this radical project of dissolving (rather than *placing*) one's self into the play of textuality: that is, Writing in its most engaged sense. In fact, pseudonymity as a Sign (to the artist orand to society) for the distancing, the fictionalizing, the dissemination, the projection, the injection, the presentation, the transfiguration, the fracturing, the catalyzing, the negation, the putting-into-play, the disappearance, the textualization of self can be seen as one particularly endemic motif within the Yellow Sign. In case you should not believe me, I shall list a number of the pseudonymous adepts of the Yellow Sign here; though, naturally, I am very far from declaring it definitive:

Alexis
Bertrand Aloysius
Guillaume Apollinaire
Jean Arp
Bibergeil
Georges La Boeuff
Johannes Baargeld
Aloysius Bertrand
I.K. Bonset
Monty Cantsin
Lewis Carroll
Blaise Cendrars
Jean de Cilra
Christian
J.P. Contamine de Latour
Tristan Corbière
Arthur Cravan
Dadamerika
Dada-Oz
Dadasopher
Paul Dermée
Daimonides
Theo Van Doesburg
Karen Eliot
Paul Éluard
Imogene Engine
Jean Ferry
Edgar Firn
Bruno Franklyn
George Grosz
John Heartfield
Iliazd
Isidore Isou
Bob Jones
Comte de Lautréamont
Maurice Lemaitre
Olchar E. Lindsann
Mina Loy
Aurélien Lugné-Poe
George Maciunas
Augustus MacKeat
Walt Merin
Ephraïm Mikhaël
Jean Moréas
Crabb Murlock
Lt. Mernau
Musikdada
Mynona
Gérard de Nerval
Chadwick Niral-Nelson
Klaos Oldanburg
Philothée O'Neddy
Opach
Alexander Partens
Walter Petrie
Pharamousse
Progress-Dada
Rabelais
Rachilde
Raimon Rajky

Man Ray
Hugues Rebell
Jehan Rictus
Mac Robber
Mario Rossi
Sandomir
Alberto Savinio
Walter Serner
Alexander Sesqui
Superdada
Supermusicdada
Tristan Tzara
Ippolit Wheeden
World-Dada

-Olchar E. Lindsann, *The Yellow Sign*.

The subject never *is*. The *subject* is only the *signifying process* and he appears only as a *signifying practice*, that is, only when he is absent from *within the position* out of which social, historical, and signifying activity unfolds.

    -Julia Kristeva, *Revolution in Poetic Language* (1974).   (Kristeva 1984, p 215.)

Everything occurred as if the mind, having reached this crest of the unconscious, had lost the power to recognize its position. In it subsisted images that assumed form, became the substance of reality. They expressed themselves according to this relation, as a perceptible force. They thus assumed the characteristics of visual, auditive, tactile hallucinations. We experienced the full strength of these images. We had lost the power to manipulate them. We had become their domain, their subjects. In bed, just before falling asleep, in the street, with eyes wide open with all the machinery of terror, we held out our hand to phantoms… We experienced this mental substance in its concrete power, its power of concretion. We saw it pass from one state to another, and it was by these transmutations which revealed its existence to us that we were also informed of its nature. We saw, for example, a written image which first presented itself with the characteristic of the fortuitous, the arbitrary, reach our senses, lose its verbal aspect to assume those fixed phenomenological realities which we had always believed impossible to provoke.

    -Louis Aragon, *Une vague de rêves* (1924).   (Nadeau 1973, p 89.)

But is one obliged to accept the invitation to think what one is invited to think?

    -Jacques Derrida, *Psyche: Inventions of the Other* (1987).   (Derrida 1991, p. 219.)

My dearest reader:

    Your turn:

Appendix: A Library.

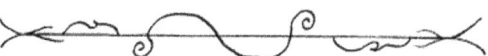

He found the library of St. Victor most magnificent, especially certain books which he discovered in it, of which the catalogue follows, and *primo*:

Bigua salutis (The Props of Salvation).

Bragueta juris (The Codpiece of the Law).

Pantofla decretorum (The Slipper of the Decretals).

Malogranatum vitiorum (The Pomegranate of Vice).

The Thread-Ball of Theology.

The Long Broom of Preachers, composed by Turlupin.

The Elephantine Testicle of the Valiant.

The Henbane of the Bishops.

Marmotretus, de babouynis et cingus, cum commento Dorbellis (Marmotretus on Baboons and Monkeys, with commentary by des Orbeaux).

Decretum universalis Parisienis super gorgiasitate mulierculariumad placitum (Decree of the University of Paris on the Gorgiosity of pretty Women, for pleasure).

[. . .]

The Nonsense of the Law .

The Goad of Wine.

The Spur of Cheese.

Decrotatorum scholarium (On the Foulness of Scholars).

Tartaretus, de modo cacandi (Tartaret, on methods of Shitting).

The Fanfares of Rome.

Bricot, *de differentiis soupparum* (On the Varieties of Soup).

The Tail-piece of Discipline.

The Old Shoe of Humility.

The Tripe-pod of Big Thoughts.

[. . .]

Marforii bacalarii cubentis Rome, de pelendisque mascarendisque Cardinalium mulis (Marforio, Bachelor of the See of Rome, On the skinning and scorching of the Cardinal's Mules).

Protest by the same, against those who say that the Pope's mule only eats at his hours.

Prognosticatio que incipit, Silvi Triquebille, balata per M. N. Songecrusyon (The Prophesy which begins, *Sylvi Triquebille,* a ballad by M.N. Songecreux).

Boudarini episcopi, de emulgentiarum profectibus enneads novem, cum privilego papali ad triennium, et postea non (Bishop Boudarin, Nine Enneads on the Efficacy of Emulgences, with papal sanction for three years and no more).

The Maidens' Shittery.

The Bald Arse of Widows.

The Monks' Hood.

The Mumblings of the Coelestine Fathers.

[. . .]

The Body-odours of the Spaniards, supercockcrowed by Brother Inigo (de Loyola).

[. . .]

The Ramblings of Ballad-makers.

The Bellows of the Alchemists.

The Hey-presto of the Begging Friars, pocket-walleted by Friar Graspit.

The Shackles of Religion.

The Lecher's Lattice.

The Elbow-Rest of Old Age.

The Muzzle of Nobility.

The Ape's Paternoster.

[. . .]

The Morris-dance of the Heretics.

[. . .]

The Chimney-Sweep of Astrology.

Campi clysteriorum per S.C. (The Use of Suppositories, by Symphorien Champier).

The Wind-Dispeller of the Apothecaries.

The Kiss-my-arse of Surgery…

-François Rabelais, *Gargantua and Pantagruel* (1532).   (Rabelais 1985, pp 187-192.)

Mr. Merritt always confessed to seeing nothing really horrible at the farmhouse, but maintained that the titles of the books in the special library of thaumaturgical, alchemical, and theological subjects which Curwen kept in a front room were alone sufficient to inspire him with a lasting loathing. Perhaps, however, the facial expression of the owner in exhibiting them contributed to much of the prejudice. The bizarre collection, besides a host of standard works which Mr. Merritt was not too alarmed to envy, embraced nearly all the cabbalists, daemonologists, and magicians known to man; and was a treasure-house of lore in the doubtful realms of alchemy and astrology. Hermes Trismegistus in Mesnard's edition, the *Turba Philosophorum*, Geber's *Liber Investigationis*, and Artephius' *Key of Wisdom* all were there; with the cabbalistic *Zohar*, Peter Jammy's set of Albertus Magnus, Raymond Lully's *Ars Magna et Ultima* in Zetzner's edition, Roger Bacon's *Thesaurus Chemicus*, Fludd's *Clavis Alchemiae*, and Trithemius' *De Lapide Philosophico* crowding them close. Mediaeval Jews and Arabs were represented in profusion, and Mr. Merritt turned pale when, upon taking down a fine volume conspicuously labeled as the *Qanoon-e-Islam*, he found it was in truth the forbidden *Necronomicon* of the mad Arab Abdul Alhazred, of which he had heard such monstrous things whispered some years earlier after the exposure of nameless rites at the strange little fishing village of Kingsport, in the Province of the Massachusetts-Bay.

-H.P. Lovecraft, *The Case of Charles Dexter Ward* (1927).   (Lovecraft 2001, p 102.)

My books, at this epoch, if they did not actually serve to irritate the disorder, partook, it will be perceived, largely, in their imaginative and inconsequential nature, of the characteristic qualities of the disorder itself. I well remember, among others, the treatise of the noble Italian Coelius Secundus Curio, "*De Amplitudine Beati Regni Dei*"; St. Austin's great work, "The City of God"; Tertillian's "*De Carne Christi*," in which the paradoxical sentence, "*Mortuus est Dei filius; credible est quia ineptum est; et sepultus resurrexit; certum est quia impossible est*," occupied my undivided time, for many weeks of laborious and fruitless investigation.

-Edgar A. Poe, *Berenice* (1835.)   (Poe 1975, pp 645.)

[Coleridge] spoke slightingly of Hume (whose Essay on Miracles he said was stolen from an objection started in one of South's sermons—*Credat Judaeus Apella*!) I was not very pleased with this account of Hume... He however made me amends by the manner in which he spoke of Berkeley. He dwelt especially on his *Essay on Vision* as a masterpiece of analytical reasoning. So it undoubtedly is. He was exceedingly angry at Dr. Johnson for striking the stone with his foot, in allusion to this author's Theory of Matter and Spirit, and saying, 'Thus I confute him, Sir.' Coleridge drew a parallel (I don't know how he brought about the connection) between Bishop Berkeley and Tom Paine.... He considered Bishop Butler as a true philosopher, a profound and conscientious thinker, a genuine reader of nature and his own mind. He did not speak of his *Analogy* but of his *Sermons at the Roll's Chapel,* of which I had never heard. Coleridge somehow always contrived to prefer the *unknown* to the *known*.

    -William Hazlitt, *My First Acquaintance With Poets* (c. 1823)   (Hazlitt 1982, pp 52-53.)

    In brief, he could find no sustenance either among these writers or even among those in whom literary dabblers delight: Sallust, admittedly less dreary than the rest; Livy, sentimental and pompous; Seneca, turgid and lackluster; Suetonius, lethargic and spineless; Tacitus, who in his calculated concision is the most virile, the most biting, and the most vigorous of them all. In poetry Juvenal, despite some very sprightly lines, and Persius, despite his mysterious insinuations, left him cold.

    -J.-K. Huysmans, *A rebours* (1884).   (Huysmans 1998, pp 24-25.)

And yet, 'tis strange he had never read Cicero, nor Quintilian *de Oratore*, nor Isocrates, nor Aristotle, nor Longinus amongst the ancients;—nor Vossius, nor Scioppius, nor Ramus, nor Farnaby amongst the moderns;—and what is more astonishing, he had never in his whole life the least light or spark of subtlety struck into his mind, by one single lecture upon Crackenthorp or Burgersdicius, or any Dutch logician or commentator;—

    Laurence Sterne, *The Life and Opinions of Tristram Shandy* (1760-77).   (Sterne 1996, p 38.)

Finally, in the fifth century, we have Augustine, Bishop of Hippo. Him Des Esseintes knew only too well, for he was the most revered of the writers of the Catholic Church, the founder of the Christian orthodoxy, the theologian seen by Catholics as an oracle, as a supreme authority. The consequence was that he no longer ever opened St Augustine's works, even though, in his *Confessions*, he had proclaimed his loathing of this world…

He much preferred browsing through the *Psychomachia* of Prudentius, the inventor of the allegorical poem, a form which was to enjoy such a long run of popularity in the Middle Ages, and he enjoyed dipping into the works of Sidonius Apillinaris, whose correspondence, studded with witticisms, conceits, archaisms, and enigmas, he found enticing…

After Sidonius there was also the panegyrist, Merobaudes, whom he frequently read; Sedulius, the composer of rhymed poems and alphabetical hymns, certain parts of which the church has appropriated for use in her services; Marius Victor, whose obscure treatise *De perversis moribus* is lit up in places by verses that glow like phosphorus; Paulinus of Pella, author of that trepid work, the *Eucharisticon*; Orientus, Bishop of Auch, who in the distichs of his *Commonitorium* denounces the licentiousness of women whose faces, he claims, bring ruin upon the nations of the world.

    -J.-K. Huysmans, *A rebours* (1884).   (Huysmans 1998, p 30.)

But although the day was spent without books or reading, it was not profitless. For in that fine meadow they would repeat by heart a few pleasant lines of Virgil's *Georgics*, of Hesiod, or of Politan's *Husbandry*, and quote some Latin epigrams which they would turn into French rondeaux and ballads. While they were feasting, too, they would separate the wine from the water, according to Cato's instructions, in his *De re rust.*, and also to Pliny's, with a cup of ivory root.

    -François Rabelais, *Gargantua* (1534).   (Rabelais 1985, p 93.)

At dinner-time [Coleridge] grew more animated, and dilated in a very edifying manner on Mary Wolstonecraft and Mackintosh. The last, he said, he considered (on my father's speaking of his *Vindiciae Gallicae* as a capital performance) as a clever scholastic man… He thought him no match for Burke, either in style or matter. Burke was a metaphysician, Mackintosh a mere logician… Coleridge added that Mackintosh and Tom Wedgewood (of whom, however, he spoke highly) had expressed a very indifferent opinion of his friend Mr. Wordsworth, on which he remarked to them—'He strides on so far before you, that he dwindles in the distance!'... He did not rate Godwin very high (this was caprice or prejudice, real or affected) but he had a great idea of Mrs Wollstonecraft's powers of conversation, none at all of her talent for book-making. We talked about Holcraft...

-William Hazlitt, *My First Acquaintance With Poets* (c. 1823) (Hazlitt 1982, pp 49-50.)

He was a close correspondent of the notorious Baudelairian poet Justin Geoffrey, who wrote *The People of the Monolith* and died screaming in a madhouse in 1926 after a visit to a sinister, ill-regarded village in Hungary.

[...]

Derby's parents took him abroad every summer, and he was quick to seize on the surface aspects of European thought and expression. His Poe-like talents turned more and more toward the decadent, and other artistic sensitiveness and yearnings were half-aroused in him...Always a dweller on the surface of phantasy and strangeness, he now delved deep into the actual runes and riddles left by a fabulous past for posterity. He read things like the frightful *Book of Eibon*, the *Unaussprechlichen Kulten* of von Junzt, and the forbidden *Necronomicon* of the mad Arab Abdul Alhazred, though he did not tell his parents he had seen them.

-H.P. Lovecraft, *The Thing on the Doorstep* (1937). (Lovecraft 2001, pp 342-343.)

But what if my own line, that admittedly twists and turns, passes through Heraclitus, Abelard, Eckhardt, Retz, Rousseau, Swift, Sade, Lewis, Arnim, Lautréamont, Engels, Jarry, and a few others? From them I have constructed a system of coordinates for my own use, a system that stands up to the test of my own personal experience and therefore appears to me to include some of tomorrow's chances.

-André Breton, *Prolegomena to a Third Surrealist Manifesto or Not* (1942). (Breton 1972, p. 285.)

In the premises detailed above, entry having been effected by M. Lourdeau, locksmith at Paris, no. 205, rue Nicolas Flamel, with the exception of a bed of polished copper mesh, twelve meters long, and without bedding, of an ivory chair and of an onyx and gold table; sequestration made of twenty-seven assorted volumes, some paper-backed and others bound, with the following titles:

1. BAUDELAIRE, a volume of E. A. POE translations.

2. BERGERAC, *Works*, volume II, containing the *History of the States and Empires of the Sun*, and the *History of Birds*.

3. *The Gospel According to* SAINT LUKE, in Greek.

4. BLOY, *The Ungrateful Beggar*.

5. COLERIDGE, *The Rime of the Ancient Mariner*.

6. DARIEN, *The Thief*.

7. DEBORDES-VALMORE, *The Oath of the Little Men*.

8. ELSKAMP, *illuminated Designs*.

9. An odd volume of the *Plays* of FLORIAN.

10. An odd volume of *The Thousand and One Nights*, in the GALLAND translation.

11. GRABBE, *Scherz, Satire, Ironie und tiefere Bedeutung*, comedy in three acts.

12. KAHN, *The Tale of Gold and of Silence*.

13. LAUTREAMONT, *The Lays of Maldoror*.

14. MAETERLINCK, *Aglavaine and Sélysette*.

15. MALLARME, *Verse and Prose*.

16. MENDES, *Gog*.

17. *The Odyssey*, Teubner's edition.

18. PELADAN, *Babylon*.

19. RABELAIS.

20. JEAN DE CHILRA, *The Sexual Hour*.

21. HENRI DE REGNIER, *The Jasper Cane*.

22. RIMBAUD, *The Illuminations.*

23. SCHWOB, *The Children's Crusade.*

24. *Ubu Roi.*

25. VERLAINE, *Wisdom.*

26. VERHAEREN, *The Hallucinated Landscapes.*

27. VERNE, *Voyage to the Center of the Earth.*

In addition, three prints hanging on the walls, a poster by TOULOUSE-LAUTREC, *Jane Avril;* one by BONNARD, advertising the *Revue Blanche;* a portrait of Doctor Faustroll, by AUBREY BEARDSLEY; and an old picture, which appears to us to be valueless, *Saint Cado,* issued by the Oberthür printing house of Rennes.

-Alfred Jarry, *Exploits and Opinions of Dr. Faustroll, Pataphysician* (1911).   (Jarry 1996, pp 10-12.)

"Conrad pursues the obscure and mystic as some men pursue romance; his shelves throng with delightful nightmares of every variety."

Our host nodded. "You'll find there a number of delectable dishes—Machen, Poe, Blackwood, Maturin—look, there's a rare feast—*Horrid Mysteries,* by the Marquis of Grosse—the real Eighteenth Century edition."

Taverel scanned the shelves. "Weird fiction seems to vie with works on witchcraft, voodoo and dark magic."

"True; historians and chronicles are often dull; tale-weavers never are—the masters, I mean. A voodoo sacrifice can be described in such a dull manner as to take all the real fantasy out of it, and leave it merely a sordid murder. I will admit that few writers of fiction touch the true heights of horror—most of their stuff is too concrete, given too much earthly shape and dimensions. But in tales such as Poe's *Fall of the House of Usher,* Machen's *Black Seal* and Lovecraft's *Call of Cthulu*—the three master horror tales, to my mind—the reader is borne into dark and *outer* realms of imagination.

"But look there," he continued, "there, sandwiched between that nightmare of Huysmans', and Walpole's *Castle of Otranto*—Von Junzt's *Nameless Cults*. There's a book to keep you awake at night!"

"I've read it," said Taverel, "and I'm convinced the man is mad. His work is like the conversation of a maniac—it runs with complete clarity for awhile, then suddenly merges into vagueness and disconnected ramblings."

Conrad shook his head. "Have you ever thought that perhaps it is his very sanity that causes him to write in that fashion? What if he dares not put on paper all that he knows? What if his vague suppositions are dark and mysterious hints, keys to the puzzle, to those who know?"

-Robert E. Howard, *The Children of the Night* (1931).   (Carter 1971, pp 174-175.)

My dearest reader,

I, like you, am a reader; that is to say that writing is not so much an *action* here as it is a reflex; reading is an act of writing before it ever comes to a matter of writing, or not writing, anything *down;* writing into the gaps in the reading. Writing as *how* you read what you read, writing as *why* you read what you read, writing as *what else* you read than what you are reading now, writing as *who* you are while you read, writing as where you *are* when you read, writing as what you do *while* you read, writing as what you *think* while you read, and—*most especially*—writing as what you do *with* what you read, *after* you have read, *what you create through you reading.*

Etc., etc.

My point (insomuch as I could, at any time, ever be said to have a *point*) is this: there is nothing constant about reading, on any level, except what *has been* read; the modalities of those *emphatically multiple* readings are irretrievable, we have only the constant, the text, which in itself refuses to tell us *how* it has been read, or what actions have preceded or followed it, by *any* of its readers. Everything else is speculation. Reading and writing are not two separate actions; nor are reading and thinking. Nor are thinking and writing. They all inhere in each other. This observation has been underscored in psychoanalysis, in semiotics, in economics, and through a number of other discourses.

I do not know how you, *you,* my very individual reader, (will) have read this book: in several extended sittings, or on and off for a couple of years; on your commute to work each day on the bus, or at home at nights on a sofa; silently or aloud; from beginning to end, or in random order (god (sic) help you!). Do you, like I do (I might recommend the practice) read a score of books at once, hopping from one to the other, discovering the hidden correlations one would not otherwise make? And if so, are any of those books the ones I have placed parts of within my own? And will you therefore discover the details of the sophistry that I have so lovingly nurtured, and discovered everywhere? Will you, as I do, physically *mark* your reading, further dismembering this already dismembered text, converting my writing of my reading into *your* writing of *your* reading of that writing, underscoring passages, bracketing others, contravening my arguments, or augmenting them, in the margins? I might recommend such an approach. Have you discussed it with your friends and comrades (and have they read it, and how, and how many of them, and when?) or have you kept silent, and if so, then why? Much less can I know how you will feel as you read each specific passage, what incidents of the day will float in your mind, or what physical postures will occupy your nerves, and what connections or readings these conditions may evoke, far beyond anything I could possibly have anticipated. I could *certainly* not conceivably have guessed at all of the intricacies of your psychology and your history, which after all is inevitably to a great extent opaque even to yourself, the obsessions that you will project into this text, anywhere that its gaps and ambiguities allow. Indeed, quite possibly I do not even know *you,* and could never have guessed even so relatively simple a matter as which of the people and passages presented in this book you are familiar with, or how your reading of these writers, and your history with that reading, diverges from my own.

Etc., etc.

At the same time, as *you* read *my* readings (both the readings I have written by writing *about* the readings, and the readings I have written by cutting them out and placing them *here* for you to read), you do not know how I—who while merely one *voice* of the 'author' am nonetheless also, or am *part of* (and which part?) a *person* who produced this book, but who cannot altogether be discovered within it or equated, without excess, *with* that voice—I say, you can not fully know how I, your very individual 'writer' (and reader), have written this book, in *any* of the hundreds of sessions it took to write. Nor do you know how I read the books I have written you my readings of: in several extended sittings, or on and off for a couple of years; on my commute to work each day on the bus, or at nights on a sofa; aloud or silently; from beginning to end, or in random order. Within these readings, what passages have I physically *marked,* and how, and why, and what have I written in the margins? And what have I *not* marked or written, and why not? What have I discussed with my comrades, and who were they, and what was said? Much less can you know how I felt as I read each specific passage, what incidents of the day, floating in my mind, or what physical postures occupied my nerves, and what connections or readings these conditions may have evoked, without being explicitly coded in the text. And what convoluted psychologies and multivalent histories have been at play, in such obscure ways—you have *even* less of an idea than do I.

Etc., etc.

The book you are reading is not the one I wrote; instead, it is the book I want you to *read*. The former's only function is to create, with you, the latter; and I could never predict, and will never know what you have read.

On the other hand, of course, there is that ~~thing~~, the book that we have in common, though that commonality is nonetheless beyond us. Even had you never even *heard* of this book, I *still* would not know how you felt on such and such a day, and you *still* would not know how a certain minor or major event may have changed my thinking on such another. But such a question, of course, would never even come up. The *book* that we have in common, if nothing else gives this non-knowing some kind of significance. We can each speculate (and I have been doing so, now, exhaustingly, for nearly two years, about you, whomever you are) and something productive might emerge from that space, because the space of *speculation* is the space where anything unexpected might grow and take form. I say that this takes on significance, not so much because I have 'written' *this* book, but because, as I have pointed out, I have *read*. With or without *this* book, that (anti-)relationship might still exist; I no more know where you were the day you first read Poe (if you have) than you know where I was when I first read him; and for *me* (I'd might as well tell you), reading Poe was, after all, probably where all of this started.

And from there I learned what Poe read, and who read Poe; and I tracked them down, and I wondered *why* Poe read it, and *how* they read Poe. And who read *them?* And who else read what he read? And why? And how?

Etc., etc.

And through this *reading*, which has unfolded for nearly twenty years, gradually I learned to *think;* and discovered that the difference between the two was merely one of modality.

I have given you this banal story, which I have attempted (since, as you have found, or will, I pride myself on nothing if not on brevity) to keep short, in order to reiterate once more that in this (anti-)*exchange* which is the book, the most important things are those that we cannot fully know, the most important intellectual spaces are the ones where we fail to meet, but can feel each others' presence. That is why it is not enough, as you read this, simply to note what I have read, what part of it I have used, and mark it off on some kind of mental checklist, as an *abstract* reading. It is the unknowable *specificity* of the conditions of reading, of the *agent* of that reading, of what is projected *into* its gaps without leaving their trace for you to read except through a projection of your own, that are most important in this exchange. There are a few *clues* that narrow the range of this projection, for better or for worse: What edition have I read? When did I first read it? Have I read it many times? What other texts did I read it through?

Etc., etc.

This is no doubt why, for instance, Paul Éluard, after reading Isidore Ducasse's *Poems* (which is composed primarily of corrected plagiarisms), set off on a several-year programme of locating and reading every book Ducasse was known to have read. He could, of course, never come to *know* Ducasse the better, but his *unknowing* could take on a much more intimate and specific form; the *context* of Ducasse's thought could be more closely apprehended, even if that thought itself remained always beyond the pale. Éluard even managed to find a copy of one book with Ducasse's own marginalia; and while having more relics of *how* what was read was read, etc., etc. would, of course, still never yield the thought, that *absence* might be so sensitively known— what a perfect *hallucination* of the thought might be induced—and without being *the* thought, *would* be *thought*, and would stand in some kind of intimate relation…

If you are reading this, now, *after* having battled your way through this book, cutting *your own* paths through the impenetrable thicket I have attempted to evoke, you know a good deal of *what I have read*. If you are reading this first, you shall soon find out. I'd might as well add, of course, that it is obviously not *everything* that I have read, nor have I read the entirety of all the books that I list. There are things I *should* have read that, for various reasons, I have not gotten around to yet; there have no doubt been countless times, or will be, as you read this book, when you have thought of some example that I really *ought* to have included, with obvious significance, whether an essay by Benjamin or an episode of *The Muppet Show*. After all, I'm only human; I am only human. On the other hand, there are editions I have used that *you* really *must* avoid, my dear reader, should you choose to go through any of the doors I have attempted to point out to you.

For all of the reasons I have lain out above, I shall not give you a simple 'bibliography', designed to provide 'proofs' of the outrageous *speculations* that permeate *this* book; a bibliography is the *ghost* of a reading, and not an interesting species of ghost—such as you might find in Henry James, in Le Fanu, in Onions, in Blackwood, in Jackson, etc.—but simply an anemic *abstraction*. The citations in this book serve several purposes, none of which is to provide 'proof'. One primary function is to approximate, as much possible, the gesture with which I would greet you if in person you remarked upon a passage, which reaction would be: half springing from my chair, with the fingers of one hand dancing as the other knocked against my leg, excitedly offering in a loud voice to fetch you the book at once from my bookshelf so that you might experience it yourself. Upon which I would proceed, while clutching the back of my head distractedly in my hand, to convey to you the wonder (or even the disappointment) of the book that you held in your hands, as you impatiently waited for me to shut up so that you could open it and read it yourself.

In order to spare you the latter frustration, I have provided citations that are discrete, simple—someone with a more classical (or academic, which is to say classical without the grace) bent than my own might say *elegant*. I, however, find them boring in the extreme; and so, for your perusal on your own time, I offer you whatever commentary I might, were I given the chance, in handing you the book itself, spout off; as to the effects of what I tell you on my reading or on my writing of it (and as to what I am *not* saying), you can, needless to say, only speculate. Of course, these comments would be dependant upon the specific conditions of that moment, what we had been talking *about*, where we were, what we had each been doing that day... Etc., etc. In any event, this is a palimpsest not of the *texts* which you are supposed to understand as leading inexorably to the complex absurdity of this book that you are holding in your hands (or which perhaps lays open before you on the table as you eat), but of the *library* which has constituted one essential aspect of a life that you know, in any case, very little about, and from which this book has simply *emerged*. Never fear, they are still in alphabetical order; there is virtually no aspect of this book that I have intended to be *easy* or straightforward, with this one exception: I want to create no barriers between you, my very, *very* dearest reader, and the books that have (among a few other things) created the part of me that is disappearing from this text even as you read. I *want* you to read these other books (except a few; and those I shall warn you of).

There has, of course, been an empty spot on those shelves of mine for a long while, though its absence was not entirely noticeable, diffused as it was through the margins, between and underneath the lines of all of the 'actual' books of this library; and that is the book that you are reading now, for whose physical quality I apologize; but, after all, the production and publication of a book is as subject to circumstances—both economic and *ethical* (read some of my other writings, after all)—as is its writing and its reading; and a book bound in seal-skin is not the only kind which takes on a physical significance; I much prefer a paperback traversed with marginalia, creased and scuffed and half-unbound; such a book has been half-sublimated into *thought*, and what remains, like Des Esseintes, are the worn-out tatters of the body that, having traded so much of its pulpy vitality into the life of the mind which is not *of* it but which cannot exist *without* it, has been unable to follow, and remains as a *relic* of what it never really *contained*.

-Olchar E. Lindsann.

A Library

Ackerman, Blaster Al. (2006). *Corn & Smoke: Stories, Performances, Things.* **Baltimore: Shattered Wig Press.**

Anybody who enjoys fun, or cares about our culture, should read the Blaster. The first book in the alphabet is the initiator of the most recent self-designated *collective* (is this the right word?) explicitly *discussed* in the book you are now reading, Neoism. (It goes without saying that another is always already at play in everything that I read and that I write, because I am in the midst of it as it continues to grow, and there is no need in this particular context to speak 'about' Post-NeoAbsurdism.) It is also the first example of my admitting to the embarrassing situation which continually recurs, of my coming to him far too late, and being much less familiar with his work at this stage than I ought to be. Ackerman has begun an essential (if not necessarily exclusive) return of the 'Avant-Garde' tradition (this seems like the wrong word here, but for lack of a better…) to its roots in pulp, from which it split in the early 19th Century, with the result that one can read in it all of the annihilations of the Yellow Sign, or simply a fucking funny story, and most essentially both; the ethic and critical rigour (in an inimitable form) of the one and the visceral appeal and lack of pretension of the other (The precise opposite of the text I have produced here, which is after all merely one term in a growing dialectic, or heterolectic). And his 'writing' itself, of course, is but a small part of his life and activity, of which myths are beginning to proliferate… I shall not go on… The book I have was sent to me by him in return for a copy of *Synapse* in which I had published two of his 'Hacks' of John M. Bennett.

Ades, Dawn, ed. (2006). *The Dada Reader: A Critical Anthology.* **London: Tate Publishing.**

For many years, the standard Dada anthologies in English have been Motherwell's *Dada Painters and Poets* and Huelsenbeck's *Dada Almanac*, both of them indispensable. It is therefore these two anthologies that have set what constitutes, for most of us, the poetic Dada canon. Ades' excellent book serves as a much-needed corrective for this situation and broadens our understanding of the Dada *community*. While each of the older anthologies presents us with a monumental selection of works—concentrating on definitive statements, on core figures, on 'major works'—and in so doing brings together without distinction texts from all kinds of contexts to present a picture of Dada as a single, homogenous phenomenon, Ades brings to bear a large selection of usually more modest and unassuming works that have escaped the canon—the kind of work from which most of each issue of the various Dada journals were comprised, and which thus comprised the main mode of artistic communication between the various Dada communities scattered across Europe, the Americas, and Japan. Furthermore, the work is organised by journal, allowing us to get a glimpse of the very different dynamics of the various local Dada communities who produced them, the ways in which Dadas from other communities participated in those journals and thus articulated international relationships, and even the ways that journals within a particular community would articulate different aspects of a broader field of activity, thought, or idiom. This provides a much-needed context for the canonical Dada poems and pronouncements, and reinforces their status as *social gestures* within an international community, and not simply polemics or 'artworks' directed outside of the group. Ades gives representation to a number of individual Dadas, Dada groups, and Dada journals that have received almost no attention in the Anglophone world, such as the *Stupid* Group, *Ventilator*, and many others. It would no doubt have been more directly at play within this text had it not been on loan to Bradley Chriss and Megan Blafas. An excellent collection, filling in the gaps of the more canonical sources.

Apollinaire, Guillaume & Revell, Donald, trans. (2004). *The Self-Dismembered Man: Selected Later Poems.* **Middletown, CT: Wesleyan University Press.**

Apollinaire is one of those people who (like Rimbaud), if one engages with a certain tradition *as* a tradition—that is to say, as an ongoing, multi-generational project in which it is *irresponsible* to practically re-invent the wheel with every generation so that minimal progress is made while hegemonic structures continue to develop more rapidly and effectively—one cannot *entirely* ignore (though I have managed to ignore a number so far…). One must at least give it a try to see if there's something one is missing. Apollinaire, in life, served admirably as a transmitter of myths between two generations who both did far more interesting things; Vaché had a point when he accused him of patching up lyricism with telephone wire, and Kristeva's dismissal of him seems reasonable. These poems cover his military service in the war he so loved, for the Nationalism for which he was so proud, and which killed him, which is just fine, for you get what you ask for. He died on Armistice Day to the cheers of a crowd shouting, 'down with William', thinking they were celebrating his own death; and this too was just as well, for after all he had worn his uniform as if it were a badge of honour, and had probably killed a good many young men through his public support of bureaucratized xenophobia; and if writing poems in which the deaths of hundreds or thousands of men was balanced just about equally by the *love* he bore for his mistress, then no doubt there was some other egotistical bastard who loved his mistress just as much, which by the same logic renders Apollinaire just another picturesque literary *effect*. But hey—he's got some very nice lines, though.

Artaud, Antonin and Hirschman, Jack, ed. (1965). *Artaud Anthology.* **San Francisco: City Lights.**

I have not yet read *more* Artaud yet, partly because, since I bought it in A.Da. 87 (that's 2002 for the uninitiated reader), I am still digesting it. Artaud sticks like a blood-clot in the throat: you are choking, there is blood everywhere and you don't even know if it is yours, and you can't think why you swallowed it in the first place; but there is no turning back.

Ball, Hugo, Elderfield, John, ed., and Raimes, Ann, trans. (1996). *Flight Out of Time.* **Berkeley: University of California Press.**

The only reason that there are no quotations from this, Ball's diary, is that it was lost somewhere during my (mostly financially induced) move from England back to the United States. It is, however, central to the matrix of ideas from which this book emerges. It is essential in *engaging with* one aspect of Dada, especially its relationships with major cultural shifts and its association with Mystical systems; the second part of the book is one of the more intelligently articulated accounts of that recurrent plague of this tradition, the conversion to Christianity; Ball's approach also represents one of the more admirable forms such a conversion can take.

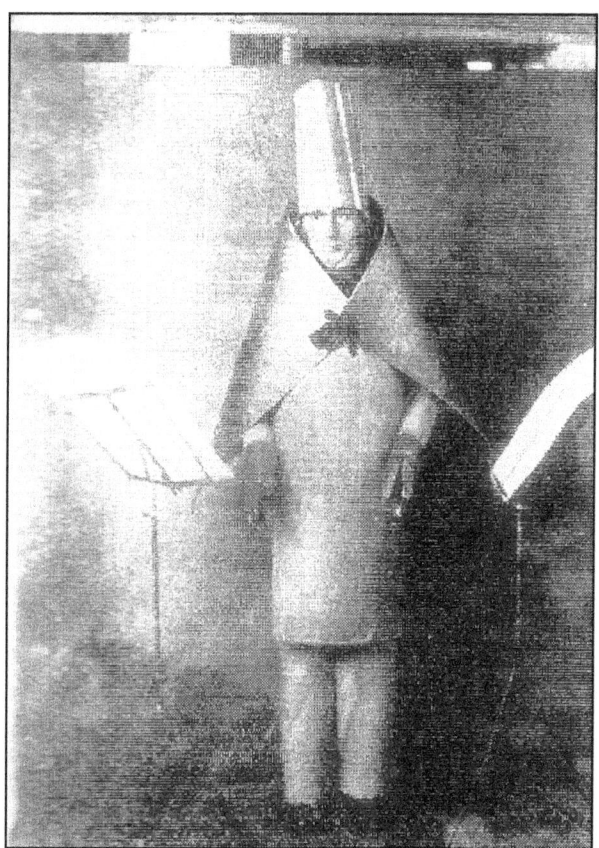

Hugo Ball in costume to perform *Karawane* at the Cabaret Voltaire, 1916. (Gamard 2000, fig. 34.)

Ball, Hugo, Huelsenbeck, Richard, Serner, Walter, and Green, Malcolm, trans. (1995). *Blago Bung Blago Bung Bosso Fataka: First Texts of German Dada: Fantastic Prayers/ Tenderenda the Fantast/ Last Loosening Manifesto.* **London: Atlas Press.**

This was the first book I ever bought from Atlas Press. From it, and from Atlas Press, I began to become aware of the complete paucity of the mainstream historiographic treatment of Dada, especially in English; for these three very different, and all brilliant works announced themselves as being part of an aspect of early Dada I had not so much as been informed of previously. Through memorizing and developing my performances of Huelsenbeck's *Plane* from the *Fantastic Prayers* I first learned that words are movements of the body, impulses of the nerves, aching muscles, sweat, a raw throat. Malcolm Green's wonderful introduction to the volume—one of the best introductions I have ever read, and the most influential on my own understanding of the cultural implications of how one speaks about creative activity—introduced me to the notion that Dada (and by extension, any collective venture) was part of an intricate project involving multiple groups cooperating and interpenetrating; it also introduced me to the very *concept* of historiographic responsibility, of re-examining what has been ignored and the *readings* of what has not, of keeping the *discourse* of history always in the present, always in flux, always evading the calcifying historiography of the *dominant canon*. It was the first time I recognised the *value* of translation, the canonical power involved. And this, in turn, extended to the Press—with Atlas, in experiencing this book, I first recognised Publishing not as a purely practical act, but as an ethical and ideological undertaking, as a tool for creating and maintaining communities and traditions. So while there are few quotations, per se, from this text in the book, my reading it has been a precondition not only for the *writing*, but the *publication* of the book in your hands; while Atlas itself is not a micropublisher, if I had never read this book, mOnocle-Lash might not exist as such.

Barthes, Roland & Miller, Richard, trans. (1975). *The Pleasure of the Text.* **New York: Hill and Wang. Original Publication 1973.**

The ideas of Barthes permeate the base assumptions of the book you are reading so pervasively that, like many of the deepest influences on this book, it has scarcely anywhere been necessary to cite him specifically. *Image: Music: Text*, which I have lent to a friend and therefore cannot list here, was my first text of 'critical theory'. The ideas in *The Pleasure of the Text* are obviously heavily at play in this book, but I foolishly lent that out as well at the critical stage. Unfortunately for Barthes, I soon *fell into* Derrida and have not gotten back to shore; I don't get lost in Barthes in the same way; it is too much like he is *speaking* to me.

Baudelaire, Charles & Verèse, Louise, trans. (1970). *Paris Spleen.* **New York: New Directions. Original Publication 1869.**

I have borrowed a copy from Warren Fry; I must buy my own and spend more time with it.

Baudelaire, Charles & Charvet, P.E., trans. (1972). *Selected Writings on Art and Literature.* **London: Penguin Books.**

Baudelaire has grown slowly on me over the years. I first came to him because I knew he had been an admirer of Poe, and tried intermittently to enjoy him more than I was ultimately able to. It was not until I learned about Dandyism that things began to make sense; after which I found him popping up in nearly every avenue of investigation I embarked upon, and finally came to understand. His critical theory still seems to me the most relevant of his published work.

Baudelaire, Charles & Howard, Richard, trans. (1993). *Baudelaire.* London: Everyman's Poetry.

Decent translations; the fruit of my second-to-last attempt to understand what so many people I respected were on about.

Baudelaire, Charles & Diamond, Stacy, trans. (1996). *Artificial Paradises.* **New York: Citadel Press. Original Publication 1860.**

Interesting on a number of levels; its subject matter is treated in the book in your hands, and is in fact somewhat disappointing in that he ends up at times sounding a bit like a non-asinine version of Nancy Reagan with his intermittent warnings against the evils of the use of the drugs to which he is dedicating a whole book; Flaubert reproached him for this as well. However, he also included a *re-presentation* of De Quincey's *Confessions*. Not a translation per se, but a blow-by-blow punctuated by translated quotations and occasional commentary. Baudelaire's contribution as a traditionally/communally-engaged translator is enormous, this is particularly interesting however as an extension of that canonizing role through blurring the lines between the text and its inevitably inflected re-presentation. This exercise was forced upon Baudelaire by his publisher, but he made interesting and fairly responsible use of it.

Baudelaire, Charles & McGowan, James, trans. (1998). *Flowers of Evil.* Oxford: Oxford University Press. **Original Publication 1857.**

Alright, I am beginning to understand...

Bennett, John M. and Kostelanetz, Richard. (2007). *BACKWARDS/Furtherest Fictions.* Hartford, Blue Lion Books.

Kostelanetz has made a huge contribution to the historiography of experimental and marginal artistic communities through his critical work; and as he is at great pains to point out in the introduction to his half of this superb collaborative book, his own creative work has been unjustly ignored in some circles whose opinion he apparently cares about. The nature of the debt that I owe to his collaborator in this book, John M. Bennett, can be summed up *in part* by the fact that he *has* no introduction to his half, but spends nearly as many words as Kostelanetz's introduction in listing every single micropress journal, anthology, and performance event that any of his hundreds of poems presented in this book have appeared in. Utterly without ego and intensely, and quietly, committed to strengthening and maintaining communities that refuse any dependence upon commercial structures or dominant discourses, Bennett's work has not *at all* gone unrecognised within the communities within which he *chooses* to work. As will be discussed below in relation to micropress publication, Bennett's work cannot be read or spoken about in the same way as most of the work in this palimpsest of a library I am presenting to you. To read Bennett's work, to really *read* it is to *possess* another body, to inhabit the relics of what Kristeva might (at least through my reading) call a certain duration of another's thetic becoming; everything is in a state of near-incomprehensibility, words, like sensations, seem to appear but their cohesion has not yet been established, there is no ego and barely the faintest glimmer of an unconscious, a preconscious; they are articulated through an erratically rhythmic network of ruptures and unmotivated mergings, a network that itself is only half-articulated, not yet even *defin*itively temporal or spatial. The reader finds him or herself in the midst of this *process*, and lets the possible articulations of this strange meeting play out, the simultaneous dissolving of her or his own 'self' and the physical rhythms and drives underlying it as it reads, and the partial and momentary crystallization of the text as it finds itself caught up in the process of becoming (of) the reader. This has everything—everything to do with the book you are reading now. The copy of *BACKWARDS/ Furtherest Fictions* that I own used to be Bennett's own; after looking through it while visiting at his home upon my return from the United Kingdom, I inadvertently stole it and discovered it with a stack of recent Luna Bisonte publications he had given me; I e-mailed him to arrange to return it, and he told me to keep it. He had already *apologized* before the incident for not giving me a copy, but at around 400 pgs., he very understandably couldn't afford it. Refer to my earlier point.

Bergson, Henri & Paul, Nancy Margaret and Palmer, W. Scott, trans. (2004). *Matter and Memory.* **Mineola, NY: Dover Publications.**
Original Publication 1896.

I recommend the following regimen: For every five pages of Bergson's *Matter and Memory*, read one chapter of Kristeva's *Revolution and Poetic Language* and four pages of the poems of John M. Bennett. You will come to *feel* thought. This is nearly the precise regimen that I followed while writing this book; for perhaps two months, usually on several cups of coffee (Mallarmé's drug of choice, need I remind you, and among Jarry's repertoire as well), until 3 AM, in the kitchen of our apartment. This copy is *heavily* dog-eared and marked. Bergson brings together several discourses to create a dense landscape of text, he manipulates his rhetoric brilliantly so that his argument, though always balanced on the very outskirts of comprehensibility, is at the same time always inevitable (in a strange way, not entirely unlike Schreber…), and he is relentless, allowing the reader no rest; in reading him I was constantly on the edge of my own comprehension, my brow furrowed, training. Attempting to 'condense' it (and not only that, twist and manipulate it) for the discussion in this book has been one of the most difficult things I have ever done; thinking itself became painful. I had made a note to read Bergson some time earlier when I heard of *Time and Simultaneity* (which ironically I have yet to read), but finally took the plunge when I learned he had taught Jarry. Reading Bergson has brought Jarry into (yet another) radically different focus.

Blair, David, ed. (2002). *Gothic Short Stories.* **Hertfordshire: Wordsworth Classics.**

When I decide I need to become familiar with a certain arena of thought or activity, I start with whatever collection/ anthology/ compilation/ etc. I can get my hands on, blind as I am, and work from there toward the best work, which I know will generally be obscure. Thus this book.

Blake, William. (2000). *The Complete Illuminated Books.* **London: Thames & Hudson.**

Blake is possibly more central to this book than anything that actually appears within it. There are several reasons he has not appeared more; the best of which is that while the various themes and ideas at play all extend in their applicability and in their sources far beyond the confines I have had, for the sake of (my much-vaunted) brevity, to place around my discussion, I have focused, among other things, upon models who have created from Modernity itself the strategies, modalities, and discourses through which to attack it; Blake, while mounting a comprehensive, incisive, and inspiring attack on that emerging order, it seems to me did so primarily through re-charging, and detourning, the weapons of what was being displaced. Moreover, I am not capable of inhabiting Blake's work in the necessary way; he is still too monumental, I am still in awe of him. And no useful critique can be made from a position of *awe*, only of *respect*. I have mentioned my predilection for beat-up books; my volume of Blake is an exception. The corners are still sharp; I use only my best pens to trace my own characters into it; I bought a magnifying glass explicitly to study it. Never read a typeset transcription alone; Blake writes for the eyes as well.

Breton, André & Howard, Richard, trans. (1960). *Nadja.* **New York: Grove Press.**
Original Publication 1928.

Everything in this book—which is *neither* (and not *all*, for none of these compartments is valid) fictional, nor biographical, nor factual, nor theoretical—is relevant to the book I am now finishing. The literary 'products' of Surrealism are generally too comprehensible to be of much value; if you're going to come this far, go all the way (*some* way) and read some Tzara, Leftwich, or Lautréamont. What *Nadja* snares so well is the way of *living* developed by the Parisian Dadas and further explored by the Surrealists in their five or six years of real vitality. *Nadja* is a gorgeous document of *something*.

Breton, André, Seaver, Richard, trans., & Lane, Helen R., trans. (1972.) *Manifestoes of Surrealism*. Ann Arbor: University of Michigan Press.

I got hold of this book somehow or other soon after I became interested in Anti-Art, but did not read it for several years due to my hatred for Surrealism—and especially Breton—whom I blamed (only somewhat unfairly) for getting scared of the implications of Dada, turning it into an orthodoxy, and bringing down the movement with it. When I finally got around to reading it some years later, I was surprised to find that Breton's theoretical writings (whatever his *behaviour*) were remarkable, if still too drenched in the ideological left-overs of Romanticism; and a new trajectory of my thought and investigation was set. My mistrust of Surrealism as a phenomenon remains, but the factors that led to this splendid idea being first turned into an orthodoxy, then recouperated by the institution, are far more complex. What Breton did was to bring back into the open a number of issues that had been implicit, and I would argue quite conscious, in the ways of living created by the Dadas and the generation or two preceding them, but which needed to be articulated *vocally* every few generations lest they be lost, especially the notion of a *tradition* of revolt; and, implicit in this, a refusal to be dominated *by* history, while also refusing to *ignore* it and let it go its way unmolested. In his way, Breton articulated notions I had been developing myself (on very little information), and provided a framework within which to begin such a project, as well as a model for what strategies seemed to work, and to fail.

Breton, André, Éluard, Paul, Soupault, Phillippe & Gascoyne, David, trans., Melville, Antony, trans., & Graham, Jon, trans. (1997). *The Automatic Message/ The Magnetic Fields/ The Immaculate Conception*. London: Atlas Press.

Automatic writing was mis-*conceived* by the Surrealists, and I tend to agree with Stewart Home that their theological *faith* in the unconscious as an easy answer for the ills of mankind was a major factor in their eventual ideological failure, much like the Situationists' later theological faith in the 'coming' Revolution. As a social practice among others, automatic activity—especially *collective* automatism such as that currently being explored by Warren Fry, D.B. Edwards, and others, can have great value; as a personal practice, it can be invaluable; but it must be situated *within*, and not *at the helm of* new modalities of living, and consciousness is ultimately no less interesting, unpredictable, or enigmatic than the unconscious; it is simply received, abstract, and structurally passive *models* of consciousness that create this illusion. Breton recognised, at least, that the *products* of automatic writing were fast becoming a fetish that distracted from the *process* which gives the activity its greatest value; consequently, these texts have—can have and should have—a primarily historic value.

Breton, André & Polizzotti, Mark, trans. (1997). *Anthology of Black Humor*. San Francisco: City Lights Books.
    Original Publication 1945.

The *Anthology* is one of a number of key texts in the tradition of the Yellow Sign—along with Verlaine's *Damned Poets*, Huysmans' *A Rebours*, Gourmont's *Book of Masks*, and Home's *Assaulting Culture*—concerned with delineating, concentrating, and re-figuring that tradition, (re)creating it, catalyzing a community through presenting it as already-formed, always already at play. Elaborating on Verlaine's more modest strategy, Breton juxtaposes passages from the original to his own commentary, thus allowing the reader to read for her- or himself and, possibly, become intrigued and track the authors down, while at the same time suggesting a certain *way* of reading, establishing a model for how a practice of reading might be *strategized*. It is key to note that despite Breton's role as Surrealism's most vocal polemicist and theoretician, this is not positioned as a 'Surrealist' tradition (though the *Manifestos* would have provided some precedent for such a maneuvre), indeed Surrealism is scarcely mentioned, although the tradition overlaps greatly with it; and, while most of those included do come from the 'literary' world, there is at least an attempt to suggest the artificiality of this boundary with the inclusion of people such as Brisset and Fourier.

Breton, André & Polizzotti, Mark, trans. (2003). *Selections.* **Berkeley: University of California Press.**

Whatever else one might say, Breton, when he is not being derailed by tedious 'Love Poems', is the only Surrealist who, as far as I am concerned, did not fall to shit as a writer of verse after his conversion to Surrealism, with the exception of Péret, who has always felt Dada to me throughout his life. This is also to say that Breton's poetry *works on me* in a way that very little from the 20th Century does. This particular volume, which is slim but excellent, is for me metonymically encapsulated in a single poem, for which I value it highly: *Lethal Relief*, reprinted in full in this book ('The statue of Lautréamont…'). The indescribable *physiological* response to my first reading of this poem, the feeling that every word was a key to some obscure relationship to *Maldoror* that I myself could not articulate, yet Breton had somehow *addressed*, forced me to think without any definable reason: only someone with a relationship with the text of *Maldoror* that was as deeply *unsettling*, on the most basic level, as my own has been, could have written this poem; and only someone with a relationship to it as deeply unsettling as *my* own, even though that relationship could not have been the *same*, could have fully *read* it. It came to me as a kind of communication across generations (and even translation), invisible to anyone not *initiated*. This may be when I came to understand—if that is the right word—the Yellow Sign.

Brotchie, Alastair, Ed. & Gooding, Mel, ed. (1995). *A Book of Surrealist Games.* **London: Shambhala Redstone Editions.**

I have only played a few of these so far; again, one of the things which speaks in Surrealism's favour was the value it placed on games, and the fun that the Surrealists had playing them. I do not keep this in my bookshelves, but on the living room table. Anyone is invited to mark it, because such a book must be *played*, like an instrument, by everyone.

Carter, Lin, ed. (1971). *The Spawn of Cthulu.* **New York: Ballantine Books.**

The story about this book is far better than the book. It is yellowed and tattered as hell; the cover, title page, and first page are no longer connected to the spine. It was found by my friend Aaron Howard, whom Warren Fry and I met in a maze in New York and ended up making noise and poems with in the display window of a storefront for two hours before introducing ourselves and learning each others' names. He attended an Anti-Soiree at my and Fry's apartment, where I was excitedly discussing how, under the influence of Ackerman and Home, I was re-addressing my long-time relationship with H.P. Lovecraft, and planned, once the book you are now reading was finished, to try to find time to engage more fully with the Cthulu Mythos as a writer. Several days later, on the streets of New York, he stumbled upon a huge box of books thrown out on the sidewalk, and began to stuff them into his bags, pockets, and arms. He came upon this anthology—focusing upon a number of writers involved with the mythos—and recognised the name. He put it aside, and called me before heading to New Jersey for the next Anti-Soiree, and told me of his find. He gave me a choice: he had considered tearing pages out, one by one, at every step from Brooklyn to Penn Station to New Brunswick to our apartment; but then again, this might be of more use to me to actually read. Tormented, I weighed the decision; this was indeed *just* the kind of anthology I'd been looking for, it was free and I was working sporadic temp jobs at warehouses on the outskirts of the city as I strove to finish the book in your hands, and moreover it sounded like a beautiful and well-loved copy; on the other hand, a trail of horror stretching from Brooklyn to central New Jersey was not something I could ethically stand in the way of. I closed my eyes and told him to flip a coin, or follow his inclinations. He arrived three hours later with the book wrapped up in a thick rubber band.

Carruthers, Mary. (1998). *The Craft of Thought: Meditation, Rhetoric, and the Making of Images, 400-1200.* **Cambridge, University of Cambridge Press.**

I discovered this book far too late, and moreover, it does not belong to me, it was lent to me by Charlotte Whalen; I plan to buy a copy quite soon, however. I have been able to read only the part most explicitly relating to what I have written here. It provides the groundwork for tracing nearly *all* of the ideas floating around in the present text back to a very highly developed state in what was, if still an elite minority in a closed microsociety—Medieval European clerical communities—at least not as utterly bereft of cultural capital as 'the arts' in our present society. Looked at from the standpoint of a history of *what was* it is fascinating; from the standpoint of a *model of what forms of thought might be created*, though it would take generations and would have to be differently articulated in response to vastly different cultural models, its *potential* seems huge.

Caws, Mary Ann. (2001). *Manifesto: A Century of Isms.* **Lincoln: University of Nebraska Press.**

There are a number of huge anthologies of theoretical writing centred on creative activity (most of them tilted toward the visual arts), all of which would likely be good to have and read, but having read this, I feel very little urgency to acquire them. It was through this book that I came to a much fuller conception of how creative activity was organized and discussed in (especially) the first half of the 20th Century than in standard 'histories', and was introduced to at least a dozen movements and groups ignored by mainstream history. The picture painted by 'Post-Modern' history of a creative discourse in which polemic is an anomaly was effectively destroyed. The book is invaluable for creative currents—both subversive and semi-dominant—until the Second World War, after which strange gaps begin to appear; for instance there is no representation of Situationist or Neoist tendencies—though there is an excellent Feminist manifesto by Cixous and Clément.

Cendrars, Blaise & Padgett, Ron, trans. (1992). *Complete Poems.* **Berkeley: University of California Press.**

I am not as fond of Cendrars as I would dearly like to be. Like a simulacrum of Cravan.

de Certeau, Michel & Rendall, Steven, trans?. (1984?) *The Practice of Everyday Life: A General Introduction.* **Retrieved 10 July 2007 from the World Wide Web: http://en.wikipedia.org/wiki/The_Practice_of_Everyday_Life**

I am ashamed not to have read this whole book yet. I will do so *soon*.

de Certeau, Michel & Massumi, Brian, trans. (1986). *Heterologies.* **Minneapolis: University of Minnesota Press.**

I borrowed this book from Charlotte Whalen, far too late in the game. While it cannot be said therefore to be an influence on the present text in the *strictest* sense, the essay *History: Science and Fiction* is entirely relevant to the project that it is intended to imply.

Chambers, Robert and Joshi, S.T., ed. (2000). *The Yellow Sign and Other Stories.* **Chaosium.**

Chaosium, along with a few other presses such as Necronomicon Press, is not unlike a counterpart to Atlas Press in world of Horror. They are particularly interesting in that they also publish *The Call of* Cthulu, a role-playing game that I have not myself played (Warren Fry asserts that it is particularly intelligent in design and structure) but that extends the correlations made in the body of this text concerning the mythology in this community and the role of myth in Avant-Garde communities. The Cthulic mythology is not the exclusive property of the *writers,* the readers too can write their conceptions of it; and these writings they *play* will feed back into their reading of the texts, which continue to be produced. The applicability and correlations between role-playing and what I speculate upon in this book as 'hallucinatory practices' should be fairly evident. I was turned onto Chambers through Lovecraft; though his later work is apparently (none of it has been reprinted) a huge embarrassment even to his greatest admirers—the turn-of-the-20th Century equivalent of grocery-store romances—the stories collected in *The Yellow Sign* are stunning. Chambers was on to *something*, and then he turned away. But not before he gave it a name: the Yellow Sign.

Coleridge, Samuel Taylor. (1847). *Biographica Literaria: or, Biographical Sketches of my Literary Life and Opinions.* New York: Wiley & Putnam.
    Original Publication: 1815.

At the time that I was given this—by my grandmother, at the last Christmas before her death—the 1847 edition was the only one that could be found; so I read it directly from this delicate, beautiful, two-volume set. I did not even dog-ear or mark it (when I re-read it, I probably shall). This was the first book I read in which I was conscious throughout of having no real notion of what was going on—and persevered. I was familiar with virtually none of the theorists or writers to whom Coleridge referred, was forced to reconstruct the whole intellectual climate in which his thought developed through his comments about them (I was familiar with the literary context but this was not nearly as much help as I had expected), had no frame of reference for the arguments he was making or the language he employed—and I kept going, and at the end had constructed through the experience a system of thought. This might, in truth, be the first book I ever really *read*.

Cravan, Arthur; Rigaut, Jacques; Torma, Julien; and Vaché, Jacques. (2005). *4 Dada Suicides.* London: Atlas Press.

It is interesting to note—this is not, you will understand, necessarily a criticism—that of the four authors here, only one is *known* to have committed suicide, and only one was a Dada in the (relatively) strict sense; moreover, they were both the same person, Rigaut. (One might wonder why Crevel and Loringhoven, who also met both of these criteria, were left out, while Torma was included despite having virtually no connection to Dada whatsoever; though as it happens he was *very* highly regarded by the College of 'Pataphysics...) It really doesn't matter, because they are all brilliant and sobering texts, not because of the nihilism per se, which is of course quite charming, but because they are relics of engagements more complete than most of us can even aspire to; they remind me that I am, ultimately, a coward. This is the only set of texts by Cravan that I am aware of in translation beside the *Independants* review in Motherwell's anthology, and Rigaut is mindblowing; *Lord Patchogue* is a masterpiece. This is a particularly nice book by Atlas, with a classy slipcase that has been crushed all out of shape due to my never keeping the book in it.

Dawkins, Richard. (2006). *The Selfish Gene.* Oxford: Oxford University Press.
    Original Publication 1976.

The concerns of Meme theory are obviously at play in the conception of this book, but I have not investigated its theorization enough to be able to speak about it; this was the first step in that direction.

Deak, Frantisek. (1993). *Symbolist Theater: The Formation of an Avant-Garde.* Baltimore: Johns Hopkins University Press.

The title of this book is misleading; for the real emphasis, and the inestimable value of this book is in the subtitle rather than the title. Deak's working conception of 'Theater' in this text is *the performative* in all of its manifestations, and the 'theatrical production' of the play is only one subset among others; and even then, he analyzes the dynamic of the audience as much as that of the performers, producers, and writers. Deak looks at *how* Symbolism as such came to constitute itself as a mode of sociality responding to economic conditions, changing social forces, and developing ideas regarding the re-creation of the self; it is a study of a community simultaneously forming itself, and examining how to articulate and conceive *of* itself. I read over half of it at the library in the UK, and when I returned bought a copy for myself to re-read and complete.

De Quincey, Thomas. (1995). *Confessions of an English Opium-Eater.* New York: Dover.
    Original Publication 1821.

I bought this Dover edition for $1 at the Book Loft, a 30-odd-room independent used book store in Columbus, Ohio. Thank god (sic) for Dover Thrift Editions, realizing that poor people also like to read. In addition to the aspects of it about which I have spoken in the body of this book, De Quincey's constant addresses to the reader regarding the act of reading (which I am sure you will notice in my own work, my dearest reader, as in many others in this tradition, Tzara and Lautréamont especially), his idiosyncratic prose style and sentence structure, and the constant self-reflexivity of the text prepared me for Lautréamont, Derrida, and others. In going back to the book I was surprised to see how much my original notation, inscribed perhaps six years ago, dealt with these aspects of the text. One of the first conversations with future Post-Neo co-founder Aaron Andrews that I distinctly remember concerned Thomas De Quincey and Frank Zappa.

Derrida, Jacques and Kamuf, Peggy, ed. (1991). *A Derrida Reader: Between the Blinds.* **New York: Columbia University Press.**

Like several others, if Derrida makes only a few explicit appearances in this book, it is because his writing has so thoroughly permeated every aspect of my life and self-conception that the influence can scarcely be isolated. I bought this book around the same time I began reading *Maldoror*, and am still only a third of the way through it—caught up in re-reading *Tympanum* or *Envois* I have yet to work through everything. Only Lautréamont has affected *who I ~~am~~* as profoundly as the writings of Derrida. For a year I would spend an hour a day reading and re-reading a paragraph at a time, until something emerged from it. And things began to collapse; my conception of 'reality' progressively imploded like the House of Usher. And it was not so much his 'ideas' (which anyway are not 'ideas', his thought is not that simple) that initiated this, but his *writing*, of which the various notions that emerge are merely the by-products. Derrida's writing is a crucible within which the reader is annihilated. A way must be found to force society to this same crisis.

Derrida, Jacques and Bass, Alan, trans. (2001). *Writing and Difference.* **London: Routledge.**

Though I haven't yet finished the 700-odd page reader with which I started, I bought this as well, also only half-completed. *Play and Signification*......

Ducasse, Isidore and Lykiard, Alexis. (1978). *Poésies: and complete miscellanea.* **London: Allison & Busby.**
    Original Publication 1870.

This 1978 edition is completely included in the Lykiard edition of *Maldoror*. Ducasse anticipated a great deal, from plagiarist technique and détournement to the gift-economy of micropress and mail art; I've discussed him enough in the main text. As I discuss there, there is endless debate concerning whether the *Poésies* represent a renunciation of *Maldoror*, or are to be taken sarcastically, and such an argument, in conceiving Lautréamont as a 'mere' pseudonym, manages to miss several points simultaneously; the issue is both much simpler and infinitely more complex than that: *Maldoror* is a text. The *Poésies* are a text...

Duchamp, Marcel & d'Harnoncourt, Anne and McShine, Kynaston, eds. (1973). *Marcel Duchamp.* **New York: Museum of Modern Art.**

I feel it incumbent upon me to take a highly critical stance regarding Duchamp, considering the way he has been twisted into a catch-all excuse permitting all kinds of intellectual apathy and ethical bankruptcy—a darling-child of the Post-Modern Establishment and enabler of all of its elitist, consumerist mechanizations. That he has been used in this way is largely, but not entirely his own fault. It is in any case unfortunate, because he could in many ways have been an inheritor of Mallarmé, and translated the intense engagement of the latter into visual languages and discourses; but he continued and in some ways deepened those faults of Mallarmé that ought to have been *corrected* by later generations—the deferral of explicitly social responsibility, the lack of active engagement with how his work and his myth was employed to bolster various parties in ideological struggles—and thus Duchamp became not only recouperated, but set up as a legendary screen behind which the machinery of the 'Art Market' has been able to package human potential and sell it to the isolated economic-pseudointellectual Elite as a status-commodity. Manipulative capitalists from Andy Warhol to Matthew Barney have all been justified by pointing at the sorry figure Duchamp allowed himself to be turned into; if this is not *failure*, I don't know what is. But it is sad, because he was so close to being brilliant…

Edwards, David Beris. (2006). *Ballyhoo.* **Dartington, UK: self-released.**

Edwards would doubtless express astonishment were one to speak of him as an heir to Baudelaire's most radical practice, and indeed he came to it through completely different means; yet I have quoted somewhere in this book Gautier's description of Baudelaire as a living textual mode, of 'speaking in italics and capital letters'; and although I am far from alone in my own community in exploring these kinds of practices—Kathy Karpilov, Alan Reed, and Bradley Chriss, in particular, are models to learn from—I can think of no one who better answers this description of Baudelaire than David Beris Edwards. Edwards himself is unthinkable except *as* a fiction, and a distinctly *literary* fiction emerging from Wodehouse, Lear, Carroll, Spike Milligan, and many others. Since he cannot possibly exist in this world—that is to say, he *refuses* to exist in *such* a world—Edwards has made himself into a walking rift in the banality of 'reality', and carries *with* him a fiction, so that everyone close to him comes to share this world of nonsense which is quite simply life as it *ought* to be, and which Edwards insists, with such rollicking charm, it *must* be. And thankfully for all of us, this world and this superior logic that he carries with/in him is one that is generous, fun, hilarious, excited, and emphatically *never* dull. It is a world—which perhaps can exist *only* against nature and outside reality but which Edwards nonetheless forces *upon* nature and into reality—that is devoid of anything petty (unless delightfully petty), anything vindictive, anything complacent. It is unnecessary for Edwards to rail *against* anything, because he has already made himself into a walking revolt against the banality in which the rest of us, even as we fight to swim, are nonetheless constantly in danger of drowning; and he has made it to shore so successfully and so long ago that he no longer needs to shout about it, and can get on with making the most of it—and having *FUN*.

Engine, Imogene. (2007). *The Iuk Kide.* **New Brunswick, NJ: mOnocle-Lash Anti-Press.**

It was primarily through Imogene Engine that I was introduced to rigorous theoretical discourse, and the dizzying scope and avidity of her learning, her insistence upon engaging with every realm and structure of intellectual activity, is inspirational and humbling. Both my thought and my writing were developed in the first several years of Post-Neo during our frequent six-to-ten hour sessions writing, conversing, reading, comparing, and revising in the Blue Danube in Columbus, Ohio, where we would set up a creative and intellectual workshop in the booth where, we are told, Rod Serling once wrote episodes for *The Twilight Zone*. Her writing is continually in flux, all of her poems being continually taken apart, recombined, re-figured, like Schwitters' physical *Merzbilder;* and her life is a continuous looping *through* writing, they are two terms of a single movement, Jarry's 'diastole and systole'. Like *A Rebours,* like the stories of Lovecraft and Chambers, like the 'Book' of Mallarmé, and like the book you are holding in your hands, the Iuk Kide is a book *wherein* the book both focuses and annihilates, where personal mythologies are teased out, dismembered, and refigured, and where language comes to die and be reborn.

Ernst, Max. (1976). *Une Semaine de Bonté.* **New York: Dover Publications.**

The Dadamax is òne of the practitioners of hallucinatory practice who was most explicit about the *fact* of his involvement, but the details of whose engagement have been hardest to track down. There is, I suspect, much more yet to be learned from Max Ernst. This is probably the most consistently haunting and deeply disturbing collection of visual art that I own, and one of the few full bodies of visual work which communicates to me a sensibility regarding the Yellow Sign that is comparable to that of Lautréamont, Derrida, or Jarry. The more time one spends with this work the more *intimately* disorienting it becomes.

Fink, Bruce. (1997). *A Clinical Introduction to Lacanian Psychoanalysis: Theory and Technique.* **Cambridge: Harvard University Press.**

In general I have become increasingly less fond of 'introductions' to 'difficult' texts, for reasons fairly obvious from other comments. In Lacan's case however, the obscurity (at least in the lectures—I do not yet have *Ecrits*) is not due so much to the textuality itself but to the fact that most of what Lacan has left behind was not *intended* to be read, much less by non-specialists; this was compounded for me by a lack of thorough familiarity with even traditional Freudian discourse. This book was recommended to me for this reason by Alan Reed, whom I trust when it come to reading *and* to Lacan, and who pointed out that a *clinical* approach to Lacan is the most productive, because his theory grew *out* of clinical practice, it did not start (as I was inevitably predisposed to do in my reading) *out of* discourse on language. This proved to be an excellent recommendation, and I have refrained from bringing more thoroughly or forcefully into this book the *specific* applicability of the Lacanian perspective to these practices primarily due to my lack of familiarity with Lacan's texts themselves (so far). Though on another level, the fact that a book specifically aimed at practicing specialists in a discipline I have no training in, and no extensive reading in, was nonetheless a straightforward and *relaxing* read makes me more than a bit nervous regarding the state of psychology in the Anglophone world today… a fact that Fink diplomatically addresses at several points.

Fisher, Ben. (2000). *The Pataphysician's Library: An Exploration of Alfred Jarry's livres pairs.* **Liverpool: Liverpool University Press.**

Following, in condensed and much more obscure form, Huysmans' example in laying out both an alternative canon and an alternative way of *reading* that canon through his embedded criticism with Des Esseintes' library, Jarry also presents a library in *Dr. Faustroll, Pataphysician* which is then re-figured on the course of his journeys to the several islands dedicated to the authors included. Fisher presents a description and analysis of these authors and works included, a number of whom are not available in English aside from a few scattered anthologies. This throws light on the aspect of Jarry's work as an intervention in the Symbolist community and an internal act of communication within it as well as external utterance; it is also a good introduction to that community, one of my first. Unfortunately, the many quoted passages are not translated.

Foucault, Michel and Howard, Richard. (2001). *Madness and Civilization: A History of Insanity in the Age of Reason.* **London: Routledge.**
    Original Publication 1961.

It is obvious that large sections of the present book would be unthinkable without Foucault, and the implications of his work are so basic to it that it has not been necessary to discuss him explicitly. As Derrida points out, Foucault takes on an impossible task in *Madness and Civilization*, an attempt to historicize from the space of History's impossibility as such; one aspect of my own book is not entirely far from a response to both this attempt and this failure.

Franck, Dan & Liebow, Cynthia, trans. (2001). *Bohemian Paris: Picasso, Modigliani, Matisse, and the Birth of Modern Art.* **New York: Grove Press.**

Due to the *essentially* meaningless (except, of course, for the fact that they unfortunately represent, *de facto*, the Truth-producing machinery of the controlling order) set of bureaucratic conventions instituted by 'academic' discourse since the Second World War in order to set itself apart from and above the 'impurity' of 'popular' writing, it is very difficult to find anything dealing with culture, and not published within small communities, that is not either uselessly pedantic on the one hand or entirely missing the point on the other (not that 'academic scholarship' does not generally miss the point as well). This issue comes to the fore when one is attempting to trace in print the relics of a mythic tradition. Either the subject is treated in such a way as to crush the mythic character of these stories into the dirt, desperately searching for a way to 'prove' or 'disprove', to 'cite sources', in other words to reduce this ongoing social activity into a *history*, in the most stupid and contemptible sense of the word, as a recourse to (and thus bolster of) 'Truth' as a transcendental guarantor to which the discourses of Power might appeal; or else it is treated simply as a diversion, as an example of 'how crazy artists are, and ooh, they used to be even *crazier*.' Ultimately the latter type is preferable, because behind it at least the myth is living and tangibly *at play;* if you don't like the way the story's told to you, you can change it; in fact this is exactly how it *ought* to work. Nonetheless it is a bit like listening to a slightly annoying interlocutor for 12 hours (or 300 pgs.) in order to get a few dozen stories to spruce up and go tell to your friends in a more interesting version: worth it in the end, but more of a chore than it ought to be.

Fry, Warren Clippenger. (2007). *The Dada Cabaret, Happenings, and Brute Salon: A Disquisition on Collaboration and Indeterminacy.* **Unpublished Thesis, Mason Gross School of Art, Rutgers University.**

My conversation and activity with Warren Fry has been invaluable in placing me in a state in which to read the histories I have *traced*, and he has through his conversation during its writing had a greater direct influence upon the writing of the present text than any of my comrades; without his engagement with the ideas at play here in the midst of their development, they could not have been articulated. His uncompromising example and support have kept me (I hope) constantly alert to the many dangers of such a project, which might be recouperated or invalidated as an act of *praxis* at the slightest faltering of ethical or intellectual discipline. The most recent explorations of alternative social modes carried out by the New Jersey Post-NeoAbsurdist group, a direction of activity initiated by Fry, have begun to explore regions contiguous with the collective automatism, a-semic conversation, and socially-shared hallucination that has been discussed in relation to the Bouzingos gatherings, the Club de Hachichins, Jarry's circle as transcribed in *Days and Nights*, the Zurich and Paris Dada circles, and early Surrealist games, meetings, and 'séances'. This activity (in which I myself have of course been heavily engaged during the writing of this book, and which has largely been carried out in the apartment that Fry and I share as I type this) has been extended into psychogeographic projects involving elements of Situationist derive merged with a group application of strategies in some ways similar to Jarry's and Rimbaud's 'projective' practice, with the 'projected' element not being perceptive but rather a 'hallucinated' history or hallucinatory *causal order* itself modeled on the Cthulu mythos. All of this activity, and our many hours of discussion concerning it and its potential, has constituted a kind of silent parallel to the production of the book you are reading now. Fry's text here historically situates a part of the larger set of explorations now being carried out, and includes contributions by myself and fellow Post-Neos D.B. Edwards and Tomislav Butkovic.

Fuseli, Henry & Myrone, Martin. (2001). *Henry Fuseli.* **Princeton: Princeton University Press.**

This is simply a relatively inexpensive book with decent plates that I picked up at the Detroit Art Institute, which has one of the two painted versions of the iconic *Nightmare*. This painting, like Arnold Böcklin's *Isle of the Dead* and Moreau's *Salome*, has taken on an almost talismanic role in the tradition I am delineating that is not confined to the visual arts; it is referred to in literature both explicitly and through gesture from the Romantics through the Surrealists, and is constantly reworked by generations of graphic artists (Böcklin's piece has also been referred to in similar ways in literature, re-worked in visual form by Doré, Kubin, Klinger, Dali, and

Gieger, and treated musically in Rachmaninoff's tone-poem of the same title). In this way what began as an 'picture' has evolved into a talisman and a relic, so that almost regardless of the surface itself it can be engaged with through the generations of readings and re-writings that adhere to it. Fuseli is wildly uneven, but at his best he can be chilling, as for instance in his study for the head of a damned soul from the *Inferno*, which is displayed at the Art Institute of Chicago in the same room as Moreau's *Hercules and the Hydra*. The room also contains paintings by Böcklin and Puvis de Chevannes; despite my implacable hatred for the way in which the museum system has sold out its responsibility as a *civic institution* that ought to serve the public that cannot afford to 'buy work' for itself, rather than cater to the rich donors who want the price of their investments to go up through the museum's investment of status-capital, I must confess that this (along with David Beris Edward's living room, with its floor strewn with collage material and noisemakers and Fronty Beaky the unemployed thingey pinned to the wall) is one of my favourite rooms in the world.

Gamard, Elizabeth Burns. (2000). *Kurt Schwitters' Merzbau: The Cathedral of Erotic Misery.* **New York: Princeton Architectural Press.**

This is an excellent book. In addition to delving into the development of the Merzbau, both physical and conceptual, and teasing out the complex symbolic language at play, Gamard uses the Merzbau as the focal point of a more comprehensive situating of Schwitters' life, thought, and work in relation to hermetic, alchemical, and mystical systems. This was the book that first introduced me to the potential significance of these systems, and it was in reading it that I first realised the significance—the *full* significance—of Anna Blume.

Gammel, Irene. (2002). *Baroness Elsa: Gender, Dada, and Everyday Modernity.* **Cambridge: Massachusetts Institute of Technology Press.**

See my comments under 'Lane' below for my tirade concerning the indisputably sexist exclusion of the Baroness Elsa von Freytag-Loringhoven even from most internally-generated canons of the Avant-Garde. Gammel's book helps to alleviate this problem to *some* extent, and as a biography it is thoroughly exhaustive and not likely to be superceded unless someone eventually gets around to publishing the fragmentary autobiography that Gammel refers to. For that reason, this book is absolutely essential. Gammel's readings of Loringhoven's behaviour and productions are not precisely 'off' in

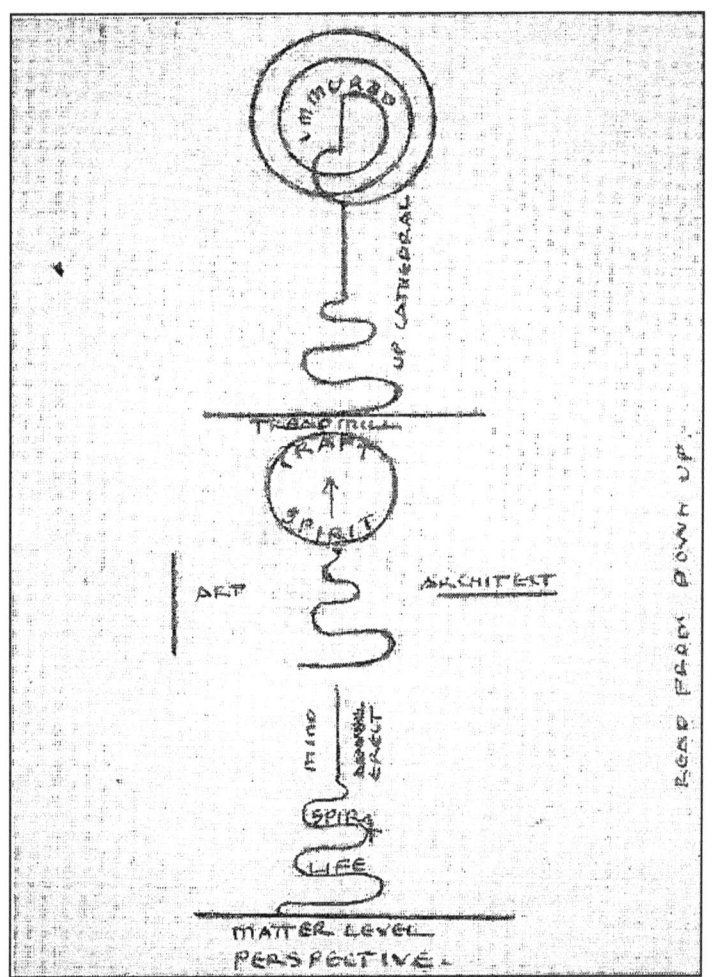

The Baroness Else von Freytag-Loringhoven, *Matter Level Perspective* (1922-23). (Gammel 2002, p 340.)

their arguments, but are framed in an academic fashion that seems destined to (unknowingly) recouperate them as 'art'; that is to say that Loringhoven's practice is framed as part of a 'historical' or 'finished' *moment* of revolt rather than as part of an *ongoing revolt* toward which the historian still owes a duty; this is in fact the major reason that Loringhoven does not figure more than she does in the book you are holding now; the relevant information could only be imported, with the methodology employed, by importing the text itself of Gammel, which despite the information it describes lends itself in its very terms to the framing of Loringhoven's practice as 'Body Art', etc. etc. Loringhoven's life is far too courageous and committed for me to risk contributing to her recouperation as a mere fore-runner of Cindy Sherman. This leads to my other complaint about the book: given the fact that there has been not a *single* concentrated collection of her work in any discipline, it is frustrating that Gammel provides only short snatches of poems, cut up by her commentary; this wouldn't bother me, of course, if it were possible for me to compare it to an existing volume… be all of this as it may, Gammel is enthusiastic, there is a huge amount of research and a wealth of detail upon which a close examination of her practice might be made, and there is also a good deal of information about Fin-de-Siècle communities in Germany that I have not come across elsewhere; and at least it *exists*, and is long overdue.

Gibson, Michael. (1999). *Symbolism.* **Köln: Taschen.**

Symbolist visual art was closely intertwined with literary symbolism in its discourse, social structures, and theory, and (as one can see, for instance, in Huysmans' treatment of visual art in *A rebours*) interpenetrated and directly communicated with literary communities much more than in previous generations or intellectual currents; one can see the nature of intertextual reference develop within painting into something more akin to the concept of an enclosed, hermetic tradition under this influence, as visual artists within Symbolist communities begin to abandon earlier models of building their personal and influential canons as if the predecessors they modeled themselves upon were so many independent agents, and began taking heavily into account those artists relationships, or potential relationships, to the emphatically heterogenous *traditions* they were themselves building through this very process; certain works within this tradition came to be identified with this stance, fetishes *of* tradition, as the reworking themes such as Böcklin's *Isle of the Dead* (reworked either explicitly or implicitly by Keller, Klinger, Rachmaninoff, and Giger) and Fuseli's *Nightmare* (for instance Klinger, and a host of writers such as Lovecraft and Blackwood, and later filmmakers) across generations came to act as affirmations of involvement in this continuing community. The resulting heterogeneity of the actual artistic *products* of this community is probably a key reason for the relatively lax treatment of it by mainstream art history (which may in fact work in its favour). This book is a decent, inexpensive edition of colour plates, organizing the presentation of the movement around its various national manifestations; the best basic introduction to the visual element of the Symbolist movement that I have found, though predictably enough the text concentrates almost exclusively on the production of works, and the nature *of* those works, not really investigating the ways in which those works, their production, their reception, and the discourses with which they interacted, *functioned* socially or personally. (The closest I have found to such a presentation of the movement is not explicitly 'about' Symbolism but rather the geographic, temporal, and cultural moment from which one particular manifestation of it emerged, Philippe Roberts-Jones' *Brussels: Fin de Siècle* which traces the artistic and social relationships in that city between literary, architectural, musical, philosophical, and visual arts communities.) While there is a good amount of excellent work emerging lately concentrating on the *full* significance of literary Symbolism, such as that by Richard Candida-Smith and Frantisek Deak, I have yet to come upon any such work even professing to treat the movement's visual element with the same respect; one has to figure out on one's own what *seems* to have been going on.

Gorey, Edward. (2001). *Ascending Peculiarity.* **New York: Harcourt, Inc.**

Besides the basic enjoyability of his work, Edward Gorey is an example of the potential fluidity between vernacular and 'intellectual' traditions. While this is far from the only book of Gorey's in my collection—the 'Amphigories' 1-3 include most of his smaller books, which are however quite nice for mass-produced trade editions—I include it because it is a series of interviews with Gorey, which highlights the extent to which Gorey represents a continuation of one very important aspect of Decadence, that of active consumption, of reading treated as an over-writing of cultural significance. Many parts of Gorey's interviews read almost like the long lists of cultural products and criticism that we find in *A Rebours;* a strong case could be made for Gorey representing a real continuation of Aesthetic practice, as a full-fledged member of the Decadent community—which, mediated as it is *through* the reading of cultural artifacts (especially as figured by Huysmans), is not inherently bound by time or any possibility of 'direct' interaction with other members of the community.

de Gourmont, Remy. (1994). *The Book of Masks.* **London: Atlas Press.**
   Original Publication 1896/98.

The publication of *The Book of Masks* markss one of the key moments of canonical condensation in the history of the Yellow Sign, much more ambitious than Verlaine's *Damned Poets*. It is the relic of a community presenting itself *to* itself as well as to others. While still quite valuable, this edition is one of the very few instances where I feel that Atlas Press has slightly dropped the ball. On the one hand, they have included texts from most of the writers included, many of whom have not been translated elsewhere, which is wonderful (the original edition included only Gourmont's commentary). On the other hand, they have not included the entirety of Gourmont's own writings on them, explaining that they deal with specific texts that readers will not be familiar with; I am constantly reading about things I am not familiar with, I find it quite interesting. Still, this may have been an unavoidable practical compromise, and it is far more valuable to have rare translations than commentary on unobtainable texts. My larger concern is their decision to cut 11 people out of the book—including several whose names are consistently evoked by Jarry, Huysmans, Mallarmé, etc, such as the Goncourts, Vielé-Griffin, René Ghil, Max Elskamp, etc. because, 'it proved impossible to find anything of interest.' (!) Furthermore, verse is not presented even when it is specifically the verse that Gourmont is concerned with, because, we are informed, translating it is too hard. Nonetheless there is some wonderful work—Rachilde's *The Frog-Killer*, in particular, is chilling and elegant.

Green, Malcolm, ed./trans. (1993). *The Golden Bomb: Phantastic German Expressionist Stories.* **Edinburgh: Polygon.**

I haven't dealt a great deal in this book with German-language manifestations simply because I'm not familiar enough with the specifically German Avant-Garde (this excepts Dada, and most of my understanding of German Avant-Garde communities is in relation to German Dada) to be able to approach it with a sensitive awareness of its traditions, the terms of its discourse, and the modalities of its socialization. Dandyism seems to have been as strong an influence in Germany as in France by the late 19th Century, and I suspect that it may have taken on more socially appropriate form there—Ball and Huelsenbeck have both associated themselves explicitly with it at some point, and Green does give some account of the influence of Dandyism on Expressionist communities in the introduction to this book; but I have not been able to gather enough information to really investigate the German manifestations of Dandyism or related practices. I suspect that

Arnold Böcklin, *The Isle of the Dead* (1880).   (Gibson 1999, p 118.)

Stephane George and Frank Wedekind could have fruitfully discussed in relation to my themes, as well as a number of the Expressionists with whom I have simply not been able to familiarize myself yet; this book is a step in that direction, translated and edited by Malcolm Green, who has done a huge amount to attempt to correct the blind-spot in English-language communities regarding German dissenting movements. I have not yet worked very deeply into the book, but there is some excellent work.

Halsey, Alan. (2001). *The Text of Shelley's Death.* **Sheffield: West House Books.**

Halsey's book provides a perfect (and much shorter) counterpart to the book you are reading now, and presents—entirely through juxtapositions of the accounts of people involved in the circumstances of Percy Shelley's death—the way in which the assumption of some kind of 'Truth' that magically inheres in historical events breaks down in the very process of that 'Truth' being coded in writing. It is a kind of clinical cross-section of a particular mytheme from the 'history' of the Yellow Sign at the moment of its passing *into* myth. An excellent text and a beautifully made book from Halsey's West House Books. I was recommended to this book by the poet John Hall after a(n Anti-)lecture I gave on the Yellow Sign. I explained to Halsey when ordering the book that I was investigating similar ideas, hoping for some dialogue on the implications of this notion, but his response was politely dismissive. When, several months later, I mentioned the same to Jim Leftwich of Xtant Press, he compiled nearly ten pages worth of notes and relevant material he had come upon in his own work. This to me exemplifies the difference in attitude between a 'Small Press' and micro-press communities.

Hazlitt, William. (1982). *Selected Writings.* **London: Penguin Books.**

Hazlitt is something of a old friend I had not visited for quite some time until I started preparing for this book; upon meeting him again, I found that I and/or he had grown into the possibility of a more thorough and productive engagement than before. This was a pleasant discovery, because it is not always the case.

Hendricks, Geoffrey, ed. (2003). *Critical Mass: Happenings, Fluxus, Performance, Intermedia and Rutgers University 1958-1972.* **New Brunswick, NJ: Mason Gross Art Galleries, Rutgers University.**

I borrowed this book this book from Warren Fry, and have only been able to read a few snatches of it. Of course any involvement of a *defiantly* marginal movement (there are some elements of Fluxus that fit this description, other elements that do not) with an institution represents a compromise, but it can be a *strategic* compromise, for better *or* for worse. Of the dominant institutional triumvirate governing the discourse of the 'Visual Arts', and of performance practices that associate themselves with this discourse and power-structure, the university is the least pernicious; it is at least a place where (amidst a great many sheep looking for job-training) intelligent people gather to prepare to *apply* whatever potential they have to affect the world around them, whereas the galleries are, and the museums have become, the places where they go to hand that potential over to cultural prison-guards in return for a few laurels. Despite the fact that the primary social function of the university is to channel and constrain intellectual activity and growth into the directions, boundaries, and structures established by the dominant ideological order, the fact remains that incursions from marginal communities into the communities centred on a university, and the infiltration—*if* it is vigilantly self-critical and strategic—of those structures themselves by people intent upon undermining that normalizing prerogative might be essential, in our particular historical moment, to the continuance of this tradition. The people who have the *potential* to intelligently engage—and at this stage, certain modes of 'artistic' training represent the skills that those coming *out of* this field have to offer to larger comprehensive revolutionary projects—must be made aware that this attempt does in fact *exist,* and moreover that it still *continues* and is not consigned to the pages of a dead 'history'.

Home, Stewart. (1991). *The Assault on Culture: Utopian Currents From Lettrism to Class War.* **Stirling: AK Press.**

Here is a book I *very much* wish I would have come upon sooner; in fact I came upon Home only half-way through the writing of this book, and to *Assault on Culture* toward the end; perhaps the most recent community-condensing book in the tradition of *The Book of Masks* and the *Anthology of Black Humor*. A long footnote toward the beginning of the book in your hands articulates the position of this project in relation to Home, who is the only contemporary I have come across who is positioned firmly *within* the politicized dissenting current (shall we call it the Avant-Garde?) and is addressing historiography firmly head-on, dealing not with vague ideological generalizations but with concrete issues of organisation, discourse, positioning, canonization—all from the deeply engaged standpoint of openly polemic *strategy*. The large preponderance of 19th Century and 'classical' Avant-Garde figures and texts in this book is due largely to not finding this book, and Home's other writings, two years ago, and I am therefore only beginning to become aware of similarly focused groups of the past thirty years, and without direct connections to Post-Neo. Absurdly, this book was only available in the UK, and cost more to ship than to buy; but it is worth the expense, it is vital. AK Press needs to re-issue this.

Home, Stewart. (1995). *Neoism, Plagiarism, and Praxis.* **Edinburgh: AK Press.**

A collection of assorted writings by Home after *Assault on Culture*, including a number concerning the Art Strike. Home is uncompromising, his voice is something of a cross between Debord (despite Home's criticism of his praxis) and Arthur Cravan, and I suspect some vernacular influences I am missing. Again, Home is one of the few theorists aggressively addressing issues on the levels that they *need* to be addressed, and committed to unsettling the self-satisfaction that has plagued dissenting communities coming out of 'Artistic' discourses for the past several decades. I don't always agree with him, and his published arguments can lean toward the overly-reductive or dogmatic in his search for an uncompromisingly polemic discourse, especially one designed to unsettle those clinging to the social 'legitimation' of academia; in fact I suspect that he would attack a very large part of the approach that I take in this book, which is after all hardly populist. As I have attempted to suggest in various places, I have my reasons; but it is essential that the kind of rigour that Home demands regarding the way one positions one's activity in relation to the ideological and economic associations clinging to any kind of 'intellectual' or 'creative' realm be aggressively voiced, and that an engaged, unsentimental, and openly polemic discourse be more fully developed and maintained among those engaged in this fight.

Ferdinand Keller, *Böcklin's Tomb* (1901-02).
(Gibson 1999, p 16.)

Hood, Thomas. (1873). *The Poetical Works.* **New York: James Miller, Publisher.**

I came to Thomas Hood primarily through Poe, who admired him greatly. His work has not been reprinted, aside from a few anthologies, since the 19th Century, hence my owning the 1873 edition (I own another 19th Century edition of Hood as well). Hood was deeply involved with social struggles, and wrote work responding to the Romantic 'intellectual' tradition of Shelley and Leigh Hunt as well as popular ballads for a more general public; publishing with Coleridge, De Quincey, and Lamb, he was also a contributor to *Punch*.

Huelsenbeck, Richard, Kleinschmidt, Hans J., ed., and Neugroschel, Joachim, trans. (1991). *Memoirs of a Dada Drummer*. Berkeley: University of California Press.
   Original Publication 1969.

If, in the triumvirate of English-translation memoirs by Dadas, Ball's *Flight Out of Time* represents the mystical, philosophical, and macro-historical perspective and Richter's *Art and Anti-Art* represents the perspective of the personal and social *experience* of the movement, *Dada Drummer* represents the hard-lined realism characterizing the Berlin Dada community. *Dada Drummer,* like both of those other texts, seems to me *essential* for any understanding of the lessons of that movement. If Ball coveys the cultural and personal *scope* of the implications of Dada as a way of living and Richter conveys the excitement and the *plausibility* of putting such ideas into practice within a community, Huelsenbeck conveys the intransigence, aggressiveness, and both cultural and physical *courage* of Dada at its best. (His fellow Berlin Dada Raoul Hausmann also wrote a memoir which, for some inexplicable reason, has never to my knowledge been translated.) Unfortunately, the older Huelsenbeck writing this memoir is not as intransigent as the younger Huelsenbeck he describes, and it is painful to see him down-playing the revolutionary political activity of Berlin Dada; this is most likely due to Huelsenbeck's status as a foreign national living in McCarthy-era New York during the book's writing. This edition also includes several smaller essays by Huelsenbeck of varying quality; his essay on the emergence of the gallery-and-critic-controlled infrastructure in American art is quite cogent, as is his essay 'On Leaving America for Good', which I re-read on the plane to the UK when I moved there two years ago (and here I am, back).

Huelsenbeck, Richard, ed.; Green, Malcolm, ed./trans.; Brotchie, Alastair, ed.; Wynad, Derk, trans.; Hale, Terry, trans.; Wright, Barbara, trans.; Melville, Antony, trans.; & Barnett, Susan, trans. (1993). *The Dada Almanac*. London: Atlas Press.
   Original Publication 1920.

The only international anthology assembled within the Dada movement that is available in English; Tzara and Huelsenbeck had planned a huge, and more comprehensive anthology called *Dadaglobe* that would have presented a much fuller scope of the size and variation of the movement, while the *Almanac* focuses, though not exclusively, on Berlin and Zurich (the Atlas edition does include some extra material to help alleviate this situation). Financial difficulties intervened, as they so often do in the publication of anti-institutional projects. Nonetheless, The *Almanac* helps to counteract the Francophone bent of Motherwell's anthology, and these two constitute the standard and indispensable Dada anthologies, though I would recommend Ades' as well. Though not as large as Motherwell and obviously without the memoirs that are sprinkled through the latter by Huelsenbeck, Buffet-Picabia, and Ribemont-Dessaignes, this represents the movement in its moment, and contains several essays coming out of Berlin that throw light on aspects of the activity there, especially theoretical and (anti-)historiological activity, not indicated elsewhere that I have seen, such as Alexis' account of a Dada Cabaret, Serner's account of the Dada tour of Japan, and Daimonides' essay on Dada Philosophy.

Huidobro, Vincente; Guss, David M., ed./trans.; Fredman, Stephen, trans.; Hagen, Carlos, trans.; Merwin, W.S., trans.; O'Brien, Geoffrey, trans.; Ossman, David, trans.; Palmer, Michael, trans.; Rothenberg, Jerome, trans.; Weinburger, Eliot, trans.; and Young, Geoffrey, trans. (1981). *The Selected Poetry of Vincente Huidobro*. New York: New Directions.

While his poetry remains poetry, it is very *good* poetry, and Huidobro's *Althazor* is, after Tzara's *Approximate Man*, the most moving a-syntactic epic I have read.

Hustvedt, Asti, ed. (1998). *The Decadent Reader: Fiction, Fantasy, and Perversion from Fin-de-Siècle France.* **New York: Zone Books.**

I've only begun to make my way through this huge reader, which includes several complete novels—d'Aurevilly's *Les Diaboliques,* Rachilde's *Monsieur Vénus,* Huysmans' *A Haven,* and Villiers' *The Future Eve*—Moréas' novella *La Faënza,* sizable extracts from Péladan's *Le Vice supreme* and Huysmans' *Saint Lydwine of Schiedam,* and short stories by Maupassant, Mendès, Lorrain, Gourmont, and Mirbeau. I found this on the same day that I found Pierrot's book, though at a different shop. Each author's selection is prefaced by an essay by a different writer; these are not bad essays though they tend to focus upon particular thematics within the author's work, a rather odd approach for a reader. In relation to the book you are holding, these stories tend not to address Decadent *Aestheticism* as I have discussed in relation to *A rebours* (the ones I have read so far), aside from Péladan's selection, which is quite relevant; it can nonetheless be detected as a latent force from which they emerge, especially in Villiers' work and of course Huysmans'.

Huysmans, Joris-Karl & Anonymous trans. (1931). *Against the Grain.* **New York: Illustrated Editions.**

When living in England, I did not have a phone for the majority of my sojourn. Alan Reed left the country several months before I did, and due to this circumstance we were unable to meet a final time before he left. I returned to the home of the head librarian of Dartington College Arts, John Sanford—who was generously letting me share his flat after my previous, horrendous living conditions had finally fallen apart completely—to find this book, which looks precisely how one would hope a 75-year-old copy of *A rebours* would look—that is to say, intact but faded, stained, a bit peeling, its cloth binding curling up—reclining on the stairwell with a short note from Alan. A further irony emerged after a bit of research; for, on the basis of its date and publishing information and its garish, utterly unrelated illustrations, this would appear to be what is described by Terry Hale as, 'at least one American version, possibly a pirate edition, with "garish illustrations". This book given to me in England by a Canadian before we both returned to the American continent is, apparently, a pirate American edition. How did it end up in Rural England? Possibly through a combination of as many chance circumstances as resulted in an American farm-boy ending up there to receive it.

Huysmans, Joris-Karl & Mauldon, Margaret, trans. (1998). *Against Nature (A rebours).* **Oxford: Oxford University Press.**
    Original Publication 1884.

I really don't think it's necessary to go on more about *A rebours,* 'the breviary of decadence'; my discussion of it takes up nearly a fourth of this book.

Huysmans, Joris-Karl & Hale, Terry, trans. (2001). *Là-Bas/The Damned.* **London: Penguin.**
    Original Publication 1891.

I did not really know what to make of this book, quite different from *A rebours,* as I was reading it; it requires a long digestion, and I am still in the midst of that process after over a year; I have had to approach it, as it were, *through* the earlier book not so much because I happened to have read the former first, but because it provides some kind of fulcrum outside *Là-Bas* from which one can lean into the later without falling into the unsettling nebulosity that permeates it. Like *A rebours,* the latter book lacks a proper 'plot'—or rather, the only real narrative arc is the one that Durtal is reading and re-*writing,* about the Medieval Satanist and child-murderer Gilles de Rais. But whereas the lack of a traditional plot in *A rebours* is a reflection of the life that Des Esseintes has chosen for himself, the plotlessness of *Là-Bas* has the feeling of a crisis, of a slipping away of all the various coordinates according to which the individual's grounding in the social order are pinned; whereas the story of Gilles de Rais, running alongside and through it, is genuinely wicked, rich, dynamic, the crisis in which Durtal and his associates are *stranded,* rather than immersed, takes the form merely of a stasis, a formless malaise, and the Satanism through which some of them try to escape cannot regain the grandeur of its predecessor in de Rais; it comes off merely as sordid, and one gets the feeling that this realisation is slowly creeping into everyone involved. And, of course, Huysmans followed the self-projected character of Durtal through two more books as this crisis progressed, ending eventually with his conversion to Catholicism. The questions this leads me to are: for what was this agitated confusion a symptom? And would we be able to recognise it as acutely were we to find ourselves in the midst of its return, or continuance? And—ultimately—could we, or can we, within our various communities and as a society, construct a better and less passive response?

Jarry, Alfred & Lykiard, Alexis, trans. (1989). *Days and Nights: Novel of a Deserter.* **London: Atlas Press.**
    Original Publication 1897.

Really, simply read my treatment of *Days & Nights* in the body of this book, there's no point in reiterating it all here…

Jarry, Alfred & White, Iain, trans. (1993). *Visits of Love.* **London: Atlas Press.**
    Original Publication 1898.

This was lent me by Nathan Shaffer; of the Jarry I've read, this has been the least revolutionary to how I live my life, its interest—aside from the Berthe Courrière letter reproduced in this book—remains essentially literary. Nonetheless, it is interesting to watch Jarry approach a book written on contract explicitly for an 'erotic' publisher, and to wonder how he got away with it; it is worth noting that while the opening chapter of his historical novel *Messalina* begins with the heroine going to a brothel and being graphically and almost violently fucked by three men in ten minutes and half as many pages, his book written for a pornographic publisher in fact portrays no sex at all.

Jarry, Alfred & Taylor, Simon Watson. (1996). *Exploits and Opinions of Dr. Faustroll, Pataphysician: A Neo-Scientific Novel.* **Boston: Exact Change.**
    Original Publication 1911.

I lived for a year or more off the copy of the Dartington College of Arts library, and now am using Warren Fry's; it is quite strange that I do not yet own my own copy, but then it is for some reason very hard to find, none available on Amazon or ebay…. What can one say about this book? I have trouble reading it; while not, *on the surface*, as complex and impregnable as some of Jarry's other work—and Jarry the stylist is never, in anything else I have read, the slightest bit *nervous*, he is always in control, he has arranged everything just the way he wants you to encounter it—*Faustroll* seems to exude a nervous, intense, but unlocalizable agitation, so that I can scarcely handle more than a few pages at a time before my nerves begin to physically cry out at me. Why is this? *Why* is this? I am neither the first nor the last to ask this question.

Jarry, Alfred, Brotchie, Alastair, ed, Edwards, Paul, ed./trans., Melville, Antony, trans. (2001). *Adventures in 'Pataphysics: Collected Works I: Black Minutes, Caesar-Antichrist, Essays, Speculations.* **London: Atlas Press.**

One can only speak about Jarry in pieces, he refuses to *cohere* (this is his brilliance—to be able to write in any mode is to be able to *live* in any mode, if one is really writing). The *Black Minutes of Memorial Sand* is an utterly and beautifully incomprehensible text, probably, along with *Caesar Antichrist*, Jarry's most verbally dense, permeated with Lautréamont. If *Days & Nights* presents a world transfigured *by* textuality and *Faustroll* a world transformed *into* text, then *Black Minutes* and *Antichrist* represent the world *of* textuality itself, and suggest the depth and richness of the linguistic function underlying Jarry's later life and work. When I bought this—the first book I bought when I arrived in the United Kingdom—I had read only Jarry's *Ubu Roi*, and was utterly blown away to find that he was also capable of such dense beauty. Writing for Jarry is not a matter of style but a way of modulating the very coordinates of his thought and self-conception, as this collection hammers home; and his meticulous stylistic perfection is not an 'Artistic' exercise but a finely-honed tool for crafting himself.

Jenkins, Janet, ed. (1993). *In the Spirit of Fluxus.* **Minneapolis: Walker Art Center.**

I borrowed this book from Warren Fry, and have not been able to read all of the essays included yet. Simon Anderson's essay concerning Fluxus publication is interesting and fully competent, which is rare enough. The first essay in the book is by one of the two curators of the museum exhibition for which this it is a companion (and whose name is listed on the book's spine while its actual *editor's* is not, and is hidden halfway down the publishing information on the inside), and is entitled 'Fluxus and the Museum'. The extent to which the commercial art *market* (which the museums, despite their social charter to do *just the opposite*, have essentially become part of, setting prices and determining the 'status' that is in fact what is being marketed, with creative lives as collateral) has come to see the *Institution* as such as *synonymous with* creative activity is evident in that the essay by and large does not deal with Fluxus' ambivalent relationship with the Museum system and its role in canonization—a worthwhile study though that would be—but instead merely *oohs* and *aahs* over 'intermedia', the fact that Fluxus continued to work in an a-disciplinary mode that had been constantly in place in many creative communities for many, many generations. The fact that they worked primarily outside mainstream systems is presented as some kind of anomaly without substantial historical precedent, and bemoans the fact that because they worked outside the art market and created an operative community on their own terms, 'they did not engage a wide audience or, what is perhaps more significant, a critical voice or champion.' Certainly they *did* fail to reach a 'wide audience,' and while this *is* a failure, would an isolated non-community of self-declared elites with a great deal of money and no cultural capital *count* as a 'wide audience'? And Fluxus *did* of course have *many* critical champions—for instance George Maciunas, George Brecht, Henry Flynt, etc.—those who engaged critically with Fluxus cared enough about it, and were *genuine* enough in their engagement, not to sell it off to collectors. This introductory essay finishes with the rhetorical question of whether, through museum retrospectives such as that curated by the author of this essay, Fluxus is in danger of recouperation; though of course this word is not used, since the notion is presented as if it is strange, new, and slightly amusing. Of course, no answer is give to this question, the curator does not genuinely interrogate her own role, saying only that, 'Hopefully this book and exhibition will offer insight into Fluxus without limiting it, and will open up new areas of study rather than putting them to rest.' Obviously the point has been utterly and *willfully* missed here: as soon as its activity has been subjected to the kind of inanely recouperative structures such as that of Huyssen elsewhere in the book, speaking about Fluxus as 'that crucial fluid space between modernism and postmodernism', i.e. as a contingent secondary *bridge* between two meaningless *terms* in the ongoing march of the dominant discourse, all the 'new areas of study' in the world will serve only to dig the hole deeper.

Klinger, Max, and Varnedoe, J. Kirk T., ed & Streicher, Elizabeth, ed. (1977). *Graphic Works of Max Klinger.* **New York: Dover Publications.**

Klinger is an important and under-recognised influence on Dada and Surrealist thought and work. A great many of his prints perfectly embody the Surrealist notion of the uncanny, and his sensibility—both visual and (anti-)narrative, permeates Ernst's collage work; indeed, some of Klinger's later intaglio prints feel more like collage than Ernst's work from *Une Semaine de Bonté*. Breton's *Nadja* contains a graphic reference to Klinger's seminal series 'a glove', which (like much of his work) virtually reads as Surrealist not in some vague 'strange' sense but almost as a doctrinaire illustration of the Surrealist conception of the Object, in all its phenomenological and philosophical implications. Moreover, Klinger was one of the visual artists most committed to explicitly engaging in the changes in canonization taking place within and through the Yellow Sign, one literary aspect of which I have traced in this book. Klinger engaged in canon-making by rendering it inseparable from his own creative output, importing the social, ideological, and political realms into it: in his own 'field' through reworking themes such as Böcklin's *Isle of the Dead* (not included in the Dover book but there is a print in the collection of the Chicago Art Institute) and Fuseli's *The Nightmare* (in Klinger's *The Dead*

Child), and making them into traditional talismans touched upon by each generation as a token of this continuing project. At the same time, he refused to allow this traditional engagement to be restricted to the visual arts, engaging especially with music—his own methodology was largely derived from Schumann's—producing for instance a series of prints based upon Brahms' *Fantasies*, which in turn involved a number of poets such as Almers and Hölderlin, and one specifically inspired by Flaubert, the Goncourts, and Zola.

Kristeva, Julia & Waller, Margaret, trans. (1984). *Revolution in Poetic Language.* **New York: Columbia University Press.**
    Original Publication 1974.

This edition is the only one available in English, but it does the trick. Nonetheless, it is something of a travesty. It is a translation of only 1/3 of Kristeva's text, the 'theory' underpinning the radical, literally Self-destroying *praxis* of textual subjectivity that the rest of the book—omitted here—examines as *practice*. In other words, this edition reduces Kristeva's praxis to theoretical exposition by killing over half the book. The excised portion reportedly identifies how the notions and ways of existing built up in the part that *has* been published are played out in *practice* in the writing of Mallarmé and Lautréamont. The translator's excuse is essentially that translating the entire book would be too hard, and a lot of people wouldn't have the patience to read it anyway. This person should not be a translator, this is disgraceful. If it's 'too hard', go fucking translate something you're actually up to, and have someone good actually do the job. If it requires three translator's notes per line to explain the intricacies, so be it. And anybody who actually makes it through the first third of the text is obviously *engaged*, is not a casual reader who will say, 'oh, now I have to read *poems?*' Moreover, the book is poorly designed, the typeface clunky and inelegant, left justified only, practically no margins, it feels slapped together—irresponsible in light of Kristeva's arguments. But there's no other way; so if you don't read French, buy it. This is one of those books that you have to fully *read*, or else throw up your hands. Kristeva deploys so many discourses, uses them with such fluidity, that it is nearly impossible to be on your feet all the time; and in the process one finds that everything can be approached productively through anything else; the principles of the constitution of matter inhere in the shortcomings of the materialist dialectic, the vagaries of grammar are intricately related to the energy discharges of our musculature. Kristeva revolutionized my approach to the *subject* and forced me to approach it with a rigour, and to conceive of it in a broader field of relations, than I had even thought to before. I started this book four times; I would not get back to it for a week, and would re-read the last chapter and find it utterly incomprehensible. The very tangible things under discussion, without losing their tangible *relevance,* are reduced through their very analysis, the fine nuances that constitute their action, into systems of abstractions whose implications are so exciting, and whose nature is so *unthinkable*, that one is constantly operating within, and developing, a systemicity of thought that can only be held *in suspension* until its significance sinks into the operational principles of the mind itself; to try to *understand*, per se, to treat the thought as a 'fact' or an 'idea' that can be kept in the brain's pocket, would be to touch it and watch it crumble away. Reading this book taught me think beyond the *possibility* of thought, to think the body.

Lacambre, Geneviève. (1999). *Gustave Moreau: Between Epic and Dream.* **Chicago: Art Institute of Chicago.**

Huysmans' criticism on Moreau in *A rebours* is the best I have seen. This book's plates are as good as you are likely to find, but Moreau cannot be reproduced. I'd never paid a great deal of attention to him until I saw his *Hercules and the Hydra* at the Chicago Museum of Art; I stayed staring at it for over an hour. I stopped painting several months later; the sensitivity and love of *paint* that permeates the piece was something I realised I did not share and had no right to continue to ape. His work seems nearly classical at first glance, but one examines it and discovers that in fact everything is wrong, perspectives are reversed, forms are in disintegration, eroded under the weight of their own caustic articulation; a half-dozen painterly discourses are colliding with each other, seeming to form a synthesis but in fact undermining each other viciously, a surface laying out on the slab of canvas the corpse of a mass of visual and symbolic languages in the midst of their own collapse.

Lacan, Jacques, Sheridan, Alan, trans. and Miller, Jacques-Alain. (1981). *The Seminar of Jacques Lacan: Book XI: The Four Fundamental Concepts of Psychoanalysis*. London: W.W. Norton & Company.

This book was misplaced during my move back to the U.S., and is presumable in a box someplace in Toledo, Ohio, along with Ball's *Flight Out of Time* and Reed's *City Poems*, and no doubt some other things as well. I attempted to begin it, with no background in Psychoanalytic discourse, shortly before going to the UK; it did not work. If I find the book I shall try again, though perhaps I should just buy *Ecrits*. Fink's *Clinical Introduction to Lacanian Analysis* is quite helpful.

Lane, Christopher. (1998). *A Short Biography of the Baroness Else von Freytag-Loringhoven, Including Some of Her Writings*. Retrieved 14th April 2007 from the World Wide Web: http://home1.gte.net/zzyzlane/write/essay/baroness.html

The fact that the work of the Baroness Else von Freytag-Loringhoven's work is so difficult to find *even* for those who look is a historiographic *disgrace*, and I defy anyone to argue that it is not the result of a latent sexism on the part of her Dada comrades—much as they might have attempted to escape it—*and* of every generation of historians of the Avant-Garde up to and including the present time. The innovator of the readymade, she has been shoved aside in order to convince generations of Post-Modern dupes that that this was the 'invention' of Duchamp, who, by placing them in a gallery, legitimated the readymade as an 'art object' that could be imported into the consumerist-institutional market/discourse, while Loringhoven treated it as a talisman, a fetish, a part of *life*. A developer of calligraphic poetry and its integration into mail art, scarcely any of her poems have been reproduced in their graphic form; one of the leading poets of American Dada, along with Picabia, there is *no* collection of her verse available today—not even her verse in English, which would not so much as require translation. We should all be ashamed. This is the best repository of her work I have found online; the biography by Lane has been mostly superceded by the publication (thankfully!) of Irene Gammel's exhaustive biography.

Lash, W.Q. (1947). *Christian Prayer and Approach to Christian Mysticism*. Bombay: Hind Kitabs Ltd.

It was late in the writing of this book that I discovered the depth of the *technical* influence of monastic and mystic practices on those speculated upon within it. I was in a used bookshop attempting (unsuccessfully) to find a reputable edition of Loyola (see my entry on that book), and came upon this little book, which was priced at $4. It is a little brown saddle-stitched tract, and its picturesque nature combined with its origin in India the year that that country gained its independence, made it inevitable that I would buy it. I flipped through and it quickly became apparent that I was on to something. Obviously, I now need to find more than a 40 page book…

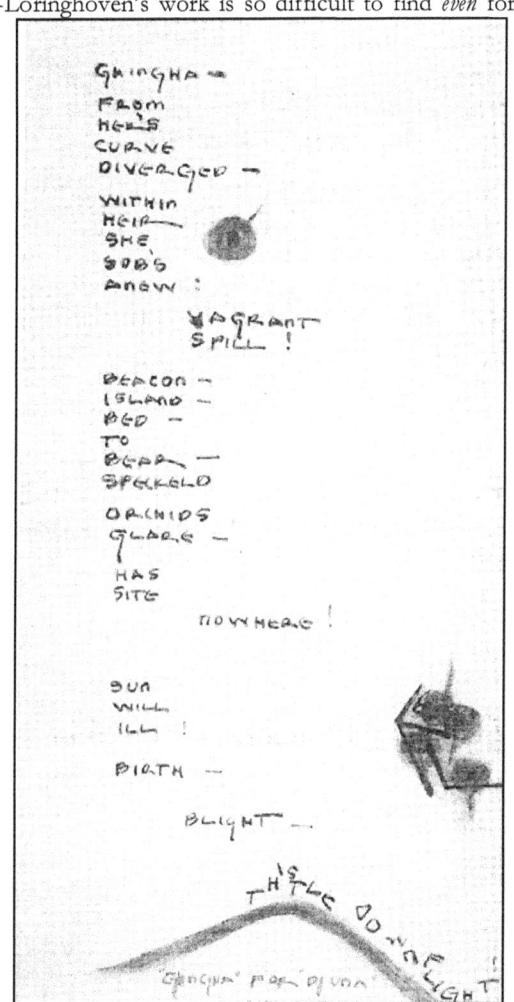

the Baroness Else von Freytag-Loringhoven, *Ghingha* (1924).

(Gammel 2002, p 343.)

Lautréamont & Lykiard, Alexis, trans. (1998). *Maldoror & the Complete Works.* **Cambridge: Exact Change.**
Original Publication 1869.

Maldoror is incomparable. I had heard it crop up from time to time in a number of contexts; Breton spoke of Lautréamont of course, as did Ball; Tzara read passages from *Maldoror* at the Cabaret Voltaire; finally I bought it. For the past three years, I have carried a copy with me everywhere I go, unless it will be in danger of being lost (as *I* always am, now); it is a reminder of my inevitable inadequacy. I never finish with it, I simply read it in continuous rotation, if I finish it one day I will begin it again within the week. My first copy, which I shall never give away, is so tattered and thoroughly marked-up that it has been retired, and sits now on my shelf. That copy was the Penguin edition, and it was enough to grasp me; the Lykiard translation is *far* better, and is annotated. I cannot speak about the text itself. I have written through it in *The Yellow Sign,* several sections of which are included in this book.

Lewis, Matthew. (1809). *Romantic Tales.* **New York: M. & W. Ward.**
Original Publication 1808.

One indication of the importance I attach to the high Gothic form is the fact that I bought this nearly 200-year old book, around A.Da. 86 (2002 if you choose to count from the birth of Christ), in order to read more from the author of *The Monk,* none of whose other works have been reprinted since their original publication. This is the first American edition, published the year before Poe's birth; though the front cover is no longer attached to the spine, the book is in otherwise good condition, with that dusty yellowed tan binding so instantly recognizable as belonging to the first quarter of the 19th Century. Interestingly, the stories here do not have the darkness of that novel, but do include, to a somewhat lesser extent, the same system of nesting narratives. A good amount of Lewis' shorter work is reminiscent of Voltaire's *Zadig,* which I read around the same time.

Lewis, Matthew. (1998). *The Monk: A Romance.* **London: Penguin Books.**
Original Publication 1796.

The Monk was, so to speak, the first *full-on* Gothic that I read. That is to say that while I have a very long history with *Frankenstein,* the latter is Gothic more in theme than in structure; it is, ultimately, comprehensible. *The Monk* is *proper* Gothic, sub-plots within sub-plots within *side*-plots to the main plot which is in the book being read by characters in the outermost plot…the kind of book where three chapters on a character interjects and suddenly you, the reader, become utterly disoriented, you'd forgotten this was a story being *told,* and wait, who is this speaker again? And you flip back to find out, but the characters are all basically indistinguishable anyway, and what's going on? Where are we? Who is this? Yes, *that's* what I call a story. It is similar to Derrida's grammar—a sentence runs on for a page, with countless parenthetical asides, *each* containing arguments one could build an entire book around, with conditional clauses whose object you have forgotten, you are retracing your steps… the Gothic, like Derrida, and like Lovecraft, and like Mallarmé, is the experience of losing one's way.

Lindsann, Olchar E. *The Yellow Sign.* **Unpublished manuscript.**

The book you are holding at the present time is merely a threshold, for me as much as anyone.

LIP, Department of Dogma and Theory; w/Brotchie, Alastair; Chapman, Stanley; Foulc, Thieri; & Jackson, Kevin, ed. (2003 Vulgar.) *'Pataphysics: Definitions & Citations*. London: London Institute of 'Pataphysics.

A very nice small book, lent to me by 'Pataphysician Nathan Shaffer. A series of (alphabetized) quotes, it is not structurally unlike much of the present book; and interestingly, a text that I started some time ago, and which is continually expanding, called *What is Pataphysics*, was a prototype for the poetics of juxtaposition here. This latter should have been published a year ago in the *Collected Reports of the Post-NeoAbsurdist Institute for Anti-Rational Affairs*, which has been plagued with problems ever since and has yet to be released. The latter, however, is composed mostly of quotes not referring directly to Pataphysics, whilst the Atlas edition is composed of those that do.

Lottman, Herbert R. (2001). *Man Ray's Montparnasse*. New York: Harry N. Abrams Inc.

My comments regarding Franck's *Bohemian Paris* can apply equally well here; a wealth of myth, but in a context which situates Avant-Garde activity as a *part* of Bohemia, rather than situating Bohemia as a deployment *of* the Avant-Garde (which in turn serves to illustrate the way in which the Bohemian project has ultimately failed).

Lovecraft, H.P. (1982). *The Best of H.P. Lovecraft: Bloodcurdling Tales of Horror and the Macabre*. New York: Del Rey.

This is the first volume of Lovecraft I ever owned. I couldn't say how many times I have read Lovecraft; I own only a relatively small part of his body of work, but every year or two since, I suppose, the early 'nineties, I find myself going back to it; I think, 'man, Lovecraft is fun, I haven't read Lovecraft in awhile—' and soon I am compulsively going over every story I own yet again. Why? I have begun to address this question to myself forcibly since my last re-reading, spurred on by a number of excited conversations about Lovecraft with Kathy Karpilov and Nick Hallam—the kinds of conversations, ranging from the stories themselves to the mythos to the time of one's life when they were first encountered, and all the life since where they have remained a presence—the kinds of conversation one can only have with other people who have been initiated into him; and those who haven't read him, and those who can't 'get' him, can only shake their heads. The three of us attended and performed at a Lovecraft Festival in Exeter, and I got a clue; there were people in this room who could probably find nothing else in common but this unrefined *germ* of deviance, of the recognition of its *value*—people who had moved from Lovecraft on to Derrida, people who had not read a book *except* Lovecraft for a decade, people who live their whole lives as a constant revolt against capitalism and conformity, people who eat McDonalds each day and just love horror movies, people who have turned their experience of Lovecraft into a love of music, of literature, of occultism, of gaming, of film, or even of nothing in particular *except* Lovecraft. How many things could bring all of these people together, inspire the feeling that they all held in common a kind of *open secret*, that a fan of Lovecraft is a friend of mine, and could create the atmosphere of a kind of extended family among all these disparate people? Many things could, of course; but the Avant-Garde, to its detriment, is not one of them.

Lovecraft, H.P. (1986.) *H.P. Lovecraft Omnibus 3: The Haunter of the Dark*. London: Grafton Books.

This book was given to me, upon my leaving England, by Nick Hallam. It was his first volume of Lovecraft, and I value the gift very highly, because for those who *read* Lovecraft, you do not forget your first copy; there is some kind of strange recognition that strikes you for the first time, and you will do *something* with that recognition that there is some thing very *wrong* with *what is*, and that whatever this wrong thing is, it is something you must claim as your own and empower. This is of course what happens to Lovecraft's characters as they read that fateful text, stumble upon that fateful bit of arcane knowledge that will lead them inevitably to the brink of madness; and it is, in a more subtle way, what happens when the right person *reads* Lovecraft, and goes on to pursue that rift in the 'real' that he has unveiled. You see this rift open and close for a moment in

Lovecraft's text, and you find a way, *some* way to force that rift again in life, wherever you have the opportunity—whether you do so through writing complex arguments to reveal the world as always already on the verge of collapse, or you do so through facing off against an audience each night with a guitar, spitting on them, fomenting a situation where hatred and adoration fall into each other and the negation of everything becomes an addictive revelation (this could equally be a description of a proper Punk show or a Dada cabaret). Hallam and I played a Noise set based on the syllables of Cthulic rights at a Lovecraft Festival in the basement of an Anarchist bookstore on All Hallows Eve—can you imagine anything more perfect, because *wrong?*

Lovecraft, H.P. and Joshi, S.T., ed. (2001). *The Thing on the Doorstep and Other Weird Stories.* **London: Penguin Books.**

If I were to recommend one of these three volumes of Lovecraft to buy, I would recommend this one, which is copiously annotated and nicely designed, with a cover by Doré. Buying Lovecraft is a bit chancy because there are dozens of different collections out by several different publishers, with the result that you inevitably end up with a good deal of overlap; each of my three volumes has perhaps one or two stories not in the others; it is best to start with one series by a publisher and stick with it. Anything edited by Joshi is likely to the best bet.

Loyola, Ignatius, and Anonymous. (1999). *The Spiritual Exercises of St. Ignatius* **(sic.) Rockford, IL: Tan Books.**

The reason that Loyola has not played a greater role in this book is due to my buying this edition, which it turned out is an adulterated translation by some unnamed second hand, who has put into Loyola's mouth discussions of Napoleon, etc. Since I don't generally deal with theological writing, publishers, or scholarship, I don't know whether this is typical of the field or an anomaly, and that being the case I could not afford, on my very small budget, to buy another copy at the risk of it too being a mere summary of what the text 'says' (sic) rather than a translation *of the* text. Bookstores do not seem to have it in stock anywhere, and I refuse to go through the doors of an 'Inspirational Store'. So here I am…

Lucan, Medlar & Gray, Durian, and Martin, Alex, ed. and Fletcher, Jerome, ed. (2000). *The Decadent Traveler.* **Sawtry, U.K: Dedalus.**

One of a series of Decadent handbooks—also anthologies—assembled by the elusive Lucan and Gray. Though not quoted directly in this book, Lucan and Gray have been invaluable in my getting a grasp on Decadence and situating myself in relation to it. In view of that aspect of Decadence I have focused upon in this work, the activation of cultural *reading* through the appropriation and interpretive détournement of cultural artifacts, Lucan and Gray have identified the perfect Decadent form in the Anthology; and the ways in which those anthologies play out—while always evolving from one to the next—reinforce this strength. They have also reaffirmed the continuation of the Decadent community and discourse since the point of its 'literary' zenith in the 1880s, as indeed has the press with which they are associated, Dedalus, which through its roster continues providing a space for both continued production and re-interpretation of existing writings and themes. While I have, naturally, never met either of the secretive authors in person, their editor Jerome Fletcher has been invaluable in the preparation of the present book.

Lucie-Smith, Edward. (1972). *Symbolist Art.* **London: Thames & Hudson.**

Decent enough as a primer of Symbolist visual art, though thoroughly pedantic and unimaginative; I wouldn't bother with more than a scan of the text, but it deals with a fair number of artists. It attempts to deal with the literature as well, which is in theory somewhat to its credit, but in this area it is not only pedantic and unimaginative, but also in well over its head. It's about what one expects from Thames & Hudson when they're not republishing texts produced without then remotely in mind (i.e., Richter's *Art and Anti-Art*)—when one tends to think of a particular book primarily in relation to the series by a major publisher of which it is a part, rather than to its author, one does not expect great things.

Mallarmé, Stéphane & Lloyd, Rosemary, ed. (1988). *Selected Letters.* **Chicago: University of Chicago Press.**

The Myth of Mallarmé as a recluse is an odd one, because of course he served—I would argue, quite deliberately—as the catalyst and hub of a community. His conversation is of course legendary, and many of those around him implied that the most vital application of his thought was articulated through his social relationships and personal discussion, both individually and in groups. Friends remembered that often they were unable to actually 'understand' what he was saying, but that through listening, absorbing, and entering into the conversation anyway, they came to develop new modes of thinking; this is of course the sense of *reading* that I most value, and is also a description of the functioning of the Symbolist poem, when it *works*. Mallarmé's letters do not approach this part of his practice, which we can never recover, but rather makes its withdrawal more pronounced, more painful. The letters themselves refer constantly to their own inadequacy, and in reading them that necessity of speculation, of reading *into* as a surrogate for reading *behind*, is extended. They imply, but do not delineate, the extent to which the *practice* of his writing was a practice of life, and indicate as well the multiplicity of its effects. His early letters, dating from the period of and after his crisis with the Void, are harrowing and—in a very different idiom—the only account of such an experience I have read that is (remotely) comparable to Artaud's. In the later letters, one can trace—though again, one is tracing on air—his engagement with the community he was gathering up and making aware of *itself*, the keen *practical* application to this practice of *writing* social structures—a practice which must be collective, collaborative, but which often demands a person to *empty themselves*, as Mallarmé had already learned to do, in order to transform a part of themselves into a *hole* through which the energy of a community can multiply itself as it passes.

Mallarmé, Stéphane & Weinfield, Henry, trans. (1996). *Collected Poems.* **Berkeley, University of California Press.**

It took me some time to be able to engage with Mallarmé; I came to him via Derrida, who might well be considered his inheritor. Mallarmé, through this engagement with syntax—which is to say the structuration of thought—shows how a system can be inhabited by its own negativity, utilized as a tool in its own overturning. His poems are emphatically and explicitly machines for multiplying thought; they are not objects to be consumed, they are objects into which the subject hurls itself and begins to come apart. I have discussed Mallarmé enough in this book to be able to leave it at that. This is an excellent volume, the translations are excellent and Weinfield provides detailed translation notes and very engaged, if sometimes rather reductive, notes on each poem. This is the edition to find.

Marcus, Greil. (1990). *Lipstick Traces: A Secret History of the Twentieth Century.* **London: Secker & Warburg.**

Marcus brings together fractured narratives of Dada, Punk Rock, Situationist tendencies, Medieval heresies, and the Lettrist International in a laudable attempt to break the Avant-Garde tradition out of its isolation from vernacular culture and within 'Art', and is written primarily with an eye for those not terribly familiar with the Avant-Garde trajectory. This is in fact the book where I first learned of Lettrism and the SI. There is a part of me that is put off by certain aspects of the book, such as its traditional reliance upon the rather shaky connections between the SI and the Sex Pistols, which tends to do a mythic disservice both to the 60s/70s Avant-Garde and to Punk, both of which are far broader and sometimes more radical than the two groups chosen to epitomize them. On the other hand, I am not one to criticize the kind of mythology that Marcus is engaged in, which at least *is,* I believe, being read outside 'artistic' circles and thus hopefully preparing openings of potential dialogue and closer co-operation and understanding among various manifestations of cultural disgust; it has been a long time since I read it and my understanding and engagement has evolved hugely since then, so I can't speak to how effective or responsible the employment of that myth is.

Maturin, Charles. (1989). *Melmoth the Wanderer.* **Oxford: Oxford University Press. Original Publication 1820.**

A splendid book; in some senses *Melmoth* is situated midway between *The Monk* and *Frankenstein*. I could not possibly give even the vaguest synopsis of Lewis' book, where some of the nested narratives carry as much weight and force as the ostensibly 'main' narrative, and bear a less explicit relationship to it than here; while in Shelley's book one can easily give a blow-by-blow of a single plot. Maturin employs the topographical narrative of the high Gothic, but a sense of continuity and identity is not so irremediably beyond recovery, the nested narratives are more easily situated within the arc of the story, and Melmoth emerges as a recognizable *character* who bears a number of parallels with the emerging Byronic type, and who would serve as models for Maldoror and others in literature, and for Borel, Baudelaire, and others in life and the construction of their myths.

McDonough, Tom, ed. (2004). *Guy Debord and the Situationist International: Texts and Documents.* **Cambridge, MIT Press.**

This is not the time or place for a full-fledged critique of the Situationist International; on the one hand they provide an inescapable and essential model for any dissenting stance emerging from artistic or 'theoretical' discourse, and have a growing influence on the thought and practices of myself and many of my closest collaborators. On the other hand, Stewart Home is quite obviously right in his assertion that they are being elevated to an inflated canonical status within marginal communities (and even some institutional discourse—this book is after all published by *October*) that prevents them from being rigorously *critiqued*. Therefore I will simply say that in relation to the book you reading, the Situationists, as most Avant-Garde groups from the Futurists forward had done (with the partial exceptions of Surrealism and Neoism), publicly denied their debt to the tradition from which they stemmed, while continuing that tradition in such radicalized forms as to render them nearly undetectable (for instance the derive as a development from Surrealism's Objective Chance, which derived in turn from the 19th Century Flaneur, which derived in turn from Poe's *The Man of the Crowd*; the Bohemian behaviour in the Paris group, a continuation of Lettrist social modes, which were ultimately forms of behaviour devised by the early 19th Century Bouzingos and La Bohême Doyenné; or détournement, an elaboration of certain Surrealist Games and the plagiarisms of Ducasse—one debt that *was* openly recognised by Debord). While historical precedents are obviously not *inherently* necessary for the *immediate* efficacy of such strategies—much less is my argument a matter of bourgeois 'giving credit'—such an approach, whatever its intention, is bound to reinforce the positivist notion of The Heroic Innovators, and in the process contributes to the positioning of those strategies among practitioners as finished 'tools' which either 'work' or 'don't work', and must therefore be either stuck *to* stubbornly and dumbly or *discarded*, rather than constantly developed and modulated. In view of these *particular* arguments then, the historiographic aspect of this project might be seen in part as an attempt to depart radically from this a-historical approach to present a conception of subversive activity as ongoing, never finished, and necessarily self-reflexive concerning its own strategies and tactics, successes and failures across generations—without, it is hoped, presenting a finished 'history' which allows itself to be taken as a picture of 'what happened' and thus to be recuperated and re-deployed as a weapon of apathy. This particular collection of Situationist texts has the advantage of containing a number of 'Editorial Notes' from various Situationist journals that focus on immediate issues and tactical-level points of discussion (though not, unfortunately, 'tactics' per se, most remain essentially rants) rather than more abstract macro-critiques such as *Society of the Spectacle*. As the title would suggest, the collection focuses almost entirely on Debord and what Home labels the 'specto-Situationists', aside from a bit from Constant.

McGann, Jerome J., ed. (1994). *Romantic Period Verse.* **Oxford: Oxford University Press.**

After immersing myself in British Romanticism through Perkins' Anthology, I had an inkling, through engaging with 'minor poets' included there such as John Clare, Hunt, Landor, etc., that the standard pantheon of Shelley, Byron, Keats, Coleridge, and Wordsworth was merely a small part of a much larger discourse, and this collection gives the best indication I have found of the larger literary climate from which Romanticism emerged, representing not only Romanticism itself (and a few smaller marginal currents) but the institutional poetry which they were up against. The anthology is presented by year as well, giving an idea of the development and conversations being played out as the movement began, recognised itself, and then reinvented itself after the apostasy of its originators, and recontextualizes even the most enthusiastically canonized deployments according to the (relative) situation at the time of their publication. If my reading of Perkins initiated me into a real *engagement* with poetry itself, this book first made me acutely aware of the politics of canonization, and by extension of the act of writing not merely as an 'artistic' gesture but as a *social activity*.

Mension, Jean-Michel & Nicholson-Smith, Donald, trans. (2001). *The Tribe.* **San Francisco: City Lights.**

This is the *only* book in English I have been able to find dealing specifically with Lettrism, an interview with ex-Lettrist Mension. I am roughly half-way through. It is interesting in establishing in great detail the context from which Lettrism and the Situationist International emerged (and, at the same time, in seeing how the models established by La Bohême Doyenné and the Bouzingos had evolved in the intervening 120 years), the extreme fluidity that was at play between petty crime and the Avant-Garde, youth delinquency and political agitation, alcoholism and intellectual engagement. On one hand this represents the extent to which politically-engaged intellectual activity had become genuinely open to *some* of society's most disenfranchised components (though it should be noted that while, for instance, Mension was a 16-year-old alcoholic begging for change or stealing from cars for ether-money, this was still essentially a bourgeois luxury, slumming—he went home each day to sleep in his Communist parents' house while they were at work). On the other hand, the growing inaptness of the Bohemian model to a society that has come to cheerfully and dismissively accept the caricature of the 'Bohemian artist' is also revealed, in the way that the romanticism of the Bohemian lifestyle overshadows the issues of its social role or efficacy even in the interviewer's questions and Mension's answers; how much they drank, and at which bar, and what they drank, and when they moved from one bar to another, is apparently deemed much more important and interesting than why they lived their lives in the way they did.

Motherwell, Robert, ed. (1981.) *The Dada Painters and Poets: An Anthology.* **2nd Ed. Cambridge: Belknap Press of Harvard University Press.**
    Original Publication 1951.

One of the essential resources for primary texts on Dada in English, my first introduction to Dada writing aside from the examples in Richter, and Tzara's *Approximate Man*. An important historiographic exercise in its own right, this massive compendium is decidedly Francophile in its emphasis, but is actually considerably less so than the few earlier treatments of the movement. I bought this book around the time that *The Appropriated Press* was founded.

Nadeau, Maurice and Howard, Richard, trans. (1973). *The History of Surrealism.* **Middlesex: Penguin Books.**
    Original Publication 1964.

Nadeau wrote this book during the Nazi occupation, and the primary thematic thread around which Nadeau organises his narrative is the political and extra-artistic aspect of the group, in particular their ambivalent relationship with organised Communism and the their progressive movement from a more radical social stance drawing from Dada into a more purely 'artistic' trend, to the point where they even championed Dali and allowed themselves to be recouperated as a 'weird' joke (though Nadeau's history ends with the War, as Surrealism itself ought to have done, finding itself where it was). Interestingly, Nadeau shows how Pope Breton was in fact instrumental in the move from the Surrealist project of 'research' and new modes of collective living that were their focus for the first few, vital years of the movement into the more traditionally 'artistic' direction that they eventually settled into.

Nerval, Gérard de & Wagner, Geoffrey, trans. (1970). *Selected Writings.* **Ann Arbor: University of Michigan Press.**

My concentration so far has been on Nerval's mythic activity and on his role within various group dynamics; I've only begun to become familiar with his published work. Nerval's hallucinations are legendary and are sure to have exerted a great influence on later initiates who consciously evoked hallucinations; I have not addressed them here because his hallucinations were for the most part not self-induced or conscious; that is to say they were hallucinations proper, and were not a part of any 'practice'. At the same time, they were heavily inflected by (and quite possibly partly due to) the modes of thinking that he *had* cultivated through his mythic activity, which he pursued so rigorously and which operated with such fluidity between the 'literary', social, and psychological registers. Had I all the time and room in the world, he would be interesting to look at in this connection.

Perkins, David, ed. (1967.) *English Romantic Writers.* **New York: Harcourt Brace Jovanovich.**

I was once a painter, who also wrote poems. This is to say that I was unconcerned with language as such, and 'writing' (if it could really be called such) was essentially a hobby. Then, at roughly the same time (I was I think 20?) I began to study under the poet Edward Lense, and I bought this giant, nearly 2,000 page collection, printed in miniscule type on exceedingly thin paper, and resolved to read it from beginning to end. This convergence eventually led to the book in your hand (via a number of strange and circuitous maneuvres). It took me nearly two years to plough through the anthology—which in itself is nothing special, a fairly standard canon with predictable commentary—but by the end of it I had come first to approaching poetry as a craft, then as a discipline, and finally as a way of thinking. This sustained attention to a fairly coherent milieu, in retrospect, prevented me from falling into the fallacy of simply taking a poet here, a poet there, treating various currents or schools merely as 'styles'; virtually *living within* British Romanticism for several years, absorbing and internalizing the coordinates of its thought, involving myself intellectually and emotionally with its inner struggles and learning to think through its discourse, prepared me to approach creative activity as a socially, historically, and politically *situated* engagement in which, as they say, the devil's in the details; it is the sensibility that I have since applied to every historical creative endeavour I have encountered and been intrigued by, and more importantly have attempted to apply to my own modes of sociality and social positioning within the communities, groups, and collectives with which I have had the privilege to be involved.

Pierrot, Jean & Coltman, Derek, trans. (1981). *The Decadent Imagination 1880-1900.* **Chicago: University of Chicago Press.**

I found this book by chance in a huge used book shop in Chicago (I can't recall the name but a native would probably know it) while visiting my sister. It kept me engaged for about half its length, and was helpful in disentangling the Decadent from the Symbolist communities (there was a great deal of overlap between the two, both synchronic and diachronic, and Pierrot does endeavor successfully to establish Decadence as an autonomous phenomenon). It is, however, painfully academic and eventually one becomes burdened down by the formula: 'I propose that X____ is a characteristic of Decadence; to prove it, here are two dozen examples of people mentioning X____ in their work.' This is a splendid technique, but only if it yields interesting results.

Poe, Edgar Allan. (1975). *Complete Tales & Poems.* **New York: Vintage Books.**

I was probably about eight when I was given this volume of Poe, and it is still the one I use. I read through all 1,000 pages or so and revisited them repeatedly over a number of years, alongside the complete Sherlock Holmes, Mallory's *Le Morte d'Arthur*, Homer, and Tolkien. The stories that fascinated me initially were the crowd pleasers (there is not a hint of criticism when I say this): 'The Tell-Tale Heart', 'The Premature Burial', 'The Pit and the Pendulum'. I continued to pull it out occasionally over the years, but did not thoroughly re-read it until around 20, when I read through it alongside Perkins' huge volume of British Romanticism. Whereas I had not thought of Poe before outside the Horror tradition, in light of my current reading I came to look at him in relation to Romanticism and, through his separation from that tradition and his relationship both to it and to the American society *out of which* he wrote, to begin examining the role of Nationalism in creative endeavour, and the peculiar and burgeoning sickness that seems lodged at the very heart of American society. This was also the first time that I read *The Rationale of Verse* and the *Poetic Principle* with any degree of comprehension, and Poe's emphasis on self-awareness and precision, his rejection of transcendental notions of 'genius' and abstract 'inspiration' revolutionised my thinking in a way perhaps analogous to those essays' effects on Baudelaire and Mallarmé, whose reminiscences of their own first contacts with these texts I recognise perfectly. My second exhibition of paintings consisted entirely of treatments of Poe. And so, on that first *return* to Poe, I learned from him that writing was a philosophical engagement, and that it needed to be *well-done*. The pieces that fascinated me in addition to those essays were 'William Wilson', 'The Conqueror Worm,' 'The Masque of the Red Death', 'The Black Cat', 'Hop-frog', 'For Annie', 'Ligeia', 'Berenice'. A couple years later I returned again, discovered his criticism in other volumes, and *Eureka;* the *variety* of his output, and the potential of being able to inhabit so many modes, struck me; and I took another look at pieces such as 'Maelzel's Chess-Player', 'The Case of M. Valdemar', 'The Gold-Bug', 'The Colloquy of Monos and Una', 'The Imp of the Perverse', 'The Murders in the Rue Morgue', and *The Narrative of Arthur Gordon Pym*. I have just now begun yet another return, have discovered the full depth of social comprehension involved in 'The Man in the Crowd', the annihilation of 'Descent into the Maelström', must re-read 'The Purloined Letter' in the light of Lacan and Derrida, and everything else in the renewed light of Lovecraft, of Maturin, of Lewis; and am anxious to see what new readings and implications will emerge from this creator of texts that seem to endlessly renew themselves just when you think they have finally been fully assimilated and exhausted.

Poe, Edgar Allan & Foye, Raymond, ed. (1980). *The Unknown Poe: an Anthology of Fugitive Writings by Edgar Allan Poe, with Appreciations by Charles Baudelaire, Stéphane Mallarmé, Paul Valéry, J.K. Huysmans & André Breton.* **San Francisco: City Lights.**

Not a bad little book, including some letters (not a comprehensive selection); a number of poems unpublished or removed from standard editions of his work, many written when he was 14; several short essays from his *Marginalia;* some other short topical essays, including one on Shelley and, for some reason, the standard *Imp of the Perverse;* and selections from writings on Poe by Baudelaire, Valéry, Breton, Mallarmé, and Huysmans. Most of these latter are only partial, and the full texts readily available elsewhere (most of them are included in my own library, though they were not when I first bought this collection six years ago or so).

Poe, Edgar Allan. (1997). *Eureka: A Prose Poem.* **New York: Prometheus Books.**
    Original Publication 1848.

In this book, Poe begins with a statement insisting that what follows is emphatically a *poem;* then comes a quasi-comedic science-fiction satire attacking all contemporary wisdom concerning the prerogatives of logical thought; after which he launches into a novella-length speculative tract involving astrology, physics, philosophy, and very unconventional theology, and ends up proposing a version of the Big Bang theory 115 years before it became generally accepted within scientific discourse. Yet another example of why I keep coming back to Poe.

Poe, Edgar A. & Cassuto, Leonard, ed. (1999). *Literary Theory and Criticism.* **Mineola, NY: Dover Publications.**

It is worth remembering that, aside from the unexpected popularity of *The Raven,* which did not extend to the rest of his fiction or verse, Poe was known in his own country almost exclusively as a critic until his reputation was re-imported from the Continent after his influence had been so strongly felt in France. Aside from the readily available (but superb) *Rationale of Verse* and *Philosophy of Composition*, this book gives a sample of the character of that criticism, which was consistently vitriolic and provocative. The majority of the books reviewed here have probably not seen publication since the first half of the 19th Century, but there are criticisms of Dickens, Cooper, and Hawthorne. Even without knowledge of the books under discussion it can be a worthwhile read; it was largely through this criticism that Poe plays out his attacks upon commercial interference with creative discourse and upon artistic Nationalism, campaigns which underlie his whole critical project. This volume also deals with Poe's one-sided battle with Longfellow: after launching a public assault against him, the hoped-for response was not forthcoming, so Poe adopted a pseudonym, and wrote and published an essay refuting all of his own arguments; this was a pretext for him to answer, in turn, his own objections, and thereby broaden and deepen his own thesis. Brilliant. This book was essential to my conception of Poe, and through him of artistic activity in general, as *socially situated*, and as taking up a self-conscious—and critical—stance in relation to the way that this field of activity is organised and mediated through its relationships to economic structures.

Punch Annual, Vol. LXXIV. (1878). London: Punch.
Punch Annual, Vol. LXXV. (1879). London: Punch.

All in all, one of the few ways in which British society is inferior to its American counterpart is in the quality of its Thrift Stores (or Charity Shops). This is a serious issue in my line of 'work' (or rather, play); one mitigating factor however is that one is far more likely to find excellent *and* affordable old *books* in the UK, to whit: when Warren Fry and I visited in March, A.Da. 91 (that would be 2007 Anti-Vulgar), we found two volumes of *Punch* (1878 & 1879) selling for under 10 quid a piece. Beautiful. In direct relation to the book you are now reading, I was startled to come upon a number of satires of Aesthetic communities, which indicated a span and scope of Aesthetic practice in England I had been unaware of; here, years before Wilde even began writing, was evidence of an Aesthetic community that was not merely a small, obscure Avant-Garde circle centred on Walter Pater, but a social phenomenon broad enough to become the object of satire for a vernacular weekly, from which Wilde *came*. The most important implication is that, while the *lifestyle* obviously represented a mere fad for many practitioners and so remained *merely* a 'lifestyle' (at best) rather than anything approaching a real re-invention of self, the community was nonetheless not restricted to 'artists', and was able to integrate with broader social structures with at least a certain amount of success.

Rabelais, François & Cohen, J.M., trans. (1955). *Gargantua and Pantagruel.* **London: Penguin Classics.**
    Original Publication 1532-52

Once again, if only I had known sooner! I made a note to get around to Rabelais when I learned the esteem Jarry held him in, and when Sterne referred to him as 'my master' (along with Cervantes, who I need to revisit), I picked it up; I am still quite early on, but it is a kind of womb where I can see the beginnings of Jarry, D.B. Edwards, Lautréamont, Monty Python, Sterne, the Gothic…

Ray, Gene, ed. (2001). *Joseph Beuys: Mapping the Legacy.* **Sarasota: Ringling Museum of Art.**

I borrowed this book from Warren Fry, and have not read enough of it to comment upon it. Beuys of course has dealt with *lived myth* more thoroughly than nearly any *artist* since the Second World War, but never, to my knowledge, really integrated it into the continuing *development* of this tradition; he maintained an isolated stance that encouraged an a-social mythic isolation. His was not so much an engagement with mythic *literature* as the cultivation of *a* myth, which limits the potential of his practice as pointing toward new modes of sociality, though his engagement might well be applied *within* such a project. This is in keeping with his major fault, which he shares with Broodthaers, Duchamp, and a number of others; engaging a great many of the psychological, philosophical, and social implications of creative activity, he maintained throughout his life a blind-spot in relation to the ways in which the power-structures mediating discourse, and the relation of that discourse to economic concerns, curtailed the actual *functioning* of the full potential of his work, with the result that the 'legacy' of his work remains boxed up inside the Museum, several generations of 'Post-Modern' status-brokers cite him as an influence, and his activity remains merely 'Art'. As with Duchamp, I *want* very much to like Beuys, he was on to a great deal; but after crafting a myth of himself so carefully, thoroughly, and beautifully, he failed to take responsibility for the ways, the discourses, and the venues within which it was deployed, and not only squandered it but ended up a subtle advertisement for the 'professional' system. Beuys was never really engaged in any serious way with the project of the Avant-Garde, but he became very good at adopting their trappings, quite literally a sheep in wolf's clothing.

Redon, Odilon & Gibson, Michael. (1996). *Odilon Redon: The Prince of Dreams.* **Köln: Taschen.**

Henri Fuseli, *The Nightmare* (1781).   (Gibson 1999, p 23.)

The tradition I have traced in this book deals mainly with practitioners coming out of a literary tradition, partly due to the need to set limits *somewhere* to the realm of investigation, and largely because visual artists have tended, due to the nature of their medium which does not facilitate the *same* kind of fluidity between 'art' and reportage as writers, not to leave what might be picked up as evidence for such practices; this is especially true because most of the practices described here do not leave a significant visual trace that can announce itself as such in the way that it can in a narrative (incidentally, this also explains the lack of quotations, etc. by a great many visual and asemic poets, the very nature of whose work renders it deeply connected to the themes of this text but which, due to the specific nature *of* that involvement, does not leave relics that can be read according to the logics applied within this particular text). In practice however, visual and literary communities have always been shared within Avant-Garde currents, and so the practices described were most likely not unique to writers (Piranesi' and Fuseli's connections with hallucinatory practice have been noted). Redon (along with Moreau, Manet, Bonnard, and Rops) was central in the thought and canons of those engaged with these practices in the 19th Century, even in primarily 'literary' communities or discourses.

Reed, Alan. (2006). *Imagining Revolt*. Unpublished Thesis, Dartington College of Arts, Totnes, United Kingdom.

In comparing the book you are reading to Reed's (smaller!) text here, one can see a number of different points at which our thought both converges and diverges, often practically in the same movement. As is the case with several other books or documents included in this virtual library, such as those by Warren Fry, Imogene Engine, and David Beris Edwards, this *text* is largely a token of a much greater influence on the course of this paper and the system of thought—and the life—from which it has emerged, influence which has come through hundreds or thousands of hours of conversation, correspondence, shared explorations, actions, and experience. In this connection, Reed's most effective book is the one he has made himself into, and which he is constantly re-writing; so that the initiatory experience I have written about in connection to the books of Derrida, Kristeva, etc. is one that Reed's conversation encapsulates in a differently articulated, but equally decisive way. Without many, many hours spent over coffee, losing arguments and unsure what was even being argued, finding myself continually contested and probed on every nuance of my developing ideas, until finally the probing and questioning became mutual and the arguments became collaborative derives of thought in which the *form* of argument merely became the ambulatory mechanism by the means of which ideas and potentialities were traversed and transfigured, this book could never have been conceived. Were I to provide a dedication to the book you are now reading, Reed would, I suspect, immediately berate me for succumbing to a lyrical gesture that would undermine the larger social efficacy for which it strives, positioning it as a 'personal' gesture more appropriate to 'Art' than to the other registers on which it must operate. So, instead, I inscribe such a sentiment here, in the appendix, within a library, where it cannot, I think, do much harm and is perhaps *precisely* where it ought to be situated.

Richter, Hans & Britt, David, trans. (1997). *Dada: Art and Anti-Art*. London: Thames & Hudson. Original Publication 1964.

This is one of the most important books of my life, and I know for a fact that I am far from alone in this. Richter taught me that it is not only *possible* to achieve something beautiful, but very easy; you simply have to *actually want to*. It is the first book I recommend, lend, or give to a friend; Bradley Chriss keeps extra copies on hand for those who need to read it; Warren Fry and David Beris Edwards have both been deeply inspired by it. What I was officially 'taught' concerning Dada, and what I took for accurate for many years, was essentially that it *was* the cheeky use of the Readymade, and was basically synonymous with Marcel Duchamp. When I finally realised that there may have been something to it that I had missed, a particular image recurred to me, one that had been flipped past for not more than five seconds in a slideshow several years earlier, a man inside a large awkward cardboard costume, looking like a cross between the Tin Man, a stovepipe, and a lobster, with a very earnest, very direct, and at the same time very *lost* look on his face. It was most certainly *not* Marcel Duchamp. And I decided that there *must* be something else, and that I needed to track it down. Going to the bookstore, Chance—which that day vouchsafed to me its devious kind of (Anti-)trustworthiness—led me to Hans Richter. Richter was, in many ways, the most grounded of the core Dada group; among the least 'absurd', the least polemic, and most importantly in his later role as scribe of the movement, the least histrionic and least given to post-mortem internecine strife. He was also, and perhaps for these very reasons, perhaps the *nicest*. The result is that *Dada: Art and Anti-Art* is not, like Ball's history, one of otherworldly mysticism; like Huelsenbeck's, one of political upheaval and ideological combat; like Tzara's version, one of impersonal destruction of all personal and social guarantors of subjective comfort; like Duchamp's, one of formal innovation or 'artistic' concerns. Richter's history is the history of a group of friends, some of whom had never personally met, who galvanized that friendship into a force that profoundly transformed hundreds of lives, made all of those *other* histories thinkable and achievable, and *in the process* established the groundwork for a programme of joyous, deep-seated social revolt upon which we are still attempting build new ways of living; and, as Richter shows, they did this simply by *actually caring*. The most essential thing to be gleaned from *Art and Anti-Art* is not anything unique to

Dada, it is the realisation that the Institution has somehow managed to dupe us all into thinking that *we need it;* Richter, in his generous, humble, unassuming way, taught me that a 'movement' is not something that one assembles like an army of ready-made Heroes to launch on the grand battleground of Art History; it is the experience of a few *dedicated* friends who love nothing more than what they are doing, finding other dedicated friends who all *make each other* into something none could have imagined on their own, until one day they all look around, realise with astonishment what has come into existence through them, and get back to what they love to do together, as that intangible *thing* that has evoked itself between them continues to grow.

Rimbaud, Arthur & Mathieu, Bertrand, trans. (1991). *A Season in Hell & Illuminations.* Brocksport, NY: BOA Editions.
       Original Publications 1873 & 1874 respectively.

Artaud's arguments in *Coleridge the Traitor* can, I think, be applied to a number of people, including Rimbaud. There are many people with less representation in this book than one might expect. In many cases, this is due to oversight or inability to gather and work through the material; in Rimbaud's case (as with Dali's, for different reasons) it is intentional.

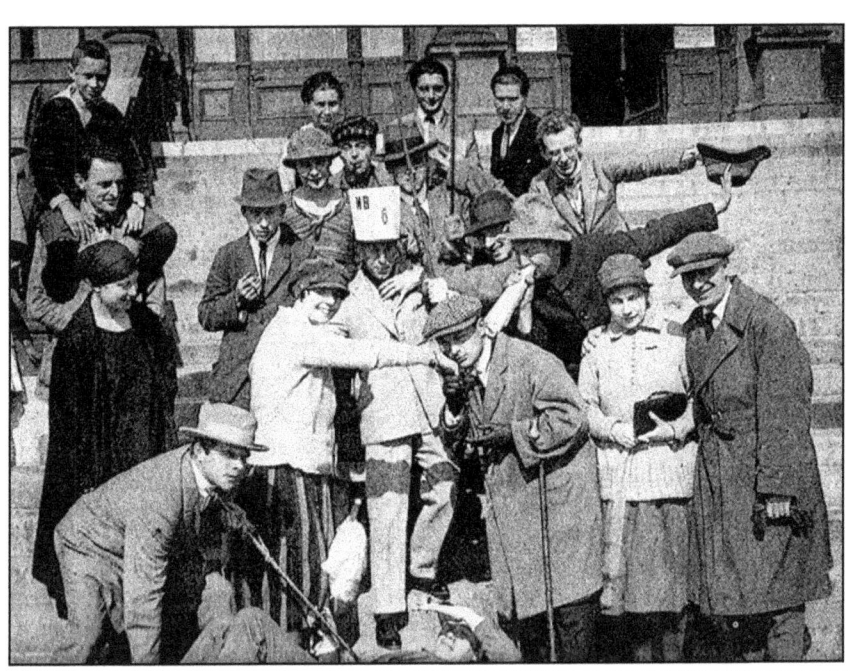

A group of Dadas from several different Dada communities hanging out at the Constructivist 'congress' they collectively crashed at the invitation of I.K. Bonset, and turned into an international Dada gathering in Weimar, 1922. (Motherwell 1981, p xx.)

On the one hand, Rimbaud was heavily involved with many of the practices and engagements presented in this book—much more heavily than is indicated within it—he heavily influenced later initiates, and is a major mythic figure. On the other hand, I have serious issues with the ways in which that myth has been used, as discussed in the main text of this book. Rimbaud was an *apostate*. To romanticize the fact that he abandoned any cultural engagement in order to run off and become a *slave-trader* (let's not mince words here) is to encourage generation after generation to abandon any kind of collective project in favour of a perpetual adolescence.

Schreber, Daniel Paul and Macalpine, Ida & Hunter, Richard A., trans. (2000). *Memoirs of my Nervous Illness.* New York: New York Review Books.
       Original Publication 1903.

I have not been able to get as far *into* Schreber yet as I would like; though his hallucinations, since they are not self-aware (for the most part—though certain devices such as the *fleeting-improvised men* begin to unravel this distinction), they throw a good deal of light on the practices treated here from several interesting directions. Moreover, Schreber's rhetorical strategy of constant *deferral*, which is not entirely dissimilar to that employed at times by Bergson (though the latter is tidier and therefore less clever in how he eventually *accounts* for these deferrals), and his success in establishing a workable logic that in its turn is able to *account* in its own way for all of the points—both phenomenal and 'causal'—where perceptual 'reality' and hallucinatory 'reality' meet, demonstrates in great detail the workings of a hallucinatory logic (in this case, because un-willed, working from the inside of hallucination out), and reinforces the notion that the mechanics of hallucination as proposed here are in some form basic to thought itself.

Schwitters, Kurt and Rothenburg, Jerome & Joris, Pierre, trans. (2002). *Poems Performance Pieces Proses Plays Poetics.* **Cambridge, MA: Exact Change.**

Schwitters, despite Huelsenbeck's arguments to the contrary, was by no means an 'Artist' in the narrow and derisive sense of the term; creation was for him a transformatory process, a metonym of the continual emergence of the subject, and Huelsenbeck would have been on somewhat firmer ground had he accused him of hermetic religiosity than of bourgeois complacence. Schwitters' work is subject to a rigorous, complex, highly personal and therefore ultimately unknowable system of thought and symbolic structuration that positions his productions definitively as relics, as texts baring their own inadequacy as a kind of mirror, they evoke my own speculation in order to fill those voids. As a result, I return to Schwitters for reinvestigation every few years and so far the ~~significance~~ of what he has left behind—and especially of what he has not—continues to unfold itself.

Shelley, Percy and Reiman, Donald, ed. & Fraistat, Neil, ed. (2002). *Shelley's Poetry and Prose.* **New York: W.W. Norton & Co.**

After Poe, Shelley was the second poet whom I made it a point to read *completely*; to this day I own several volumes of Shelley that I bought simply for a single poem or three- or four-page essay I did not own. As a poet, my opinion of him has scarcely ever flagged, though I no longer explicitly write like him (often). It is due to Shelley, more than anyone else, that I first *engaged* poetry. As a figure, I am aware of his faults. One must, at the same time, not forget his strengths; it was Shelley who first convinced me not only of the 'philosophical' duty of the artist but of the *political* element of creative endeavour that cannot be separated from it. The strange juxtapositions of Shelley's glaring moral blind-spots and his vicious ethical stances are worth investigating, especially in the attempt that I have suggested must be made to investigate such early, radical attempts to combat modernity before a firm cultural footing had been found from which such a battle could be waged. Shelley was never able to escape a number of the co-ordinates of thought that had been ground into him from every side; despite his hard-fought, even desperate attempts to escape from the modes of living and thinking of the class that he recognized as responsible for the perpetuation of a political and economic system that he loathed (unlike Byron, who never really tried), Shelley was never able to completely escape his Aristocratic modes of thought, either in his most intimate relationships (an idealist philosophy of Free Love resulting in practice with the suicide of his first wife), or in his least intimate (a trail of huge unpaid sums owed to the lower-class tradesmen for whose rights he fought). At the same time, he put himself fully on the line for his radical political commitments—expelled from Oxford for refusing to apologise for distributing an Atheist pamphlet to every Bishop in Britain, trailed by Government spies from the age of 16 until his virtual exile from England, the target of several assassination attempts as a result of his refusal to back down when helping to organise early labor unions among poor Welsh mining communities. Neither of these facets of Shelley's life invalidates or excuses the other, but it is worth examining him as a *subject* desperately attempting to extricate himself from the social forces that have created him, and simultaneously succeeding *and* failing spectacularly.

Smith, Richard Cándida. (1999). *Mallarmé's Children: Symbolism and the Renewal of Experience.* **Berkeley: University of California Press.**

An excellent book, recommended to me by Alan Reed, which I am only half-way through. It examines Symbolism, via Mallarmé presented in the roles of theorist, practitioner, and pedagogue, in a thoroughly wide-ranging context, locating it as a multifaceted reaction to Modernity on a number of registers. The discussions of the Symbolists' reactions to the rapidly enclosing professional and financial structures through which creative exchange was being thought and mediated, and of the physiological basis of Symbolist poetics and reading practices have been especially central in informing certain aspects of the book you are reading now. Richard Cándida-Smith (like Deak in *Symbolist Theater*) manages to do what very few studies of creative communities do, to address such a community not as an epoch in the production of artistic products, but as a collective effort to reconcile aspects of human experience and activity that capitalist ideology insists upon separating—philosophy, economics, biology, communication, psychology, sociality—and to draw from this synthesis (provisional as it may be) new ways of living.

Starkie, Enid. (1954). *Petrus Borel: The Lycanthrope.* **New York: New Directions.**

Max Klinger, *On Death, Part II: The Dead Mother* (1889). (Klinger 1977, p 74.)

There is a frustrating tendency—see my tirades concerning Freytag-Loringhoven—to produce biographies without translating the work of the poets involved. Therefore, there is no English translation of Borel's work—or indeed any of the Bouzingos with the obvious exceptions of Nerval and Gautier—available. One frustration about Starkie's book is that she includes a number of full poems and some fairly extensive passages, but does not provide English translations even for those. Nonetheless, it is a good thing that this book exists, for Borel and the group that formed around him had a seminal influence on the modes of sociality that dissenting communities would adopt over the next two-hundred years, and his role is virtually unknown and unexamined in English. An academic would likely be irritated by the 'lax scholarship' that seems to characterize most work from this period, but I find it quite refreshing. Borel is not so much the raison-d'etre of the book as the focus through which Starkie can evoke the confused politico-artistic underworld of France in the 1830s, with the result that several poetic, political, and heretical religious figures are resuscitated; Théophile O'Neddy plays almost a co-starring role apparently for no other reason than that Starkie feels he deserves to remembered; which is good enough for me. I prefer her enthusiastic storytelling to a text peppered with citations, and one gets the sense that she is relying to a large extent on a continuing oral tradition, so that this book truly operates mythically, with versions of, for instance, the Nerval myths concerning the beds and his skull-mug, and the Battle of Hernani, that differ from versions I have seen elsewhere.

Steadman, Ralph. (2002). *Doodaaa: The Balletic Art of Gavin Twinge: A Triography.* **New York: Bloomsbury.**

My mother by Chance—that eternal Anti-Ally—saw that 'Dada' was mentioned on the back of this book during the very first days of my interest in it and picked it up; I began reading it simultaneously with Richter's *Art and Anti-Art*. Steadman's connection with Gonzo is rather secondary to my interest simply because I have not had the chance to really become familiar with it; this book however, which details the dynamic of the obscure, hermetic, and fiercely anti-institutional Doodaa group had a great influence on a number of elements on my own thought while Post-NeoAbsurdism was in its infancy; the account of the publication of Twinge's first Doodaa journal—a single copy of a single poem on a broadsheet, given to a random passerby, brought home to me for the first time how straightforward and liberating such publishing could be; several days later David Hartke mentioned that he had been thinking along similar lines. We found Aaron Andrews, the three of us ended up at Hounddog's Pizza where a good number of Columbus Post-Neo's antics were hatched, we drew up a long list of names for the projected publication, and finally settled on Hartke's suggestion: *The Appropriated Press*.

Stein, Gertrude & Van Vechten, Carl, ed. (1990). *Selected Writings.* **New York: Vintage Books.**

I have only read the shorter pieces in here yet; Stein was the first writer I came into contact with that abandoned 'communication' without exactly being absurd, in which the reading experience itself, and the mind's contact with the text, was foregrounded as an only slightly and gradually modulated *movement*; in this way it helped to prepare me for the work of Bennett, Leftwich, Taylor, Altemus, et al.

Sterne, Laurence. (1996). *Tristram Shandy.* **Hertfordshire: Wordsworth Classics. Original Publication 1759-69.**

Yet another book I ought to have picked up much earlier; its description as an 18th Century Sentimental comedy made me mistrust it; it came up several times in the conversation of Jerome Fletcher and I thought I'd better give it a try. It is a revelation—in Tristram Shandy (I am only half way through) we find the point where Python's *Flying Circus* meets *Maldoror*. I could not ask for much more.

Tzara, Tristan & Caws, Mary Ann, trans. (1974). *The Approximate Man and Other Writings.*

I do not have the full information for this book, because I do own the book itself; and, oddly enough, there is almost nothing explicitly 'from' it in this book, though there are certain *tics* that make their way in, and so many others, and so many others. This is one of the four or five most important books of my life. After the first Post-NeoAbsurdist exhibition with David Hartke and Aaron Andrews, I decided to look into Dada; so I picked up a copy of Richter's *Dada: Art and Anti-Art*. Among so many other things, I thought, 'ah, poetry! Who's this Tzara fellow?' I found this book at the library; within ten pages something had *changed*; reading *The Approximate* was an experience I will not even attempt to describe. The course of my life was set. *The Approximate Man* brings one to the point at which all coordinates of the 'Self' has collapsed, and before disappearing they are pulled together in a kind of sustained explosion of subjectivity. This book established the coordinates of my verse—in fact my rationale for its continued existence—in a way that was not matched by anything until my introduction to the post-lettristic and visual poetry collected in Bennett's *Lost and Found Times*, and Tzara still peeks out of everything I do. It was through him that I learned that to manipulate syntax is to manipulate thought; from Caws' detailed analysis and meticulous translation notes, I derived my poetics. When I learned that no new edition of this book existed and that copies sold for between $80 and $200, I photocopied every single page, and that thick stack of photocopies, stapled in six batches, is still what I read today. (A new edition has just, finally, been printed in paperback, but that does me little enough good now.) As for Tzara's role in catalyzing and maintaining the Dada community, certainly he was not perfect, and there is some good reason that he seems to be so universally and severely criticized within dissenting discourse; but despite the egotism with which he is constantly charged, let's not forget: it is not Tzara who allowed himself to be recouperated and defanged by Institutional history in return for 'legendary' status in the establishment as 'THE' Dadaist, but Duchamp; from Paris Dada, it was only him and Ribemont-Dessaignes who refused the return to order organized by Pope Breton; and unlike the latter and almost everyone else who found themselves in a similar position between Dada and Neoism, Tzara never positioned himself as 'the' leader, never took upon himself the 'power' to throw anyone out of the club.

Valéry, Paul & Folliot, Denise, trans. (1958). *The Art of Poetry.* **New York: Pantheon Books.**

Valéry seems to have acquired a reputation for pedanticism, which I cannot understand. I actually still need to track down his poetry itself, but his writing *on* poetry is cogent and incisive. While he might be criticized for confining 'poetry' within its own name, so to speak—he is certainly no Situationist—he is deeply engaged with poetry as a way of training *thought,* as a form of mental discipline, of restructuring the mind, of exploring the relationship of the mind to the body (why does Kristeva, of all people, get on his case?). He worked and re-worked poems as a meditative practice for twenty years without any intention of showing them to anybody; this is *not* somebody simply playing the role of 'Man of Letters', trying to make something pretty.

Vian, Boris & Chapman, Stanley, trans. (133 E.P. / 2006 Vulgar). *'Pataphysics? What's That?* **London: London Institute of 'Pataphysics / Atlas Press.**

This, a beautifully designed, printed, and constructed chapbook as one expects from Atlas, was lent to me by Nathan Shaffer. It is the transcript of a radio show about the College of 'Pataphysics by Boris Vian from 1959. It is worth a read but I have been dragged, kicking and screaming, to the conclusion that if you've read one statement about 'Pataphysics from a member of the College, you've heard them all. Their thought seems not to have developed since the '40s.

Villiers de l'Isle-Adam & Miles, Hamish, trans. (date unknown). *Vera.* **Retrieved 8th April 2007 from the World Wide Web: http://gaslight.mtroyal.ab.ca/vera.htm**
    Original publication 1883.

Vera, as Huysmans argues in *A rebours,* is a minor masterpiece, and could have formed the basis for an extended analysis in this book. (You will have to analyze it yourself, which is far better). Villiers' name popped up often as I was attempting to get a grip on French Decadence and Symbolism, and my interest in him became piqued by *The Swan Killer,* reprinted in Breton's *Anthology of Black Humor,* and Frantisek Deak's discussions in his *Symbolist Theatre.* I am currently working my way through *The Future Eve* in Hustvedt's anthology, and Villiers is *vastly* underrated. His work is fully engaged with the basic ideological underpinnings of society in a way that few writers, especially at his time, were; his work has not, to my mind, dated at all, his prose is instantly recognizable, elegant but terse, tongue always lodged subtly in his cheek, and he is capable of reconciling extremely odd scenarios, complex philosophical underpinnings (he was deeply influenced by Hegel), and apparently disparate argots and worldviews into work that is a joy to read.

Walpole, Horace, Beckford, William, Shelley, Mary, & Fairclough, Peter, ed. (1986). *Three Gothic Novels: The Castle of Otranto, Vathek, Frankenstein.* **London: Penguin Books.**

I have just bought this book, and while I have a long history with *Frankenstein,* which I first read, I think, around the age of eight or nine and revisited perhaps three or four times since (I am nearly due for another), I have been meaning to get around to *Otranto* and *Vathek* for some time. Walpole seems particularly interesting.

Wikipedia. *Entry for 'Chaos Magic'.* **Retrieved 30th August from the World Wide Web: http://en.wikipedia.org/wiki/Chaos_magick**

Chaos Magic *seems* quite pertinent to what I have been discussing. Someplace in this book I lay out my reservations about the efficacy of occult/spiritualist/magical discourses, but the ideas seem valuable and the discourse here appears to be less annoying than it might be. I have not yet had the opportunity to delve deeper than wikipedia however, and that's not much. Justin McKeown of SPART Action has recently begun a project exploring some of these relationships.

Wilde, Oscar & Beardsley, Aubrey. (1996). *Salome / Under the Hill.* **London: Creation Books. Original publications 1894.**

This is illustrated by Beardsley, which is perfect. This text is gorgeous, I wish that Wilde would have engaged language in this way more often. Lush prose that has a reason for its floridity, it is not decorative or flowery, it is terse and precise and cutting; there are so many cutting edges that it takes the form of a deadly arabesque. One of the less misogynist treatments of the *Salome* theme to emerge from Decadence and Symbolism, though of course everything is relative in those realms…

Wilde, Oscar. (2002). *De Profundis, The Ballad of Reading Gaol & Other Writings.* **Hertfordshire: Wordsworth Editions.**

I had always kept away from Wilde, thinking of him as a kind of British Fitzgerald; much to my surprise I felt, when I finally opened it, like I was reading myself in many places. Having said that, I am speaking only of his critical writings, the *Ballad* does not look promising… While in many ways the British Aesthetic movement's French Decadent counterparts were more interesting and complex in their response to the structures against which they rebelled, Wilde has the advantage, unlike the majority of the French Decadents, of being much more explicit and nuanced in *how* he appropriated aristocratic modes; an avowed Socialist, he made it clear that his was an aristocracy of 'taste' and not of *power*.

Williams, Emmett, ed, Noel, Ann, ed., and Ay-O, ed. (1997). *Mr. Fluxus: A Collective Portrait of George Maciunas 1931-1978.* **London: Thames & Hudson.**

My introduction to Fluxus came through this book; it was a gift from Sue Lense, who was justifiably horrified to find that I had not been aware of the movement. This discovery came on the same evening that I first met John M. Bennett, though it was only later that I was given the book. As any book dealing with Fluxus ought to be, it is virtually impossible to go back to it and find anything that you have read, you are forced to sit and flip carefully through it, scanning it, re-reading half the book in order to confirm something you're *certain* you read in here and just need a slight detail of… Of all of the people over the past century and a half who have taken on the function of becoming a conduit or catalyst for the formation and maintenance of a community—Borel, Hugo, Baudelaire, Mallarmé, Marinetti, Tzara, Huelsenbeck, Hausmann, Breton, Isou, Debord, etc.—Maciunas as presented in this book has left the most detailed record of not only the politicizing and public face, but of the administrative details and organizational strategies—the 'boring' jobs that nobody else is willing to do—that are generally underappreciated but essential, making this the best and most detailed portrait I have found through which to understand the strengths and weakness of his approach. At the same time, Williams' book is a splendid example of a concentrated encoding in print of a figure who engaged with the *mythic* literature more than most working in this tradition after the Second World War, and has done so in a form that retains its mythic quality; nothing is detached here, it is a series of juxtaposed documents and scores of reminiscences by his comrades (and as such is obviously a structural influence on the book in your hands). For a man's biography to be composed solely through the relics he left behind and the reminiscences of his friends and enemies is proof that he did, at least, accomplish *something*, and one could scarcely hope *realistically* for more.

The reading of all of these books, and development of the various threads of thought that has emerged and been released again into the book you are reading, has been even more the result of the conversation and *example* of many people, without whom not only this text, but *I 'myself'* would be unthinkable in quite a different way than is now the case, and to whom I am deeply in debt for far more than the production of any text, but am *emphatically* in debt, in ways they may or may not realise, to varying degrees and through weeks or years of influence and collaboration, for the book you are reading now. These people include—but are from limited to—Alan Reed, Warren Fry, Mark Leahy, Jerome Fletcher, Emily Panzeri, Bradley Chriss, Kathy Karpilov, David Beris Edwards, John M. Bennett, Edward Lense, dadaDavid Hartke, Aaron Andrews, Nick Hallam, bela b. Grimm, Jim Leftwich, Tomislav Butkovic, Megan Blafas, Justin McKeown, Chadwick Niral-Nelson, Nathan Shafer, Robert Inhuman, Sue Lense, Kathryn Wynne, Rhiannon Chaloner, Tom Russotti, Casey Bradley, Emilie Lennard, Chi-Kit Kwong, Natalie Waldbaum, Reed Altemus, Terri Lennard, John Sanford, Tracy Warr, Shelley Smith, Oriana Ascanio-Reale, Charlotte Whelan, Netel McBurgenger, Scott Lennard, Krista Faist, Pete Niemershein, Scott MacLeod, Angee Lennard, Jessy Kendall, Tomas L. Taylor, C. Mehrl Bennett, Chris Lennard, Fast Sedan Nellson, Max Ensslin, Mark Greenwood, Imogene Engine, Jon Ludd, Alastair MacLeod, Nick Solsman, Celine Smith, Eric Schickel, Professor Aristotle, and so many others (and so many others).

Appendix: Concerning Another Library.

Comparing the (anti-)library encoded in the other appendix to the 'real' library of which it is a palimpsest, there appears to me to be a major flaw, a gaping space. For there are many modes of textual exchange, and the books listed there, for the most part, represent only books subject (though not exclusively) to a particular *model* of textual exchange, the *mimetic* model. Most of the books there, to a lesser or greater extent, choose to play along, at least on the surface, with that odd but persistent notion that language is a carrier of 'meaning', that is to say, that it *refers* to 'things'. And of course I too have pretended to play along with this game, acting *as if* I was saying something that I could possibly expect you to 'understand', as if in reading these words you were not putting yourself into (a) *process* but were merely 'getting' information.

The amount of writing that plays lip-service to this extraordinary notion is remarkable, and it is worth asking why a *writer* would structure an entire text according such an odd 'logic'. This will also lead us toward the related question of why I myself have chosen to concentrate in the book you now reading (and consequently in the other appendix) on texts that inhabit this absurd pretense that language can be used to 'say' something, and (even more rich) that that 'something' might be either 'true' or 'false'—might have 'happened' or 'not happened'—might have been either 'intentional' or 'coincidental'; and (this must, I suppose, be the punchline) that language can be used to 'establish' which of these arbitrary distinctions such-and-such a 'statement' might fall into! Many people have noted what I am about to relate, of course; I merely need to reiterate it in order to pretend to make my point.

Now, this point of view is not *quite* as utterly unbelievable as it at first appears; really, it's simply a gross oversimplification. We can all find ourselves lost in a text, 'filling' the text *out* by projecting *into it* our speculations as to what it is that is missing; and what is missing is inevitably—precisely because it *is* missing, heterogenous to what we can feel as 'present'—ourselves. And if more than one of us is lost in the same text, we are both, so to speak, *in* the text, where we have projected ourselves, or those *aspects of* ourselves that the text seems to elicit. We are *together in* the text, but cannot precisely know *how* we are together. This is true as well if one of *writes* (or speaks) a text, from which whatever of the writer that is *not* the text withdraws, leaving the spaces *into* which the reader (or listener) projects herself or himself; we are both in the text, and in fact the text is a space where we *co-exist*, though only through being transformed into gaps and speculations. This is simply the human condition, of course.

Now, in this way the relics of a moment of the thought of one withdrawn subject (the writer) come into contact with a moment of another subject (the reader), and what results is the *reading*, such as will happen when you, my dearest reader, read the following text:

for the postal monks

rant trash your scabs send blooms of lust rain down dust
pushed last live said drinks fall touch ready shoe trailer
vent bottom sack guess finds slow tongues behind press
lung wire twelves diner saccharine head juice for senses
wanders grow ghosts which yawn long since fridge rung
fills out such crutches rat come to run plural findings sin
saturated gouge jingle line tried trial spent grows hot tumble
wastecan suffers ounce the limbs cut nostril ticket blink
rested tricks rind advance sex utters post fence drawer
jangle present and single hung wiper drum ladder bleeds

Reed Altemus

A connection has just been established between all of the unknowable contingencies of *your* moment of reading—its place, your history, your muscles and nerves and wandering thoughts, just now, as you read this—and the equally unknowable contingencies of Altemus' moment of writing. That you have in some sense been together, that something has been *communicated* from one system of experience to another, is clear: the rhythms of your body, the shiftings of the shades of thought you can yourself scarcely catch, have been changed by the relics left by the rhythms and shiftings of him; but this is communication in the way that energy is communicated to one body from another through a wire, or the air; it is not 'understanding', the transference of 'knowledge'. Nor is it necessary for *words* to be involved here; for instance if you look, really *look* at the following asemic text by Jim Leftwich, allow your own thought, rhythms, shades, *encounter* this relic of a gesture determined by a similarly complex system of physiology, psychology, and *moment*:

Now, the intersubjective relationships that are, as we have just seen, established through the textual act are *necessarily* matters of *speculation,* of the projection of a *subjective* hypothesis into the space of the withdrawal of the writer, which renders the text itself a productive *relic*. It is, of course, quite obvious then that the idea of 'truth' being somehow of the same order as writing, of being something *knowable*, is a notion of paramount absurdity. *But,* before you go dismissing any text that seems to pretend to 'comprehensibility', hear me out.

The issue that we are faced with when we consider the above, is that the relationship established is very vague, there are *so many* contingencies at play that the idea of sociality remains all but unthinkable, and remains in fact impossible.

Let us say that, in relation to writing, we mutually (insomuch as we can 'define' mutuality) agree to *suspend our disbelief* and *pretend* that language could in fact 'refer to' 'Truth', even though we know that it can of course only *create* it. The writer pretends to be 'referring to' rather than *evoking*, the reader pretends to 'evaluate' rather than *speculate*. Essentially we have, by bracketing out of consideration an infinite number of contingencies, created a very limited compass of thought, in which we have surrendered a huge number of ways of thinking *in relation to* each other, but have gained a much stronger and more tangible connection between us—enough, let us hope, to make sociality possible.

Of course, it is no more possible within this imaginary system we have agreed upon to transfer 'meaning' between each other as if it was cargo than it was before we decided to provisionally hoodwink each other and ourselves; we still *must* speculate in order to read, to listen, to 'evaluate', and we must still yield the pipe-dream of being 'understood' when we write or speak. Due to the very character *of* language, we *must* speculate. But by narrowing our field of associations, those speculations can be more finely honed; if we are all speculating according to a similar set of coordinates, we will *still* not 'understand' each other or be living in the 'same' 'world'; but our speculations, and the actions which respond to and perpetuate them, will be *close enough* that they will, most of the time, re-inforce and even enrich each other. We will, so to speak, be close enough to get by.

So really, it's not hard to see why writing is so often used *as if* it merely *refers to things or thoughts*, even though in reality it is a principle of structuration *through which we construct ourselves:* it is useful to do so, and allows us to use writing—a principle of ruptures and rhythms—for something it cannot *in fact* do. If you have already read the main text of this book, you will see that, according to the schema we have *derived from* Bergson, communication is a *hallucination*, a parasite *on language;* it does not in fact exist, but can fulfill the right requirements to make it *seem as if it did exist;* and at that point, of course, in many of the most important ways it *had might as well be said to exist.*

It is this hallucination that supports human sociality, which all in all is a very fine thing; the danger, of course, comes when we, as individuals or as a culture, begin to forget that, after all, we are just pretending. Suddenly 'truth' as a provisional meeting-point we have collectively created and through which we can come together, becomes 'Truth', that thing outside of us which dictates how we can think. Nature becomes the status quo that we cannot think our way out of. Writing is twisted and deformed into something that continues to create the 'Truth' of whoever is charge of that writing, and denies anyone else the right of creating it for themselves, of creating new 'truths' that could lead to other ways of thinking, to other ways of constituting the self as subject or society as community.

So you can see, perhaps, why I have used writing throughout this book in such a way as to seem to 'say' something, while all along I simply want the reader to *experience* something infinitely complex and infinitely productive (as well as emphatically *negating*). Writing has become what it should never have become, and can never really *be:* a weapon of History in that word's most insidious sense, a prison-guard of the mind and a killer of human potential. It must be reclaimed; and for many generations writers have been inhabiting this form of writing that involves sentences, characters, sentiments, ideas, and pretending that they are (which they are not, for *nothing is*) something other than avatars of writing, of manifestations of subjective and intersubjective processes, because by doing so they could activate the fiction inherent in History, in Theory, in Science, in everything that claims to be *beyond re-writing* and therefore *in control.*

For this reason, it has not been possible to use, in this particular book, texts which do *not* make any pretence about *what they are*. This is by no means to say that they are not relevant to the practices described within it; on the contrary, they can scarcely be anything *but* relevant to it, for through them the experience of textuality is not mediated through either the screen of mimesis itself—of narrative texts—or the practices of reading to which those texts have habituated so many readers. Once sociality has been established through the *constraining* of language (and consequently of *thought*), through its *naturalization*, non-mimetic texts, and those who engage with them as writers *and/or* as readers, take on the duty of ensuring that this constraint remains mobile, that it never be taken as 'Truth', that the possibility of re-establishing the coordinates *of* our sociality and *of* our thought remains always *thinkable*. These direct texts, these texts-as-texts, constitute the library absent from the library figured within the other appendix to this book.

The communities centred around the kind of textual exchange indicated above by the texts of Leftwich and Altemus organise reading in a radically different way than do more mainstream communities (and markets), not only in the way in which one reads a *particular* text as demonstrated above, but in the way in which such textual exchange is situated within readers' lives and the way in which it functions as part of the social network. On the level of the discreet text, this difference has been indicated, and it is evident how a text such as Altemus', much less Leftwich's, could not be *deployed* in the same way, in this *particular* book, as can for instance a description of Des Esseintes' habits or a letter from Mallarmé. On the level of its sociality, I shall, for the sake of relative simplicity, designate the model by which this writing is circulated as *micropress*, a term I heard somewhere or other and which seems to me fairly adequate.

When I speak of Micropress I do not mean precisely 'self-publishing' which is at best a much vaguer term that does not account for its relationship to a community and which very often is not even apt as far as it goes, since micropress is quite often not a publishing of one's own work. I have discussed this in the essay opening my book *Puking Trolley* for Luna Bisonte. Much less when I say Micropress do I mean 'Small Press'; a 'small press' is generally merely a smaller copy of a large press; more dedicated and less financially driven perhaps, but generally not markedly different in the distance it keeps from the communities to which it relates, who remain to a large extent in the role of a 'market'.

Such presses conceptualise the 'Press' as a *producer of*, as an organisation which, at best, *serves* a community. Their role is unidirectional, to send texts *out from themselves*, to mediate between 'authors' and 'audiences'. Writers working within such systems typically produce a discreet number of texts, each organised around unique themes, ideas, projects. To finish such a text is something of an event. And to the *readers*, who then *decide* to acquire that particular book, it is therefore too an event, and they will evaluate the book, they will, if it is worth it, turn it into something of a fetish. Now, fetishes have value, and my other appendix is nothing if not a display of fetishized texts that have, for that very reason, had an immense and long-lasting effect on me. The book you are now reading is most likely destined to act to a fairly large, if (hopefully) not complete extent, according to that model, if for no other reason than the sustained effort that has produced it, the concentrated nature of the engagement through which it is articulated, and the *size* of it which renders it impossible, in a practical sense, to treat it *fully* as a micropress gesture as described below.

The communities of which I am writing now—the communities with which I associate myself most strongly and from which any truly comprehensive re-writing of creative sociality *must* develop—do not form *around* textual exchange but *through* it. Within these communities the 'Press' is conceptualised as a communal *signifier* and a communal *function*, as that part of the individual who *belongs to* a community and serves as a conduit through which its social articulations pass. They do not provide any 'means of production' unavailable to readers or writers themselves; they operate primarily through gift-economy, and as such work to distribute material from anywhere within a community regardless of its point of production; and they present their publishing function as entirely continuous with both their other creative activity and their everyday lives, which are after all one and the same. Writers working within these communities are the source of an endless or intermittent stream of relics which enter into the communal economy, circulate, are modified and intermixed with countless others through reading, re-writing, and over-writing, and are then pushed aside as an endless surge of text continuously upwells, a function of social life. The completion of one text is merely the gathering of energy that will be expended in the next. And the reading of these texts is no different, not an act of evaluation or even of reflection, but one of *immersion* which immediately gives way to another immersion, another meeting of two unknowable moments of contingency that will constitute in turn another moment in the continual re-writing of the reader who writes the spaces left by these texts that are not so much *fetishes* as relics, such that the micropress 'library' becomes, as well, an *archive*.

In micropress communities, nearly every reader is a writer, not because only writers read it, but because to read it *is* to write, and because writing is not a matter of status but of *involvement* in the social body, in contributing one's own rhythms to the complex of rhythms constituting that social body. Every day, members of such communities are faced with texts and produce them in all kinds of formats—one sends, receives, and alters texts through the mail, through e-mail, in blogs, in books, on postcards, on disk, in posters. Publication outstrips any possibility of complete digestion; the creation of texts is so exuberant and so unbridled that the possibility of the 'masterpiece' is drowned under the sheer volume of relics; the *mastering* of textuality remains as in any other mode of writing, but refuses to constrain itself to a few key texts, refuses to separate itself as a timeless *investiture* of value, but insists instead upon maintaining its direct connection with the succession of moments from which in fact it arises, it insists upon *expending* itself, on wearing its own continual decay upon its sleeve, it insists upon remaining always in the present, or as a *relic* of a vanished present which has been supplanted by a thousand others, because in this way the possibility of *change* is always already on the verge of actuality.

One can fully *read* the creative activity of these communities—which are quite obviously nearly inseparable from Mail Art communities when operating at their highest pitch—only through *sustained engagement;* through receiving packages full of artwork, books, broadsheets, video and sound every week or every day; through receiving a half dozen poems through e-mail each day; through viewing dozens of works on online archives every day. One does not read *a* book or *a* poem or view *a* collage, one *absorbs* these texts because they pervade one's atmosphere.

If you have read the body of *this* book in your hands, my dearest reader, you will see that we are approaching a space not altogether distinct from the knot of themes that pervades *it*. To read these works in this way, from *within* a community that lives its life *through* them, is to habituate oneself to thinking *differently*, to projecting into these unknowable and constantly proliferating *relics* of unknowable moments the hallucinations of your own experience, and to watch them subtly inflect it. It *can* be to allow yourself to dissolve, and to observe yourself in the midst of dissolution, reconfiguring your thought and your relationship to it by means of the marks left by an other, which refuse to allow you to make an easy and comfortable sense of them. In learning, through long and sustained engagement, to *inhabit* these corpses of other people's thoughts, one learns how one inhabits one's own. In learning not to read a text from the standpoint of the subject, but to read the subject from the position *of the text*, from the standpoint of the hallucination which has insinuated itself *into* the gaps of the text, one can learn, from that space of annihilating *absence*, to rewrite the subject itself.

Anabasis, *Thomas L. Taylor*. 814-318 Pl., Ocean Park WA 98640, United States.

Answer Shirker Press, *Jessy Kendall*. P.O. Box 392, Lewiston ME 04243, United States.

Avantacular, *Andrew Topel*. 1 Lakeview Acres, Rushville IL 62681, United States.   andrewtopel@hotmail.com

Editions sRL, *Ficus Strangulensis*. Rt. 6 Box 138, Charleston, WV 25311, United States.

Fluxus Canuks/Imp Press, *Ross Priddle*. 21 Valleyview Dr. SW, Medicine Hat AB 11A 7K5, Canada.

Luna Bisonte Prods, *John M. Bennett*. 137 Leland Ave., Columbus OH 43214, United States. bennett23@osu.edu

Marymark Press, *Mark Sonnenfeld*. 45-08 Old Millstone Dr., E. Windsor NJ 08520, United States.

mOnocle-Lash Anti-Press, *Olchar E. Lindsann*. 221 Howard St., Apt. #3, New Brunswick, NJ 08901, United States.   olindsann@hotmail.com

    British Division, *David Beris Edwards*. 31C High Street, Totnes Devon TQ9 5NP, United Kingdom. goodygoody_yumyum@hotmail.com

Peyronie Press, *John M. Bennett & Blaster Al Ackerman*. 137 Leland Ave., Columbus OH 43214, United States.

Textimagepoem, *Jim Leftwich*. www.jimleftwichtextimagepoem.blogspot.com   jimleftwich@mac.com

Tonerworks, *Reed Altemus*. PO Box 52, Portland ME 04112, United States.   raltemus@gwi.net

X-tant Press, *Jim Leftwich*. 535 10th Street SW, Roanoke VA 24016, United States.   jimleftwich@mac.com

(all addresses as of Oct., A.Da 91/2007 A.D.)